EARLS OF CREATION

RICHARD BOYLE, 3RD EARL OF BURLINGTON
Portrait by G. Knapton now at Chiswick House
Reproduced by permission of the Trustees of the Chatsworth Settlement

EARLS OF

CREATION

Five Great Patrons
of Eighteenth-Century Art

BY

JAMES LEES-MILNE

ILLUSTRATED

HAMISH HAMILTON
LONDON

First published in Great Britain, 1962
by Hamish Hamilton Ltd
90 Great Russell Street, London WC1
Copyright © 1962 by James Lees-Milne

PRINTED IN GREAT BRITAIN
BY EBENEZER BAYLIS AND SON, LTD.
THE TRINITY PRESS, WORCESTER, AND LONDON

CONTENTS

List of Illustrations   page 7
Preface   9
Introduction   11

I

ALLEN BATHURST, 1st EARL BATHURST
(1684–1775)

i   Politics and Friendships   page 21
ii Cirencester House   33
iii Cirencester Park   37

II

HENRY HERBERT, 9th EARL OF PEMBROKE
(1693–1750)

i   Eagle and Dove   page 60
ii The Architect Earl   67
iii The Palladian Countess   71
iv Marble Hill   79
v   Houses and Bridges   92

III

RICHARD BOYLE, 3rd EARL OF BURLINGTON
(1694–1753)

i   Italy and the Arts   page 103
ii William Kent and Marriage   122
iii Architectural Doctrines and Renown   135
iv The Gardens at Chiswick   140
v   The House at Chiswick   148
vi Later Buildings and Declining Years   156

IV

EDWARD HARLEY, 2nd EARL OF OXFORD
(1689–1741)

i   Wanley and the Harleian Library   page 173
ii Literary Friends and Down Hall   185

iii Architectural Tours   *page* 206
iv Gibbs and Wimpole Hall   212

V

THOMAS COKE, 1st EARL OF LEICESTER
(1697–1759)

i   Youth and the Grand Tour   *page* 221
ii Paterfamilias and Collector   232
iii The Conception of Holkham   244
iv The Creation of Holkham   254
v   Disenchantment and Death   261

ILLUSTRATIONS

Richard Boyle, 3rd Earl of Burlington	*frontispiece*
Allen Bathurst, 1st Earl Bathurst	*facing page* 32
The 'Hexagon', Cirencester Park	33
Cirencester Park House and the Broad Ride	33
Jonathan Swift	48
Alexander Pope	48
Plan of Oakley Great Park, Cirencester	49
Alfred's Hall, Cirencester Park	54
Pope's Seat, Cirencester Park	54
Ivy Lodge, Cirencester Park	55
Grisaille of Farnese Hercules	64
Marble Hill, Twickenham: Chimneypiece in the Saloon	64
Henry Herbert, 9th Earl of Pembroke	65
Henrietta Hobart, Countess of Suffolk	80
Giulio Capra's Palace	81
Marble Hill, the Entrance Front	81
Wilton House, The Palladian Bridge	96
Palazzo Thiene, Vicenza	97
Palazzo Iseppo De'Porti, Vicenza	97
Sevenoaks School	112
Burlington House	112
The Man of Taste	113
Chiswick, The Exedra	128
Chiswick House from the South-east	128
Rocca Pisana	129
Villa Capra, or the Rotunda, Vicenza	129
Chiswick Villa	144
Pope in his Grotto at Twickenham	145
York Assembly Rooms	160
John Gay	161
William Kent	161
Humphrey Wanley	176
Edward Harley, 2nd Earl of Oxford	176
Matthew Prior	177
James Gibbs	177
Wimpole Hall, The Library	224
Wimpole Hall, the Chapel	224
Thomas Coke, 1st Earl of Leicester	225
Margaret Tufton, Countess of Leicester	240
Lady Mary Coke	241
Edward, Viscount Coke	241
Holkham Hall, the South Front	256
Holkham Hall, the Triumphal Arch	256
Holkham Hall, the Marble Hall	257
Holkham Hall, the Saloon	257

PREFACE

THE HOPEFUL STUDENT of architecture in leafing these pages may complain that too many are devoted to irrelevant particulars of the men who created the buildings he is in search of, and too few to the buildings themselves. The casual browser of period fodder on the other hand may well be bored with the architectural descriptions. To both I could easily point out which passages to leaf and which to leave, were these not sufficiently self-evident. I am however impenitent in maintaining that architecture wholly unleavened with historical association is unpalatable stuff. Architects, especially amateur ones, are after all human beings with other interests and frailties than bricks and mortar. Indeed the greater the architect the more profound his knowledge of the kindred arts, literature and life, the more intense his pursuits both sacred and profane.

In writing the five following sketches I have been immensely beholden to the descendants of the subjects and wish to record my gratitude to them individually. Earl Bathurst courteously answered many tiresome inquiries and made arrangements on my behalf for photographs to be taken of several pictures at Cirencester Park. The Earl of Pembroke generously gave me access to those papers at Wilton which relate to the 9th Earl, lent me the photograph of his ancestor's bust, and read through and corrected the proofs of Chapter II. Since he is the ultimate authority on the history of Wilton and the Herbert family he has greatly reassured me about many facts concerning his ancestor and his building activities. The Duke of Devonshire allowed me to spend several days transcribing the papers and correspondence of Lord Burlington in the Library at Chatsworth. Mr. Christopher Harley gave me permission to have photographed and to illustrate the interesting portrait of the 2nd Earl of Oxford in his possession at the ancient Harley stronghold of Brampton Bryan. The Earl of Leicester put at my disposal the numerous account books in his Library, and let me roam at will round the rooms and park at Holkham. Lady Silvia Coombe, his sister, gave me much help and hospitality.

Mrs. George Bambridge very kindly entertained my wife and me at Wimpole and showed us round that beautiful house, to which she has done so much in such good taste, while cherishing the memories of the 2nd Earl of Oxford. I am also greatly beholden

to Earl Spencer for allowing me to read through and make use of
Lord Burlington's letters to Lady Burlington in his possession at
Althorp: to Dr. W. O. Hassall for help in directing me to the
appropriate papers in the Holkham Library: and to Mr. T. S.
Wragg for his invariable kindness in directing my steps about the
Library at Chatsworth, in producing material hitherto unknown
to me, and in himself specially taking several excellent photo-
graphs.

I warmly thank Mr. John Harris of the R.I.B.A. Library for
some greatly needed help in his department and for several fertile
ideas: Mr. John Fleming for kindly informing me about Sir John
Clerk's visit to Chiswick: and Mr. Hugh Honour for introducing
me to William Kent's brief but invaluable Italian journal. Once
again I am indebted to Mr. Alec Clifton-Taylor, who after reading
my typescript nobly gave me the benefit of his suggestions and
advice. Lastly, I am most grateful to my wife for many pertinent
criticisms and her constant encouragement.

J. L-M.

Alderley Grange,
Wotton-under-Edge,
Gloucestershire.
August 1962.

INTRODUCTION

THE FIVE EARLS, who are the subjects of these essays, were almost exact contemporaries. The active life of each practically spanned the reigns of the first two Georges. Three of them were born in the 1690s and died in the 1750s between the ages of fifty-eight and sixty-two, which in their generation amounted to longevity. Lord Oxford, the first to die, only lived to be fifty-two. Lord Bathurst, however, who came into the world well before the others, left it long after the last of them. Having been born when Charles II was still King, he survived the first fifteen years of George III's reign and reached the almost incredible age of ninety-one.

That these five Earls enjoyed a similar upbringing and moved in the same social orbit, owing as much to their interests as to their birth, goes without saying; that they were all Palladian requires perhaps a little qualification. Three of them, Burlington, Pembroke and Leicester, were avowed disciples of the great sixteenth-century master from Vicenza. Indeed Palladio was their architectural god, whose cult they were more largely responsible for reviving than any of their contemporaries, with the single exception of the commoner and professional architect, Colen Campbell. So successful were they in this respect that they brought about a neo-Palladian era in England. Whereupon the plausible deduction ensues that Bathurst and Oxford, because they belonged to this era, were Palladian Earls likewise. This they surely were, only with a difference. There was for them no avoidance of the new Palladian teaching in the spate of books and treatises then issuing from the printing presses, which advocated a return to Vitruvian sources of architecture, any more than there is for the most conservative artists today total escape from the current 'abstractionism'. Painters, sculptors and architects cannot fail to be affected, whether they like or detest it, by the prevailing style of their own time. It must inevitably colour their works, however ostensibly hostile to it these may appear, when they are viewed through the distant eyes of posterity. Bathurst and Oxford may have professed to ignore Palladianism, preferring to adhere to the outmoded architectural style (Wren or baroque, whichever we care to call it) favoured by the departed Stuart dynasty. They were, as we shall discover, Stuart sympathizers, Tories and defenders of lost causes, whereas Burlington, Pembroke and

Leicester were Hanoverians, Whigs and positive protagonists of a new national style in architecture. Even so the buildings designed or sponsored by the two dissident Earls express much of the spirit if not the letter of the Palladian era in which they were active participants.

Admitting then that my five subjects were contemporary Earls living in a revived Palladian era we come to the common quality which they all shared. They were to a man deep-dyed aesthetes and creators of country house domains. There were other contemporary Earls—Islay, Orford, Strafford, Chesterfield—whom I might just as well have selected. But one has to draw the line somewhere. There were also contemporary Knights and Squires with the same interests and no less erudition, only with a little less influence because of their humbler rank in society. They too may equally well repay investigation. Another important factor is that the principal country houses of my five chosen Earls (with the single exception of Wimpole Hall, where indeed Lord Oxford's Harleian Library and Chapel are intact) still remain little altered since they were contrived. In one way and another they are masterpieces of architecture or landscape gardening, which are moreover available at stated times for any visitor who is curious enough to study and admire them.

The main point is therefore that all five Earls were amateur architects or landscape gardeners (if not both) of no mean order. Lord Burlington's architecture is now generally recognized as marking a turning-point in eighteenth-century style. Its importance can hardly be over-estimated. It constitutes the great triumph of the amateur. Never before in the long history of British art did the fashionable amateur exercise such an influence as in the reigns of the first two Georges. Never before did he have the wealth and the means to create on so magnificent a scale; nor did he have the knowledge and the inclination to do so. For their enthusiasm alone the early Georgian amateurs deserve the highest commendations. I have attempted in the following pages to show why and how my Earls were impelled to build. The best method seemed to me to ascertain as far as possible from exiguous sources what sort of lives they led and what sort of characters they were. None of them played a very prominent rôle in public affairs so that records of their activities and behaviour are fairly scanty. With the strictly honourable exception of Lord Burlington they were not, judged by our standards, particularly estimable characters although by those of their day their manners were fairly representative of their class and wealth. To our way of thinking these noblemen were over-indulged and spoilt. On the other hand they had a most pronounced sense of duty towards not only their own generation but posterity as well in that everything they created and collected was of the very highest quality.

The interests of the neo-Palladians, like those of true renaissance men, seemed all-embracing. Sport, politics, religion, music, literature, painting, sculpture, architecture and gardening absorbed them. Collecting on a far-reaching scale was their passion. Their self-confidence was robust and overweening. In what other age than theirs would a dignitary of the Church, who was also a scholar of renown, have the temerity to exhort a poet to tamper with Milton's verse? 'I wish you would review and polish that piece [meaning *Samson Agonistes*],' wrote Bishop Atterbury to Pope in 1722, '. . . it deserves your ear, and is capable of being improved, with little trouble.' Their judgments were arbitrary and unconciliatory. 'The taste of most of our English poets, as well as readers,' complained Addison eleven years previously, 'is extremely Gothick.' No adjective at that time had a more pejorative meaning, whether applied to verse or architecture. In the latter context Smollett spoke his mind just as positively. 'The external appearance of an old cathedral cannot but be displeasing to the eye of every man who has any idea of propriety and proportion.' There were no two opinions on any question of taste. The early Georgians knew what they disliked, and discarded it; they knew what they did like, and produced it. Fashion dictated taste in art as well as literature. By 1748 when the Palladian Earls were long past their prime Lord Chesterfield was extolling the rococo style; and in 1750 Mrs. Montagu, who was remodelling her London house in Hill Street, announced that she was sick of 'Grecian elegance and symmetry'.[1] Instead, she wrote, 'we must all seek the barbarous goût of the Chinese.'

What I find remarkable about the Palladian Earls is their sincere friendship with, as well as generous patronage of, men of letters and artists. They did not merely employ them as useful and obedient instruments with which to embellish their magnificent houses and estates. They did not condescend to them. On the contrary they exalted them to their own Olympian heights, treated them almost as social equals, even deferred to them as to their intellectual and artistic superiors. 'Lady Berkeley after dinner clapt my hat on another lady's head,' Swift recounted to Stella, 'and she in roguery put it upon the rails. I minded them not.' The

[1] By 'Grecian' Mrs. Montagu really meant Roman. In 1750 she was not aware of the imminence of the one-Grecian 'goût' to be brought to England in the wake of Stuart and Revett in the 1760s.

poet did not deem the incident the least bit untoward. We cannot picture a lady even of the Merry Monarch's loose court stooping to the same horseplay with a man of letters, were he as eminent as Dryden, a quarter of a century before. Lord Oxford could address the linen-draper's son, Alexander Pope, in this strain: 'I will allow nobody to esteem, to value, or love you more than I do from the conviction that you are the best poet, the truest friend, and the best natured man'—which from any disciple to his master would be tribute indeed.

Pope's name constantly recurs throughout these pages; I had no idea, when I embarked upon them, quite how constantly it would recur. It goes to prove, I submit, the great and various parts this astonishing man played in the history of his time. How was it that a poet became so involved with painting, architecture and landscape gardening? Pope was seldom out of the limelight, whether it were focused upon Lord Bathurst's rides and follies, the terraces, the boudoir and even the ice-house which Lord Pembroke was constructing for Mrs. Howard, Lord Burlington's pictures and galleries, or Lord Oxford's library. Of the five Earls only Lord Leicester, the least in touch with men of letters in spite of his zeal in collecting ancient manuscripts, seemed able to keep him away from his seat, Holkham. It is this peer's very deficiency that gives the answer to our question. The country house domain of the English Palladian age was as much a literary as an architectural and horticultural composition. It was inspired as much by the writings of the ancients and moderns as by the rules of Vitruvius and Jones, as much by the verse of Pope and Thomson as by the layouts of Bridgman. Through his wide reading Pope was better versed in the classics, and incidentally in the writings of his fellows, than any other living scholar and author. He also happened to be deeply versed in the moral philosophy of Anthony Ashley Cooper, 3rd Earl of Shaftesbury (1671–1713). For these reasons he became the accepted monitor of the aristocracy in its craze for country house building and landscape gardening during the new Palladianism.

Lord Shaftesbury had been a William of Orange Whig and a deist; and he evolved a philosophy of aesthetics which was to imbue the age ushered in with the Hanoverian dynasty.[1] Pope, who was a Tory and a Catholic, did not approve of him on political and religious counts. But the poet found the Earl's philosophy irresistible and irrefutable. Briefly, Lord Shaftesbury's thesis was

---

[1] For a very succinct analysis of Lord Shaftesbury's aesthetic philosophy, see Christopher Hussey's brilliant Introduction to Margaret Jourdain's *The Work of William Kent*, 1948.

that harmony, symmetry and proportion were the prerequisites of morality and beauty. In the words of Mr. Hussey: 'He applied to ethics the same principles that, for him, governed the arts of design, arguing that taste, as pursued by a cultivated man, is expressed in conduct no less than in architecture and painting, and vice versa. Beauty of life and beauty of form are identified as complementary aspects of the ideal.' By an extension of the argument the more developed a man's taste in the arts, the greater was his title to moral superiority. In consequence, the aristocrat with pretensions to the ideal spiritual good must acquire a sensitive appreciation and a correct judgment of all things; he must eschew vulgarity and excess, even to the extent of checking unseemly laughter. He must become an arbiter of taste, a lover of the arts; a *virtuoso* rather than a scholar and practitioner. It was not befitting his high and detached status in society to become too much a proficient in any artistic sphere. Hence the criticism of Burlington by Lord Chesterfield (who himself neatly fulfilled the Shaftesbury ideal of dilettantism) for having overstepped the bounds of propriety by actually designing buildings. He demeaned his authority and imperilled his immaculate soul by undertaking work which should have been left to masons and artisans. There is no doubt, however, that Lord Shaftesbury's philosophy was interpreted by gentlemen amateurs of the early Georgian reigns in various degrees of seriousness. They read into *The Characteristicks of Men, etc.*, that difficult and disjointed omnibus of the philosopher's complete works first published in 1711 and enlarged in 1714, what they could and often what they would. Some like the exquisite Lord Chesterfield recognized the necessity to become superfine beings on a remote plane; others were content to improve their speaking knowledge of the arts while leaving their rough manners to take care of themselves. In most cases annual incomes were the determining factor. But one and all learned from *The Characteristicks* that correct breeding and correct architecture went hand in hand; that gentlemanliness was enhanced by an understanding of Palladianism. 'To employ an inappropriate column in a building,' writes Christopher Hussey, 'was tantamount to a social solecism; too great freedom of design was licentious; and that which savoured of Baroque was gross vulgarity.' It is enough to say that Shaftesbury's influence upon the attitude to beauty, the arts, and to nature by the generation succeeding his own was paramount. Pope was his oracle, and the aristocracy were the elect, who strove to attain the ideal of the cultivated man through the pursuit of his philosophy.

The most concrete result of Shaftesbury's teaching was the early Georgians' approach to nature. He was the first person to propound that nature deserved more than exploitation and use, and that it was something deserving contemplation for its own sake. It did not of course in his eyes belong to the same high category as a work of art. Since it lacked that harmony, symmetry and proportion, of which true beauty consisted, it was inferior. Nonetheless, nature in its own poor way revealed God's majesty and should be treated with reverence. 'The vast deserts of these parts,' Shaftesbury wrote of mountain landscapes, 'ghastly and hideous . . . want not their peculiar beauties. The wildness pleases.' This reasoning was an important first step in an entirely new direction, namely towards the appreciation of natural scenery. It eventually led later generations to a respect for wild life and vegetation.

Such days still lay far ahead, and were not to be reached before Wordsworth and the Lake poets arrived on the English scene. Meanwhile Shaftesbury did not advocate that the cult of nature ought to result in landscape gardens becoming irregular in plan. Far from it. When he declared nature to 'have a magnificence beyond the mockery of princely gardens', he did not envisage primeval nature in the raw, a kind that disgusted all eighteenth-century persons, but a nature that never properly existed. It was that idyllic landscape such as he imagined the ancient Romans like Pliny to have fashioned as the perfect villa setting for classical temples, obelisks, columns, sarcophagi and urns on plinths: in fact such as Claude Lorrain and Poussin had depicted on canvas in the previous century. Just as the Palladians learned from Shaftesbury to design 'correct' houses comformable to the buildings described by Vitruvius, so they followed his directions in the lay-out of idyllic gardens on the ancient pattern. Both English Palladian country houses and gardens were therefore no less associative and traditional than strictly mathematical and purist, which they are generally held to be. Classical they might be, romantic they surely were, diffusing the very spirit and virtue of antiquity. No artist understood this seeming dichotomy of qualities better than William Kent, whose approach to architecture and landscape gardening under the direction of his learned friends like Pope, Burlington and Leicester was essentially historical and pictorial. Kent in short became the most versatile artist and the most representative executant of the Shaftesbury doctrine in the English Palladian age.

Kent, the son of poor parents, uneducated and gross in habits, had all the imagination, fire and genius which most of his noble patrons and friends lacked. But without their learning, guidance and companionship he would never have achieved his successes. He was in a sense their product, their crowning fulfilment. The combination of interests, the co-operation of talents, the resources of money and opportunity brought about by the several partnerships in which he was engaged, enabled Kent, artistically speaking, to be the dominating figure of the age. In no other age have the arts in England been more blessed. All endeavour has to be judged by results. And no one can deny that the country houses, collections, and landscape gardens, which this remarkable little group of Palladian Earls created, still amount to some of the nation's greatest treasure.

BATHURST I

ALLEN BATHURST

1st EARL BATHURST

1684–1775

i. Politics and Friendships

DURING HIS ninety-one years Allen Bathurst was able to carry out the most ambitious as well as the dearest scheme of his heart, namely the creation and embellishment of his estate. Since he began the task when he was a comparatively young man, and followed a persistent course of operations, he was able to enjoy its fulfilment. And enjoy is the appropriate word. For he was one of the unashamed enjoyers of everything life had to offer. Seldom is a man so fortunate as he was. And seldom is a great arboriculturist granted by the fates nearly three-quarters of a century in which to watch the trees he has planted grow to maturity.

The subject of this essay was not, properly speaking, born in the purple; and he was a Tory. Neither of these contingencies was a disadvantage to him. He redressed the first, with an ease that was habitual, by getting himself made a peer at a very early age. He profited from the second by having to leave political office on the brink of a career, which many lesser men would have regretted, and by devoting himself to the pastime from which he has earned a lasting reputation.

Although Allen Bathurst was not exactly patrician by birth, he came of gentle and distinguished stock. The Bathursts had long been settled near Boteherst, which is the name of a wood near Battle in Sussex. The foundation of their fortune was laid in Henry VI's reign by the progenitor of the family who was a clothier. Lord Bathurst's great-grandfather rose to aldermanic rank and built himself a country house, called Franks[1] in the Darent Valley in Kent, where he reared a large family. His fourth son, George, bought a Northamptonshire estate. George Bathurst

---

[1] Franks was bought early in Queen Elizabeth's reign by Lancelot Bathurst. In 1748 it passed from Bathurst ownership, but was bought back by the 7th Earl about 1911.

had a still larger family than his father. His fifth son, Ralph, was President and re-founder of Trinity College, Oxford, after the Restoration. His sixth, Benjamin, was more successful than any of his brethren. He became a Member of Parliament and a knight. At one brief period he was Governor of the East India Company. His greatest triumph was the entry into royal circles. He was made Treasurer to the Princess Anne of Denmark on the establishment of her household, and, when she succeeded to the throne, her Cofferer. In this enhanced position he flourished but two years, and died in 1704.

Sir Benjamin Bathurst married as satisfactorily as he did everything else. In fact, he probably owed his entry into court circles to his wife's family. Lady Bathurst was Frances, second daughter of Sir Allen Apsley of Apsley in Sussex. Her father, having fought with the cavaliers in the Civil War, was rewarded with the post of Falconer to Charles II. Although the Apsley wealth derived from the iron trade, the Falconer's wife and daughters were soon accepted by the Princesses Mary and Anne on a footing of close intimacy. Many letters, abounding in nicknames and exclusive, if rather infantine jokes, passed between the Princesses and the young Apsleys, and are preserved at Cirencester House.

Of this union Allen Bathurst was born in St. James's Square on 16th November, 1684. The boy was educated at Trinity College, Oxford, of which his uncle Dean Bathurst was still President. The Dean was then nearly eighty, a man of vast learning and some wit. The undergraduates were devoted to him because of his pleasantries and eccentricities. His only weapon of correction was mild ridicule. At the same time he used to keep a whip, which he would brandish in the college gardens for the innocent pleasure of arousing an ill-founded alarm in the breasts of freshmen, as yet unacquainted with his benevolent disposition.

Before being sent to Oxford Allen Bathurst was already betrothed, if not more solemnly plighted. His grandmother, Lady Apsley, the friend of royalty, was autocratic as well as grimly humorous. She arranged a contract between her son Peter Apsley's daughter, Catherine, and the child's first cousin, Allen Bathurst. So in 1692 when the boy was eight and the girl four they were married 'in jest to please their grandmother'. The tiny wedding and guard rings have survived. Evidently the children viewed the affair with no displeasure, for when they were practically grown up a wedding ceremony was re-enacted in 1704. The marriage proved a fruitful, and probably a happy one. Catherine Bathurst produced four sons and five daughters. If her epitaph in Cirencester Church is to be believed, 'by her milder virtues', compared with those of her lord, she 'added lustre to his great qualities. Her domestic economy extended his liberality, her judicious charity his munificence; her prudent government of her family his hospitality. She received the reward of her exemplary life' in 1768 at the mature age of seventy-nine. A cynic might interpret from the careful phraseology of the epitaph that Lady Bathurst was just the very slightest bit mean.

In the year of Allen Bathurst's proper marriage his father Sir Benjamin died. The young man now found himself a person of affluence and a landed gentleman with a stake in the county of Gloucestershire. Nine years previously old Sir Benjamin had purchased the Oakley property, to the west of the town of Ciren-cester, from Anne Poole, Countess of Newburgh. The son felt it incumbent upon him to assume the responsibilities of his newly acquired station. He did not have long to wait before others felt the same way on his behalf. In 1705, before he had reached his majority, he was elected Tory Member of Parliament for Ciren-cester. He was at once plunged into debate upon the Union with Scotland, which he supported. For seven years he assiduously attended the House of Commons, where he became an ardent champion of his two friends, the brilliant and equivocal Tory malcontents, Henry St. John and Robert Harley, in their efforts to stop Marlborough's wasteful and expensive campaigns on the Continent. In 1712 he was one of a dozen Tories raised to the peerage in order to induce the Lords to accept the Treaty of Utrecht, which his cousin, Thomas Wentworth, 3rd Earl of Strafford, at that time Ambassador at The Hague, had negotiated. As Baron Bathurst he continued to serve The Tory cause. For two more years his party remained in power until, with the death of Queen Anne, all hopes of a Stuart succession quickly evaporated. The Tories being discredited, the Whig supremacy was sum-marily established. It was to last for two generations.

Bathurst did not allow this reversal of political fortune to dis-tress him unduly. With his natural equanimity he cheerfully accepted whatever the future held in store. He may even have welcomed the social changes he saw ahead. He was lucky perhaps not to suffer the more serious deprivations which, with the advent of the new dynasty, befell certain Stuart supporters more promi-nent than himself. He had been present at Kensington Palace that August afternoon when Queen Anne, whose health for years caused apprehension and speculation about her successor, finally expired. 'Everything has been so quiet since her death,' he wrote to his cousin Strafford, 'and we go on so unanimously in both Houses of Parliament.' And he added, either to tease his cousin or else deliberately to perplex the censors if his letter to Holland should be opened, 'the Tories in the House of Commons are the persons that appear most forward to do the King's business.' Such a way of meeting adversity certainly implied a calm resignation and a cool fearlessness. The last quality was one he displayed on later occasions. He was utterly indifferent to public opinion when adherence to his loyalties was called upon. No considerations of place induced him to swerve from them. During Walpole's administration he boldly spoke against the persecution of Lords Bolingbroke and Oxford—which St. John and Harley had long since become—Queen Anne's ministers then in deep disgrace. He publicly charged the Directors of the South Sea Company with intentionally defrauding the public and urged that they might be brought to justice. When his old friend, Francis Atterbury, Bishop of Rochester, was impeached in 1723 for Jacobite treason, Bathurst in the House of Lords leapt to his defence, although he must have realized that his case was indefensible. He bitterly attacked the bishops for their relentless hostility. He could hardly understand their inveterate hatred and malice, he declared, 'unless they were infatuated like the wild Indians, who fondly believe they will inherit not only the spoils, but even the abilities, of any enemy they destroy'.

How far Bathurst himself was implicated in the same activities as the Bishop of Rochester is doubtful. It is fairly certain that the Old Pretender looked upon him as a likely supporter, and with some reason. Two years after the abortive landing of James in Scotland in 1715, the Prince's agent, the Earl of Mar, was advised that his master would do well to thank several English sympathizers for their financial assistance. Amongst them was named Lord Bathurst who, Mar's correspondent wrote, had advanced £1,000. Again, Mar in a letter of the same year to James referred to Bathurst 'as a very pretty gentleman of a plentiful estate and a true lover of Patrick [the Pretender's pseudonym] as his father was. . . . This is not the first money he has given for his service to my knowledge, nor will it be the last, I believe.' Whether these advances of money meant more than an understandable sympathy for the unfortunate heir to the Stuart dynasty, to whom the Bathurst family owed its present happy position in the world, may never now be revealed. A letter, written several years after Bathurst's death by Horace Walpole to the Rev. William Mason, suggests that it did. Walpole was referring to the

2nd Earl Bathurst, then Lord Chancellor of England. '*Cette tête à perruque*, that wig-block the Chancellor, what do you think he has done? Burnt all his father's correspondence with Pope, Swift, Arbuthnot, etc.—why do you think? Because several of the letters were indiscreet. To be sure he thought they would go and publish themselves, if not burnt, but indeed I suspect the indiscretion was that there were some truths which it was not proper to preserve, considering *considerandis*. That is just what I should like to have seen. There was otherwise so much discretion, and so little of anything else except hypocrisy in all the letters of those men that have appeared, that I should not so much regret what discreet folly has now burnt.' If, then, Allen Bathurst was in his youth involved in the Atterbury Plot, a commendable discretion in middle age did not prevent him from doing all in his power to serve his old friend during, and even after, his trial and exile. Bathurst's concern in the Stuart predicament inevitably waned with the course of time. During a debate in the Lords in January 1726 he said there was no longer occasion to mention the Pretender's name in order to raise fears in the public, 'when all were agreed his was an expiring interest'.

Horace Walpole's innuendo may have been actuated by malice, since he never cared for Bathurst, who was his father's consistent opponent. On the Whig Prime Minister's fall from power in 1742 Bathurst was made a Privy Councillor and Captain of the Band of Gentlemen Pensioners. Horace greeted these returns to favour, brought about as they were by his father's disgrace, with an ironical ode in the style of *The Country Maid*, of which one stanza runs thus:

> *Dear Bat, I'm glad you've got a place,*
> *And since things thus have changed their face,*
> *   You'll give opposing o'er:*
> *'Tis comfortable to be in,*
> *And think what a damned while you've been*
> *   Like Peter, at the door.*

In 1757 Bat was made Treasurer to the young Prince of Wales. Horace, alarmed by the accumulating honours, fervently hoped he would not be made the Prince's Governor. This particular fear was groundless, but with the succession of George III Lord Bathurst was granted a pension of £2,000 a year from the Irish revenues. Sinecures and pensions were in the eighteenth century the expected rewards of honourable, as well as dishonourable, men in public life. And Bathurst, who consistently inveighed against corruption, had never wavered from the Tory cause. In 1772—the year his elder son was made a peer for sitting on the woolsack—he was created Earl Bathurst. By then he was an almost legendary figure, venerated in parliamentary circles for his prudence, his integrity and his longevity. In 1775 Burke in one of his greatest speeches in the House of Commons occasioned by the outbreak of the War of American Independence paid a flattering tribute to the old statesman, then in the last year of his life. In moving certain resolutions for conciliating America, Burke drew attention to the fact that Bathurst's life had coincided with the development and, as it seemed then, the decline of England's colonial prosperity.

In spite of being a Tory Bathurst was a man of liberal principles. When the brutal Captain Porteous of the Militia was killed by the mob in Edinburgh, Lord Carteret in the Lords spoke vehemently against them, and the Scots in general. Lord Bathurst expostulated that the Scots were, on the contrary, a brave people who had been provoked beyond endurance by ill usage. He always took the part of the persecuted, and his natural benevolence favoured peace and freedom of the individual. 'The liberty of the press,' he wrote on one occasion to the Earl of Strafford, who was anything but liberal in his views—Lord Chesterfield once referred to his 'excess of bloated pride'—'is the greatest liberty of the subject, and therefore all little inconveniences which arise from it, are to be submitted to.'

Allen Bathurst was one of those carefree creatures who fairly swim through life, for whom the current is seldom treacherous, and the winds of heaven never too boisterous. He was astute and well-informed, without being intellectual. The chief gift the gods gave him at his birth was that least definable, often least desirable, yet always most covetable attribute—charm. The recipient of it may get away with murder. He will come unconsciously to rely upon it as the unfailing stand-by in every difficulty or emergency of his life. It will finally seduce him from effort, possibly nullify his talents, and destroy his soul. It will almost certainly make him unreliable in day to day affairs and in business relationships. Bathurst did not escape some of these pitfalls. There are frequent references in the letters of his friends to his volatility and his erratic behaviour. These failings, which exasperated them, were nevertheless the occasion of much banter and invariable forgiveness.

'The account you send me of my brother,' Benjamin Bathurst writes in 1738 to their staid cousin, Strafford, 'does not in the least surprise me, he has more than once in my opinion quitted his best friends for those I think very indifferent. He flys about in life as in his journeys, still pursuing something new, without taking the least delight in anything he once has known.' Such strictures may be thought a little too severe, but coming from a younger brother are perhaps excusable. Alexander Pope, who loved Bathurst unfeignedly, alludes in letters to his unpredictable movements. He never knows, he says, where he will be off to next. To their mutual friend, Edward, Lord Harley, he complains of his unpunctuality and inability to keep appointments. Matthew Prior has the same criticism to make. 'Lord Bathurst's proceedings with the prose man [by whom their shared correspondent and gossip, Erasmus Lewis, is meant: he, Prior, being Bathurst's 'verse man'] is admirable; T'is a picture,' he writes in 1720 to Harley, half vexed and half amused. 'His lordship having chid me that I never saw him, and desiring me to ride over to Riskings [Bathurst's property at Iver in Buckinghamshire], I did so on Monday, and when I came thither I found he was gone to Cirencester the Friday before; good again, I think this may be added to the piece.' Nevertheless, Prior's resentment did not last for long. Within a few days he wrote again to Harley: 'I am at Riskings with Batty: we drink to your health; moderation.'

A gad-about, he was in Pope's opinion one of the two most impetuous men he knew, the other being Lord Peterborough, the shifty, intriguing *condottiere*, whom Bathurst in no other respect resembled. Always 'pursuing something new', was one of his brother's diatribes, as though a perpetual curiosity and a certain inventiveness in his restless nature was unbecoming to a lord's station in society. Here we have a typical instance of it. 'Lord Bathurst came here the other morning,' Lady Strafford is writing to her husband from her house in St. James's Square. 'He has a most extraordinary fancy for a conveyance at Cirencester that outdoes your contrivances, but I am sure I wou'd not goe in it; he designs to buy the bottom of an old barge that holds twelve people, and to put it upon the carredg of a waggon, and so to have it drawn about with six horses, and a table in the middle. . . . I find he sees Lady Suffolk often.' This was in 1735.

The tart and very feminine postscript in Lady Strafford's letter reads like one of those sly allusions to Bathurst's habitual gallantries, about which he himself was engagingly frank. In the case of Lady Suffolk there was at the time no shred of evidence to suggest an amorous intrigue. Ten years before, Lady Strafford's little shaft might have been nearer the mark. Then Bathurst was an assiduous visitor at Marble Hill, where he helped Mrs. Howard, as she then was, with the layout of her garden. It is true ill-disposed persons—Lady Mary Wortley Montagu was one of them—disseminated rumours with the result that the Prince of Wales, who was supposed to be Mrs. Howard's lover, dismissed him from his drawing-room. The two were old friends by now and Lady Suffolk was just about to embark upon a second, extremely happy marriage. Besides, there is reason to suppose that Bathurst's amours were conducted upon a less exalted plane. Pope in his letters to his friend frequently teased him about his fascination for women and the coming and going of his mistresses. Any casual encounter was grist to his mill; and he let who cared know it. The promiscuous nature of Bathurst's liaisons was attended with occasional threats to health and purse. Swift congratulated him in 1730 on his recovery from what he described as 'the disease of a young man, [which] foretells a long life, if that be any satisfaction in such a world'. Only five years before he had been at death's door, apparently from the same cause, as well as deeply in debt to the amount, so it was being put about, of £25,000. And 'which way has this money gone?' was the inquiry. 'In wenching? I never heard that he played.'

Good living, however, does not seem to have impaired an exceptionally robust constitution. Good fun was always at his elbow from youth to extreme old age. We hear of him at the age of twenty-nine with Lord Jersey, 'two of the prettiest peers in England . . . tucking up' in bed some other lord 'with a young lady'. He loved dancing immoderately. 'He loves a glass of good wine,' wrote his aunt, Lady Wentworth, about this time. He also loved snuff, and would beg his cousin Strafford, when Ambassador at The Hague, to send him the best procurable in Holland. One of the last glimpses of Lord Bathurst is through the eyes of a dinner guest at Cirencester when his host was already a nonagenarian. Bathurst's son, the highly principled and abstemious Lord Chancellor, was present. Shortly after the meal he withdrew, and the father cried: 'Come, now the old gentleman's gone, let us crack another bottle!'

John Gay in some verses, entitled 'Mr. Pope's Welcome from Greece', written to celebrate his brother poet's completion of the translation of Homer, referred in one line to Bathurst,

whom you and I strive who shall love the most.

There can be no doubts in the mind of a peruser of the letters which passed between the leading writers of the age that his contemporaries were deeply devoted to him. His spontaneity, his uninhibited pleasure in their society, his affectionate welcome of,

and his unstinted generosity to, his friends were irresistible. Bolingbroke and Oxford were unvarying in their love for one on whose
public support they could always depend. Congreve, Prior, Swift
and Gay were his constant guests for months at a time. A country
parson from one of Bathurst's Northamptonshire livings reminded
his patron in a fulsome dedication of his translation of Gelli's
Circe how one night at his lordship's dinner table he met assembled
no less a company than Lord Lansdowne, Prior, Congreve, Gay,
Fenton and Pope. It could never be said of Bathurst that he
treated a man of genius like the glow-worm, whose light is admired
but left to adorn a ditch. The men of letters among his friends
were mostly a feckless lot; when they had any money they did not
know how to keep it. So Bathurst acted as their banker, invested
their surplus capital in his own estate development, and saw that
they received a regular and safe return. 'The two hundred pounds
you left with me,' Gay writes to Swift on 16th May, 1728, 'are
now in the hands of Lord Bathurst, together with some money of
mine, all of which he will repay at Midsummer.' On Pope's death
one of his bonds for £2,000, on which he had already received
£1,500 interest, was released by Bathurst, who had been his
financier, to the poet's executors.

Of all these men, the one who was most intimate with him, who
best understood and valued his good qualities was Pope.

> *Oh teach us Bathurst! yet unspoil'd by wealth!*
> *That secret rare, between the extremes to move*
> *Of mad good nature, and of mean self-love.*

Thus from his heart the poet addressed his noble friend in
Epistle III of the *Moral Essays*. The Epistle is dedicated to
Bathurst, and takes the form of a dialogue between the friends.
The poet, who has been charged with toadying to the great, and
whose words of rancour have been likened to poisoned barbs that
spare neither enemy nor even ally, was consistently loyal to
Bathurst. He termed him 'a preserver of ancient honour'. He
found in the extrovert character, and the robust physique of the
imperturbable Bathurst a refuge from the thoughts that tormented
his own hypersensitive mind and the pains that racked his own
misshapen body. 'Your head and your limbs are of so good a
make,' he tells the peer less with envy than with admiration, 'that
the more active the machine is made to play, the better it works:
with such weak ones as mine, the least extraordinary motion puts
'em out of frame.' There are, on the other hand, frequent petulant
complaints of Bathurst's utter neglect of him. Bitterly he asks him

to recall 'that there was at the latter end of Queen Anne's reign, a poet of the name of Pope'. More often his letters express volumes of unashamed, exquisite adoration, which are touching in their simplicity of meaning and childlike lack of restraint. 'I never leave you,' he writes on 6th August, 1735, 'but I wish to say a hundred things to you, and when you go away for any time, I feel my sense of the loss of you tenfold, as men do of the loss of life, when it nears its end, though they never know how to make a right use, or possess a full enjoyment of it. You cannot know how much I love you and how gratefully I recollect all the good and obligation I owe to you for so many years. I really depend on no man so much in all my little distresses, or wish to live and share with no man so much in any joys or pleasures. I think myself a poor unsupported, weak individual, without you.' A more sincere profession of attachment and dependence could hardly be imagined.

We do not know how Bathurst responded to these effusions. It was not in his nature to reciprocate in the same measure. He may indeed have been slightly perplexed, for he was too sympathetic towards human frailty to be embarrassed by words like the following, addressed to him three months later: 'I dream of you still, and you are the object of my dotings; like an old woman that loves the man that had her maidenhead.' His letters to Pope express a tender concern for him and breathe the gentle affection of an elder brother towards the man who was, indeed, four years his junior. He too can reproach his friend for not writing. 'You are perpetually roving,' he writes in what one suspects is a mild offensive calculated to parry a similar charge against himself; 'and one must shoot flying (to speak in the language of the country) to hit you.' He indulges in a fraternal badinage which he knows will flatter the poet's sensibilities like nectar laced with laudanum. 'I have often seen you write in your sleep, nay to my knowledge you translated half Homer when you were scarce awake; how easy then,' he pleads, 'wou'ld it have been for you to have write me half a dozen times in all this time.' He urges Pope either to let them meet in London, or to come and stay. 'I would quit the finest walk on the finest day in the finest garden to have your company at any time' is meant as a concession not to be treated lightly. And on another occasion: 'If you refuse coming I'll immediately send one of my wood-carts & bring away your whole house & gardens, & stick it in the midst of Oakley-wood, where it will never be heard of any more, unless some of the children find it out in Nutting-season & take possession of it thinking I have made it for them.' It was protective and affectionate injunctions such as these which warmed the cockles of the lonely and hypochondriacal poet's heart and made him feel wanted and cared for. He must come and stay, Bathurst repeats, and bring John Gay, if he is not too busy with his new work, *The Beggar's Opera.*

It is a fact that a large part of the painful translation of Homer's *Odyssey* and *Iliad* into rhymed couplets was accomplished by Pope either while staying with Bathurst at Cirencester or Richings,[1] or while his friend was his guest at Twickenham. Pope regarded the truly immense undertaking as the one work by which his name would be ensured remembrance by posterity. He translated at incredible speed, with an apparent facility which was deceptive. The tension and sweat involved were mitigated to a large degree by the presence in the house of some friend, with whom he felt perfectly at ease, and with whom he need exercise no ceremony. Bolingbroke and Bathurst were far and away his closest companions. Of the two Bolingbroke had first place in his esteem. The brilliance of his mind matched his own. Pope admitted that there was no man whom he admired more unreservedly. But to be with him was an intellectual exercise which, however stimulating, was exhausting over a long period. Bathurst, as we have seen, appealed to Pope as the very complement of himself. His openness, his disregard of all obstacles, and his gay vitality were balm to the other's jangling nerves. Moreover Bathurst was wiser, if less incisive than Bolingbroke. And his company made less demands. Pope probably took liberties with him which he would not have dared to take with the other. Bathurst hints at it obliquely in a letter to Pope. 'My charitable vanity or folly supplies bread to many industrious labourers, and therefore I would think no further,' is an allusion to Pope's *Epistle to Lord Burlington*, sent to him for his comments before publication. And he goes on, 'I have often thought myself the better for your company, though you have slept all the time you have been with me'—a slightly rueful recognition of their intimate relationship, but one implying the highest tribute a friend can pay to another. Certainly Bathurst used to recount, long after the poet's death, how Pope would translate Homer in the mornings, the words tumbling over each other before he recaptured them on paper. At breakfast he would recite, first the Greek text with

---

[1] Riskins, Riskings or Richings Park, near Iver, Buckinghamshire, was inherited from the Apsleys. Here Bathurst carried out grand improvements to the gardens. Lady Hertford, whose husband finally bought it from Bathurst, described Richings as 'nearer to my idea of a scene in Arcadia than any place I ever saw. . . . The house is old and convenient . . [There were] a cave overhung with periwinkles . . . little arbours interwoven with lilacs . . . high beech tree walks', etc. Both house and gardens have long since disappeared.

great rapture, then his own translation. Having done this, he would subside into his chair in a state of utter exhaustion. After a while he would ask his host for comments, when the old eager light would return to his eye, as he rebutted or accepted each criticism in its turn. He was so anxious for friends' approval that once he sent to a lady the present of some cherries wrapped in his manuscript translation, for lack of other paper, with the request that each scrap be returned, with comments, by the bearer.

'Bathurst was negative, a pleasing man,' was the terse and ungracious verdict of Samuel Johnson, who would admit no other of Pope's circle of noble friends to be 'such as that a good man would wish to have his intimacy with them known to posterity'. Whatever diversity of opinions historians have reached in interpreting the characters of Bolingbroke, Oxford, Lady Mary Wortley Montagu, Lady Suffolk and others of the noble circle whom the doctor censured in one explosion of middle-class disapproval, at least his contemporaries agreed over that of Lord Bathurst. 'That excellent lord,' Edward Digby, a co-publisher in 1729 with Oxford and Bathurst of the *Dunciad*, calls him in a letter to the poet. And he says in words that must have made the recipient's little heart glow with pride and love: 'With him I know not by what connection, you never fail to come into my mind, as if you were inseparable.'

On his death in 1744 Pope bequeathed as a small gesture of gratitude to his protector and patron three canvases in grisaille by Sir Godfrey Kneller of the statues of the Farnese Hercules, the Venus de Medici, and Apollo. They had been expressly done for him by the painter, as we are to understand from the following lines in Pope's *Miscellanies*:

> What God, what genius, did the pencil move
> When Kneller painted these?
> T'was friendship warm as Phoebus, kind as love
> And strong as Hercules.

They hang today in the house at Cirencester which Lord Bathurst built for himself and where the poet used to stay, sometimes for months on end.

These strange, full-length pictures in chiaroscuro were, indeed, Pope's last gift to Allen Bathurst. They are by no means his only memorial at Cirencester. On the contrary, the whole vast property owes much of its inception to the poet. For the strongest bond between these men was not the political sympathy of two Tories over a long period dominated by Whig philosophy and govern-

ALLEN BATHURST, 1ST EARL BATHURST
Portrait by Sir Godfrey Kneller, 1719
Reproduced by permission of Earl Bathurst

Phot

THE 'HEXAGON', CIRENCESTER PARK
Probably designed by Lord Bathurst

CIRENCESTER PARK HOUSE AND THE BROAD RIDE
A view from the Church Tower

Photo

ment, not literary interests, nor intermittent bursts of ageless conviviality—strong as these ties undoubtedly were—but the love and practice of silviculture and landscape design. It was in these sciences that Bathurst was a master. In Pope he found an eager participator, albeit the amateur to his professional, who was also a scholar of that deep classical learning which in the eighteenth century went into the composition of gardens and parks. Pope's brain and vision, and Bathurst's taste and practical experience of forestry combined to produce the largest area of Early Georgian landscape layout to survive in Britain.

ii. Cirencester House

The correspondence which passed between the friends until Pope's death in 1744 began at least as early as 1718, in which year Pope made his first visit to Cirencester. A broken chain of letters from that date onwards has been preserved. It is very likely that the peer and the poet had been acquainted long before. Since they moved in the same circles and since Bathurst's villa at Richings and Pope's at Twickenham were within easy reach of London and each other, earlier visits were possibly exchanged and views on gardening pooled during Queen Anne's reign. Unfortunately, much of their correspondence has been destroyed, or lost, so that little sequence in the progress of the work at Cirencester can be gleaned from what survives.

The house which Sir Benjamin Bathurst went to live in when he bought property at Cirencester in 1695 was known as Oakley Grove. It bore little resemblance to the present Cirencester House, which stands on the same site and incorporates some of the ancient walls. An engraving by Kip, dated 1712, shows Oakley Grove to have been an E-shaped structure with gables and end wings projecting towards the town. It had been built for Sir John Danvers early in the seventeenth century. Danvers cannot have lived in it for more than a very few years, because he sold it in 1615 to the Pooles. His ancestors had acquired what was known as the tything of Oakley fairly soon after the Dissolution of St. Mary's Abbey of Cirencester, founded in the twelfth century by the Black Canons of the Order of St. Augustine. It amounted to that half of the monastic property which lay to the west of Cirencester town; the other half, lying to the north-east, went to a Richard Master, whose descendants, the Chester-Masters, still own the greater part of it today.

It was the Jacobean house to which Allen Bathurst was brought

3

when eleven years old, which he inherited, and where he entertained Queen Anne and her husband one August night of 1708 on their journey to Bath. After the Queen's death six years later Bathurst found himself out of office. An entirely different sort of life confronted him. It held no terrors for him. Unlike most of his Tory colleagues who clung to politics and the court Bathurst was relieved that his public services were at least temporarily suspended and that he was obliged, as much from prudence as inclination, to retire to the country. He proceeded to set about improving his inheritance. Two things were immediately necessary: the rebuilding of the out-of-date Jacobean house and the creation of a park according to the latest notions of taste and propriety. He began with the house.

Allen Bathurst was, at this turn of his fortunes, just thirty years old, with another unforeseen sixty years before him. He had for a decade combined the rôles of serious politician and gay Lothario. There were no adolescent pranks of his companions to which he was not party. He drank, he danced with the best. He wore the most expensive and finely chosen clothes. He had a splendid physique and a handsome face. He was, we are told, by no means displeased with the figure he cut in the world. It would have been surprising had he any misgivings about his person, which was attractive according to written accounts. There is a portrait of him at Cirencester taken in 1714 by Kneller. It shows him in the plenitude of youth and power. But it is of a stiff dummy in Coronation robes. The face is sadly prosaic, a stodgy pudding of a face, and, one surmises, hardly a living likeness. Another portrait taken ten years earlier in company with his demure and fawn-like child wife, by Michael Dahl, is more revealing. The face here is that of a boy, but that of a personage. The long, rather protruding, pointed nose, and the cleft chin are distinguishing features, repeated in an even better portrait by Kneller taken in 1719. Yet another likeness is the bust done by Nollekens when Bathurst was advanced in age and dignity. This bust, of which one copy was provided for Lord Cobham's Temple of Friendship[1] at Stowe, and another, now in the library at Cirencester, has been set beside that of Lady Bathurst (also by Nollekens) over their monument in Holy Trinity chapel of Cirencester church. Both are so skied in front of a window, and so obscured by dirt that it is very difficult to see them properly. The wife's bust is that of a woman advanced in age, frail and gaunt, with hair scooped back from hollow temples over her ears to hang in a neckerchief behind

[1] The Temple still stands after a fashion, but the bust has gone.

the head. The sinews of her throat are scraggy, the nose is sharp and thin, the cheek bones are high. In spite of her wan and tired air she carries her head proudly and defiantly. The husband looks comparatively robust and was perhaps younger than the wife at the time of his sitting. At any rate his face is full; the chin is heavy, the eyebrows are arched, the look is quizzical. He wears a Roman toga across his chest. Altogether he is jovial and complacent.

Nowhere in the surviving correspondence does Lord Bathurst refer to any plans for the alteration of his house. Yet if he did not totally rebuild Oakley Grove, then he certainly transformed it. To all outward and inward appearances the present Cirencester House is a different building from its predecessor. Having demolished the wings of the Danvers house Bathurst was left with a rectangular structure which he then proceeded to play about with. Work was probably begun in 1715 and finished by the end of 1718. In August of the last year Bathurst wrote to Pope that he was still being 'disturbed with the noise of saws and hammers, which has no other ill effect whatsoever attending it but only that it is apt to melt money sometimes'.

The finished thing, it must be admitted, was not an outstanding success. With its two plain fronts, without orders and almost devoid of ornamental features, Cirencester House can hardly be termed a gem of architecture. But it has its points of interest. The chief is perhaps its old-fashionedness. Its style accords with the Bathurst family's declared Toryism. On the whole Tory builders still favoured the old Wren style of country house, which was homely, with its straightforward plan of two large rooms on either front and two entrance doors upon an axis. The Tory landowners were stoutly opposed to Italian ideals and foreign craftsmen. It was the progressive Whigs who were to sponsor the Palladian villa type of country house, which they usually magnified two- or three-fold, and sometimes decorated with contemporary rococo patterns, often by Italian stuccoists imported from Venetia. The Whig process had only just begun, and in 1710 William Benson's Wilbury Park near Amesbury was the first country house to be built on a Palladian model, taken from an unpublished drawing by Inigo Jones. The architect of Cirencester House was very possibly Bathurst himself. Mr. Hussey has suggested that Bathurst may have had at the back of his mind his old college, Trinity, which his uncle largely re-edified in a very insipid style with, it is said, the advice of Wren, and that he even engaged an Oxford builder, such as one of the Townesend family, to conduct operations. Whoever the designer was, his work was neither very inspired nor very well executed. After Bathurst's death in 1775 his son's agent reported that the structure was already extremely unsound. The 2nd Earl feared he would have to pull it down and begin all over again. His Countess even protested, 'I shall be quite afraid of sleeping in it', owing to the roof timbers being in so rotten a condition. Curiously enough, Allen Bathurst did not seem to interest himself unduly in the form or style of his new house. Beyond replacing the Jacobean structure, which to his eyes must have been quite barbaric, he was not very particular. His remark to Pope, when the work was finished, 'I trust to you to give an account how it comes to be so oddly bad', strikes a note rather of indifference than surprise.

A second point of interest is the house's closeness to the town. The Whig grandees went to great pains to isolate their country seats, sometimes at the expense of numerous lesser dwellings and cottages in the near vicinity. In order to dwell in detached splendour, remote from the common herd, it was no uncommon thing to remove a whole village out of the way and re-erect it in some more discreet spot. The Tories on the other hand still liked to maintain the time-honoured squire's connection with the village community, of which they prided themselves on being members if autocratic ones. Bathurst evidently associated himself with this squirearchical notion. One front of his house can almost be described as being on the town street, from which it is only separated by a high wall and a massive semicircle of yew, reminiscent of the baroque forecourt of St. Peter's, Rome, in extreme miniature. This conscious conceit was possibly suggested by Pope.

Bathurst's motives for rebuilding on so extensive and costly a scale were, then, more political or social than aesthetic. He was simply following the prevailing rage of the day for some sort of change. Sir John Summerson has calculated that between 1710 and 1740 as many as one hundred and forty-eight great country houses were built, or rebuilt, in England alone. They were a symbol of the general confidence of the age and a token of the security and wealth of the newly established class of gentry to which Bathurst belonged. His friend, Jonathan Swift, had satirized this very propensity for building in *Gulliver's Voyage to Laputa*. When Gulliver arrived at the country house of the Lord Munodi, he was overcome with admiration of the noble structure, raised according to the best rules of ancient architecture, by the fountains, gardens, walks, avenues and groves which adorned it, all disposed with exact judgment and taste. He gave unqualified praise to what he saw. To his surprise his encomiums were received in melancholy silence. After supper, when no third person was by, his host confided to him with a sad air that he had been obliged utterly to destroy his beloved old home and its plantations, and to rebuild and re-cast them 'after the present mode', unless he were prepared to submit to 'the censure of pride, singularity, affectation, ignorance [and] caprice', as well as to earn his sovereign's lasting displeasure.

There was much similarity, as of course Swift intended, between the Lord Munodi's absurd situation and that of Bathurst and his contemporaries in that both the inhabitants of Laputa and Great Britain often felt driven to greater expense than they could well afford merely to keep abreast with their neighbours, and to maintain their prestige in ministerial and court circles. Only in Bathurst's case the difference lay in his not feeling compelled to adopt the latest 'mode', which in poor Munodi's involved employing 'a most ingenious architect who had contrived a new method of building houses, by beginning at the roof, and working downwards to the foundation'. His methods, on the contrary, were unimpeachably conservative and traditional, perhaps defiantly so, in order to flaunt his Tory allegiance. He appeared to show no ostensible interest in the new Palladianism notwithstanding his subscription to Leoni's English translation of Palladio's *Four Books of Architecture*, published in 1715. The curious factor is how Bathurst earned some little reputation as a builder in these early days. Lord Bute in a letter of 1715 to Lord Strafford compared his own low taste in architecture to the consummate experience of Lord Bingley (the builder of Bramham Park house and creator of its then unrivalled gardens), 'and the rising merit of Bathurst'. Lord Strafford eagerly sought his cousin's approval of his new gallery at Wentworth Castle.[1] And yet the man whose knowledge of building he so much admired had written to him not long ago: 'I think any house good enough to sleep in,' and consistently discouraged other amateurs from dabbling in architecture.

iii. Cirencester Park

If Bathurst's house shows little originality, his park is quite another matter. The first was undertaken by himself alone, the second in collaboration with Pope and other friends, who furnished him with the most convincing arguments drawn from classical precedent. His own first-hand experience of the growth of trees and shrubs supplied the necessary, practical knowledge.

[1] In the West Riding. At that date known as Stainborough.

Kip's view of the old Danvers house showed the lands to the west of it, before they were covered with Lord Bathurst's plantations. Those lands then appeared to be open, rolling wolds and thinly-scattered woodlands of no unusual contour or beauty. In 1716 Bathurst bought from the executors of Sir Robert Atkyns, who had been Gloucestershire's first and eminent historian, a large area to the west of, and contiguous to, his own property. It comprised Oakley Wood and the manor of Sapperton, where, on the east slope of a valley and close to the parish church, stood a picturesque Tudor manor house, the home of the Atkyns family. With that utter disdain of the eighteenth-century man of taste for all non-classical architecture of whatever period or style—unless it were deliberately mock medieval, Moorish or Chinese—Bathurst razed the old house to the ground some years later. The distance of Sapperton from Cirencester is five miles as the crow flies. Bathurst proceeded to make of the intermediate area a series of conjoined parks, united by one immensely long avenue, and, in the words of Mr. Christopher Hussey, 'the finest example surviving of plantation on the pre-landscape model'.[1] The extended property on which he was now free to impose a uniform layout was remarkable for this reason: it comprised the original estate, a flat table-land, whose springs feed the infant Thames (its source was actually on his acreage) and the western valleys, whose streams belong to the Severn watershed. Thus the property offered that variety of contour which to the landscape creator is a boon seldom granted. Bathurst lost no time in profiting to the full from what his own good fortune and astuteness had acquired.

As Christopher Hussey has pointed out, Cirencester Park is a forest, with rides and glades cut out of it, rather than grassland streaked with woods and coppices. The difference probably accounts for its survival after two hundred years. Bathurst's method was to amalgamate several different regions by planting trees where none previously existed, and out of the dense growth created to carve and mould the shapes he had in mind. If beech was his staple crop, chestnut, elm, and oak were liberally introduced, with a sprinkling of wild cherry, yew, and occasional coniferous trees. He laid great emphasis upon seasonal colouring, and his calculated efforts to achieve it contribute to his deserved reputation as a great planter.

It is not improbable that one of Bathurst's first motives was to emulate his rich and powerful neighbour, the Duke of Beaufort at Badminton. The newly-risen in early Georgian times were

[1] *Country Life* articles, 16th and 23rd June, 1950.

incredibly naïve in their efforts to assert their social equality with the old-established families. The contemporary park at Badminton, now only known to us through plans by Kip and others, embraced an immense area of the countryside. It belonged to the seventeenth-century Le Nôtre style of layout. A rectangular area, enclosing the house, was plotted into strictly formal lawns, orchards, mazes and parterres. Outside this area long, straight avenues, crossing open country, radiated from one focal point, a mile or more from the house. If Kip's accuracy may be relied upon, no less than twenty-three rides met at the *rond-point*. It is significant that Bathurst did not follow this particular style of landscape, and, in fact, studiously avoided making his house a prominent feature of the layout. It might, as it turned out, have been better had he done so, for the relation of house and park at Cirencester is oddly equivocal.

Horace Walpole in his chapter on Modern Gardening[1] had the grace to concede that Bathurst's influence upon park landscape was very considerable. He praised him for having made planting subservient to utility and ornament and, more important still, for having created scenes of unsurpassed beauty. He recognized in him one of the first to explode the false taste of Le Nôtre and King William's gardeners. Bridgman and then Kent, whom Walpole admired inordinately, were in fact the very first to break away from the tyranny of the formal strait-jacket, of which Versailles is the most notable victim. But Kent evolved another type of garden, which, important though it was in its influence, did not approximate so closely to the picturesque landscape (universally accepted in Walpole's middle age) as Bathurst's at Cirencester. What Kent aimed at was a limitation of landscape. At Chiswick and at Rousham he may have 'leapt the fence', but he created small elysiums of confined dimensions. Bathurst on the other hand was centrifugal in his aims. There was nothing confined about his bold conception, which sought to embrace the wide world as its domain. And indeed Bathurst's park, although conceived at a time when Le Nôtre's was still the accepted form of layout among country house owners in England, had certain affinities with the picturesque school of the future. Bathurst lived to witness and even to be affected by the dominant ideals of Capability Brown. He may have remained faithful to the scheme he had formulated in his young manhood, but he inevitably modified it in certain particulars as the years proceeded. Furthermore, the park, though far advanced, was not completed until after his death. The Home

[1] See *Anecdotes of Painting in England*, for Chapter XXIII, Vol. III: 1876 Edition.

and Oakley parks were still separated during his lifetime, and quite a mile of the eastern extremity of the great Broad Walk was planted by his successor after 1775.

The decisive influence upon Bathurst's original conception may well have been the famous short essay which Pope contributed to the *Guardian* in 1713. In it were laid down several maxims which Lord Burlington and Kent adopted, and instantly put into practice at Chiswick. I shall come to them in a later chapter. But Pope's cogent theme, with which he opened his essay, established an entirely novel principle in garden layout. His words began as follows:

'There is something in the amiable simplicity of unadorned nature, that spreads over the mind a more noble sort of tranquility, and a loftier sensation of pleasure, than can be raised from the nicer scenes of art.

'This was the taste of the ancients in their gardens, as we may discover from the descriptions are extant of them [*sic*].'

He thereupon proceeded to quote from Virgil and Homer in order to illustrate those principles which the Burlingtonians so avidly adopted.

To us, accustomed to admire the simplicity of unadorned nature, Pope's exordium may at first seem trite, and hardly worth reiterating. But in 1713 his words were considered subversive. Until that date the gardens of Europe had, ever since they were first made in medieval times, remained thoroughly formal and artificial. They were a silent protest against the savage wildness of the country outside their bounds. At first they amounted to a few beds in the shape of knots of flowers, or herbs, within high palings. As the Renaissance advanced, terraces expanded, and statues and fountains were introduced. In all their varieties gardens remained cabined and confined. Straight canals, straight alleys, straight vistas always intersected at right-angles. Nothing was allowed to grow naturally. Flowers were regimented, hedges were pleached, yews were treated in topiary and trees trimmed. By the time Queen Anne was on the throne English gardens had truly adopted the grand manner of the Continent. They were still formal, and axial. Then Alexander Pope in one short essay announced that all such gardens were in a deplorable taste, that the ancients had known better and should be imitated, in that they allowed nature to rampage, untamed and unadorned. Instead of gardens being controlled and ordered so as to produce 'nice scenes of art', they were to blend with and even ape hostile nature, hitherto only found outside a domain and shunned by all persons with pretensions to civilization as rude and horrid.

Bathurst was one of the first landowners to carry out Pope's injunctions on an immense scale. He truly 'saw', in the phrase of Horace Walpole, 'that all nature was a garden', but unlike Kent, to whom these words were applied, he made his garden literally comprise fields and valleys, streams, woods, open spaces and prospects. Compared with the parks of a later generation Bathurst's will strike us as formal enough, for straight vistas, often with classical temples punctuating the extremities, are still the rule with him, as they were with Kent. But the irregularly shaped woods through which they cut, the glades upon which they opened, and the occasional serpentine walks which threaded a way from one section of the park to another, constituted the revolutionary beginnings of the new movement in landscape design. Added to these innovations, the romantic buildings, with which Bathurst diversified his grounds, had never before been seen in England.

Pope was well pleased with Bathurst's beginnings on his park. After a first visit to Cirencester around midsummer of 1718 he wrote delightedly: 'My Lord, to say a word in praise either of your wood or you, would be alike impertinent, each being, in its kind, the finest thing I know, & the most agreeable. I can only tell you very honestly (without a word of the high timber of the one, or the high qualities of the other) that I thought it the best company I ever knew, & the best place to enjoy it in.' The reference to high timber is presumably ironical, for Bathurst's new plantations must at this stage have been in their infancy. The gentle irony is borne out by the verses Pope enclosed in his letter:

> *Woods are, not to be prolix,*
> *Collective bodies of straight sticks;*
> *It is, my Lord, a mere conundrum*
> *To call things woods, for what grows und'r 'em,*
> *For shrubs, when nothing else at top is,*
> *Can only constitute a coppice.*
> *But if you will not take my word,*
> *See Anno quart. of Edward, third.*
> *And that they're coppice calld, when dock'd,*
> *Witness Ann. prim. of Henry Oct.*

These instructive lines about Oakley Wood the poet put into the mouth of John Gay, who had not yet visited it, but was enthusiastic over Pope's account of its natural beauties. 'He has already planted it with myrtles and peopled it with nymphs,' Pope added. In any case Pope was making his mother spend a month or two at Stanton Harcourt in Oxfordshire in order to facilitate his journeys to her from Cirencester where 'I will not fail to be with you, whatever time you shall pass there in August'. However, on 14th August Bathurst was pressing Pope to seize the 'opportunity of this warm weather to inhabit the silvan seat' in Oakley Wood. 'It will destroy the pleasure if I perceive that you are not as free with it as if it were entirely your own.' To which Pope replied, 'I never was more earnest for any innocent thing than to enjoy the Silvan Bower this season.'

The Silvan Bower has disappeared. It may have stood on the site of Alfred's Hall, which was not begun until 1721. It must not be confused with Pope's Seat, which survives, a Doric temple with raised centrepiece, flanked by niches, facing south across the Seven Rides down an avenue, focused upon the spire of Kemble church, and down another terminated by Queen Anne's Column. Pope allowed himself to be driven to the Silvan Bower, where he would compose an hour or two in the mornings, be served with refreshments by an attentive servant in livery, and brought back to the house later in time for dinner. On other days, when he felt more robust, so he told his dear friends, Teresa and Martha Blount, he would go hunting on the downs, 'eat heartily, talk tender sentiments with Lord B or draw plans for houses or gardens, open avenues, cut glades, plant firs, contrive water-works, all very fine and beautiful in our imagination'. It is unlikely that he would be allowed by his solicitous host to sleep the nights in the Bower. In a letter of the 18th September Pope revealed that his August visit did take place, and that he and Bathurst after heated discussions in the daytime fell asleep over their game of commerce in the evenings. 'I believe you are by this time immers'd in your vast wood,' refers to the rides and vistas which Bathurst must have been cutting through Oakley Wood as a consequence of their daily discussions and evening ruminations before the effects of port overcame them. 'Everywhere I think of you, and everywhere I wish for you,' the poet added wistfully on his return home.

Pope is soon back again. These early days are critical for the future of Cirencester Park, and there is endless planning still to be done. On 8th October he is writing to the two Blount sisters: 'I am with my Lord Bathurst, at my Bower, in whose groves we had yesterday a dry walk of three hours. It is the place that of all others I fancy & I am not yet out of humour with it, tho I have had it some months: it does not cease to be agreeable to me so late in the season; the very dying of the leaves adds a variety of colours that is not unpleasant. I look upon it as a beauty I once loved, whom I should preserve a respect for, in her decay. And as we should look upon a friend, with remembrance how he pleased us

once, tho' now declin'd from his former gay and flourishing condition.' This condescending assessment of the beauties of autumn
strikes us, who no longer feel obliged to seek excuses for our
appreciation of them, as either insincere or affected. And why,
unless the season induced melancholy reflections, Pope should
have regarded his Bower, which must have been newly built and
was to him a matter of only a few months' acquaintance, in this
nostalgic spirit, remains unexplained.

Two years pass, and Pope is writing to Bathurst in 1720 about
Cirencester's elysian groves. 'I could say, almost in the style of a
sermon, the Lord bring us all, etc.! *Thither* may we tend, by
various ways, to one blissful bower; *thither* may health, peace, and
good humour wait upon us as associates; thither may whole
cargoes of nectar (liquor of life and longevity) by mortals called
Spa-water, be conveyed; and there (as Milton has it), may we,
like the deities

> *on flowers reposed, and with fresh flowerets crowned*
> *'Quaff immortality and joy'.*

In September 1721 Pope is at Cirencester once more. He is still
enthusiastic over the improvements. On 15th he writes to Lady
Mary Wortley Montagu: 'how had I despis'd, & totally forgot my
own little *colifichies*, in the daily views of the noble scenes, openings, & avenues of this immense design at Cicester? No words,
nor painting, nor poetry (not even your own) can give the least
image proportionable to it. . . .' And in May of the next year he
makes claim to much of the results that unfold before his eyes.
To a friend he speaks of the glories of Oakley Wood: 'I look upon
myself as the magician appropriated to the place, without whom
no mortal can penetrate into the recesses of those sacred shades.
I could pass whole days, in only describing . . . the future, and as
yet visionary beauties, that are to rise in these scenes: the Palace
that is to be built, the pavilions that are to glitter, the colonnades
that are to adorn them; nay more, the meeting of the Thames and
the Severn, which (when the noble owner has finer dreams than
ordinary) are to be led into each other's embraces thro' secret
caverns of not above twelve or fifteen miles, till they rise and openly
celebrate their marriage in the midst of an immense amphitheatre,
which is to be the admiration of posterity a hundred years hence.'

By 'the Palace that is to be built' Pope is not, of course, referring
to Cirencester House which by 1722 was already finished, but to
the Wood House in the middle of Oakley Wood. It is interesting
that Bathurst was already contemplating the junction of the

Thames and the Severn. Posterity did not, in fact, have to wait a hundred years, and Bathurst died a mere fourteen before the $2\frac{1}{4}$-mile Sapperton Tunnel, with its crenellated Gothic and its sober classical openings, was dug under his property and the Thames and Severn Canal formally opened by King George III in person. The ceremony took place in 1789. One cannot help wondering if on that notable occasion any tributes were paid to the man, whose finer dreams had conjured up the very vision then being enacted on land, which his taste and judgment had so signally beautified.

The next letter in the series comes from Bathurst and is dated 21st October, 1723. It concerns the Wood House. Bathurst had been suffering from giddiness, for which he was blooded and purged on successive days. In spite of this disability he boasts—and how well he knows that Pope will admire his courage and resilience—of having daily visited his plantations either on foot or horseback. 'I am resolved,' he says, 'to begin the alterations of my wood house, and some little baubling works about it, which you shall direct as you will. I have tired myself with computations and designs of things which cannot be completed in my own time, and I am now resolved to follow the rules of Horace, who in one place says,

Vitae summa brevis spem nos vetat inchoare longam:

and in another,

Carpe diem, quam minimum credula postero.'

That Pope interested himself in the form the Wood House took is indisputable. That Bathurst was chiefly responsible for the design and entirely so for its execution there is little doubt. A great deal of thought, work and correcting was put into a concoction of small importance—small, architecturally, yes: but, as it turned out, of great consequence academically. The Wood House, King Arthur's Castle, or Alfred's Hall, as it was ultimately named when it had assumed the shape it presents today, was the ancestor of Sanderson Miller's tower on Edgehill (which in Horace Walpole's words 'preserves the true rust of the barons' wars', and has been held to be the archetype of all such castellated follies, although actually built twenty years after the Cirencester one was begun), of Dunstall Castle at Croome, the tower at Hagley, the eye-catcher at Wimpole, and, later still, of those countless imitation castles with which James Wyatt, John Nash, and Thomas Hopper adorned the romantic landscapes of the early nineteenth century Bathurst evidently began upon this toy in 1721, for in that year

CIRENCESTER PARK

Bishop Atterbury in a letter hoped 'my lord may have as much satisfaction in building the house in the wood and using it when built, as you have in designing it'. In 1732 he was still busying himself about it, as he explained to Pope on 24th July: 'I have now almost finished my hermitage in the wood, and it is better than you can imagine, and many other things are done that you have no idea of. However there is enough remaining to employ you for a week at least, and occasion the consumption of a quire of paper in draughts. I will venture to assert that all Europe cannot show such a pretty little plain work in the Brobdingnag style as what I have executed here.'

By the Brobdingnag style—although Lilliputian would seem a more accurate standard of measurement—Bathurst must have had his friend, Dean Swift, well in mind. For Mrs. Pendarves (later Delany) writing to the Dean of St. Patrick's from Cirencester on 24th October, 1733, says: 'My Lord Bathurst talks with great delight of the pleasure you once gave him by surprizing him in his wood, and showed me the house where you lodged. It has been rebuilt; for the day you left it fell to the ground, conscious of the honour it had received by entertaining so illustrious a guest, it burst with pride!' It is regrettable that Swift's reply does not exist to tell us whether he was more gratified by the honour done him, or by relief at his miraculous escape from destruction. He may have had very different memories of his sojourn there, if a sentence in a letter of his to Bathurst in 1735 can be taken seriously. He then reminded Bathurst of an occasion when 'Mr. Pope, poor Gay, and I, were forced to lodge at one of your farmers, and walk two miles to dinner, with your two thousand five hundred acres of garden, and not a codling to eat'. The Wood House, Mrs. Pendarves continued in her epistle to the Dean, is 'now a venerable castle, and has been taken by an antiquarian for one of King Arthur's'. This misunderstanding must have pleased its creator inordinately. That his folly of only a few years' existence should take in some self-important, omniscient, old professor of archaeology was just what the gay lord hoped for above all things.

A comfortable capacity for self-deception is, we all know, the first essential ingredient of the successful folly-maker. Bathurst did not lack it. And the more far-fetched a learned allusion to antiquarian derivations, the more plausible and the more acceptable it became to him. A pedantic friend advised Bathurst that the old scribal name for Oakley, *Achileia*, was to be identified with the *Egleah* of Asser's *Life of Alfred the Great*. Since it was common knowledge that Alfred had not a little to do with the peaceful sojourn of the Danes at Cirencester, after their defeat by him at Edington, the association of the Saxon monarch with Oakley Wood was quickly taken for granted. Hence the re-christening of the erstwhile Wood House, or King Arthur's Castle.

Alfred's Hall is today very romantic in its secluded clearing of Oakley Wood. The ruin is draped with ivy and enclosed by a grove of appropriately melancholy yews. Its round tower has one pointed window, which should not deceive the least discerning antiquary. The hall, to which the tower is attached, contains two inserted windows of genuine Tudor date, brought by Bathurst from Sapperton Manor, which he had ruthlessly demolished. Indeed the folly has much Tudor, and even some medieval masonry oddly inserted in its walls. Bathurst confessed that he had brought a 'great quantity of very good hewn stone from the old house at Sapperton to the great centre of Oakley Wood'. The hall itself has an open roof, its heavy timbers supported on projecting corbels. The windows are suitably filled with coloured glass, on which a baron's coronet and two stag supporters are emblazoned. Whenever he came to decorative detail the most hardened Georgian 'Goth' found it difficult entirely to escape from his own Vitruvian age. The fireplace has a large stone lintel, on which are carved impeccably classical swags. The whole building outside is crenellated, it is true, but remains transparently, delightfully sham.

Bathurst had spoken of 'some little baubling works' around the hall. Many of these have now gone. Rudder's *History of Gloucestershire*, published in 1779, gave two little engravings which showed a gatehouse at the rear and some carefully contrived ruins, as of cloisters, on the east side of the main building. Some walls survive, and a decayed, pointed gateway of tufa stone, piquantly hollowed by artless time so as to resemble a heap of skulls: and, strangely indeed, in the open yew grove a genuine Renaissance chimney-piece of interlaced carving and, casually thrown within the ghostly fireplace, a quatrefoil window-head covered with moss.

It is unlikely that Alfred's Hall was used for accommodating Lord Bathurst's guests. But it was a useful objective for *al fresco* meals on summer evenings, when the shadows cast by the black yews evoked in the breasts of romantic Georgians suitable nostalgic yearnings for Saxon deeds of valour. It was also the scene of an annual music meeting, where the country people assembled to pass the day in fiddling, dancing and drinking. After an immense bucolic feast at their lord's expense they all dispersed, as best they could, at nightfall.

Throughout the latter part of the 1720s few letters between Bathurst and Pope relating to the progress of the park and its adornments survive. But there is no reason to suppose that there was any break in the correspondence. In October 1724 Bathurst wrote as affectionately as ever a long letter, mildly complaining about his social duties in the neighbourhood. 'I was forced to entertain [to dinner] . . . two or three odd people, who were not fools enough to be laughed at and yet were far from having sense enough to make a conversation; a most accursed mediocrity. After this I was obliged to make a visit to a country neighbour. I found him in his hall. I may properly say I found him, for I looked sometime before I could discover him, being enveloped in thick clouds of tobacco. So much civility was paid to me that I was obliged to remove out of the great hall into a little parlour, which by misfortune had just been washed. The honest friends who had just been entertaining him before were to follow us into this parlour, and the agreeable smoke which had filled a larger hall was to be transferred to the little room, with the addition of a good deal of other smoke which proceeded from a chimney that had not been incommoded with fire since last Christmas, and consequently the soot helped to the delightfulness of the smell. Not to trouble you further with this description, our drink was as bad as our conversation, and I have had too much of each.' The most aloof arcadians—and the good-natured and convivial Bathurst was not one of them, nor, one suspects, so bored as he pretended to be—are obliged to suffer worse afflictions than these described. It was certainly not the only occasion on which Bathurst would have liked to be better employed. Six years later, in describing Cirencester to Swift as 'this dominion, which I prefer to any other', he added darkly: 'There are Yahoos in this neighbourhood.' ~~Women.~~

In the autumn of 1725 he went on a long northern expedition to Derbyshire and Staffordshire on private business. His travels included a visit to Lord Carlisle at Castle Howard to see the works in the grounds there and, in its owner his cousin's absence, to Wentworth Castle. He found Lord Strafford's house, gardens and menagerie much improved since his last visit. The columns in the long gallery had just been set up, to make that apartment very magnificent; and the gardens, by being opened to the park, had benefited considerably.

In September 1728 Pope visited Cirencester while Bathurst was away. Posts were so slow and unreliable, journeys so long and exhausting, and inns so few and often unaccommodating, that the owners of large country houses expected their friends to turn up without warning. If they happened not to be at home, the servants decided who were cherished favourites and set about to make them comfortable as their masters would have done, had they been there. When however Pope got to Bath he wrote a collins to his absent host that was slightly critical. 'I saw the steeple of Ciceter stand on one side over' the house. He disliked the resulting asymmetry, which he must have overlooked on countless previous visits, and advised the steeple's forthright demolition. He noticed 'the great vista in Oakley Wood to the said steeple by being widened beyond its former hedges, bordered now only with some low thing, which I took to be a box-hedging on either side'. This was the great Broad Ride now five miles long which is the axis of the whole park. It was, as Pope implied, cut out of Oakley Wood, and was focused upon Cirencester church tower, although in his day it had not yet been extended by a mile towards the town end. The Ride is today completed by a mature avenue, chiefly chestnut and beech, whose low skirts sweep down and brush the scythed grass. 'I beheld,' the poet continued ironically, 'with singular satisfaction every tree that bore the least pretence to high timber, totally cut down and done away. Whereby I see with delight the bare prospect you have made.'

The devastation, to which Pope took exception, was presumably in the preparation of either the vast circus, called Seven Rides where Pope's Seat now is, about a mile from the town end of the park, or even of the wide clearing further west, where are to be found the Round House, the Square House and Ivy Lodge. It must be remembered that to derive his effects in Oakley Wood Bathurst was faced with felling, instead of planting trees. And the felling of fine mature trees always distressed Pope. The shock was all the more disturbing because he had obviously not been consulted by his friend beforehand. He furthermore noticed what he called 'High Wood' being pierced for a ride which would call for some building at one end. He would not advise an obelisk, but volunteered no positive suggestion.

In 1730 Bolingbroke wrote to Bathurst: 'Are you planting Are you levelling? What are you doing? [The Earl of] Essex thinks, with me, that the marriage of the line of the great park with the house is practicable, but that it requires the phlegm he master of rather than your lordship's impetuosity to contrive.' It was all very fine for Bolingbroke, the most impatient of men, to accuse Bathurst of impetuosity—all his friends did that. Had he, Bathurst, not already been at work on his park for at least fifteen

JONATHAN SWIFT, DEA
OF ST PATRICK'S
Bust by L. F. Roubiliac in
Trinity College, Dublin

tional Portrait Gallery

NDER POPE
t attributed to
an Richardson

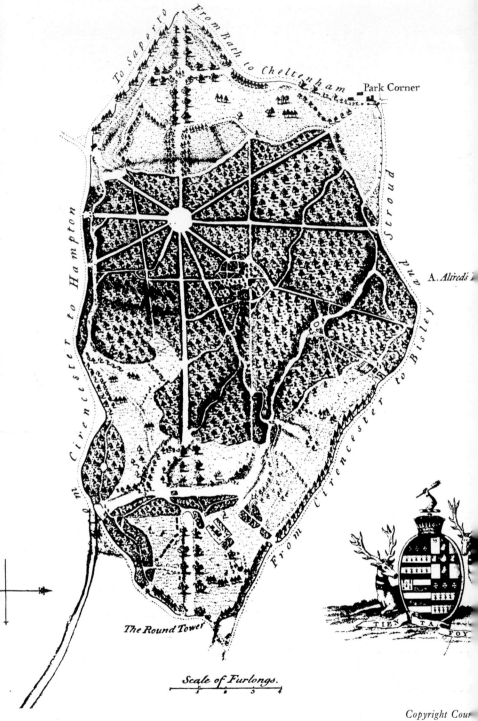

To Saperto

From Bath to Cheltenham

Park Corner

Cirencester to Hampton

Stroud

A. Alfreds

Cirencester to Bisley

From Cirencester to Bisley

The Round Tower

Scale of Furlongs.

TIEN . TA . FOY

PLAN OF OAKLEY GREAT PARK, CIRENCESTER
From Samuel Rudder's *Gloucestershire* 1779
before the Broad Ride was completed

years? And did he not intend so to continue until the last breath was left in his body? Anyway, he must have known that Bolingbroke and Essex were talking nonsense; or else their memory of his property was very faulty. Not even the phlegm of the latter peer could contrive to marry the great Broad Ride from Oakley Wood with the house, short of making a kink in its hitherto straight course to the south-east. Pope's advice was one thing. He was the inaugurator of the new garden style on which the Cirencester planting was based. Besides his visits were so frequent that he knew the park only less well than the owner thereof. Walpole was undoubtedly right in his dictum that the proprietor, if he be a man of taste, must be the best designer of his own improvements. He sees the site through all the seasons of the year, at all times of the day. 'He knows where beauty will not clash with convenience, and observes in his silent walks, or accidental rides, a thousand hints that must escape a person who in a few days sketches out a pretty picture, but has not had leisure to examine the details and relations of every part.'

On 1st October of this year Pope refers in a letter to Bathurst to his lordship's order of British elm trees from a nursery in Isleworth, and provision of leaden statuary for the park. His friend, Patty Blount, who 'has always a partiality for you, notwithstanding your eternal neglect', proposes to substitute herself as an ornament, and put herself with the statues in the waggon from London. Pope's letters were not, as we have seen, always in this facetious vein. His criticism could sometimes be bitter, if not unjust. Bathurst writing to Lady Suffolk in July, 1734, says: 'Pope endeavours to find faults here, but cannot; and instead of admiring (as he ought to do) what is already executed, he is every day drawing one a plan for some new building or other, and then is violently angry that it is not set up the next morning.'

During the ensuing two years Bathurst was again in serious financial difficulties, owing to reckless over-spending. In the late summer of 1735 he felt obliged to sell one estate; but instead of investing the proceeds—which he would have advised a friend to do in like circumstances—promptly bought another. He found it extremely hard to retrench, and was already laying designs for the next season's planting. To leave Cirencester for London, and even for Richings, was becoming increasingly distasteful to him. Nevertheless it was a duty to attend Parliament during the sessions, 'at least whilst there is any hopes that a vote may be of use', he confided in Lord Strafford. And he ended a long letter to him with the disingenuous regret, calculated no doubt to shock

4

his staid and correct cousin, that he had not had himself castrated years ago. Then he 'might not have got more children than I am now able to maintain, considering the just and necessary taxes we are all oblig'd to pay to support the exigencies of the government, who have labour'd under a long and fruitless peace'. And less than twelve months later, in July 1736, he confessed to Strafford that he had undertaken a scheme too large for his pocket, and must now leave it to a son or grandson to complete. Meanwhile he would allow his imagination of what the park might become in fifty, or sixty years' time, to supply what his exhausted purse was failing to put in train.

All these admissions of financial exhaustion read very sadly: and, as they were addressed to a close member of the family, they were doubtless meant to sound pitiful. What the true position was, we may never know. At all events, one month had not gone by when Bathurst (on 14th August) was inditing to Pope a long letter, full of very ambitious schemes indeed. It is one of the most important of his letters in all the series to the poet, because it throws a very particular light upon his activities.

He begins by exhorting Pope, who is about to stay at Stowe, to come on to Cirencester. 'One day's journey further will make but little odds,' he says in that engaging manner which brushes aside all obstacles like cobwebs, once he has set his mind on something 'Now to show you that I have a most manifest want of you at this present juncture I send you the enclosed plans.' The plans, which no longer exist, probably related to the temple, now called the Hexagon, which is set on the north side of the Broad Ride, before Pope's Seat is reached, and faces the transverse ride, leading to the main Cirencester–Tetbury road. 'That marked a,' Bathurst goes on, 'was drawn first. Afterwards I had a mind to have a cupola on purpose to try the effect of the Cornish slate, which we can have from Bristol at a pretty easy rate.' In fact no cupola was put on the Hexagon, which actually has a shallow parapet to the roof. The apex is crowned with a ball. 'In the plan marked b the building is described and the ground plot. It must be of that shape because it is to answer three walks, and the materials must be the same as those with which the seat was built, because they are already brought to the place, and because I think that rough stone exceedingly pretty, and am ready to stand all the jokes of *Rusticus expectat*,[1] etc. This building will be backed with wood, so that

---

[1] Horace's *Epistle* I, ii, 42, contains these lines:

> . . . *qui recte vivendi prorogat horam,*
> *rusticus expectat dum defluat amnis at ille*
> *labitur et labetur in omne volubilis aevum.*

nothing can be seen but the three sides.' So far this description applies correctly to the existing Hexagon, which is backed by trees, and does face three walks, so that only three of its sides, which are open, are visible from the front. As for the materials, they are the same as those used for the poet's Seat, namely what Bathurst calls a rough stone, which is very hard-wearing. The surrounds of the openings, like those of Pope's Seat, are treated in frost work. 'I design the ribs of the cupola shall be done with lead, which I will gild or paint of gold colour, which being set off by the blue slate will look admirably well. I will certainly make the three arches like that in the plan marked *a*, but I am in doubt how to settle the fascias and the cornice, etc. Now I leave it entirely to you either to come and settle this affair yourself or send the directions.'

As I have already said, the cupola was not carried out. The purpose of the long quotation is to postulate that Bathurst was his own architect of the Hexagon, with the assistance and approval of his friend, Pope, who had likewise co-operated with him to a large extent in the formation of the park. There is therefore reason to assume that Bathurst may also have designed the other temples and follies on the estate, as well as the house itself.

The letter continues: 'Another building is to be erected afterwards to answer the other diagonal which will also overlook the lake, no contemptible body of water, I can assure you. It will be at least as big as the canal at Riskins.' As for the lake, this is the first time we hear of it. Such an adjunct was considered indispensable to a Georgian country gentleman's seat. As long ago as 1718 Pope noted the deficiency when in a letter, otherwise full of encomiums, he remarked, 'there wants nothing but a cristal rivulet to purl through the shades'. With great trouble and in order to have water within view of the house Bathurst contrived to get it from a long distance. Far from resembling the formal canal popular in his youth, the lake at Cirencester was irregular in shape, and made to look as natural as possible—a complete departure from precedent and even ante-dating the large serpentine lake at Stourhead certainly not begun before 1741. At Richings Bathurst had previously deviated from the dead straight line in water so as to follow the natural contours of the land. He claimed to be the first person to have done so. Lord Strafford, thinking it could only have happened out of poverty, begged his cousin to tell him in confidence how much more it would have cost to make the canal—

He who puts off the hour of right living is like the bumpkin waiting for the river to run out; yet on it glides, and on it will glide, rolling its waters for ever.'

it was five hundred and fifty-five yards long—straight. In order to make believe the Cirencester lake was larger than it actually was, Bathurst carefully disposed clumps of trees at its either end.

Finally, Bathurst concludes his long letter of 14th August by informing Pope: 'I have also begun to level the hill before the house, and an obelisk shall rise upon your orders to terminate the view. The foundation of the building [i.e. the Hexagon], described in the enclosed plan will be laid' by the time of Pope's visit, 'and one arch up; but I will do no more before you come, if by the next you tell me that you will be so good to your faithful servant.'

The immense task of reducing the height and levelling the resulting excavation of the hill on the far side of the lake, and directly in view of the house, was certainly carried out. Bathurst had long cherished a secret determination to do reverence to that sovereign, who had been the girlhood friend of his mother and the fount of his own honours. Queen Anne was the last reigning Stuart, and the Bathursts had always faithfully served that family. Had not six of his father's brothers lost their lives fighting for King Charles I ? The years when it would have been indiscreet for him, a suspected Jacobite, to raise a memorial to the Queen, were passed. He could now safely proceed. So nice was his judgment that he deemed the existing hill where the memorial could best go, to be just too high and just the wrong shape. He did not hesitate to alter it to suit his requirements.

Pope, however, was by no means in favour of an obelisk. It 'can bear no diameter to fill so vast a gap', was his instant reply, 'unless it literally touches the skies'. He advised instead 'a solid pyramid of 100 ft. square, to the end there may be something solid and lasting of your works', which was perhaps a caustic hint that no other building of his friend was likely to bring him immortality. In the end neither an obelisk nor a pyramid was constructed. A Doric column of marked entasis with a statue of the Queen on the top, was raised in 1741. This noble monument on its regular plateau is seen axially from the house, and diagonally from Seven Rides. Moreover, it marks the end of a straight line which runs from Cirencester church tower through the centre of the pediment of the park front of the house. In other words Bathurst had borne in mind Pope's querulous jibe of September 1728 about the church steeple not appearing to be centralized with the house. Instead of demolishing it, which might, even in George II's reign, have aroused unpleasant controversy with the vicar Bathurst planted his avenue before the house in alignment with it

On 6th September Bathurst wrote once again to his cousin

Strafford. Without a trace of embarrassment or shame, as though quite unmindful of his pleas of poverty less than two months previously, he announced his hill-levelling operations. 'I have cutt through one of the hills and lett in a view up one of the diagonals, which terminates upon a little building which I have erected; next summer I shall build another to answer the other diagonal, and cut thro' that hill.' The little building, which was shortly to have a fellow, is probably one of the pair of temples, called the Horseguards. They stand on either side of the Broad Ride, to the west of Hermitage Bottom (a deep declivity dividing Oakley from Sapperton Wood), and before the clearing, known as Ten Rides, is reached. As well as facing down the Broad Ride to the church tower, they look obliquely, or at least used to do before the rides were choked, in a south-westerly and north-easterly direction respectively. The Horseguards are simple erections, each with a very tall opening, as though to accommodate a mounted life-guardsman of gigantic stature, between Ionic pilasters, which are rather too attenuated. They are frankly amateurish.

Having spoken of the levelling he had already done, Bathurst proceeded to describe his designs upon the hill opposite the house for the Queen Anne memorial. 'All this levelling work,' he wrote complacently, 'will not amount to above £50 or £60, and the situation of the house will appear as good again as it does at present.' No wonder his cousin considered Allen to be a little crazy.

Bathurst's correspondence in the latter part of his life either declined, or has not been preserved. There are occasional amused references to him by his friends. 'Lord Bathurst is in Gloucestershire, where he plants, transplants and unplants; thus he erects an employment for himself independent of a court,' was the casual remark of one friend in the summer of 1737. In October of the following year Frederick, Prince of Wales, was entertained at Cirencester, from which the obvious deduction to be made is that Bathurst was at the time not *persona grata* at the court of his father, George II. In 1739 he was obliged to part with Richings to Lord Hertford. Then in July 1741 another friend related to Dean Swift that 'Lord Bathurst is at Cirencester, erecting pillars and statues to Queen Anne'. It is the last glimpse we have through the written word, of his building activities at Cirencester.

He was in fact to be as active as ever for another thirty-four years, and his head as teeming with new ideas as it was in his youth. Bolingbroke was constantly referring to his spending most of his days out of doors, on horseback, and so remaining stronger and younger than his own sons. He must, too, have gone on building. There are no records to tell us precisely when he built the three engaging Gothic houses in and around the wide clearing before Oakley Wood. There can be little doubt that, fortified by Pope's outspoken comments, which this good-natured and un-assuming peer invariably heeded, he designed them himself. The relation they bear to Alfred's Hall precludes any other authorship. The Square House derives its name from its artificial pele tower, boasting pointed two-light windows. It and the annexe to the tower are crenellated. The Round House is distinguished by a circular tower, with pointed single-light windows. It has a sort of defensive machicolation running round the parapet, in Norman dog-tooth pattern. On the parapets are blind loops, for imaginary cross-bows. At the rear an extension bears a crenellated hexagonal chimney.

The last of these early precursors of the neo-Gothic revival is Ivy Lodge. It is a more ambitious and delightful fantasy than either the Square or Round House. It consists of a two-storey block facing south, with a double flight of steps leading to a pointed front door. There are a round-headed window and a pair of blind roundels on the façade. On either side of the block are low screens—pierced with pointed couple windows—linked to flank-ing wings which are gabled, stepped, and crenellated. The east wing conceals one end of a medieval barn facing east. The west screen and wing are in reality a blank wall, with nothing whatever behind it. The word *folly*, which conjures up an eccentric, useless piece of architecture, fit only for show, does not fairly describe these three buildings. Bathurst certainly intended them to be adornments to his great park; but also to be farm dwellings, which they always have been, and still are.

As the years went by Bathurst visited London less and less, and stayed at his beloved Cirencester for longer and longer periods. 'Your lordship who is a lover of the country,' he wrote to Strafford after one of his parliamentary visits to Westminster, 'may judge of the mortification it was to me to be kept so long away from a place I am fond off, and confin'd to a place I dislike extremely. . . .' Nevertheless, the man who once told Lady Suffolk that the four most desirable things in life were 'old wood to burn, old wine to drink, old friends to converse with, and old books to read',[1] could never become a hermit. His perpetual vivacity, of which Lady Mary Wortley Montagu had occasion years ago to complain, and his insatiable curiosity impelled him to exchange opinions in the mart of all new ideas, which is

[1] Bathurst was, without admission, quoting Saint-Evremond.

ALFRED'S HALL, CIRENCESTER PARK. BEGUN 1721

POPE'S SEAT, CIRENCESTER PARK

IVY LODGE,
CIRENCESTER
PARK
Probably designed
by Lord Bathurst

London. He positively welcomed new faces. In 1767 he introduced himself at a party to Laurence Sterne, who was delighted with him. The author of *Tristram Shandy* recounted, with customary vanity, how Bathurst declared that his company rekindled old desires to be with men of genius again. For were not all the peer's closest intimates, the pride of their generation, now dead? 'This nobleman, I say,' Sterne wrote to his daughter, 'is a prodigy: for at eighty-five he has all the wit and promptness of a man of thirty. A disposition to be pleased, and a power to please others beyond whatever I knew: added to which, a man of learning, courtesy and feeling . . . the good old lord toasted your health three different times.' The gesture was characteristic, coming from one who, with his tongue in his cheek, had solemnly averred to the Dean of St. Patrick's 'that woman's milk is the wholesomest food in the world'. He was now looked upon as Methuselah. People would nudge each other in passing him in St. James's Square, and tell old anecdotes that linked him with a past age: how he was educated by a distinguished scholar, his uncle, born in James I's reign: how as a young man once standing at the bar of the House of Lords beside a nonagenarian whom he asked how long it was since he was in the Chamber, he received the reply, 'Never, my lord, since I sat in that chair:' and, watching him point to the throne he recognized the decayed features of Tumble-down Dick, the second Lord Protector of England; and how the great Burke, in one of his highest flights of oratory, had related his life's span to the rise and disintegration of Britain's colonial empire.

To within a month of his death he rode two hours a day round his park, and drank, without fail, his bottle of claret or madeira after dinner. He died at Cirencester in 1775, and was buried off the north aisle of the church in the same tomb as his wife. The monumental inscription is worded perhaps rather more gravely than befits his true character, which, however serious at times, was never solemn. 'In the legislative and judicial departments of the great Council of the Nation'—one can picture his son, the hatchet-faced Lord Chancellor, rehearsing these pious phrases—'he served his country 69 years with honour, ability and diligence. Judgment and taste directed his learning, Humanity tempered his wit, Benevolence guided all his actions. He died regretted by most, & praised by all.' The trappings of death were in the eighteenth century invested with a traditional pomposity, and if the epitaph leaves out the lighter list of the deceased's virtues, it certainly includes nothing that is undeserved.

Bathurst's proper memorial in this transitory world is still to be seen, and what is more, enjoyed. After nearly two hundred years it has miraculously survived, owing to his descendants' unceasing care and maintenance. Of all the arts, that of landscape design is about the most ephemeral. The 2nd and then the 3rd Earl Bathurst completed, while slightly altering, the 1st Earl's layout. Their successors have, however, conscientiously cherished its original features. The skeleton of an early eighteenth-century park on an immense scale is intact.

As was only to be expected, change of taste caused the generation after Allen Bathurst's to find many faults in a style of planting, which it considered neither natural nor picturesque enough. John Byng, who visited Cirencester in 1787, recorded in his diary that Lord Bathurst 'did wonderful things here; but I cannot think with taste, as he adher'd to the formal style of his youth'. It would indeed have been strange if he had not. And Bigland's *Gloucestershire* of 1791 declared that 'The several buildings . . . are in themselves neither sumptuous nor beautiful,' and the 'park so justly admired . . . may decline a comparison with those in a modern and more correct taste.' 'The modern taste' is considered by all ages the only 'correct' one. It is a doctrine fraught with dangers. Therefore the duty of posterity should be to assess the achievements of its ancestors, not by its own, but by their standards. No opinions of Lord Bathurst's creation are so valuable as those of his contemporaries and friends, many of whom I have already quoted. On the whole their praises were vociferous. Pope was an accredited arbiter of landscape design in his day, as he was of architecture. We know how unsparing he could be in disapproval of efforts, which he deemed commonplace or pretentious. He did not hesitate to lacerate the great, if he thought they deserved it, and the Duke of Chandos in the rôle of Timon received the full measure of his disapproval, in spite of Pope's later denial of the identity. In the realms of silviculture and architecture the two noblemen whose achievements he revered above those of all others were Lords Bathurst and Burlington. Their best tribute perhaps is discovered in the following two couplets from Epistle IV of Pope's *Moral Essays*:

> *Who then shall grace, or who improve the soil?*
> *Who plants like Bathurst, or who builds like Boyle.*
> *'Tis use alone that sanctifies expense,*
> *And splendour borrows all her rays from sense.*

The creations of Richard Boyle, Lord Burlington, in which Pope again played no inconsiderable part, belong to another chapter.

PEMBROKE II

HENRY HERBERT

9th EARL OF PEMBROKE

1693–1750

---

i. Eagle and Dove

HENRY HERBERT was truly born in the purple. His background was one of tradition and culture, against which highlights of service and gallantry shone forth conspicuously. His father Thomas, 8th Earl of Pembroke, 5th Earl of Montgomery, and Lord High Admiral of England, had been for half a century the representative of a great family whose origins and territorial wealth dated from far beyond Tudor times. In other words the Herbert fortune did not spring from the Reformation although it was considerably augmented by the confiscation of monastic lands. The 1st Earl of Pembroke, Holbein's patron, unlike many of his contemporaries was no upstart raised to greatness by an implacable sovereign in return for abject subservience. He was in no need of honours to be bought by such humiliating terms. He was already a scion of noble and ancient family before Edward VI advanced him to an earldom. The 2nd Earl was married to Philip Sidney's sister Mary, the immortal 'subject of all verse'. Their children the 3rd and 4th Earls were England's greatest poet's 'incomparable pair of brethren'. And if there is still no proof that the 3rd Earl was the recipient of Shakespeare's sonnets, and his Countess the dark lady, he was undoubtedly a youth of angelic beauty and she Mary Fitton, who by a clandestine marriage enraged her jealous mistress, Queen Elizabeth. The 4th Earl was no less certainly the patron of Inigo Jones, a specimen of whose rarely authentic architecture is found at the Pembroke seat of Wilton House near Salisbury. So during Henry Herbert's childhood, which was spent at Wilton, the famous Inigo Jones south front, with behind it the Cube and Double Cube Rooms displaying a series of family portraits commissioned from Vandyke by his great-grandfather, were not yet half a century old. There were perhaps still some veteran retainers in the Wilton household who recalled the father of English architects, wearing his melon-shaped cap over unruly grey locks which streamed in the wind, as he strutted head in air about the fussy parterre beds, shouting directions to his deferential disciple and adopted son, John Webb.

It is not fanciful to suppose that the child Henry Herbert, who was seven years old when the seventeenth century drew to a close, eagerly cherished every scrap of information about the great Inigo that he could glean. For the Architect Earl, as he was one day to be called by his contemporaries, grew up to be Inigo Jones's fervent champion and played a prominent part in reinstating his prestige, which throughout the long dominance of Wren and the reign of the baroque school had lain neglected and unhonoured. Those days were still some way ahead. Meanwhile the 8th Earl was the master of Wilton. He was no mean virtuoso of the arts, being a collector on the grand scale. He bought the Arundel marbles and Mazarin busts, with pedestals, many of which remain at Wilton. He added a large number of rare books to the library. His great speciality was gems and intaglios, of which he amassed an important selection, much admired by George Vertue, the antiquarian. He employed agents in London and abroad to search for rare specimens. Pope in his *Moral Essays* refers to one such agent, who

> *Buys for Topham drawings and designs,*
> *For Pembroke, statues, dirty gods, and coins.*

The father extended his patronage to poets. He was responsible for inviting to England in 1715 or 1716 Paolo Rolli, the portentous and overrated Italian poet whose drama *Alessandro* was put to music by Handel. Rolli long before he arrived had earned an inflated reputation in this country on the strength of his translation into Italian of Milton's *Paradise Lost*. It was not that the pedestrian version particularly impressed the English—few of whom had cast an eye upon it—but that the mere fact of a foreigner taking so much trouble was flattering to their self-esteem. In return for the Earl's protection Rolli dedicated to Lady Pembroke a sumptuous edition of his *Canzonetti e Cantate*.

Henry Herbert—styled Lord Herbert from his birth in 1693 until his succession to the earldom on his father's death in 1733—followed to all outward appearances the narrow path of duty which every eighteenth-century nobleman was expected to tread. The official peerages give a prosaic account of the honours that befell him.[1] There is a certain hollowness in the conventional ring

[1] Foster's *Peerage*: Doyle's *Official Baronage*: Collin's *Peerage*.

which the rising list of promotions gives forth. One can almost
recapitulate them as one falls asleep: 1714 Lord of the Bedchamber to the Prince of Wales (an office which he retained when
the Prince became George II): 1715 Deputy-Lieutenant for the
County of Worcester: 1717 Captain and Colonel, the Coldstream
Regiment of Foot Guards: 1721 Captain and Colonel, the 1st
Troop of Horse Guards: 1733 High Steward of Salisbury and
Colonel 1st (King's Own) Regiment of Horse, Lord-Lieutenant
and Custos Rotulorum of the County of Wiltshire: 1735 Groom
of the Stole and First Lord of the Bedchamber to George II:
1742 Lieutenant-General of His Majesty's Forces: 1748 Lord
Justice of Great Britain. Thus the hackneyed but worthy catalogue
unfolds. There are moreover two incidents, not mentioned by the
official peerages, which have an important bearing upon the only
issues of Herbert's life that give him a claim to our attention,
namely architecture and archaeology. About both these pursuits
the 9th Earl of Pembroke, in that maddeningly patrician way
which must needs draw a veil across the serious facets of a man's
career and only invite attention to the frivolous or ephemeral, is
typically reticent. It was beneath the dignity of gifted noblemen
to be thought experts in any branch of science or art. It was held
incumbent upon them to deprecate the attribute of professional,
which was only fitting for those people of middling birth whose
livelihood depended upon the superior exercise of their talents.

The first incident on which the official peerages throw no light,
and on which Herbert himself is silent, is this. In the year 1712
he was travelling in Italy. The only evidence that he went on the
grand tour lies in six words of a written report from Mr. Cole, the
English Minister in Venice, to the Secretary of State in London,
dated 5th February. 'My Lord Herbert came last Saturday.'
Nothing further. On 4th March following Mr. Cole notified the
Secretary of State that the Duke of Argyll passed through on his
way to London. John 2nd Duke of Argyll was a distinguished
General whose monument by Roubiliac in Westminster Abbey is
one of the greatest works in sculpture of the century. Like his
brother Archibald, Earl of Islay, who succeeded him as 3rd Duke,
he was an intimate friend of Herbert, an enthusiastic Palladian and
a fellow patron of Herbert's architect protégé, Roger Morris. It is
then quite possible that the two men—the Duke was fifteen years
the other's senior—had been travelling together round Venetia in
the pursuit of their common interest, architecture, as well as
of objects of virtu.

The second incident, which is a culminating rather than an

anticipatory landmark in Herbert's life, was his election in 1743 as a Fellow of the Royal Society. This was a coveted honour not granted even in early Georgian times to men solely on account of their high birth. It was then, as now, the reward of merit in one of the various fields of science. Herbert's qualification must have been in the field of archaeology, but how much it amounted to seems uncertain. He was the first patron of the Egyptian Society. He was an intimate associate of that learned divine, Doctor William Stukeley, whose unbounded enthusiasm for Druidism led him to make some reckless pronouncements on the aboriginal patriarchal religion and to publish as genuine what transpired to be one of the major archaeological frauds of all time.[1] In the summer of 1719 Herbert visited Stonehenge with Stukeley on three separate occasions, helping him to take accurate measurements of the stones. At other times they opened barrows together on the Wiltshire Downs. For days on end they would examine their finds, sift their evidence and discuss the probable origins of the monuments they had disinterred. Three years later Herbert with a group of friends, including Stukeley, founded an Antiquarians' Club in London to promote the study of Roman Britain. They called it the 'Society of Roman Knights', the members, who even included some women, taking their titles curiously enough from those of Celtic princes, or notables ostensibly associated with the Roman Conquest of Britain. In such a capacity Herbert assumed the title Carvilius.[2] The purposes of the Society seem to have been confused; but the one point of view that united the members was a bitter distaste for the Gothic, which they identified with a species of barbarism in conflict with the pure classical tradition of British culture.

Herbert introduced Stukeley to his father who invited him to prepare a catalogue of the antique marbles and sculpture at Wilton, but the task yielded little result owing to Herbert borrowing the manuscript during one of those rare intervals when the Doctor visited his benefice at Stamford, transposing the sheets, adding and omitting what he thought fit, and generally making nonsense of it. Years later however Vertue referred to a small book recently published by Herbert on the statues, paintings and works of art at Wilton—it may have been a re-hash of Stukeley's catalogue—with the help and under the direction of Sir Andrew Fountaine. That celebrated dilettante and Norfolk squire, who amassed a fine collection of porcelain, pictures and

---

[1] This was Charles Bertram's *De Situ Britanniae*, purporting to be the work of the fourteenth-century monk, Richard of Cirencester.

[2] Carvilius Maximus was a Consul in the 3rd century A.D.

antiquities at his own house, Narford Hall,[1] was a lifelong friend. Vertue recorded how the two men escorted the Prince of Wales in 1722 to the Academy of Painting in St. Martin's Lane, run by the artists Charon and Vanderbank, where they stayed a whole hour. Herbert patronized, so Vertue jotted down in that magpie-nest notebook of his, John Ellis, who was to become principal painter to the Prince's son Frederick. He also patronized Vertue himself, and there is a payment to him in Herbert's House Book, kept between 1733 and 1749, of one shilling and sixpence, presumably for the engraving of some antiquarian curiosity. There are in addition frequent payments to Paul Foudrinier, described as stationer, the well-known engraver of portraits and views, and to one Thomas Pingo, for engravings of medals. Other desultory items include 'Thomas King for Lutestring' and Stephen Switzer, the horticulturist and writer on gardens, for garden mats and seeds. Mr. Griffier, who may have been John, a painter of riverside views, is repeatedly employed for cleaning pictures; and there are payments to Andien de Clermont, described as 'The Little French painter', who did grotesques for ceilings at Wilton and other country houses besides. Finally the sculptor Scheemakers receives in 1743 and 1744 £100 18s. 4½d. in all for his statue of Shakespeare 'in fine free stone with its little pedestal and ornaments', now in the entrance hall at Wilton, and Roubiliac £30 for the marble head of Sir Andrew Fountaine, also still in the house.

'Is he,' writes Dean Swift, eager for gossip in his isolated misery in Dublin on 30th July, 1733, 'Is he as good an Earl as he was a Lord Herbert? Is he spoilt by being a courtier? Can he still walk faster twenty miles than a coach and six horses?' The new Lord Pembroke had not changed a jot in character or habit because of his great inheritance and his enhanced position at court. He was still universally respected for his enthusiastic promotion of learned institutions and architectural ventures (he had contributed £20 towards the building of Peckwater Quad in Christ Church when he was only nineteen), and his patronage of scholars and artists. Nor was he yet so old—he was just forty—as to have abandoned altogether, in spite of some severe illnesses, physical feats of almost super-human endurance. The 'Hero', as he was known to his friends, was still incredibly strong. 'That Goliath, Samson and Hercules,' the effeminate Lord Hervey called him with a twinge of envy. In his youth he had been a ferocious boxer. He would walk for hours on end, covering vast distances, without showing the slightest signs of fatigue. And he swam, for fun—appalling

---

[1] See pp. 211–12 for a description of Narford Hall by Lord Oxford.

thought in the eighteenth century—like a dolphin possessed. His well-known addiction to bathing is shown by a letter addressed by Lord Chesterfield 'To the Earl of Pembroke in the Thames, over against Whitehall'. Tennis was a favourite pastime, but his swearing was so blasphemous that on one occasion the Primate of Ireland left off playing with him. With violence of action and language went violence of behaviour, for he had an ungovernable temper. There are scraps of letters and anecdotes that bear witness to his rudeness to others. A quarrel a year before his death with the postmaster at Hounslow practically led him to destroy the post-chaises. The man had a hundred devils and Jesuits in his belly, he confided to the Bishop of Chichester in justification of his own conduct. 'Lord Pemb. letter to that son of a bitch commonly called Lord Hillsborough' is the draft heading of a letter, dated July 1739 and preserved at Wilton, wherein the writer demands the repairs of a house rented from him. And the final sentence runs: 'Yr promises you know very well are not to be regarded, nor will I any longer depend upon them,' which, if it was ever dispatched, can only have resulted in a duel. Evidently his opinion of Lord Hillsborough was maintained, for three years later he wrote to a fellow peer: 'Wee heard that Ld Hillsborough was gone to ye D——l, but by yrs which I received to day I find it is not yet true . . . let the bond go to the same person as will take his lordship, to help make the flame the greater.' A letter from a certain B. Woodroffe, possibly Lord Pembroke's chaplain, survives. The writer complains ruefully, but with little apparent surprise, that after thirty years' devoted service and loyalty he had been struck by his lordship in the courtyard. 'I have strove in vain to rub off ye sad remembrance from my mind,' runs the oddly phrased but forgiving missive, 'wch in spite of all my efforts still still (when in ye Cathedral & at my prayers) revolves upon me.' The injury was soon forgotten, for subsequent letters from B. Woodroffe begin 'My Dearest Lord'.

He was, as it happened, usually forgiven. The pugnacious gestures and the torrents of anger quickly abated and turned to uninhibited practical jokes or acts of sheer kindness. The jokes from this distance of time are not always easy to appreciate. The esoteric allusions, subtle and topical, have worn threadbare in the passage of over two centuries. Wherein for example lies the significance of a joint letter addressed by the Duke of Montagu and Lord Pembroke on 26th April, 1736, to Job, the son of Solomon at Bunda, sending greetings? 'We are obliged to you and the Mussulmans of your nation,' they write, 'for the prayers you may

GRISAILLE OF
FARNESE HERCULES
BEQUEATHED BY POPE
TO LORD BATHURST
Reproduced by permission of Earl Bathurst

ARBLE HILL,
WICKENHAM
imncypiccc in the
Saloon

P.

HENRY HERBERT, 9TH EARL OF PEMBROKE
Bust by L. F. Roubiliac, c. 1750
Reproduced by permission of the Earl of Pembroke

to God for our prosperity. . . . We are sorry for the death of your father, or any other domestic misfortune. . . . We are concerned for the shipwreck of most of the things you carried home from hence.' The acts of kindness retain their pristine bloom. Rebecca Abbot, a discarded mistress, sent to her bored lover letters which were self-pitying as well as abusive. Nevertheless, he did not cease to pay her £100 a year in spite of her demands for more and he left her £800 in his will. Farmer Thorpe, a tenant, was given £80 with which to repair Moses Farm. In disregard of the agreement Thorpe pulled down Moses Farm, it being too much decayed, he declared, and made use of the materials for other purposes. A case came up in Chancery, and the Lord Chancellor's verdict was that far from any hardship having been done to the defendant, he had abused the agreement and profited to the extent of £500, which was the estimated value of the materials of the old house. The plaintiff asked for no compensation. He had won his case and that was enough. Lord Pembroke was never vindictive. He was, notwithstanding, undeniably litigious. 'In his lawsuit with my Lady Portland he was scurrilously indecent,' Horace Walpole told his crony, Horace Mann, 'though to a woman.' Walpole's uncle Horatio admitted that he had 'been very boisterous and not extremely civil in his conduct towards her. Yet she has been both untractable, and impudent with regard to her own interest', which was the paltry one of not allowing him a tract of land on which to build a terrace in front of the windows of his Whitehall house. On the contrary she deliberately planted trees to obscure his view of the Thames. Even the Prime Minister failed to temper her animosity towards the Earl and her determination to thwart him at all costs.

There was a gentle side to Herbert's nature. He was constantly generous towards unexalted people who happened to be in need, making them anonymous gifts of money and other things. Did he not give Swift a red velvet cap in the interval between receiving a challenge and fighting a duel? Is his generosity not testified in regard to Palmer's *History of Printing*, of which he gratuitously undertook the whole cost of the publication on hearing of the sudden death of the author who was unknown to him? 'The great and learned Earl of Pembroke,' Nichols, compiler of *Literary Anecdotes*, dubs him in recording this act of charity to Palmer's impecunious widow. In his will he left numerous legacies to relations, friends and godchildren, to old mistresses—adding clauses to prevent their husbands spending the money—old servants and the poor of several parishes round Wilton. We get a further glimpse into Pembroke's contradictory nature when at the time of Queen Caroline's fatal illness George II drafted a command to keep the Prince of Wales away from his mother. The Groom of the Stole suggested a palliative to the unduly harsh wording of the message. The King cut him very short, turned upon him and shouted: 'My Lord, you are always for softening, and I think it is much too soft already for such a villain and a scoundrel.' The wrath of royalty did not have the slightest effect upon his opinions. He was far too proud to be anything but indifferent to ministerial success, and ambition was a quality he did not understand. When urged to remonstrate with Queen Caroline against the ingratitude with which he had been treated by the King, he declined to pay any attention. In the Mastership of the Horse, which everyone considered to be his due, he allowed himself to be superseded by another who had not half so good a claim. He boasted of never having asked for the Garter, which in consequence was not offered him by Sir Robert Walpole, his friend and well-wisher, in the sincere belief that he would decline it, if it were.

His adoration of his animals—and his wife—was genuine and constant. In these two respects he belied Lord Chesterfield's charge of 'his lordship having given pregnant instances of all heroic virtues but love'. He left testamentary directions that on his death none of his horses should be sold, and that when those in London grew past their work they should be taken by easy stages to Wilton; 'and those horses that are at grass', the will laid down 'may be allowed hay where there is not grass sufficient and such horses as by age or other accidents may be rendered unable to feed themselves I would have such horses only to be shot without being carried out of the walls of Wilton Park or Courts there til dead and I do direct that some trusty servant may be employed to see the same executed'. His dogs too were to receive similar kind treatment. There are repeated references in his friends' correspondence to Fop and his successor, Chuff. 'I respect Lord Herbert and Fop,' Lord Chesterfield wrote to Mrs. Howard, 'not without a due mixture of fear of both.' And in 1743 Robert Herbert writes to his brother: 'Pray remember me to yr. Rib and honest Chuff, tho' not a man of his word,' Chuff having previously promised to write and tell him how his master fared. The Rib so bracketed with Chuff was Pembroke's own Genesis appellation of his wife, Mary, whom he married the year his father died. She was the eldest daughter of the 5th Viscount Fitzwilliam and herself deeply interested in the arts and architecture to an extent that was sometimes absurd and made people like the tart old Sarah Jennings, Duchess of Marlborough, mock her. 'I hear my Lady Pembroke told the Duchess of Bedford today that all the cases for knives or anything of that nature at the toy shops are now made in the shape of a pillar of some order, which she thought wonderfully pretty, for she, I mean Lady Pembroke, is not only very knowing in the stars, but she is a great architect herself.' To her Paolo Rolli, that poetical pedlar, dedicated his *David e Berseba* in 1734 just as he had paid homage to her mother-in-law with an earlier composition a generation previously.

'Often mad and always very odd' was the verdict on Lord Herbert of Duchess Sarah, who laboured under a grievance, which we shall shortly investigate. Eccentric he undoubtedly was. One form of eccentricity all but deprived him of his life. He became a fanatical vegetarian to the extent of practically starving himself to death. Parisian society was much astounded to see him walking the streets of their city—this was in 1729—wearing a bag wig, which he treated as a knapsack and kept filled, not with hair, but watercress and beetroot, which he would extract and nibble at regular intervals. For a time vegetables were the only sustenance he allowed himself. Lord Chesterfield remarked to Mrs. Howard that he supposed experience would convince Herbert that 'herbs and watercress are not preservatives against a fever; if his friendship for Fop could prevail with him to follow his example at dinner and supper, I believe it would be better for him'. Other unkind friends attributed this mania to an irrational belief that by depriving himself of meat he was thereby reducing his enormous household expenses.

ii. The Architect Earl

Henry Herbert's principal interest was architecture. That he designed a number of buildings is borne out by the written words of his contemporaries. Unfortunately no working drawings that can be proved his have come to light. Of a total seven buildings of his unquestionable authorship two have completely disappeared. Of the five survivors one is a large memorial column, one a water tower, one a bridge, and two only are complete houses. Nevertheless from them and from what we know of the appearance of the two houses which have disappeared we can conjure up a clear enough notion of Herbert's taste and style.

Of his contemporaries Horace Walpole is the most insistent

upon Herbert's right to be called an architect. He is also the most laudatory. In his monograph of Lord Pembroke in *The Anecdotes of Painters* Walpole declares: 'No man had a purer taste in building than Earl Henry, of which he gave a few specimens, besides his works at Wilton,' and 'Marble Hill and Richmond Lodge are incontestable proofs of Lord Pembroke's taste'. In a letter written shortly after Pembroke's death he is even more categorical. 'His great excellence was architecture,' he says. 'The bridge at Wilton is more beautiful than anything of Lord Burlington or Kent.' Vertue who visited Wilton in 1740 was in no doubts of the authorship of the bridge. 'Very elegant and fine' he called it. 'This is the design of the present Earl of Pembroke & built by his direction. So much skill in the art of architecture by a nobleman does great honour to the art.' Vertue the engraver had often to flatter the great and nobly born, for his livelihood depended to some extent upon doing so. Vertue the antiquary had no need to be adulatory, and his notes were meant for no eyes but his own. Swift too in his Preface to *A Pastoral Dialogue* concerning Marble Hill at Twickenham, is quite definite about the authorship of that riverside domain. 'Mr. Pope was the contriver of the gardens, Lord Herbert the architect, and the Dean of St. Patrick's chief butler, and keeper of the Ice House.' Finally there is, for what it is worth, the esteem of his social equals for his judgment in architectural matters. Lord Chesterfield, when building on a room to his embassy at The Hague in 1728 consulted Mrs. Howard about correct proportions. 'I must submit to you and Lord Herbert, who I hope will be so good as to give me your sentiments upon it.' He feared they would find five great faults in it, 'which are five great windows, each of them big enough to admit intolerable light'. This sharp comment is of interest, for it is a slighting reference to the fashionable Palladian tendency to few and narrow windows upon expansive wall surfaces. Mrs. Howard replied that Lord Herbert had been so ill she dared not trouble him. But if Lord Chesterfield promised to follow the advice given, she would instead consult Lord Burlington.

Walpole does not explain his preference for Lord Pembroke' architecture to that of Lord Burlington and Kent. But it is possible to guess the reason. Walpole was a great stickler for what he called chastity of style. It is why he was later to prefer the purer lines of William Chambers's to the fussy contours of Robert Adam' decoration. He found Pembroke's designs simpler, more truly Palladian even than those of the acknowledged arch-priest of Palladianism and his neophyte. Examination of Pembroke's build ings reveals that they are based upon Palladio, Scamozzi and Inigo Jones to the apparent exclusion of any other master. Whereas Burlington and Kent at times found precedent for their elevations, although they would not have admitted it, in some of Palladio's Mannerist contemporaries like Vignola, and even introduced rococo overtones into their ceiling and wall patterns, Pembroke utterly eschewed all such irrelevancies and deemed them impure.

In other words Pembroke's architectural compositions are less eclectic and more restrained than Burlington's, to judge by the little of his work that was carried out. His houses—none of which was of more than villa size—all follow a recognized formula with but little variation. Even the so-called Water-house at Houghton subscribes to this formula. His dwelling houses are distinguished by their compactness and their verticality. Over a deep, rusticated base, a *piano nobile* and upper floor are contained within one order, the centre either behind a wide tetrastyle portico, or upon a slightly projecting portico-like feature of which the pilasters support a pediment. On either side of the central feature there is one bay only. The roof is usually pyramidal and crowned by a ball and vane.

The first building in which we know Herbert to have taken serious interest was his own villa, called Pembroke House, on the Thames at Whitehall.[1] In 1717 he acquired the lease of a site, then neglected and covered with rubbish, of the Queen's riverside apartments in old Whitehall Palace, long since destroyed by fire. Immediately he proceeded to build, but he was not apparently his own architect. The house is said to have been to the design of Colen Campbell, who took seven years to finish it. At least Campbell in 1725 published the design in volume III of *Vitruvius Britannicus* as his own. At once it established the formula which with only slight modifications Herbert was to follow for the rest of his life.

It is a fact that Campbell was the very first of the eighteenth-century British Palladians. He had published volume I of *Vitruvius Britannicus* in 1715. His famous Wanstead House in Essex was begun the same year, and had an instantaneous bearing upon the design of houses of large size; but Wanstead was a country palace, not a villa. Campbell began Burlington House, Piccadilly, in 1716; but Burlington House was a town palace, not a villa. There is nothing to suggest that Campbell had ever visited Italy.

[1] Pembroke House, Whitehall, was altered to its detriment by the 9th Earl in 1734, and again in 1744. It was demolished by the 10th Earl in 1756–7 and rebuilt by Sir William Chambers. Chambers's Pembroke House, or No. 7, Whitehall Gardens, was demolished in 1937.

On the other hand we know that Herbert had been in Venice in 1712, which was two years before Burlington's first Italian tour and before the latter was even interested in the architecture of Palladio. It is possible—we have no proof—that Herbert found time to visit and study for himself some of Palladio's villas in Venetia. If so, then he may well have had drawings made of them, which he lent to Campbell, not only for material for volume I of *Vitruvius Britannicus*, but to serve for the design of Pembroke House in Whitehall. How else can we account for Herbert's undeviating faithfulness to the Pembroke House formula in his own subsequent architecture, in the design and execution of which he never even employed Campbell, nor in any sense appeared to acknowledge him as his master?

Pembroke House may after all have been an early vicarious essay at architecture by Herbert through the professional hand of Campbell. The fact that Campbell in *Vitruvius Britannicus* gives his own name as the architect should weigh very little with us, because for reasons best known to himself he never gives Herbert credit in this publication for any of those houses which he certainly did build. Pembroke House was soon followed in the 1720s by Marble Hill, by Royal Lodge—now called White Lodge—Richmond, and probably (for no date is given it) by the Houghton Water-house, all by Herbert himself. Marble Hill was the first to be built, but Royal Lodge, Richmond (before the wings were added in the 1760s) bore a closer resemblance to Pembroke House. The Houghton Water-house is merely the centre part of the river front of Pembroke House with every other part discarded. It consists of pedimented portico raised on a high rusticated base, which base is perforated not by low windows, but by tall arched openings derived from those which Inigo Jones used at Somerset House.

Marble Hill, the first building to be designed by Henry Herbert, was a villa on the left bank of the Thames at Twickenham for a friend, the Honble. Mrs. Charles Howard.[1] In the first half of the eighteenth century Twickenham was a very fashionable locality to which people of *ton* were wont to retire from the bustle of London, sometimes for months, more often for weeks on end. James Johnston, Secretary for Scotland, already owned a house there, later known as Orleans House,[2] a little to the west of Marble Hill. In 1720 James Gibbs embellished its grounds with a handsome octagonal room in which to receive the Princess of

[1] In 1731 she became Countess of Suffolk.
[2] Until 1927 when it was demolished.

Wales. Alexander Pope lived further up the river, and Horace Walpole was shortly to settle at Strawberry Hill, only a few hundred yards away. The choice of site had the further advantage to Mrs. Howard of being fairly conveniently placed between Hampton Court and St. James's Palace, at both of which royal residences she was in constant attendance.

iii. The Palladian Countess

In 1723 Henrietta Howard was forty-two years old. From a worldly point of view her career was just about to reach its peak, from which it gently but perceptibly declined until it found a level far more suited to her nature, which was neither ambitious for place nor covetous of power. On the sympathetic low-lying meads of Marble Hill the remaining years of her long life were henceforth to drift like the purling waters of the silvery Thames at the bottom of her garden. For Henrietta had been, and still was in a sense, the mistress of the Prince of Wales, shortly to become George II. Her position at court was an awkward and unenviable one. Her life up to date had been fraught with embarrassments and difficulties. Born a Hobart at Blickling Hall in Norfolk, she lost while still a girl her father, an irascible and quarrelsome baronet, in a duel provoked by his overbearing insolence to a neighbour. Her mother died three years later in 1701. In her teens she married a younger son of the Earl of Suffolk, the Honble. Charles Howard. Her husband was a hopeless debauchee. Lord Hervey described him with no exaggeration as 'wrong-headed, ill-tempered, obstinate, drunken, extravagant, brutal'. Howard somehow managed to obtain a minor post at the court of Hanover where the young couple lived miserably. His debts were so outrageous that no tradesman would allow either of them any credit, and to pay for a dinner party Henrietta was reduced on one occasion to cut off and sell her long chestnut tresses. Had it not been for the attentions of the son and heir to the Elector of Hanover the Howards might have faced starvation.

On the death of Queen Anne in 1714 Henrietta and her husband returned in the suite of the new King George I to London. There she became Bedchamber Woman to the Princess of Wales, wife of the man whom the world took to be her lover. Henceforth she was for a long period the indispensable companion of the Prince of Wales, the confidante of the Princess and the respected adviser of the old King. Her rôle was to minister to the exclusive and selfish needs of a philistine court, which was divided amongst itself and which jeered at her pretensions to cultivated society. At the same time she was harnessed to a husband who detested her.

Horace Walpole, who grew to love Henrietta Howard and in her extreme old age used to gossip with her for hours at Marble Hill, and Lord Hervey, who never particularly liked her, were both certain that love played no part in her relations with the Prince of Wales. In that case she sacrificed her honour for very little return. Hervey's summing-up of the situation has often been quoted: 'She was forced to live in the constant subjection of a wife with all the reproach of a mistress, and to flatter and manage a man whom she must see and feel had as little inclination to her person as regard to her advice.' So long as she retained the Prince's good graces she had to submit to regular visits from him punctually at nine o'clock evening after evening; she was obliged to sit and listen patiently to his railing against his family and his father's ministers, to his bombastic opinions on world affairs and his contemptuous references to the things in life which she held most dear. By 1729 her favour with the King, which he had by then become, was declining. As time went on Queen Caroline's early feelings of respect for her changed to jealousy, and then to contempt. In 1731 Charles Howard succeeded to the earldom of Suffolk; his wife was made Groom of the Stole and Mistress of the Robes to the Queen. Before being mercifully released from Lord Suffolk by his death in 1733 Henrietta was subjected to a final degradation. Suffolk in an access of drunken rage tried one afternoon to pull the Queen out of her carriage in public. He then forced his way into her private apartments. 'What added to my fear upon this occasion,' the Queen confided in Lord Hervey afterwards, 'was that, as I knew him to be so brutal, as well as a little mad, and seldom quite sober, so I did not think it impossible that he might throw me out of that window . . . but as soon as I had got near the door, and thought myself safe . . . je pris [sic] mon grand ton de Reine.' Suffolk's motive was no less than to extract money from the Crown by threatening to spread rumours detrimental to the King's reputation. Whether as the result of these tactics or from fear of what the world might think and say, the King eventually bought off the Earl with a pension of £1,200 a year. This encroachment upon his notorious avarice did nothing to revive the dwindling passion for his old mistress. 'But after all this matter was settled,' Caroline's story continues, 'the first thing this wise, prudent Lady Suffolk did was to pick a quarrel with me about holding a basin in the ceremony of my dressing, and to tell me, with her little fierce eyes, and cheeks as red as your coat, that positively she would not do it; to which I made her no answer then in anger, but calmly, as I would have said to a naughty child: "Yes, my dear Howard, I am sure you will; indeed you will. Go! go! fie for shame! Go, my good Howard; we will talk of this another time!" '

By now Lady Suffolk was the recipient of increasing snubs from the King as well as the Queen. In dressing the Queen one morning she handed Her Majesty a scarf. The King who was present rudely snatched it from his wife and turning to Henrietta exclaimed: 'Because you have an ugly neck yourself you hide the Queen's!'

In 1734 she had the good sense to retire altogether from court, with which she was utterly wearied. It is only right to say that both the King and Queen were just as tired of her. According to Hervey, George II resented her constant opposition to his measures, her contradiction of his opinions and her intimacy with Pope (whom in fact she never really liked) and the Twickenham literary circle, which he suspected, not incorrectly, of supercilious and disloyal criticism of his government and person.

Throughout her long reign at court Henrietta had behaved with the strictest propriety, even if her tact in dealing with the King deserted her at the end. Although perpetually besieged by tuft-hunters, place-seekers and persons desirous of the Prime Minister, Sir Robert Walpole's fall, she remained unmoved and incorruptible. Those in opposition like Bolingbroke, Bathurst, Chesterfield and Swift, who assiduously cultivated her favours to use her influence with the King, made no headway with their blandishments and yet never lost her friendship. This is all the more remarkable considering how she herself disapproved of Walpole's policy and sympathized with his Tory opponents.

Queen Caroline lived just long enough to regret Lady Suffolk's departure, if only because she became more than ever victim to the interminable boredom of her husband's society. The Princess Royal had foreseen the consequences when told of the ex-mistress's removal: 'I wish with all my heart,' the un-filial daughter remarked of her father with an acerbity which was natural to her, 'he would take somebody else, then Mama might be relieved from the ennui of seeing him forever in her room.' As for the King he suffered from no regrets and no remorse. When Lady Suffolk, who now passed her summers uninterruptedly at Marble Hill, married in 1737 her second husband, the Honble. George Berkeley, an elderly bachelor who was a martyr to the gout, the Queen wrote the news to her husband absent in

Hanover.[1] The reply elicited was characteristic of his boorishness and lack of charity: 'J'étais extrêmement surpris de la disposition que vous m'avez mandé que ma vieille maîtresse a fait de son corps en mariage à ce vieux goutteux George Berkeley, et je m'en rejouis fort. Je ne voudrais pas faire de tels présens à mes amis; et quand mes ennemis me volent, plut à Dieu que ce soit toujours de cette façon.' The marriage, doubtless to the royal chagrin, was a profoundly happy one.

Lady Suffolk's 'mental qualifications were by no means shining', according to Horace Walpole, a verdict endorsed by Dean Swift who nevertheless considered her the ideal companion of intellectuals. Both men agreed that she was remarkably shrewd and had an intuitive perception how to deal with people in all walks of life. Besides, her retentive memory made her, particularly in her old age, an asset to any company. She had an open mind and in religion was a latitudinarian. Owing to her neutral disposition in argument she was often addressed by her friends as 'The Swiss', or 'my dear Swissess'. Her noble qualities were striking in one who moved in sophisticated and literary circles. She had the strictest regard for truth which never deserted her throughout her term at court. She was discreet without being reserved; she was just, generous and ever ready to do good. In consequence she was always treated with uncommon respect as though her virtue had never been called in question. Yet her long association with the King had brought her few material advantages.

There is a full-length portrait at Blickling of Lady Suffolk as a young woman. She is wearing a pink dress trimmed with roses, and shoes to match. She holds a mask in one hand. Under a coquettish little tricorne hat appears a face half serious, half mischievous, and without traces of care. Perhaps the picture was painted before the young bride had left her early home and the rather dismal upbringing of the widowed Lady Hobart. Another portrait, the property of the present Lord Buckinghamshire, is by Charles Jervas of Henrietta seated before a background view of an unknown house, which is definitely not Marble Hill. It had belonged to Pope who left it in his will to his beloved Martha Blount. At Martha's sale Lady Suffolk bought it and gave it to Horace Walpole, who hung it in the Round Chamber at Strawberry Hill in memory of the happy hours he had spent with her gossiping about court scandals in the reign of George I. In both portraits we get a sympathetic impression of the woman described by Walpole as 'of a just height, well made, extremely fair, with the

[1] On her marriage to George Berkeley Lady Suffolk did not drop her title.

finest light brown hair; well dressed always and simply: her face regular rather than beautiful'. These charms and her mild, grave bearing she retained until the end.

Only her deafness was an increasing disability. It was the one defect, Walpole recorded, 'that prevented her conversation from . . . being as agreeable as possible'. She had to be shouted at; and like the very deaf who do not shout themselves and are inclined to whisper, she chose to answer in a low voice like a distant echo from the past. Some of her friends thereby became impatient and found the effort of conversing with her a strain. That her deafness was already apparent in her middle age is suggested by Pope's well-known *Lines to a certain Lady at Court*, which begin:

> *I know a thing that's most uncommon*
> (*Envy, be silent and attend!*)
> *I know a reasonable woman,*
> *Handsome and witty, yet a friend.*

After listing her several virtues, her good humour and 'her sensible soft melancholy', the poet in the last stanza refers a little ungallantly to his heroine's ailment.

> '*Has she no faults then* (*Envy says*) *Sir?*'—
> '*Yes, she has one, I must aver;*
> *When all the world conspires to praise her,*
> *The woman's deaf, and does not hear!*'

The deafness was often the occasion of splitting headaches. In letters to the Duchess of Queensberry Lady Suffolk bitterly complained of the insomnia that accompanied the pain. Even Bath Spa could not provide a cure, nor a visit in 1738 to Aix-la-Chapelle to drink the waters. Nor bleeding by leeches. Nor the advice of Ann Upton—whoever she was—which began: 'Take the best salad oil make it milk warm, then rub your stomach and belly with it till it is well soaked in the skin, then take as much flannel as will go round you,' and so forth, in order to draw the vapours away from the head. Nor even snuff, which merely became a habit, so that she had to deprive herself of taking a first pinch until after dinner time. Like her too frequent tea-drinking it was an indulgence which finally had to be curtailed more drastically still.

Although Pope was, until Horace Walpole's establishment on the Twickenham scene, her closest neighbour who played a prominent part in the creation of Marble Hill and took his turn with Dean Swift and Dr. Arbuthnot as her major-domo in charge of her cellar and ice-house, his relations with Lady Suffolk were equivocal. Try as she would she never really cared for him; and he, the most sensitive of men, not unnaturally was aware of it. At first he went to every length to please her, but no, she remained stubbornly indifferent to his advances. This was not at all what he was accustomed to from society ladies who as a rule tumbled over each other in their efforts to win his regard and friendship. Was she totally unmoved by his muse? Did she find poetry a bore? To be sure Lord Bathurst called her his prose-lady. Did she see through Pope's affectations, and if so, what? In an age of artificial manners her absolutely natural reactions were almost anachronistic. She could not be bothered with studied formalities between friends. She was direct in manner, whereas Pope would hover and mince around her chair, bowing and scraping. She who had walked with kings was made just as happy by the common touch. He, it can never be denied, was a snob. In August 1730 she wrote to John Gay from Windsor: 'Mr. Pope has been to see me, Lord Burlington brought him; he dined and supped with my lady all the time he stayed; he was heartily tired, and I not much pleased though I thought myself exceedingly obliged to him for the visit.' These words spell caustic indifference if any words do. Pope never forgave her for telling him that she had burnt all his letters to her: and for adding, as though in an after-thought, that in any case it was quite unnecessary to return them to him for she knew he kept copies of all his correspondence. Notwithstanding, she wished him no harm; and she was invariably kind. In 1739 she gave him an eiderdown quilt for his bed.

Towards Gay her feelings were very different. He was a man to whom a woman could be genuinely devoted, for his failings were human and spontaneous. Indeed it was difficult not to love the child-like creature, who was always in a scrape, and whenever he had money either lost or spent it within the hour, who sponged mercilessly on his friends and fell in love with the wrong sort of women. She gave him a permanent room at Marble Hill, where he came and whence he went at will, flitting between her and the Duchess of Queensberry who may herself have been a little in love with him. Lady Suffolk was consistently loyal to him even when he was in disgrace for satirizing Sir Robert Walpole in *The Beggar's Opera*. As for the Duchess she refused to go to court because Gay was in royal disfavour, thereby attracting some scandal to herself. Besides, with Gay everything was fun. The three kept up a running correspondence of delicious triviality and nonsense. 'The Duchess made these blots,' Gay wrote to Henrietta on one occasion, 'and values herself upon it. I desire you would send word whether white currants be proper to make tarts: it is a point that we dispute upon every day, and will never be ended unless you decide it.' And again: 'General Dormer refused to eat a wheat-ear, because they call it here a fern-knacker; but since he knew it was a wheat-ear, he is extremely concerned.' Sometimes a serious note crept into the correspondence, and Henrietta was never afraid of speaking her mind. 'So much for her Grace,' she writes to Gay on one occasion, 'now for yourself, John ... Your head is your best friend; it would clothe, lodge and wash you; but you neglect it, and follow that false friend, your heart.' But advice however sound was, she knew, effort thrown away. When Gay died in 1732 the two women were inconsolable and wrote each other touching letters about their common loss.

Among her literary friends Swift too was an intimate. She would sign her facetious letters to him 'Sieve Yahoo', a combination of the opprobrious terms which Gulliver gave to her profession and sex, a courtier being 'sieve' and every lady a 'yahoo'. 'I told my two landlords here,' Swift wrote in 1727 of Pope and Gay with whom he was staying, 'that I would write you a love letter, which I remember you commanded me to do last year.' To which she replied two days later: 'I did desire you to write me a love-letter; but I never did desire you to talk of marrying me.' In spite of this badinage the Dean was critical. He, the least open-handed of men, thought her parsimonious. Did he too, like his boon companion Pope, harbour little resentments against that mocking tongue of hers? Men of letters are sadly feminine when their self-esteem is at stake, and are the last people in the world to join in jokes against their own pomposities. There is a dash of rancour against his old friend in the lines composed *On the Death of Dr. Swift*.

> *Kind Lady Suffolk in the spleen*
> *Runs laughing up to tell the Queen.*
> *The Queen, so gracious, mild and good,*
> *Cries: 'Is he gone? 'Tis time he should.*
> *He's dead, you say; Why let him rot;*
> *I'm glad the medals were forgot.*
> *I promised him, I own, but when?*
> *I only was a princess then;*
> *But now as consort of a King*
> *You know 'tis quite a different thing.'*

As for Queen Caroline he never forgave her. He had brought over from Dublin at great cost to himself bundles of fine Irish linen for her; and she never honoured her undertaking to repay him with a present of some intaglios.

Far different from the poets' attitude—which, it must be conceded, was necessarily governed by deference, they being as it were dependent if not upon her bounty, at least upon her patronage—was that of her social equals. Lord Chesterfield, that polished stick, however solicitous a friend, never quite unbent from the upright tension of the monitor even towards those of his own rank, which provoked merriment between Henrietta and Horace Walpole. Lord Chesterfield was always for doing what he thought best for his friends, rather than what they might like—sometimes quite a different thing. Thus when it came to giving a present, the object's value must be conformable to the recipient's means, must encourage him or her to continue collecting only what would enhance his or her prestige in the eyes of the vulgar. 'I have bought some china here,' he wrote to Henrietta in 1728 from The Hague, '(which was brought by the last East India ships that came in) of a very particular sort; its greatest merit is being entirely new, which in my mind may be almost as well as being undoubtedly old.' It amounted to no more nor less than a service for tea and chocolate, with a basin and ewer. Its quality, he strongly implied but did not say outright (he was too patrician to be absolutely direct), was over-fine for Mrs. Howard's comparatively modest establishment. Would she instead offer it on his behalf to the Queen? And again: 'I must inform you,' he wrote portentously, 'that there is an extreme fine Chinese bed,' some chintz window curtains and chairs 'to be sold for between £70 and £80'. These were suitable for Marble Hill, he considered. If she had a mind to them, could afford them and could find a means of getting them across the Channel, 'I will, with a great deal of pleasure, obey your commands.' If he, an ambassador, could not see a way to dispatch these objects, how was she, then a solitary woman living in a London suburb, to find one? On receipt of these communications we can imagine how the missives flew from Marble Hill to Strawberry Hill and back again. There exist pages and pages of letters, composed by the two irreverent Twickenham cronies purporting to be written by Henrietta's pet dog, Marquise, to Lord Chesterfield's hound, announcing her imminent accouchement and holding him responsible. Horace penned a love letter from Henrietta's maid to Lord Chesterfield's footman, when both these innocent servants were in their seventies. Was Lord Chesterfield aware of these jokes at his and his correct household's expense? We suppose not.

But of all the strangest love letters ever published, those between Mrs. Howard and Lord Peterborough hardly have an equal. They were written when he was sixty-five and she nearly forty. Hers amount to the dullest lines she wrote. They contain no spark of real feeling, and make us wonder if there was some substance in George II's complaints of her frigidity. Yet they were deadly serious in so far as they were exercises in love letters. His are only less dull because this sexagenarian rake, who had been the arch-intriguer of his time in both politics and love, probably meant a tithe of what he professed. They abound in classical allusions to heart-burns and simpering expressions of undying devotion, couched in exaggerated heroic strains. The intrigue, if it may be so called, was barely lifted beyond a literary penmanship, and petered out leaving no scars on either correspondent. But it did yield from Lord Peterborough a delightful poem, of which the spontaneity outstrips all the letters he addressed to her. The first and the last stanzas have given it an assured place in the anthology of eighteenth-century love poetry.

> *I said to my heart, between sleeping and waking,*
> *'Thou wild thing, that always art leaping or aching,*
> *What black, brown or fair, in what clime, in what nation,*
> *By turns has not taught thee a pit-a-patation?' . . .*
>
> *O wonderful creature! a woman of reason!*
> *Never grave out of pride, never gay out of season;*
> *When so easy to guess who this angel should be,*
> *Would one think Mrs. Howard ne'er dreamt it was she?*

iv. Marble Hill

In his *Reminiscences* Horace Walpole very categorically states that Lord Pembroke—Lord Herbert as he then was—designed Marble Hill. It is unfortunate that in all the correspondence of the period there is nothing to shed further light on the discussions which led to the choice of the villa's parentage and conception. But there is no reason to dispute the statement of Horace who, as we have seen, became extremely intimate with Lady Suffolk in her later years and must often have heard from her own lips how her circle of friends combined to make a Twickenham home for her. Moreover there is ample evidence in the style of the building as well as some written data to corroborate Lord Herbert's particular contribution.

Precisely how or when Mrs. Howard acquired the property is not clear. She may have rented it on a long lease and then have decided to purchase after she realized how much money she had spent upon it. There is a very friendly and refreshingly ingenuous preamble to some legal particulars of the freehold given in a letter from a Mr. E. Rudgell, her solicitor, as late as 1727. 'Underneath is such an account of the manor of Twickenham without any of that unintelligible cant we lawyers often use (to seem wise to ourselves and keep others in the dark) that I believe upon reading it, you will understand as much of the thing as I myself can pretend to'—an amazingly frank admission, probably unique as coming from a member of the legal fraternity.

The earliest reference to her intention to build is in a letter from Mrs. Howard to Gay, dated July 1723, wherein she wrote from London: 'I beg you will never mention the plan you found in my room; there is a necessity yet to keep the whole of that affair secret, though (I think I may tell you) it is almost entirely finished to my satisfaction.' The secret most probably was that the Prince of Wales had signified his willingness to contribute to the cost of building, and that until his help was actually forthcoming, the work could not proceed. Altogether the Prince gave £12,000 towards the cost, the rest of which was to prove a great strain on her resources. In the autumn of the same year Lord Peterborough was impatient to learn whether she intended to raise outhouses and prepare for planting before it was too late in the season; and he begged Pope to let him know immediately.

By the autumn of the following year at any rate Pope, Lord Bathurst and Charles Bridgman, the King's gardener who was to create the Serpentine and lay out the park between it and Kensington Palace, were already designing the gardens at Marble Hill. The eminent trio had made a satisfactory beginning for in 1725 Pope was able to tell Bathurst 'the grass of Marble Hill springeth, yea it springeth exceedingly & waits for the Lambs of the Mountains [meaning his lordship's comparatively high ground at Richings in Buckinghamshire] to crop the same.' In return Bathurst ordered his gardener at Richings to supply all the young lime trees that could be spared for Mrs. Howard's use.

Meanwhile the builders had already made a start on the house. There is a lively extract from a letter to Mrs. Howard written by Mrs. Campbell on 24th August, 1724, which runs: 'How does my good Howard do? Methinks I long to hear from you; but I suppose you are up to the ears in bricks and mortar, and talk of frieze and cornice like any little woman! I am going in a few days

HENRIETTA HOBART, COUNTESS OF SUFFOLK
Attributed Portrait
Reproduced by permission of the National Trust, Blickling Hall

PROJECTED
DESIGN OF PALA
FOR GIULIO CAP
IN VICENZA
BY PALLADIO
Reproduced from Palladio
Quattro Libri, 1570

MARBLE HILL, TWICKENHAM
The Entrance Front

to Colonel Fane's [at Mereworth which Colen Campbell was then building], where I intend to improve myself in the terms of art, in order to keep pace with you in the winter; otherwise I know I shall make but a scurvy figure in your room.

'You are a base woman to me,' she adds in a separate paragraph, for, to be sure, you might have found one day to come to Coombank when his Highness goes to visit his dad, which he does sometimes, as the Evening Post informs me.' The Honble. Mary Bellenden was married to General Jack Campbell, a cousin of John the 2nd Duke of Argyll and his brother Archibald, Earl of Islay, and subsequently 4th Duke. Combe Bank near Westerham in Kent was Lord Islay's property, which he had let to his cousins. The actual builder of the house was Roger Morris. Islay was likewise erecting another house, to be called Whitton Park, at Twickenham the very year, 1724, in which Marble Hill was begun. There are among the Hobart papers (in the Norwich Public Library) a number of receipts relating to work both at Whitton Park and Marble Hill. Why receipts for work at Whitton came to be mixed up with Lady Suffolk's receipts becomes apparent when we find that they were all signed by the same person, Roger Morris. His name is henceforth inseparable from all Lord Pembroke's as well as Lord Islay's buildings. He was in fact Pembroke's clerk of works, a carpenter who rose to be Principal Engineer to the Board of Ordnance, a talented surveyor and finally architect, who subsequently invented designs for buildings himself. For the present he must be regarded as the professional man who executed the drawings and carried out all the building operations to the dictation of his noble clients. Certainly Lord Pembroke and possibly also Lord Islay supplied the ideas, the plans, the rough sketches of the elevations and the decoration, and generally decided the style of their houses in hand.

The first receipt we come across for the year 1724 is dated 'Feb: ye 1st' and reads thus: 'Received then of the Rt. Honble the Earl of Islay by the hands of the Rt. Honble Henry Lord Herbert one hundred pounds on account for his lordships house at Twickenham pr. me. Roger Morris.' This document suggests but does not prove that Herbert had helped design Lord Islay's house for him. And a glance at old prints of Whitton Park before it was altered by Gibbs makes this surmise not improbable. The second receipt which has no mention of Herbert's name is dated June ye 2nd, 1724, and is for £200 from Lord Islay, 'on account of an agreement made this 2nd day of June, 1724, for building the naked carcase of a house for the said Earl of Islay at Twickenham in the

County of Midsx. Roger Morris'. Mention of Whitton Park here
only concerns us inasmuch as it shows how interrelated Herbert,
Islay and Roger Morris were at this particular date. The third
receipt in 1724 is dated 25th August, the day after Mrs. Campbell
had written her amusing letter to Mrs. Howard. The sum involved
is £200 and the wording is simply 'pr the hands of the Rt. Hon
Henry Lord Herbert'. The receipt may refer either to Whitton
Park or to Marble Hill, probably the latter, if we are to believe a
sentence in a letter Pope wrote on 17th September: 'Marblehill
waits only for its roof—the rest is finished.' The fourth receipt
however, dated 3rd December, for £200 runs: 'received of the
Earl of Islay ye sum of two hundred pound on account of ye
building at Marble Hill by me Roger Morris; and the fifth
merely dated 1724: 'Carpenters Work performed by Roger Morris
for Lord Islay at Marble Hill.' Although Herbert's name is no
mentioned in the fourth and fifth receipts, at least that of Marble
Hill is. Evidently Lord Islay, who in 1724 held no government
office—he was made Keeper of the Privy Seal the following year—
was supervising from nearby Whitton the work being done a
Marble Hill for Mrs. Howard during Lord Herbert's periodi
absences at court and on military duties.

In the ensuing years the receipts relating to Marble Hill run
steadily on, and Lord Herbert once again becomes the chief inter
mediary between Mrs. Howard and Roger Morris. He now
approves every kind of bill, down to the ironmonger's. In 172
Pope for some reason orders 'a grindstone, a trough pitch'd' an
some ironwork. On the last day of July Lady Hervey writes t
Mrs. Howard that she is most anxious to see what she is told wi
be the prettiest house of its size imaginable. By 1726 the work w;
well advanced, and Morris must have had a busy time movin
from Whitton to Marble Hill and back again. There is a bi
dated 16th May for the carving of husks and leaves on doorcas
and chimneypieces, done for Mrs. Howard by James Richard
He was an important craftsman who had succeeded Grinlir
Gibbons as Master Sculptor to George I in 1722, and before th
date worked at Burlington House. Lord Herbert also approved h
bill. By midsummer of 1727 things were nearing completion. Po
wrote on 20th June to Henrietta who was away in the countr
about the birth of a calf to her cow, which was made an excu
by him and several of their mutual friends to have a feast at h
expense. 'In order to celebrate this birth-day, we had a co
dinner at Marblehill. Mrs. Susan offered us wine upon t
occasion, and upon such an occasion we could not refuse it. O

entertainment consisted of flesh and fish, and the lettuce of a Greek Island, called Cos. We have some thoughts of dining there tomorrow, to celebrate the day after the birth-day, and on Friday to celebrate the day after that, where we intend to entertain Dean Swift; because we think your hall the most delightful room in the world except that where you are.' By December 1728 Morris submitted his account for 'finishing the principal story two sweepe walls and 4 buildings in the garden at Marbell Hill', for which he charged £200. Finally a receipt dated 24th June, 1729, declared: 'Recd of the Honble Mrs. Howard by the hands of the Rt. Honble Lord Herbert the sum of seven hundred and sixtey three pound in full for the finnishing all workes done at her house at Marble Hill at Twickingham and all demand by Roger Morris.'

By now the house was to all intents and purposes finished and its proud owner comfortably enough installed. Her friends had joined together in their efforts to produce for her what amounted inside and out to a rare work of art albeit on a modest scale. Modest it may have been but she was, in consequence, if not exactly ruined, then in serious financial difficulties. We gather as much from Swift's *Pastoral Dialogue between Richmond Lodge and Marble Hill*, composed in 1727 just after he had heard the news of old King George I's death. Swift knew well enough that Henrietta had been overspending herself. He with his keen ear to the ground, and his still keener eye trained to the keyholes of high life must also have sensed a crisis coming in his friend's affair with the Prince of Wales. So he concluded that the erstwhile royal lover would seize upon his new responsibilities as a pious excuse to call a halt to further financial implication in the embellishment of Marble Hill. We detect a slightly malicious note in Swift's poem, when for instance he makes Marble Hill lament:

> *My house was built but for a show*
> *My lady's empty pockets know;*
> *And now she will not have a shilling*
> *To raise the stairs, or build the cieling. . . .*
> *'Tis come to what I always thought,*
> *My dame is hardly worth a groat. . . .*
> *But we unlucky and unwise*
> *Must fall, because our Masters rise.*

Swift's regard for Mrs. Howard was nowadays more and more tempered by criticism. References to her in his correspondence even betray an undercurrent of dislike. She was an astute and adroit courtier, to be sure. She knew how to play her cards to her own advantage. She was 'very expert', he conceded, '*to tâter le pavé*', a fine but not necessarily an attractive quality. She was cold. Besides, she was, he again insisted, stingy. She did not respond readily enough to his friend, John Gay's hints for money. She did not relish the idea of him and his literary friends having a party, uninvited, at Marble Hill in her absence. It was ungenerous of her. This was an extraordinary accusation by a man who was notoriously the meanest of his kind, and who, when he was finally shamed into entertaining his poorest friends, would carefully order the nastiest food and the cheapest wine. So the Dean, who had supped and stayed over and over again at her expense and was withal pathetically human, could not refrain from gloating a little over the straits she was now reduced to. None the less the consequences would, he acknowledged, be sad for himself and the literary coterie.

> *No more the Dean, that grave Divine,*
> *Shall keep the key of my (no) wine;*
> *My ice-house rob as heretofore,*
> *And steal my artichokes no more;*
> *Poor Patty Blount no more be seen*
> *Bedraggled in my walks so green:*
> *And here no more will dangle Pope. . . .*
> *Some South Sea broker from the city*
> *Will purchase me, the more's the pity,*
> *Lay all my fine plantations waste,*
> *To fit them to his vulgar taste;*
> *Changed for the worse in ev'ry part.*
> *My master Pope will break his heart.*

Finally the smug Richmond Lodge, to whom at this moment Herbert's and Morris's attentions were chiefly directed and which was expecting to profit from a lavish expenditure by the new Sovereign, is made to exclaim condescendingly:

> *I pity you, dear Marble-hill;*
> *But hope to see you flourish still.*
> *All happiness—and so adieu.*

to which the stricken Marble Hill merely answers:

> *Kind Richmond Lodge; the same to you.*

Matters did not however turn out so very badly. Her husband's inheritance of the Suffolk earldom gained Henrietta a higher position at court for a time and a larger income. For the rest of her long life she seemed seldom to be without builders or carpenters in the house. She was forever making improvements, adding to the north-east a two-storied wing[1] which she called her Cottage, (it comprised an underground kitchen, a laundry and her china room), and even erecting, no doubt at Horace Walpole's instigation, a Gothic farmhouse with a steeple rising twenty-five feet above the roof, which was known as the Priory of St. Hubert. In 1750 she contrived a new dining-room with Chinese hangings on battens, a new waiting-hall and a library, with a nest of pigeon-holes in the presses and wire frames over the mahogany book-cases.[2] She got Andien de Clermont, Pembroke's 'Little French painter' to cover the coved ceiling of what she called her 'Cheney room' with arabesques. Until 1903 the ceiling survived intact; so did the peculiarly shaped shelves with gilded edges on which her treasures used to be displayed. Porcelain was her passion, as her friends were well aware. They never need labour under doubts what presents would be acceptable. Lady Betty Germain, her sister-in-law, whose own prim little china closet still remains undisturbed at Knole where she lived for years a cherished guest of the ducal Dorset family, sent her 'for a Tunbridge fairing two cups and two saucers'. 'You love old china;' she wrote, 'sure I may venture to say this is really so; I being informed that these are the pictures of our first parents drawn from the life, and at that time of the year that the fig-tree ceases to produce leaves.' And in 1763 when Henrietta was extremely old her favourite nephew and ultimate heir, the 2nd Earl of Buckinghamshire, wrote to her from St. Petersburg where he was ambassador 'of the quantities of fine china' that adorned his embassy; vouchsafing particulars which made her, the true connoisseur, 'peevish', namely that 'in several instances very fine old Japan Jarrs have been cutt and broke in order to make them fit the places'. In addition to new rooms and their decoration which caused immense interest and excitement, there were recurrent routine jobs which were boring as well as expensive. Among the items in the accounts are charges for repairing the cornices and stonework outside, and replastering within the house; for mending the card table, moving the marble table out of the hall—which required the strength of several stalwart men—and then bringing it back again, fitting the busts of her friends into the hall, and providing a new seat for the water-closet.

There are no plans nor designs for Marble Hill in Lord

[1] This wing, hidden behind the curved retaining wall, was demolished by the L.C.C. soon after their acquisition of the property in 1902.
[2] These alterations were the work of Matthew Brettingham, sen., who was employed at Holkham. Charles Ross was the joiner under him.

Pembroke's hand. He was not a draughtsman. His sprawling sketches for Westminster Bridge, preserved at Wilton, testify to a lack of talent in this respect. They are even inferior to Lord Burlington's, which is saying a good deal. On the other hand there is preserved at Wilton a very professional elevation drawing of the river front of Marble Hill, showing two straight walls linking the house to a pair of pavilions, which were never built. Since the style of the drawing accords with that of a second, preserved with it, of a similar façade, not however of Marble Hill, and signed 'Rogr. Morris', it is safe to conclude that he was the author of the first. There is too among the Hobart papers at Norwich a very fine drawing of a screen of three openings, the side ones lower than the central one and filled with a grille of hexagonal perforations. This was presumably Morris's, or Pembroke's scheme dictated to Morris, for the little room to the east of the lower hall. The screen, but for the grilles, was carried out and may still be seen. Because there are no preliminary or working drawings to help us understand the part Henry Herbert played in the design of Marble Hill house, it would be a mistake to suppose for this or any other reason that Roger Morris was responsible for the form the house took. When he was first engaged by Herbert he was known as a carpenter. Indeed he was referred to in the Wilton accounts as late as 1745 as 'Mr. Roger Morris carpinter', after years of intimate collaboration, which long before this date had been recognized by a massive silver cup inscribed: 'Given me by my noble friend, Henry Earl of Pembroke.' Roger was certainly a successful man whose rise in the architectural profession was due to the satisfaction and recommendation of his noble patrons.

He had a kinsman, Robert Morris, who lived in Twickenham, was a Palladian enthusiast and, as Sir John Summerson has pointed out, the only theoretical writer on architecture within the Palladian circle. Robert held Roger in high esteem and acknowledged the 'erudition I have received in your service'. He regarded Lord Pembroke (together with Lord Burlington and Sir Andrew Fountaine) as one of 'the principal practitioners' of what he termed ancient architecture 'in so critical a juncture, when its enemies are invading and undermining its beauties'. These words were written in 1728 and were doubtless directed at the baroque school of architects comprising Vanbrugh, Hawksmoor and Archer. Robert Morris wrote a number of treatises, and in his *Lectures on Architecture, Consisting of Rules founded upon Harmonick and Arithmetical Proportion in Building*, originally delivered between 1734 and 1736 and subsequently published, his most illuminating views on the science are propounded. They are, as the long title to the work proclaims, concerned with the affinity between music and architecture. They are not concerned with 'the nice use of the orders', which on the contrary he purposely overlooked, deeming it to be of secondary importance. 'Buildings are to be perform'd by stated rules, as the several parts of music in concert are,' he declares. Beauty and proportion are inseparable. As in music there are only seven distinct notes, so in architecture there are only seven distinct proportions, 'which produce all the different buildings in the Universe'. And he proceeds to expand this engaging but slightly hazardous theme, particularly in relation to interiors. 'The cube—the cube and half—the duplicates of 3, 2 and 1—of 4, 3 and 2—of 5, 4 and 3—of 6, 4 and 3, produce all the harmonic proportions of rooms.' And if we wish to put this complicated theme to the test, we find that the elevations and the apartments of Marble Hill, down to the proportion of windows, doors and chimneypieces to walls and ceiling, answer exactly to it. Moreover the copperplates of the ideal building which he illustrates in the book correspond very closely with the features of Marble Hill, down or rather up to the pyramidal roof. In other words Robert Morris's exegesis is the Pembroke formula. It therefore seems that, just as his cousin Roger practised the formula in the technical labour of building, so Robert expressed it in writing—which Pembroke was either incapable of doing or too busy and important to attempt. As I have already remarked, Pembroke derived his formula for the perfect villa straight from Palladio either through illustrations, or first-hand by visits to the master's buildings. On page 21 of Book 2 of Palladio's famous *Quattro Libri* (1570), to which Pembroke will certainly have had access even if he did not own a copy—Burlington had eight copies in his library—there is a woodcut of Giulio Capra's projected palace in the principal street of Vicenza. The palace was never carried out. Leoni, whose English translation of the *Quattro Libri* appeared in 1715, likewise gave a plate of it which differed from the original in that he provided openings—blank sculptured panels it is true—over the *piano nobile* in lieu of slit-like windows in the frieze, shown in the original Palladio woodcut. Leoni's version thereby approximates closer to the north front of Marble Hill, where the correspondent openings are real windows instead of sculptured panels.

There were, and still are, scattered about Venetia several other country villas, built by Palladio and Scamozzi which subscribe fairly closely to the Pembroke formula, and may be deemed prototypes. There is the Villa Pisani at Montagnana (if we disregard the lower order of engaged columns) designed by Palladio for his friend Francesco Pisani in 1565; and the Villa Maldara at Rivella di Monselici (where the centrepiece is a projecting portico) designed by Scamozzi in 1588. These villas—and there are others by lesser known followers of Palladio—are cubes. Their principal elevations are distinguished by a tetrastyle projection under a pediment, flanked by single bays; and they were meant to have pyramidal roofs. Pembroke may well have visited some of them in 1712 when a boy of nineteen, with the result that years later he succeeded in transposing them, with modifications, on to British soil, so that they became a recognized pattern of the perfect, compact and elegant country villa of the smaller size.[1]

Robert Morris in his lectures on the ideal villa stresses the need for strict symmetry. It is most necessary, he says, 'to have each side of the entrance or middle of the building alike' for stability's as well as harmony's sake. There must also be a vista through a house. These injunctions were observed at Marble Hill, as we see from the plan of the house. Incidentally the elevations were not greatly altered in execution, nor in the course of a few later improvements, from the designs published in volume III (1725) of Campbell's *Vitruvius Britannicus*. Staircases must be in the middle of a house, Robert Morris continues. In rooms doors shall answer themselves, whether they be real or false. The proportions of a chimneypiece shall be determined by adding the length and breadth of the room together and extracting the square root of that sum; half of that root will be the correct height for the chimneypiece. Pedantic these injunctions may sound. Their value can only be judged by their success. At Marble Hill they were carried out to the letter. The undeniably beautiful proportions of every unit to its fellow are the result.

The staircase at Marble Hill rises from the right side of the hall when entered by the front door on the north forecourt. It and the subsidiary staircase on the left occupy that large rectangular area behind the central feature of the front. The carving of the vase shaped balusters and the stout newel posts of the main staircase i faultless. The wood used is mahogany, a gift to Mrs. Howard from

[1] And not only the country villa. In 1725-32 the Lord Mayor's House in York was buil It subscribes to the Pembroke formula. It resembles the entrance front of Marble Hill closel; and the river front of Pembroke House, Whitehall, exactly. A plaque records that it may hav been built by Lord Burlington. This is unlikely. Francis Drake's description of the Lor Mayor's House in his *Eboracum*, which he dedicated fulsomely to Burlington, is by no mear eulogistic enough to warrant the attribution; and Drake was unsparing in his praise of th York Assembly Rooms which Burlington did build. Is it possible that Pembroke was the arch tect? The names of all the craftsmen who worked on the Lord Mayor's House are known; an the man who superintended the building was William Etty, described as designer and carve

the King. It almost caused a war with Spain because, owing to
the indiscretion of the naval officer commanded to procure it, it
was cut down on Spanish soil at Honduras. The same mahogany
is used for the floorboards and the doors on the first floor. Marble
Hill and its contemporary Houghton Hall are the earliest examples
of the use of mahogany for structural purposes. Mrs. Howard had
the staircase walls painted buff, leaving the raised enrichments in a
lighter tone of the same colour. The stair landing leads into the
saloon which is the dominant apartment of the house. Its three
windows (lowered since the eighteenth century) overlook the
garden and the river in the distance. The room is a cube of 24 feet,
with a coved ceiling 4/5th the height from floor to cornice. Mrs.
Howard's colour scheme for this room was white and gold after
the Inigo Jones cube rooms at Wilton. All the superb applied
ornaments of the frieze and wall panels in carved wood and of the
ceiling in plaster, the doors, the pier-glasses between the windows
with their split pediment crests, even the exquisitely moulded
window shutters, the Carrara marble chimneypiece and James
Richard's noble overmantel with two gold *amorini* precariously
perched on the summit, not to mention the mahogany floor—in
fact the bones of the room—are exactly as she knew them. The
large wall panels facing the windows were fashioned to take three
contemporary copies of full-length portraits by Vandyke and one
of Rubens's Virgin and Child 'fixed on the wainscot'. The frames
were exact reproductions of those of the pictures in the Wilton
Double Cube Room. Canvases and frames survived in place until
the beginning of this century. The panelled overdoors, above
which gilt eagles bear palms in their claws, and the space over the
fireplace contained views of 'five Roman landscapes', possibly by
Panini. Gone however are the two large marble tables and 'the two
smaller ditto', the Japan cabinets, the pair of ivory pagodas (now
at Blickling Hall), the silver-gilt sconces and the embossed silver
perfuming set, according to the inventory taken of her ladyship's
chattels upon her decease. Gone the needlework settee and the
eight wainscot chairs with green and yellow damask and blue
covers, on which Pope, Gay, Swift and later Horace Walpole used
to recline for hours on end bawling indiscreet gossip down the
tortoiseshell ear-trumpet, while the silver kettle purred on the tea-
stand and the firelight flickered from 'the fine stove and iron
grate'. Gone too the pair of large-leaved India screens which were
carefully placed by obsequious footmen between the guests and
the windows on those chilly autumn evenings when the mists
began to rise from the lawns outside.

Standing at one of the tall saloon windows today we can survey through the grime upon the plate glass (the sashes were removed when the windows were lengthened[1] so as to throw the proportions of the south front into utter confusion) the scene of Henrietta's gardens, towards the creation of which her friends, numbering the most renowned horticulturists of their generation, contributed practical help as well as the choicest plants from their own glass-houses. Lord Herbert took the step of contracting that one, Daniel Croftes, should look after the whole garden for her, he providing all labour but having full use of her garden utensils at the rate of £130 a year. Among the common elms, ilexes, chestnuts and weeping willows that now rise dotted about the grounds in no apparent order or symmetry a huge black walnut—*Juglans nigra*—native of North America, said to be the first of its kind to be planted in England, still flourishes. Little else of rarity is left. This is hardly surprising when we consider the vicissitudes through which Marble Hill has passed since Lady Suffolk's death in 1767. Horace Walpole recorded that the introduction of foreign trees and shrubs was principally due to Archibald Earl of Islay, who kept an eye upon their well-being during his frequent visits to Whitton.

Still standing at one of the saloon windows we are just able to discern immediately below us traces of sloping terraces, now unkempt lawn, whereon Bridgman had contrived the formal parterre of which no vestiges remain. Nothing was allowed to grow so high as to hinder a view from the house of the craft sailing up and down the Thames. To left and right were calculatedly informal wildernesses and verdures of evergreens, cut through with serpentine walks and, as in Robert Morris's descriptive passage about the ideal villa precincts, 'either regularly pruned, or luxuriously shooting their branches in a wild disorder; the paths strewn with sand, to render them the more easy to walk on'. These romantic sections of the garden had always been, we fancy, Pope's cherished territory where, indeed, Swift made Marble Hill declaim:

> *My groves, my echoes, and my birds*
> *Have taught him his poetic words.*
> *We gardens, and you wildernesses,*
> *Assist all poets in distresses.*

Of the early years when Marble Hill was being created there are, alas, no surviving letters between its owner and her friend the

---

[1] In the nineteenth century.

architect. Perhaps the reason is that Lord Herbert was so constantly at Marble Hill in the 1720s that few occasions arose for
them to correspond. As a result we do not know how their relations
tended during that decade, nor whether their constant confabulations proceeded upon amicable or tetchy terms. In letters to her
friends Mrs. Howard lets fall an occasional reference to Lord
Herbert. None of them is very flattering. She remarks upon his
gallantry, it is true, and his fondness for Chuff; but she also
comments upon his bad temper. There is no letter to her from
him before 21st June, 1738, by which date Marble Hill was
already a recognized literary shrine and gathering place of artists.
'Weather, bridges, attendance [at court], reviews and some business really of consequence are the reasons that rib [his wife],
Sir Andrew Fountaine, myself and Chuff have not yet done what
they ought to have done,' he writes apologetically. 'The fault lies
. . . not . . . from an aversion to Marble Hill.' The last sentence is
at any rate reassuring. In the following summer Lady Suffolk
writes to Lord Pembroke—to use the titles they have now both
assumed—an affectionate latter, the tenor of which shows that
she assessed his character pretty shrewdly. It also points to that
ill health which was to dog her long, declining years. 'Why will you
ask us to come to Wilton for it is the thing in the world I shou'd
like to do, and I know that I must not do which is no weak argument to make my inclination stronger, but in truth this is my case.
I am troubled with such a shortage of breath that I am company
for nobody but my own husband whose vow obliges him to take
care of me in sickness, and in health. I try his patience sufficiently
but he expects his reward in the next world. You that are not so
good a christian nor under the same obligation I dare not put to
the same tryal.' George Berkeley met what Henrietta called his
reward in 1747 when he was utterly worn out with unrelieved
suffering. But he, patient and docile man, considered that his
reward came ten years previously, when she had consented to
marry him. If he gave her the comfortable stability and the devotion she needed, she in return ministered to his needs as well as
brought to his bedside the society of the authors whose books he
eagerly devoured. She never ceased to lament his death. Her letter
to Pembroke, however, continues. 'I am at this time over head
and ears in shells. I wish I had Ribs head and hands to assist me.
My Cheney Room will make you stare if not swear tho' I must tell
you 'tis the admiration of the vulgar; but my vanity would be
intirely gratified if it shou'd meet with your approbation.' She
still looked upon him with no little awe as the severe monitor in

what pertained to the Palladian correctness of Marble Hill. Could he, its creator, frankly approve of her Chinese extravaganza? Or would he condemn it out of hand as silly and frivolous? If he ever sent her his approbation, the letter conveying it no longer exists.

v. Houses and Bridges

In the 1730s Herbert became horribly involved with one who did his reputation as an architect no good at all. Sarah Jennings, widowed Duchess of Marlborough, charmed, exasperated and quarrelled with whomsoever she had dealings, whether employees, relations or friends. Impulsive, wrongheaded and often downright wicked she usually succeeded, such was the force of her personality, in getting her own way and the best of the reverberant row or litigation, of which one or other was the inevitable culmination of her contact with man or woman. Herbert's business relations with her, brought about as they were by her quarrel with somebody else, began smoothly enough. By 1730 Nicholas Hawksmoor's last baroque design, *à la Bernini*, for a Column of Victory to proclaim for all time in the park at Blenheim the great Duke of Marlborough's martial exploits had been rejected by the hero's widow. Instead the Duchess turned to Lord Herbert; and he designed and Roger Morris executed the fluted Doric column, 130 feet high, which to this day bears on its summit a lead statue of the Duke in Roman dress, by John Cheere. There the hero stands on a cylinder seemingly borne by four eagles with wings displayed. His right leg is advanced and his right hand holds either an olive branch, or a thunderbolt; to determine which from a distance is quite impossible. Proudly and rather menacingly he looks over Vanbrugh's cyclopean bridge towards the vast bulk of the palace which he never lived to enjoy. The column, which did not require extraordinary talent to design, is absolutely unbaroque and irreproachably Palladian. Hawksmoor saw the finished thing in October of the following year. 'The historical pillar,' he told Lord Carlisle, 'is set up in the park; (conducted by my Lord Herbert) . . . I must observe to you that ye inscription is very long . . . but very legible.' Indeed the four sides of the deep plinth recapitulate at tedious length verbose extracts from various Acts of Parliament granting the Duke honours and awards Evidently Hawksmoor was not profoundly impressed.

In 1732 Lord Herbert rashly undertook to design a house a

Wimbledon for Duchess Sarah. A letter from her to Herbert written on 25th March of that year mentions Roger Morris in connection with the works then in progress, and implies that he was following his master's directions. The plate given in volume V of *Vitruvius Britannicus* (which incidentally records 'R. Morris' as the *architect*) shows a house of the same stylistic motif as Marble Hill, namely a three-windowed central feature behind an Ionic tetrastyle portico, and flanking single bays, all over a deep basement: but with an additional wing of one window on either side. The whole was built of grey stock brick with stone dressings. There is a rough pencil plan (from which the finished plan departed only in minor particulars) of the house, preserved at Wilton, in the margin of which the old Duchess has made sarcastic comments about each room. At the bottom of the drawing she has scrawled 'This plan, my Palladio Dye [presumably her favourite grand-daughter, Diana Duchess of Bedford, with whom she was now on most affectionate terms] has done at my request, to oblige me, I finding that it may be compass'd with no alteration to the offices, but only changing my apartments to the other side, at the same time I must do her the justice to say that I believe she would not have done it for any other body in the world, being so great an architect, that she loves nothing but shew and Italian building.' This may have been a sly hint intended for Lord Herbert's perusal since another note on the plan was addressed to him directly. 'This room and that which answers it, I think may be done as yr. Lordp designed it in your plan with sashes to hold books or whatever one likes.' The note is civil enough but it implies that she was generally interfering with the arrangements and changing several of the rooms about.

From the start of operations however she had complaints to make. She remonstrated with Morris who, she said, 'made so many alterations in the works in doing and un-doing that the contracts are of very little use'. She accordingly dismissed him and tried to avoid paying what she owed. He was obliged to sue her in order to claim the £300 that was justly his. Then the Duchess insisted that the house must stand in a hole, as Horace Walpole put it. 'She had directed my Lord Pembroke not to make her go up any steps; "I won't go up steps", and so he dug a saucer to put it in, and levelled the first floor with the ground.' But when it was finished 'the whimsical old creature' objected that it looked as though it were making a curtsey. This may have been her opinion, but the author of *Vitruvius Britannicus* described the house as being 'very happily situated on an eminence'. In 1734 she wrote to her granddaughter, 'If I had had only myself and the Duke of Bedford's bricklayers, it would have been the finest place in the world. But I have always had the misfortune to suffer very great mischiefs from the assistance of architects. The cutting through the terrace is almost as bad as setting the house in a pit. And the wall of it is so very ill done, that I believe it must be pulled down a third time.' Nevertheless the house remained until in 1785 it was burnt down. So too did the Duchess's grievance until death released her from this and many other causes of deep resentment against mankind. The consequence was that some people felt constrained to take the Duchess's part and to abuse Lord Pembroke for having used cheap materials while charging her dearly for the cost. The story got about, was echoed in the cheap gazettes and was repeated in broadsheets and ballads that Herbert had done the old lady grave injury.[1]

Wimbledon House, owing to its wings, which stretched themselves out an appreciable distance on both fronts, was larger than the houses Herbert had designed hitherto. In Westcombe House, Blackheath, which he erected for himself about the same time as Wimbledon House on land rented from Sir Gregory Page, he returned to the villa size. Some late eighteenth-century prints and a series of oil paintings by George Lambert, in which only a corner here and there of the house is depicted, suggest that the ideas for Westcombe were culled from Palladio. The Villa Thiene at Montagnana (demolished as was Westcombe itself in the last century) has been cited as the archetype, in that Herbert may have intended to reproduce its flanking colonnades and small terminal square towers. The Villa Thiene derivation rests upon two unspecified elevation drawings (now in the R.I.B.A. library) purporting to be of Westcombe House. In the drawings similar colonnades and towers are introduced. The point is hardly worth labouring since these features in the drawings are not shown in any of the prints of Westcombe, and can never have been carried out. Westcombe seems to have resembled fairly closely the house at Whitton which Roger Morris built for Lord Islay in 1724, in being a square block with a pyramidal roof and louvre and having a projection from each of the four sides. Suffice it to say that Sarah, Duchess of Marlborough, paid it a visit when it was just finished and, as was to be expected, was highly critical. On 1st April, 1732, she wrote a description of it to her granddaughter.

[1]   *A house most commodious.'—and surely it ought,*
As it cost dear in building, tho' cheaply 'twas bought.

From an anonymous ballad entitled The Fall of Westminster Bridge.

the Duchess of Bedford, which is so lively, so entertaining and so satirical about English Palladianism and the cult of the Antique that, although lengthy, it deserves quotation almost in full.

'And now I will . . . give you an account of a place that I am fearful you once commended to me. That is my Lord Herbert's house at Greenwich, which I do think 'tis designed that your brother should buy. And that is the most ridiculous thing that ever I saw in my life. . . .

One cannot help thinking soon after one gets into the house that it must have been built by somebody that is mad. Some of the doors in the house are made in what I call a triangle, at least I don't know how to describe it better, but it is extremely fantasticall. And one of the rooms which is lowroofed and not much bigger than one of the Duke of Bedford's tables he dines upon when he receives company has four great stone pillars, which I suppose is because the Ancients had pillars to support magnificent large rooms that either wanted or at least appeared to want support. But these pillars take away what little room there is, and are plainly to support nothing.

Above stairs one of the best rooms has a passage taken out, not at all necessary to go into another room, but I suppose that it was to show an uncommon fancy or ingenuity, for instead of a partition or a wall it is divided with glass the same as is in windows from the ceiling to the floor, so that everybody that sits in the room sees those that go through the passage and they see those that sit in the room. And this I must acknowledge is extremely new.

But the alcoves for the beds to stand in are not less diverting, for they are so ordered that it is not easy to get into them but at the feet of the bed.

There is in the house a vast many wolf's and lion's heads and such sorts of curiosities made, I think, of what they call tobacco pipe clay. And there was one figure I believe my lady Delawarr would have been mightily pleased with, because the nose was broke off. There was several things, I think they call them pediments, that don't join in the middle, which is left open to set a bust made at Hyde Park. There is likewise a great deal of carving and some gilding in the house, which I suppose may be to make some amends for the furnitures being only paper.

In the first entry into the house, which is very small, but where a forest chair or two would have been convenient 'tis filled up with several pedestals. But only one of them has anything upon it, which appeared to me like a broken misshapen stone. But upon inquiry, I was told it was something of great value, and if that be so I am sure I can furnish all the rest of these pedestals by sending to pick up some of the ruins of Holdenby that have lain so long upon the ground unregarded.

The front of this house is full of niches with heads put into them of such clay as I have described. It was the custom I have heard in the time of the Ancients to put into great palaces all the great men's statues that were their ancestors who had done noble actions, and that part of this building I conclude was to imitate that, but I durst not ask who those heads represented being resolved to observe the Spanish proverb and not to laugh till I turned the street. . . .'

Presumably the noble architect was not aware of these unfavourable sentiments about his house, in the construction of which he had taken so much trouble and spent so much money, unless of course the Duchess, with her habitual recklessness, chose to regale society with them. She was perfectly ready to admit that the niceties of the architectural science meant nothing to her. She claimed to judge results by common sense. She was irritated by a sacrifice of convenience to the fashionable dictates of the moment, and she did not scruple to ridicule the follies that sometimes ensued from pedantic adherence to rules laid down by a tiresome old Roman, called Vitruvius, a thousand and more years ago. For example, she thoroughly disapproved of the Palladians' silly aversion to light. 'My Lord Herbert particularly seems to dislike extremely windows in a room,' she snorted. Our generation is inclined to be just as blind to the deficiencies and just as undiscriminating in its adulation of all the qualities of Palladian buildings as was the exclusive circle over which Pembroke and Burlington presided. The Duchess's dashes of cold water are, it must be confessed, a somewhat refreshing antidote. Naturally her prejudices were irrational and uninformed. Her tastes too were those of her heyday, which had been the reign of Queen Anne. They were old-fashioned and baroque. They are somewhat reflected in the plan of Wimbledon House which took the shape of an H made by extended wings at front and rear, a plan introduced by the Jacobeans and long favoured by the Wren school. It was reproduced by Herbert doubtless reluctantly. The Duchess admitted to her granddaughter on 21st July, 1732, that she had seen several houses by Inigo Jones, but no one that she had liked entirely. 'By which,' she said, 'I find the architects of former times had some whims, but our present architects endeavour to imitate ill whatever was useless in their buildings and add nothing but what is ridiculous of their own.'

The last building which Herbert can claim as his own creation is the Palladian Bridge across the Nadder, facing the Inigo Jones wing at Wilton House. To begin with, the layout of that part of the garden of which it is such a signal adornment was to his design. He scrapped the finicky parterres and what the 2nd Earl of Oxford

ON HOUSE

lladian Bridge
by Lord
and built by
Morris, 1737–8

Photos: Royal Institute of British Architects

termed 'the old ridiculous water works and whims'[1] which Isaac de Caux, Charles I's engineer, had with immense concentration thrashed out, as though they were a problem exercise in higher geometry. In their place he fashioned sweeping lawns, and planted cedars and groups of deciduous trees, now in their splendid maturity. He diverted and widened the Nadder river. Over it he threw the covered bridge, an Ionic colonnade with two temple-like features at either end. Ramps lead to the arched openings; and balustrades under the two sides of the temples and the colonnade protect those who cross the bridge from falling into the water. How very prosaic this bald description sounds. How utterly inadequate it is. The Palladian Bridge—pretentious, unnecessary, superfluous if you like—is one of the most beautiful buildings in all England. And this is not praise enough. It is not excelled by any building of Palladio in Venetia. Nor is it a copy of any bridge built by the Vicenzan master. The specimen bridge of which Palladio gives a woodcut in his Third Book is by comparison a heavy, cumbersome affair. Lord Pembroke extracted from it certain recognizable elements for his own design, which turned into a creation of ineffable loveliness. The noble, enduring quality of the Wilton bridge does not detract from its fragile, almost moon-spun delicacy; and its merits defy assessment in dry architectural terminology. It stands tiptoe over the pellucid stream as though it had been dropped there overnight by some superhuman hand. Yet we know from Lord Pembroke's House Book that Roger Morris, the clerk of works, and John Devall, the mason, spent the greater part of the years 1735-7 in perfecting this superb and eternal work of art. So much appreciated was it by the Georgians that at least four worthy copies were made within the next forty years, at Stowe, Prior Park, Hagley and Amesbury.

The Wilton Bridge, all grace and tenderness, is an extraordinary commentary upon the character, boisterous, overbearing and rude which Lord Pembroke presented to the world ('Thou silly fellow, thou dost not know thy own silly business!' was one of his less offensive remarks directed to Anstis, the distinguished Garter King of Arms and leading genealogist of his century). A man's

---

[1] Edward Harley, 2nd Earl of Oxford, visited Wilton in 1738. He made a reference to the new Palladian Bridge—'a most beautiful bridge over the river', he calls it—which is curious. He has taken away the old grotto, and is making a bridge which will make a communication with the other part of the garden. He has taken all the best of the columns, pilasters and carvings that did belong to the old grotto, and put them to this new building, which will be very pretty and have a very good effect. From this bridge of communication there will be about the middle a summerhouse which will look directly upon the beautiful steeple of Salisbury.' Certainly the Palladian Bridge gives no impression of being made out of bits and pieces from older buildings. It is only right to say that at the time of Lord Oxford's visit the Palladian Bridge was not finished.

soul evidently cannot be estimated by his behaviour, nor by his casual observations. 'Blasphemous', 'scurrilously indecent', 'bad-tempered' are epithets applied to him without forethought of malice by his friends. He continued to be all these things to the end. Nevertheless he was consistently public-spirited. Having designed and built a bridge for himself at Wilton he sponsored a public bridge to cross the Thames at Westminster. It was a very different sort of affair, and one which involved him in heart-breaking and seemingly profitless worries. It ultimately cost him his life. Having procured in 1738 an Act of Parliament which sanctioned the undertaking, provided funds and set up a com-mission to conduct operations, Lord Pembroke at last succeeded in persuading the commissioners to employ a Swiss resident in England, Charles Labelye, as engineer. This was done in the face of powerful interests which favoured the candidatures of, amongst thirteen others, John James and Batty Langley.[1] The appointment of Labelye, a totally unknown foreigner, caused intense antagonism among the professional body of architects who were unsparing with their criticism of the engineer and his patron, Pembroke. James King, a carpenter, was made his assistant. He too was a disappointed candidate for the post to which Labelye was appointed. His ill-feeling caused endless strife. To Labelye's instructions King wrote 'the most scurrilous and abusive answer that ever was penned', and used language towards him described as Billingsgate. Eventually the commissioners agreed to dismiss him and put William Etheridge, another carpenter, in his place.

The first stone was laid by Pembroke in 1739 with much ceremony, and the last in 1750. When it was discovered nine years after the work had begun that one of the new piers had subsided, Labelye's and the Earl's enemies could not restrain their jubilation. Pembroke, contrary to his nature, remained unmoved. His confidence in Labelye's ability was typical of his tenacity of purpose once his mind had been made up, and of his staunch loyalty. The subsidence was not in fact a serious matter, and was greatly exaggerated by the disappointed candidates. Pembroke's old friend William Stukeley came to the rescue and remedied the faulty pier by introducing some sort of relieving arch. All the same, Pembroke was never allowed to hear the end of the sinking pier. Anonymous pamphleteers gleefully seized upon the incident and did not hesitate to rake up the old charge that the Earl had swindled Duchess Sarah by using defective materials at Wimble-don House. *The Downfall of Westminster Bridge, or my Lord in the*

[1] Hawksmoor who died in 1736 left a drawing dated that year for Westminster Bridge.

Suds had a wide circulation and was eagerly read by the architectural profession and society alike.

It happened that Pembroke's and Labelye's Westminster Bridge inaugurated an entirely new era and system of bridge building in England. The old method of driving piles into the river bed thereby became outmoded. Thenceforth by means of caissons, or wooden boxes let down to the bottom and then pumped free of water, stone piers were built within them on solid foundations. When we consider that this bridge covered 1,220 feet in breadth of river and involved the laying of fourteen piers, we realize that the feat was very remarkable indeed. Portland and Purbeck stone, Devon moorstone and Kentish rag were the materials used. The finished structure admittedly was not strikingly beautiful. It was distinguished by rusticated spandrels, bold keys and voussoirs to the arches and a little domed cupola, like an outsize sentry-box, above each pier. The bridge survived until 1861 when it was replaced by the present one. It is gratifying to know that Pembroke, who never let merit pass unrewarded, especially when the road to success was made hard going by other men's spite, induced the commissioners to present Labelye with an honorarium of £2,000 in recognition of 'his great fidelity and extraordinary labour and attendances, skill and diligence'.

This act of generosity was one of Pembroke's last. He had been a sick man for several years. In October 1743 he suffered a stroke, and as a result had to spend a few idle weeks recuperating at Bath. It is a wonder that so choleric a man lasted as long as he did. A final stroke carried him off on 9th January, 1750, in his house at Whitehall at the age of fifty-seven. A letter from Horace Walpole to Horace Mann gives an account of his death which is not without pathos. 'Lord Pembroke died last night: he had been at the Bridge Committee in the morning, where, according to custom, he fell into an outrageous passion; as my Lord Chesterfield told him, that ever since the pier sunk he has constantly been *damning* and *sinking*. The watermen say today, that now the great pier (peer) is quite gone. Charles Stanhope carried him home in his chariot; he desired the coachman to drive gently, for he could not avoid those passions; and afterwards, between shame and his asthma, he always felt daggers, and should certainly one day or other die in one of those fits. Arundel, his great friend and relation, came to him soon after: he repeated the conversation, and said, he did not know but he might die by night. "God bless you! If I see you no more, take this as my last farewell!" He died in his chair at seven o'clock. He certainly is a public loss; for he was public-spirited and inflexibly honest, though prejudice and passion were so predominant in him that honesty had not fair play whenever he had been set upon any point that had been given him for right.' Horace Walpole had a strange talent for summing up character, succinctly and absolutely without cant. He then added to a faithful epitaph this sentence, at which we feel sure the Earl would not have cavilled. 'In short, he was one of the lucky English madmen who get people to say, that whatever extravagance they commit, "Oh, it is his way".' We, who are more chary than the eighteenth century of pronouncing men mad, would, had we known him, probably have considered Lord Pembroke just highly temperamental and individual. His faults, of which he was pathetically aware, ran away with him and led him to say and do things which he afterwards regretted. They were as nothing to his repeated acts of kindness and his one quite outstanding virtue as a creative artist.

In his will he directed that his funeral should be without any pomp or expense. Not more than two mourning coaches were to follow the coffin. Four servants only were to accompany him to the grave dressed in grey coats trimmed with black, and black waistcoats. He was buried in the church at Wilton in a tomb over which they placed his bust by Roubiliac. It is a noble memorial and fittingly a splendid work of art. The head is of a man of impregnable will. Under a narrow, puckered forehead a slightly Roman nose points to a projecting underlip. The pugnacious jaw is supported by a seemingly limitless substructure of jowl and double chin. It is certainly not a very prepossessing face. And yet the sculptor's genius has introduced among these brutish features just a perceptible trace of sadness in the mouth and—can it be?—of contrition in the narrow eyes.

BURLINGTON III

RICHARD BOYLE

3rd EARL OF BURLINGTON

1694–1753

---

i. Italy and the Arts

RICHARD BOYLE was ten years old when in 1704 he
succeeded his father as 3rd Earl of Burlington, 4th Earl
of Cork and 4th Baron Clifford of Lanesborough.[1] These
dignities were supported by vast territorial wealth, for he inherited
estates in Ireland and Yorkshire, at Chiswick and in London. His
London property was particularly valuable, lying as it did on the
north side of Piccadilly, bounded on the west by Lord Berkeley's
property and on the east by Lord Clarendon's. It stretched northwards towards the neighbouring Cavendish estate on the far side
of Tyburn road. During Richard Boyle's youth the outlying lands
consisted of fertile orchards and meadows which fringed the
extensive gardens of Burlington House, and dissolved into open
country up to and beyond the little village of Hampstead perched
on a hillock like a small pincushion. London however was spreading rapidly; and the Earl's adolescence coincided with a demand
for noblemen's and gentlemen's town residences outside the precincts of the City and in the new fashionable quarter close to
St. James's Palace. It was fortunate for him, and incidentally for
posterity, that he was soon able to release a large part of his
London inheritance for profitable development. He personally
controlled and supervised the erection of the splendid new streets
(some of them still bear his name and titles) which were to be a
credit to the English genius for town planning until our own
generation. We, with that cynical disregard for the arts and beauty
which will be one of our major claims to remembrance, have
mutilated or demolished half these early-Georgian town houses
and are only waiting for the site values to rise sufficiently high
before sweeping away the remainder.

Little is known about Lord Burlington's boyhood. He was
brought up by his widowed mother who lived to be an old woman.

---

[1] Burlington did not claim his right to the Barony of Clifford until 1737 when it was
acknowledged by the House of Lords.

She was Juliana, daughter and heiress of the Honble. Henry Noel of North Luffenham in Rutland. She kept house for her son until he grew up, at Londesborough in Yorkshire and in London.[1] Presumably she cared for music because the libretto of Handel's opera, *Antiocho*, was dedicated to her in 1711. In later years she flits, a shadowy figure without face or personality, across the pages of her daughter-in-law's letters to Burlington. 'My Lady Burlington dined here today with Lady Jane,' is a casual sentence written in 1735, and again 'I have had messages from Lady Burl': At least she was not neglected by her son and his wife in her old age, but whether she was tenderly loved by them we are left to conjecture. Lady Jane Boyle, who lived and died in 1780 an old maid, was one of four sisters. Of the remaining three Lady Elizabeth became the wife of Sir Henry Bedingfeld, a Papist baronet of Oxburgh in Norfolk; Lady Juliana married as his second wife Charles Lord Bruce, later 3rd Earl of Ailesbury;[2] and Lady Henrietta married Henry Boyle, to be created Earl of Shannon. That Burlington remained on good terms with his sisters we may take for granted from what we know of his strictly upright and dutiful character. He allowed each of them £300 a year and frequently stayed at Oxburgh with Lady Elizabeth Bedingfeld on his way to Yorkshire from London.

Almost the first glimpse we get of him is in 1713 when he was nineteen. At this date he is described succinctly in a letter as 'a good natured pretty gentleman, but in Whig hands'. A Whig he was to remain for the next twenty years. At the very threshold of manhood honours fell thick upon him. In 1714 Queen Anne died and the Tories were immediately turned out of office. Thereupon the young Lord Burlington stepped into his own. Having been reared as a Whig he could not be regarded as a time-server; indeed there was little enough time behind him to have served. While he was abroad and before he had reached his majority, the new King George I, whose knowledge of British constitutional customs was abysmally deficient, appointed the youth—he was never sworn—a Privy Councillor. The noble neophyte was perhaps as deserving as many more experienced greybeards, but even in the early eighteenth century such an appointment was premature. Certainly Burlington was earnest and precocious. The following year he was made Lord Treasurer of Ireland, a position as high-sounding as it was hollow. Few duties were attached to this sinecure and visits to Ireland, where he owned property, were not appreciably aug-

---

[1] Camden House, Kensington, was rented by her soon after she became a widow.
[2] His first wife was a sister of Lady Burlington, wife of the 3rd Earl.

mented on its account. He was also made Vice-Admiral of the
County of York and Lord-Lieutenant of the East and West
Ridings. The last office was more exacting than the others. He
took his duties seriously and in 1716 wrote a very sharp letter to
the Deputy-Lieutenants reprimanding them for their persistent
disregard of his injunctions. In 1722 he was admitted a Fellow of
the Royal Society and in 1724 a Fellow of the Society of Antiquaries. In 1730 he became a Knight of the Garter, and in 1731
Captain of the Gentlemen Pensioners.

For the first three years of George I's reign Burlington enjoyed
the height of his political success, in so far as that meant anything
to him. But he was totally without worldly ambition, and absolutely
heedless of ministerial preferment. When in the spring of 1733
Sir Robert Walpole brought in the Excise Bill he went into opposition with Bathurst, Chesterfield and Cobham. On 3rd May he
wrote a dignified and courteous letter to his Sovereign, resigning
not only the Treasurership of Ireland but the Lord Lieutenantship
of the West Riding (that of the East Riding had lapsed in 1721)
as well. In vain the King pressed him not to relinquish this last
post. At one fell swoop he ceased to be a Whig, thus forfeiting all
future chances of favour from the throne so long as George II was
its occupant. Then as though to cast off for ever his association
with the capital and ministerial functions, he packed up the best of
his pictures at Burlington House and moved them permanently to
Chiswick. His motives for this precipitate behaviour caused much
speculation and mischievous people, considering how well he had
stood with the court and the ministry, whispered that the real
reason was pique at not being offered the White Staff. Lady Burlington, who at the time was in the Queen's service, was expected
to follow her lord into the wilderness. She did no such thing. She
remained at court, where after a short interval her husband was
received on terms of at least outward cordiality.

Throughout his life Burlington's interest in national affairs was
little more than perfunctory. He had become a Member of the
House of Lords at an early age, and so had certain regular obliga-
tions to fulfil. Since he lived a large part of each year at Chiswick
or in London he attended debates and voted as his conscience
dictated. At election times he bestirred himself to exercise the
patronage that was his; and there are letters between his brother-
in-law Lord Bruce and himself both before and after his resignation from office, on how to advance certain candidates and hinder
others in boroughs in which he had an hereditary interest.

The word 'patronage' is recurrent throughout these pages. Never in this country did it amount to greater consequence than during the reigns of the first two Georges. Certain privileged persons were born to it, just as they were born to nobility and riches. It could no more be divested than arms or legs, and self-deprivation of it by a nobleman was as unknown as the voluntary amputation of essential physical members. Patronage was not however always exercised to the public advantage. It was a feat as skilled as that of fencing or leaping. It could be allowed to lie fallow like the mind. It could be misdirected and abused. Often it was grossly abused. Lord Burlington on the contrary exercised it with consummate skill and righteousness. 'The noble Maecenas of Arts', Vertue called him—a sentiment which his contemporaries echoed and posterity has endorsed. It was the arts, poetry, music, painting, sculpture and above all architecture that he spent his whole life in assisting and promulgating. Everything else that came within his orbit was secondary to these interests.

What first awakened Lord Burlington's interest in the arts? And when did it first become apparent? We do not know that, apart from music, the arts had made more than a vague and general appeal before his grand tour to the Continent in 1714 with Italy and Rome as the ultimate goal. Music was the definite exception and his early love for it may have been fostered by his mother. At the end of 1712 when Burlington was only a boy of eighteen Handel came to stay for a short visit at Burlington House. The following year Haym's libretto of the composer's opera, *Teseo* was dedicated to the young host. There is one ambiguous but perhaps significant reference to him at court in the spring of this year. Lady Orkney after giving a hasty sketch of 'the Duke of St. Albans a jesting, Lord Arran sleeping' in the presence of Queen Anne, added succinctly, 'my Lord Burlington eating with his eyes'. 'Eating', we like to suppose, curiously, avidly, not so much the behaviour of this dull and philistine court, as the works of art on the palace walls around him.

The grand tour was undertaken by every young gentleman with pretensions to birth and fortune as a means of finishing off his education. Few set forth upon it with the intention of making the arts a special study. Several of the more intelligent and inquiring came to do so after being captivated by the treasures to which their social exclusiveness had given them access. Others preferred to make a study of the manners, politics or economics of the foreign countries they passed through. Some merely went with the purpose of having a good time, behaved badly and brought the English milord into disrepute. A dull minority were bored and homesick throughout, and longed to return to England as soon as they decently could. Much depended upon the erudition of the tutor or cicerone who invariably accompanied the youth, and his ability to open the eyes and touch the sensibilities of his charge during the tour. Burlington, who was of a very serious disposition, quite clearly came within the first category of young gentlemen. His keen and perceptive mind was quickly responsive to the beauties to be met with. His desire to learn was deep-seated. His readiness to take advice from those more educated than himself was always on the alert. His interest in the arts was soon aroused; it turned to love and finally amounted to a consuming passion.

Early on the morning of 17th May, 1714, Burlington set out from Burlington House with an equipage of two coaches, each drawn by a pair of horses, and a seemingly immense retinue of outriders and servants in livery. He was accompanied by Henry Brandon, Mr. Carlile, Mr. Gervais, Mr. Parry and Mr. Conyers, according to a day to day record of the tour's expenses, neatly tabulated in a calf-bound folio account book which bears no heading. Who these five gentlemen were and what part each of them played is, unfortunately, not specified. Henry Brandon may have been the young Earl's tutor and bear leader, for there is a volume on architecture with his signature in it among the books which were once at Chiswick. But since he is the only one of the five not allowed the prefix of Mr., the privilege may have been enjoyed by another. Not however by Mr. Gervais, by whom is doubtless meant Charles Jervas, the portrait painter. He had previously visited Rome, where he drew antique statues and copied the works of famous masters. So his rôle on this occasion may well have been to sketch whatever works of art particularly took the young Earl's fancy. One of the names mentioned was probably that of the accountant who made the entries. Curiously enough no mention is made of the French artist and fan painter, Lewis Goupy, who was certainly taken by the Earl to record scenes of travel; his name only appears on the return journey. In later years he was to be ousted from his patron's favour by William Kent. Wages were paid to John Jones, Charles Hilton, William Harper, John Carpenter, William Bennet and Andrew, who may have comprised a coachman, postillion or groom, footmen (of whom there were three) and a valet. Having been ferried across the Thames at Westminster the party clattered over the cobbled streets of Lambeth and Bermondsey towards Greenwich. There they halted. At Northfleet they changed horses and bought asparagus. They baited at Rochester and again at Ospringe. They

stopped the first night at Canterbury where Burlington gave
money to the poor of the town. On the 18th they reached Dover,
where having paid the town dues they confronted the custom
house officer. Dinner and supper, at which three bottles of cider
were consumed, were had at Dover. Not till 30th May did they
reach Ostend, where they disembarked and paid the crew of the
packet boat which had brought them across the Channel.

From Dover the coaches and some of the servants were probably
sent back to London, for there is mention now of a chaise and
only four horses having been ferried from Ostend across the
shallow harbour mouth to the east bank. With this reduced equipage they proceeded to Bruges, where two soldiers conducted
Burlington round the town. The months of June and July were
spent rapidly traversing Belgium and Holland. On 9th August
they crossed the Rhine into Germany with two berlins and a post
wagon. The type of vehicle hired was evidently chosen to suit
the country they went through, as was the number of guides
required to keep them to the proper roads. Düsseldorf, Cologne
Frankfurt, Darmstadt, Heidelberg were passed in quick succession. Somewhere beyond the last town one berlin got stuck in the
mire and had to be dug out with pickaxes. The coach was left
guarded all night while his lordship walked to the nearest inn to
sleep till the next morning of 21st August. On the 24th they
reached Baden. On the 29th they sailed down Lac Leman to
Geneva where Burlington's gun had to be mended.

September was spent in travelling to Rome, via Turin, which
meant passing through Chambéry and Modane, where chairs were
hired to carry the party over the Mont Cenis. On 11th September
they were in Turin. A store of coffee and a quilt for the dogs to
lie upon at the bottom of the chaise were purchased. On the 13th
they crossed the Tanaro at Alessandria. Two days later the
reached Genoa where his lordship's trunk was repaired. The
wasted very little time in this republican city, so rich in palace
and works of art, but continued along the west coast of Italy into
Tuscany. Massa, Pisa, where Burlington stayed only one night
Leghorn and Poggibonsi were next on the list. At the last town
chaise and two saddle-horses seem to have sufficed. On the 27th
they were at Siena, which held out no attractions, for they continued rapidly southwards, doubtless hoping to reach the Holy
City before the summer weather broke. The weary climb to
Radicofani on its desolate peak, affording a most primitive inn
which all eighteenth-century travellers dreaded, and the descent
to Aquapendente were accomplished with little apparent trouble

At last, after passing Montefiascone and Viterbo, a leisurely pace across the Campagna brought them to Rome on the last day of the month.

The first expense noted in Rome was '1st October. Paid for a Baskett for Dye to Pupp in'. The next, on the 12th, rather ominous, was for a visit from the Pope's doctor. Burlington, worn out by his incessant travelling, had possibly succumbed to a fever, for until 22nd October numerous doctors were being summoned. Then on 4th November appeared a strange item, which was several times to be repeated, namely, 'to a Fryar that brought my Lord some flowers'. Were these gifts ostensibly to cheer his convalescence, and really in the hope of making a convert of the ailing and susceptible youth? Henceforth wine for the party, milk for the dogs and snuff for his lordship were frequent necessities.

Until Christmas Burlington was clearly unwell, for on 27th December the faithful accountant noted down: 'At Prince Bungay's [?Borghese's] garden being the first day of My L^{ds} going abroad since ye 3rd October last.' On this day as though to celebrate his recovery he bought a brilliant diamond ring for 1,350 crowns. It was far from being Burlington's first extravagance. A month before (on 27th November to be exact) he had purchased from one 'Mr. Joseph Vintlema' The Temptation of St. Anthony after Annibale Carracci for 300 crowns, and again on 7th December from a gentleman with the improbable name of 'Mr. Bendetto Mosquita' a picture of architecture with figures of 3 men & a horse by 'Viveano' (both of which pictures were inventoried at the Earl's death as hanging in the Red Closet at Chiswick House). How came it that Burlington's first purchases of works of art took place when he was still confined to his lodgings after a fairly severe illness? He could hardly have had time to choose them the very day after his arrival in Rome before he was stricken. It happens that towards the middle or end of November William Kent returned to Rome after a four months' journey as far as Venetia in the company of young Thomas Coke of Norfolk. He was most probably sent by Coke to pay his respects to Burlington at the Earl's lodgings. In any case the arrival of so important a nobleman as Burlington would at once be common knowledge to the English community in a town of the small size of Rome. Moreover, we have George Vertue's word for it that he first met Kent in Rome. Nothing is more likely than that Kent, with his long acquaintance with the Roman dealers, brought the two pictures to Burlington's bedside for his approval and, in his capacity as experienced agent to rich milords, effected the purchases for him.

By the 1st January, 1715, the Earl was fully recovered and preparing to enjoy himself for a further month's stay in Rome As well as dried plums, quince cakes and pomegranates, coffee chocolate and tallow candles, six packs of cards, a sponge and ribbons for his cane were purchased. A map of Italy was acquired More serious expenditure was also incurred. 'A pair of harpsi-chords' were hired on a two months' rental. A visit on horseback was made to Frascati. The foot of a porphyry vase was bought and still more pictures—namely—a Madonna by Carlo Maratta from Mr. Pietro Branchi for 210 crowns, a Madonna by Pascoline from a Monsieur François Rosset for 75 crowns, and a Madonna by Domenichino (now known as the Madonna della Rosa) from the Superior of the Convent of S. Maria della Vittoria for 1,500 crowns The Carlo Maratta eventually hung in the Red Closet at Chiswick and the Domenichino, which was greatly cherished, in the Red Velvet Room. In addition to the handsome sum which he paid the nuns for the Domenichino Burlington also, according to Horace Walpole, generously presented them with a set of marble columns for their church. On the last day of January three more pictures were bought, one being of Noah Sacrificing (to be hung in the Red Velvet Room at Chiswick) by Maratta, another a Nativity scene and a third by Viviano.

Before leaving Rome Burlington at the beginning of February bought a marble table, some porphyry vases and a Madonna by Pietro da Cortona. He also took a box at the opera. On the 4th February are two curiously opposed entries in the account book, one 'for clothing Brother Stephano a Fryar', and the other 'for bottle of champagne'. On the 5th Burlington left Rome in a chaise by way of the Porta del Popolo, paid the requisite dues at the Ponte Mola and struck northwards. Already he was homeward bound by slow stages. At Siena he stayed one or two nights and that of the 10th at Leghorn to renew a broken axle tree. Before starting on again on the 11th he had his wigs powdered and bought some cinnamon water. At Pisa this time he stopped for a week or more visited the Duomo and Baptistery and climbed the Leaning Tower. By now there were five post horses to draw the chaise with one postillion and three footmen. Just before leaving Pisa 'a basket for the little white dog' was bought and a stock of coffee and biscuits laid in for the journey across the Apennines to Bologna He also ordered a harpsichord to be sent direct to Florence Having crossed the Apennines he went to the play in Bologna had his clothes washed and the chaise mended. But he soon left for Padua, where having crossed the Adige he arrived on the

24th. The following day he left by boat down the Brenta to Venice. He must have passed the vast palace of the Pisani at Stra, the melancholy Villa Malcontenta and innumerable villas, shuttered because it was still winter, which Palladio and his followers had built. These villas, which in after years were to influence him so profoundly that he played a larger part than any other Englishman in reproducing them in his own country, meant no more to him then than the dipping willows, the dusty planes, the waving poplars and the rectangular polenta fields in the fertile, well watered landscape of Venetia through which he was being leisurely paddled.

In Venice his first payments were once again for chocolate and the mending of his clothes: the next, dated 2nd March, for a hood and mask, which preparations presuppose a ball in some palace of the Grand Canal. His arrival did not escape the vigilance of the British Consul keenly on the alert at this date for news of the movements of the Old Pretender and his British sympathizers. The Consul wrote at once to General Stanhope, the Secretary of State in London: 'My Lords Essex and Morpeth with Mr. Mansell sett out this week for Rome, & my Lord Burlington is arrived from hence as I heard this moment.' On 5th March Burlington paid Mrs. Rosalba Carriera for 12 pictures in miniature, 288 crowns'. He attended a firework display and had seats specially reserved for a bull fight, probably in St. Mark's Square. Although his stay in Venice was short he nevertheless thought it worth while to hire a harpsichord.

On 8th March the British Consul again reported to London: 'Last Tuesday my Lord Burlington sett out hence for France and Rome; my Lord Peterborough is still here . . .' the latter Lord being a suspected Jacobite. Indeed, two days earlier Burlington had returned across the Lagoon and up the Brenta to Padua, his pelucca being towed the last part of the journey. Porters had to be hired to carry his luggage to the inn. The night of the 6th at Padua, and he was off next morning in two chaises for Vicenza. There he scarcely halted in spite of the Palladian palaces and the Villa Capra which he certainly cannot have had time to visit. The night of the 7th was spent at Verona and that of the 8th at Brescia. His companions seem by now to have dwindled. Some of them had perhaps already been sent home, or otherwise disposed of. The expenses recorded about this time are exclusively for his lordship, 'Mr. Goope and Self'. By 'Mr. Goope' is meant Lewis Goupy, the artist, who at last makes an appearance, and by 'Self' the still anonymous accountant. On the 15th they were re-crossing the Mont Cenis with one chaise and two horses to carry six persons, besides four saddle horses. Three unnamed Italians accompanied them to France. On the 16th they were in Savoy, already changing Italian money into French. On 27th March Henry Brandon, with Thomas Lund and Drury, whose names were not registered in the suite on leaving London, were sent independently on board wages from Lyons to Paris.

The 6th April saw his lordship and his whole retinue assembled in Paris. Two harpsichords and a bass viol were instantly purchased; so too were a set of silver dessert baskets, a sponge to clean the pictures with and 'a comb for the little dogs'. The three Italians were sent as a treat to the opera to console them for their home-sickness. Evidently Lord Burlington went into society in Paris, for he bought patches and gloves—fourteen pairs—and had to tip the footman of a Duke who sent him a present of chocolate. He bought French books and on 23rd went to Versailles by coach. On 2nd May he hired a coach to seat eight persons from Paris to Calais and enough vehicles to convey an enormous quantity of luggage. This, if the account book can be relied upon, amounted to no less than eight hundred and seventy-eight trunks and crates. The final expenditure was on a new silk quilt for Burlington's landlady, the old one on his bed having been 'Spoyle by ye Dogs'. His retinue, horses and luggage were shipped at Boulogne. They reached Dover in safety on 30th April where the custom-house officials seized upon some gifts bought for 'Ser Pope', and had to be bribed with 10/6d. before they would release them. Having paid the crew and tipped the cabin boy, the party proceeded to Canterbury. They spent the night at Rochester, and there is special mention of the three Italians and the bass viol still being with them. On 2nd May the party drove in state in three coaches—hired from the Spread Eagle for 7/6d.—to Burlington House.

From this very rapid journey of twelve months certain facets of Lord Burlington's character are revealed to us. They are his assessment of his proper station in the world, and his consideration for inferiors. Even for the first decades of the eighteenth century the large retinue of attendants and servants which this noble youth thought fit to accompany his progress was considerable. He may not have been out to dazzle the inhabitants of the countries he rushed through. Though a proud man he was not ostentatious. Yet he certainly meant his presence to be appreciated. It was. All his life he cut a figure in the world, which in return respected him and looked upon him with awe. At the same time he was kind and compassionate. His largesse to the poor of a town he passed

Photo: Royal Institute of British Architect.

SEVENOAKS SCHOOL, KENT
Design by Lord Burlington in the R.I.B.A. Library, Portland Place, W.1

BURLINGTON HOUSE, PICCADILLY, W.1
By Colen Campbell, from *Vitruvius Britannicus*, Vol. III, 1725

Photo: Royal Institute of British Architects

THE MAN OF TASTE FROM WILLIAM HOGARTH'S SER

MASQUERADES AND OPERAS

Lord Burlington carries a hod up a ladder to Pope who in whitewashing the s

of Kent bespatters the Duke of Chandos on the pavement

through was doubtless perfunctory, as was his annual Christmas gift of gowns and petticoats to the old almswomen at home in England. These were levies expected of a rich nobleman and were not withheld. But the gifts to the friar who brought him flowers, the clothes to Brother Stephano, the marble columns to the Sisters of Santa Maria della Vittoria were unsolicited. So too were the baskets, lambskin rugs and all sorts of comforts and delicacies for Dye and the other little white dogs that were his constant companions and delight on the journey.

More important still, the tour reveals the particular arts which had already touched his interests. Architecture does not seem to have been among them up to date. On the other hand pictures, objects of virtu generally and music were conspicuously favoured. Most of the paintings and some of the porphyry vases which still belong to his descendants were bought wisely and well. And if he did not during his travels buy much sculpture[1] he brought back with him from Rome, according to Vertue, a living sculptor in the person of Giovanni Battista Guelfi, who was doubtless one of the Italians sent to the opera in Paris. Another was Pietro Castrucci, who was to be the first violin, or leader, in Handel's operatic orchestras over a considerable period. The harpsichords and the bass viol, which he acquired, do not testify to any proficiency on these instruments, but they point to a very genuine love of music, which was to grow with the years.

Lord Burlington returned from his grand tour to an altered England. During the interval Queen Anne had died and the Elector of Hanover arrived to reign as George I. With the change of dynasty the Tories went and the Whigs, to whom Burlington belonged, had come to power. Life held out glowing prospects for him, as it were with both hands. We have already seen how minor ministerial posts were thrust upon him. He was young. In August of this year he became twenty-one and independent. He was immensely rich. He would be a patron of artists. The opportunity immediately offered itself. Handel was in London on his second English visit, which was prolonged into permanent residence. The composer was still poor and struggling. Moreover he was distinctly out of favour with the new King, to whom, as Elector of Hanover, he had promised to return but whom, lured by prospects of English patronage, he had failed and insulted. Burlington again took him to stay in his London house where he set him up in apartments of his own. He then persuaded George I to forgive

---

[1] The beautiful bronzes of the Four Seasons by Massimiliano Soldani (1658–1740) now the property of H.M. the Queen, were commissioned by Burlington in Rome, 1715.

the composer and even to grant him an annuity. Handel remained for at least two years in Burlington House where he composed the operas, *Silla* and *Armadigi*, of which the first was performed on a private stage fitted up in one of the drawing-rooms. In the summer of 1717 at latest he left Burlington House for Canons to become Chapel Master to the Duke of Chandos. To judge from an affectionate letter which Handel wrote to Burlington while on a short visit to Dresden in 1719 the break caused no estrangement. He called the young Earl his benefactor and protector, stressed his attachment to his person and begged him to extend those favours which were so very precious to him. Burlington's faith in Handel never wavered. Although he was later to be responsible for introducing to England the Italian, G. B. Buononcini, who became the German's malevolent rival, he loyally supported Handel throughout his career. There are entries as late as 1750 in the Earl's accounts of payments 'for the use of Mr. Handel' and of subscription tickets for his oratorios at Covent Garden.

When in 1719 the Royal Academy of Music was established under the patronage of George I, Burlington, who was the principal sponsor—he guaranteed £1,000 towards the £10,000 required—appointed Handel the first Director, with Paolo Rolli as librettist. The Academy gave a much needed fillip to British musical talent which since the death of Purcell had languished uncultivated. Because native composers and executants were lacking in brilliance Burlington, quite heedless of the resentment engendered among them and the wearisome consequences, did not hesitate to invite foreigners to London. Hence the advent of Buononcini, who probably accompanied Burlington on the return from his second tour to Italy in 1719. That a nasty competitive spirit soon waxed within the Academy was not the Earl's fault. Buononcini was vain and idle, and whatever his supporters cared to think, his talent fell far behind Handel's genius. He was vilely jealous of the German successes. John Byrom's epigram, which was bandied about society, inspired as it was by mischief and little else, yet reflects the prevailing discord.

> *Some say, compared to 'Bononcini'*
> *That Mynheer Handel's but a ninny,*
> *Others aver that he to Handel*
> *Is scarcely fit to hold a candle.*
> *Strange all this difference should be*
> *'Twixt Tweedle-dum and Tweedle-dee.*

Until his disgrace for deliberately filching a madrigal which claimed as his own composition, and his dismissal from the Academy, Buononcini was the cause of the most intense and bitter dissension in the operatic world. On the succession of George II who was an uncompromising Handelian, a new opera house was set up in Lincoln's Inn Fields by Frederick Prince of Wales and his partisans, who as vehemently championed Buononcini. For a time Handel shared the monarch's unpopularity. The King and Queen, according to Lord Hervey, 'sat freezing at his empty Haymarket opera, while the Prince with all the chief of the nobility went as constantly to that of Lincoln's Inn Fields'. They looked upon an anti-Handelian as an anti-courtier and treated him or her with the utmost disfavour. Affairs reached such an absurd pitch that 'the Princess Royal said she expected in a little while to see half the House of Lords playing in the orchestra in their robes and coronets'.

The large majority of the peerage were of course lamentably ignorant of and indifferent to music, which they merely made into a political issue. Burlington on the other hand kept aloof from these unseemly squabbles, refusing to be a partisan. He continued to help finance and in a sense direct the Academy of Music until it died a natural death of inanition. He gave musical parties in his own houses, befriended musicians and opera singers, no matter to which group they adhered, continued to play the harpsichord himself and installed an organ at Chiswick.

The young patron on his return from the Continent in 1715 established at Burlington House, in addition to the composer Handel, the sculptor Guelfi. For a time Burlington regarded him as the greatest sculptor of the age; but he quickly became disillusioned and transferred his admiration to Rysbrack. Guelfi, who was slow of speech, opinionated and quite convinced that no man was his equal, stayed in England for nearly twenty years. At first he seems to have worked almost exclusively as a restorer of antique sculpture, notably upon the Arundel marbles, and did not begin carving from the life until the middle of the following decade. None of his work for Burlington has been identified, although much of the garden statuary at Chiswick may be his, as Vertue recounts. He sculptured the Craggs monument in Westminster Abbey and a number of monumental effigies there and elsewhere. His portraits of young men and women are debonair and patrician; the heads sometimes are sensitive but few of his figures or busts have the dash and baroque spirit of his Roman master, Camillo Rusconi.

In 1715 two large folios appeared on the London bookstalls. They were to have considerable bearing upon Burlington's future

…erests. Colen Campbell's first volume of *Vitruvius Britannicus* was a collection of engravings (with prefatory descriptions) of plans and elevations mainly of country houses by contemporary architects, including himself. As the title of the folio suggested, Campbell's intention was to launch a new style of architecture by reviving what he called 'the antique simplicity' and reverting to the absolute authority of Inigo Jones. Although the book supplied illustrations of a few buildings by Wren and Vanbrugh, Campbell sought to imply that the baroque style, with its 'capricious ornaments', as practised by these masters of an older generation, was now obsolete. The majority of the buildings illustrated were in the Jonesian tradition. For example, Wilbury Park in Wiltshire by his teacher the Surveyor-General William Benson, was a house built in 1710 and the first to be modelled on a design (unpublished) by Inigo Jones. In other words Campbell's *Vitruvius Britannicus* sounded a sharp clarion call as if to announce the dawn of a new Georgian style of architecture and, incidentally, the triumph over the discredited Tories of the Whig party, with which the style was thenceforth to be identified.

The second folio to appear was *The Architecture of A. Palladio* 'in four Books, Revis'd, Design'd, and Published by Giacomo Leoni, a Venetian', translated into English by the Huguenot refugee, Nicholas Dubois. Leoni claimed to have seen most of the buildings illustrated in Palladio's original 1570 publication, and to have added from first-hand study several decorative details omitted in the crude Italian wooden cuts. In several cases Leoni's additional details were purely conjectural, a fact which Burlington must have discovered for himself in 1719 and which may explain why he never wholly approved of the author. He certainly never employed Leoni as an architect. On the other hand he subscribed in 1720 to the second edition of the book, just as his mother in his absence abroad had subscribed to the first.

There is little doubt that the two publications first opened Lord Burlington's eyes to a new and important field of the arts. Campbell's book pointed out to him what vast possibilities lay ahead for architecture in Great Britain. All that was needed was enthusiastic and intelligent leadership of a movement that was on the brink of starting. Burlington's definitive rôle in life became immediately clear to him. He would be the arch-patron of the new style which Campbell had been the first man to advocate in print. Leoni's book incidentally supplied him with the design for his earliest architectural venture. This was the entire re-modelling of Burlington House in Piccadilly.

The history of the re-modelling of Burlington House is con-
fusing. It is a surprise to learn that James Gibbs, Catholic and a
Tory, claimed that he began to transform the house, which
Burlington's grandfather had employed Sir John Denham to build
in 1665, into 'the only town residence really fit for a British
nobleman'. Why did the young Earl, so recently inspired by the
Vitruvian tenets, commission a professed admirer of Wren, whose
work he intensely disliked, and an architect schooled in the Roman
baroque tradition? The explanation must be that Burlington had
in his salad days, so to speak, engaged Gibbs before the publication of Campbell's first volume and Leoni's *Palladio*, and before
his own grandiloquent assumption of Palladianism and declared
antipathy to everything that did not subscribe to it. It happened
that Gibbs got no further than raising the eastern stable block in
the forecourt, when he was supplanted in 1717 by the author of
Vitruvius Britannicus himself. As Colen Campbell explained in
volume III of his book, published in 1725, 'the stables were built
by another architect before I had the honour of being called to his
lordship's service, which obliged me to make the offices opposite
conformable to them. The front of the house, the conjunction from
thence to the offices, the great gate and street wall, were all
designed and executed by me'. This statement is tolerably correct
so long as we realize that, in regard to the front of the house,
Campbell merely adapted a design to Sir John Denham's pre-
existing structure. In the first place the Charles II house was not
destroyed. The core of it even stands to this day, namely a centre
of seven bays with projecting wings, each of which originally of
two bays was made into one large bay after 1717. In the second
place Campbell's new front can hardly be called his or anyone
else's invention but Palladio's. The seven-bay centre is with only
minor modifications a fairly faithful transcript of the Palazzo
Iseppo di Porti in Vicenza. Curiously enough Campbell had
already dedicated to Lord Islay in volume I of *Vitruvius Britannicus* this very design as being his own invention.

Campbell never went to Italy; and Burlington, as we have seen,
only passed through Vicenza hurriedly on 7th March 1715 without even stopping the night. So presumably the general idea for
the front of Burlington House (and for that matter of the house
dedicated to Lord Islay) was gleaned from B. Picart's drawing of
the Vicenzan palace which Leoni subsequently had engraved for
his book. When Campbell came to execute the design he sub-
stituted a balustrade for the attic floor; he also left the frieze of
the great cornice plain and omitted the sculpture, which in Leoni's

ving as in the actual Palazzo Iseppo façade is inserted over between the windows of the *piano nobile*. Otherwise he did tamper with the design. Where Campbell definitely showed some invention was in the flanking wings. The single Venetian window,[1] which now takes the place of Sir John Denham's pair of ordinary windows, is the earliest example of the revived Venetian window in England—and revived, not from Palladio but from Inigo Jones, for the following reason. In Italy the Venetian window was always treated as a functional element to bridge a space in the centre of a façade. Here it merely fulfils a decorative purpose at either end of the composition just as first it was made to do in several of Jones's designs for Whitehall Palace. Campbell was to repeat this particular treatment upon the corner towers of Houghton Hall. His English successors throughout the eighteenth century trod in his footsteps.

When the Earl went abroad for the second time he left the work at Burlington House entirely in the hands of Campbell, in whom he then had absolute confidence. In August 1719 Joshua Fletcher, mason, was paid £534 17s. 6d. for the 'Rustic Basemᵗ in the front of Burlington House'. On 15th September someone on the Earl's behalf spent £2 3s. 0d. on coach hire and a dinner at the Pack Horse 'after viewing Mr. Simon's work with Mr. Campbell'. Only a few weeks later—on 3rd November to be precise—Burlington was in Vicenza, scribbling notes in the margin of a 157c copy of Palladio's *Quattro Libri* which he had recently purchased in the city. Against the woodcut of the Palazzo Iseppo di Porti, which he had just seen for the first time, although it was the model of the London house now being rebuilt for him, appear these remarks: 'There is very little of this house executed, only the front, and the rooms belonging to it, the mezzaninos are finely finished by Palladio, but all the doors, and ornaments of the rooms above stairs, except the soffito of the salon, are quite altered, the great cornice is plain [which shows the liberty Leoni took by embellishing it in his engraving], and the columns in the entrance are Doric without bases.' By Christmas, when his lordship returned to England, the front of Burlington House was finished.

During 1716, the year in which Gibbs had begun upon the east stable block at Burlington House, friends of the Earl were already referring to his building activities. Alexander Pope in a letter o 9th July to Charles Jervas, who had accompanied the Earl on hi first foreign tour, wrote: 'my Lord Burlington desires you may be

[1] By Venetian window is meant a large centre light under a semicircular head, flanked b two narrow lights under flat lintels. Sometimes this form of window is in England terme Palladian.

put in mind of him. His gardens flourish, his structures rise, his pictures arrive, and,' he adds, '(what is far nobler and more valuable than all) his own good qualities daily extend themselves to all about him: Whereof, I the meanest (next to some Italian chymists, fidlers, bricklayers, and opera-makers) am a living instance.' Pope specifically mentions Burlington's gardens and structures in the plural; and the significance of the sentence lies in the fact that his noble friend was busy at both Burlington House and Chiswick House. At the latter he was adding to the Jacobean house which he had inherited, not the famous rotunda—that was to follow in 1725 —but a large room, called the Summer Parlour, which is now pulled down. In the only surviving account book to include Burlington's expenses on building operations, mention is made in 1719, the year in which the accounts open, of bricklayers', plasterers' and carpenters' work proceeding at Chiswick House and Burlington House simultaneously.

John Gay in the first edition, printed in January 1716, of *Trivia* had composed four couplets which are perplexing:

> *Yet Burlington's fair palace still remains;*
> *Beauty within, without proportion reigns,*
> *Beneath his eye declining art revives,*
> *The wall with animated picture lives;*
> *There Hendel* [sic] *strikes the strings, the melting strain*
> *Transports the soul and thrills through every vein;*
> *There oft I enter (but with cleaner shoes)*
> *For Burlington's beloved by ev'ry Muse.*

He was referring, not to Chiswick but to Burlington House where Handel had been given apartments the previous year. The building in which the great composer's melting strains were being struck was still Sir John Denham's. Campbell had not yet begun pulling down the front in order to re-erect it along Palladian lines. The 'proportion' without, which Gay was careful to mention, doubtless referred to the additional office blocks intended to give a nice balance to the cumbersome Charles II mansion between them. Gibbs was then engaged upon the east one of these. But the 'beauty within' gives rise to inquiry. The poet would hardly have mentioned it, and certainly not 'the wall with animated picture' if he had had in mind an interior and painted wall dating from the 1660s. Such decoration would in 1716 have called for no favourable comment at all. The least said about something so old-fashioned the better. Nor can Gay have meant by 'animated picture', as has been suggested, the staircase walls and ceiling painted by Sebastian and Marco Ricci, for they were not executed until after Campbell had recast the interior. Moreover an entry in the account book under 21st February, 1721, 'Mons. Devoto for painting the ornaments in ye ceiling painted by Sig^r Rizzi' suggests that the Ricci's work was then only just completed. It is probable, on the contrary, that Gibbs had actually started to redecorate some of the rooms of the old Denham house, and that his work was summarily scrapped when Campbell became engaged upon a far more drastic undertaking, namely the practical rebuilding of both the outside and the inside of Burlington House. It must, then, have been a mural painting done during Gibbs's brief commission to which Gay was referring. An old tradition, only lately exploded, attributed the Ricci paintings to Thornhill. Is it not possible that Thornhill, who was a boon companion of Gibbs and worked with him at Wimpole, was responsible for the 'animated picture'? Its destruction after so brief an existence would explain Thornhill's and his son-in-law Hogarth's intense animosity towards Burlington, and his henchman Kent.

From what survives today of the early-Georgian rooms in Burlington House the mind and hand of Colen Campbell are very conspicuous in the decoration. Apart from three indifferent ceiling canvases, which well merited the jeers of Thornhill and Hogarth, there is nothing to suggest any contribution by Kent, who only appeared on the scene after the decoration of the interior was well in hand. The wall and ceiling paintings by the Ricci, under the inspiration of Veronese, and even the saloon ceiling by Kent still convey a baroque flavour. The saloon doorways with seated boys on the pediments tally closely with the overmantel in the saloon of Marble Hill, of which the architect was Campbell's other noble disciple, Lord Pembroke. Incidentally, the boys at Burlington House were by the same master carver, James Richards, who was paid by Burlington for constant work between 1719 and 1721.

The inhabitants of London were amazed to see rising in their midst a palace taken from a north Italian city. Few of them were sufficiently well versed in Vicenzan palace architecture to appreciate that the difference in the Piccadilly mansion lay in its being given wings, pavilions and a spacious forecourt, instead of a straight façade flush with an extremely narrow street. The greatest glory of Burlington House was the semi-circular colonnade which joined the ends of the pavilions, flanking the house, to the gateway and thus completed the courtyard enclosure. Campbell claimed the gateway (based on the York House watergate, which he

erroneously supposed to be to Inigo Jones's design) and the wall
in which it was set as his. Burlington however was unquestionably
the designer of the colonnade. Its conception was bold and novel.
John Macky, in his *Journey through England in* 1724, assumed that
Burlington's colonnade was inspired by Bernini's before St. Peter's.
This may have been the case, because for all his protestations
Burlington was often unconsciously influenced by other than
Palladian buildings. On the other hand, although Palladio never
carried out a semicircular colonnade before a villa, he certainly
planned one for the Villa Serego at Santa Sofia. It may then have
been this unexecuted plan, or even Inigo Jones's quadrant colonnades at Stoke Bruerne which suggested themselves to Burlington.
Nothing quite like the graceful, curved Doric screen at Burlington
House had appeared in England before. The Earl's contemporaries
were justly enchanted with it; and Horace Walpole's description
of how it dawned upon him for the first time is not so well known
that it cannot stand re-quotation: 'As we have few samples of
architecture,' he wrote in a letter, 'more antique and imposing than
this colonnade, I cannot help mentioning the effect it had on
myself . . . Soon after my return from Italy I was invited to a ball
at Burlington-house. As I passed under the gate by night, it could
not strike me. At daybreak, looking out of the window to see the
sun rise, I was surprised with the vision of the colonnade that
fronted me. It seemed one of those edifices in fairy-tales that are
raised by genii in a night's time.'

Until his second and momentous visit to Italy Burlington
remained under the tutelage of Colen Campbell, to whom undoubtedly he owed his first practical experiences of building.
Whatever suggestions the Earl may have contributed to the
designs of the new Burlington House, Campbell carried them
through and was responsible for the replanning and decoration of
the interior.[1] If the 'new casina in the gardens of Chiswick' was,
as Campbell admitted in volume III of *Vitruvius Britannicus*, 'the
first essay of his lordship's happy invention', it bears the stamp of
the tutor's style. It is stiffly pretentious without being original, a
triumphal arch with a Venetian window stuck above it, the whole
crowned with a prim, Wren-like cupola. The general idea was in
fact lifted from the centrepiece of one of Inigo Jones's or Webb's
drawings for Whitehall Palace, which was in Burlington's collection. It was carried out by Burlington in 1717.

A portrait of Lord Burlington, with a view of the 'new casina'

---

[1] Burlington himself made alterations inside the house long after he had freed himself from
Campbell's tutelage. The elliptical library on the ground floor (east wing) and consequent
alteration to the ballroom above were his.

in the background has recently come to light.[1] It shows him as a young man of about twenty-three or -four in the undress of the period, that is to say with open neck, wearing a long coat and a turban cap. He is leaning rather nonchalantly with his right arm upon a pedestal. The hand holds a pair of callipers. Already there is a slight tendency to embonpoint. The face is not handsome: the eyes are small but discerning; the nose long and patrician, and the mouth small but stern. The figure is that of a man reserved, sensitive and idealistic. The portrait has been attributed to Hayman, Dahl and Richardson. Because of the subject's youth and justifiable pride in his first building it must have been done soon after the bath-house was finished and before the second journey to Italy. There is in the account book under the date 9th January, 1720, an expenditure of £31 10s. 0d. 'To Sir Godfrey Kneller being for 2 copies of his lord[pps] Picture' taken just before the journey, of which this may conceivably be one.

ii. William Kent and Marriage

In the summer of 1719 Burlington set forth on his second foreign travel. There was no question this time of drifting rather aimlessly round the Continent. He knew in advance precisely where he wanted to go, what to see and for what purpose. Venetia and in particular the buildings of Palladio were now his main objective. He also hoped to acquire whatever papers, drawings and records of the master might still be on the market. An incidental objective was to find and bring back to England Italian musical talent for the Royal Academy of Music which he was about to inaugurate. One result of this search was, as we have already seen, the introduction to London of Buononcini, who perhaps came over in Burlington's company. The journey lasted no longer than six months, for by Christmas the traveller was home again.

From a letter of 15th November by Kent to one of his early patrons, Burrell Massingberd, it is clear that the painter had met Lord Burlington by pre-arrangement at Genoa before the Earl proceeded to Vicenza and Venice, in order 'to get architects to draw all y[e] fine buildings of Palladio . . . I hope', Kent went on in his half literate style, 'by his Lordship's encorgement and other gentlemen who may have a better gusto, than that damned gusto that's been for this sixty years past'. This ungrammatical sentence shows the missionary zeal behind the expedition of the two men

[1] In the possession of Mrs. Lancaster, Haseley Court, Oxfordshire.

Since Kent's (admittedly scrappy) Italian journal of 1714[1] that his interests were then almost solely in painting, it is p that Burlington had in the meantime inspired him with an in in Palladio and the conviction that correct architecture mu reintroduced to England—and not the other way round. Burlington spent some months in Vicenza and from there went to Venice towards the end of October. On 3rd November Mr. E. Burgess, the Minister at Venice, reported to the Secretary of State: 'My Lord Burlington went from hence ye day before yesterday, in order to make the best of his way home through France. He left the inclosed letter with me, which I beg you will be so kind as to send to his house;' and again on the same date: 'My Lord Burlington was here ten or twelve days, but left us the day before yesterday.'

On the very day that Mr. Burgess sent his report to London Lord Burlington bought in Vicenza, whither he must have returned on his way home, one of the many copies of Palladio's book that were to adorn his library shelves at Chiswick. This copy, signed and dated at Vicenza, is the only one to be annotated by him. The marginal comments, which are sometimes revealing, indicate which buildings of Palladio impressed him most. Against San Giorgio Maggiore in Venice he carefully noted down several unorthodox details, and observed that 'behind the great altar, there is an intercolumn which discovers the choir; it ends in a semi-circle and is one of the most beautiful buildings in the world'. In later years Burlington, at Chiswick and at Kirby Hall, Yorkshire, was to remember how thrilling a plan can be which 'discovers' to the visitor walking through a large rectangular room a lesser chamber with a semicircular, octagonal or hexagonal apse. The Palazzo Thiene in Vicenza aroused his most ardent commendation. 'If any of Palladio his designs, can claim a preference to the rest, this in my opinion has the best rule in it, it is certainly the most beautiful modern building in the world, there is hardly any part of architecture that does not enter into the composition of it and it is the best school that ever was for rustics. In the entrance, the whole shaft of the columns excepting about an inch below the astragal, and as much above the cimbia to show the diameter, is rough rustic.' Did he perhaps regret that he had not taken the Palazzo Thiene as the model for his London house? His reference to the Palazzo Iseppo di Porti, which was the prototype, is cool by comparison. Opposite a woodcut of the Palazzo Chiericati he wrote an ambiguous note: 'I was extremely surprised (in my second journey to Vicenza) to meet with a bricklayer, who told

[1] For some extracts from Kent's *Journal* see pp. 227–8.

me that he built this house from the ground, after Palladio's design, about thirty years agoe, and upon further search, I found that there were several people, who remembered the building of it, but I could not meet with the least account, of the occasion of its being rebuilt, for it is very certain that this design was executed by Palladio, he himself says so, and the excellent cast of the whole inside of the house, demonstrates that it is an exact copy from a former.'

The Palazzo Chiericati was built in 1550, so that if by 1690 or thereabouts the structure called for drastic repairs it is not very surprising; but there are, as Burlington himself said, no records of it having been totally rebuilt. Of the famous Villa Capra (the Rotonda) just outside the city, which was to have a profound influence upon Palladian villas in England, including Chiswick House, Burlington remarked: 'This is the only house in Vicenza that is quite finished by Palladio, and one plainly sees, by the ornaments and exquisite tast that is in the most minute part of it, that he executed his design without restraint.' And he added: 'The present owner has done it great injury by inlarging the chamber doors, and dressing them in a most extravagant manner, but those in the salon have escaped.'

Finally he has something to say about the Villa Foscari, now called the Malcontenta on the right bank of the Brenta. 'It is easy to see how much he [Palladio] was cramped in the execution of this design, by the portico, which stands upon a plain brick stucco wall, whereas he intended a beautiful pedestal to the whole.' He goes on to point out that the windows are of smaller compass than the architect meant them to be. 'The top of the house is finished in the middle with a plain attic wall and pediment and not in the manner that it is published . . . but as the present Sig^r Foscari is a great architect in the modern way (as may be seen by the many monstrous buildings in his gardens) I conclude that they are his alterations.' Burlington was quick to resent any alterations to the master's designs. He was right in noticing how the great hexastyle portico has an unfinished look without the stepped and moulded basement which Palladio provided for it in his woodcut. The rather melancholy and haunted aspect which is so suited to its present name, La Malcontenta, is largely due to this deficiency as well as to some others Lord Burlington noticed, namely the reduced size of the windows and the lack of the cheerful curved side scrolls to the topmost gable feature. Moreover the absence of the flanking walls with syncopated ball coping has resulted in an accentuation of the villa's height and gauntness.

In his Italian text of the *Designs of Ancient Buildings by Palladio*[1] published many years later Burlington explained how during his last journey to Italy he made the most diligent researches of which he was capable for unpublished drawings of the master. Palladio had mentioned that many such existed in his lifetime. Burlington told how in the Villa Maser, which lies near Asolo at the foothills of the Dolomites, he came across some papers relating to Palladio's private life and several designs (but failed to find any annotated drawings). He purchased the papers and designs from the owner who was a descendant of Palladio's great friend and protector, Daniele Barbaro, and claimed to have published all the designs without making the least alteration to any. He only omitted a few working drawings (which he had acquired previously) of certain details because they were too big. Palladio's designs appearing in Lord Burlington's publication are all of Roman baths. We can detect clearly several features, such as the continuous row of split pediments in the Baths of Vespasian, the colonnades in the Baths of Nero, and the exedrae, niches and oval rooms in the Baths of Antonine, which Burlington reproduced later at Chiswick, in the York Assembly Rooms and elsewhere.

On his return to London by way of Paris, where he picked up William Kent again, Burlington lost little time in acquiring from John Talman[2] his collection of drawings by Palladio, Inigo Jones and John Webb. There are payments to John Talman on 3rd May, 1720, for a book of Jones's designs and plans, and on 7th April, 1721, 'for a parcell of architecticall designs and drawings by Palladio', for each of which the Earl paid £170. The transaction was probably arranged by Kent, who knew Talman intimately, having embarked upon his Italian travels in 1714 in his company. Yet a further consignment of Palladio's drawings was bought by Burlington from Dr. Richard Mead, to whom they had passed from a Bishop of Verona.

When Burlington and Kent returned to London for Christmas of 1719 they were brimful with experiences and ideas for future projects. Each had seen for himself the chief works of Palladio and had investigated through the master's drawings the sources of his architecture, which were principally Vitruvius and Augustan Rome. These first-hand contacts revealed to them that the path they were resolving to follow had already been trodden step by

[1] Entitled *Fabbriche Antiche Disegnate da Andrea Palladio Vicentino e date in luce da Riccardo Conte di Burlington, Londra MDCCXXX.*

[2] John Talman (1677–1726) was the son of William Talman the architect. John Talman was one of the greatest collectors of architectural drawings, many of which now repose in public museums and libraries.

step by Inigo Jones well over a hundred years previously. In consequence their admiration for this fellow-countryman pioneer turned
to profound reverence. They saw that their mission was to continue where Inigo had left off, and their sacred duty to re-promul-
gate his teaching. Thus Burlington financed and assisted Kent in
the publication of *The Designs of Inigo Jones* (1727), which in
reality comprised only a few drawings by Inigo, many by his pupil
Webb and one or two by Burlington himself. Furthermore they
were determined to re-edify those of Jones's surviving buildings
which were in decay. So they repaired at Burlington's expense
St. Paul's Church in Covent Garden and the Barber-Surgeons'
Hall in Monkwell Street. In 1738 Burlington bought from Sir
Hans Sloane and re-erected in Chiswick garden Inigo's gateway
which formerly stood in front of Beaufort House in Chelsea.

From now on the two men worked in the closest partnership
and harmony. Kent was taken to live at Burlington House and
there given apartments which he never quitted until he was
removed to a niche in the Burlington family vault in Chiswick
churchyard. That was still nearly thirty years ahead. In these early
days Burlington does not seem to have recognized the least architectural talent in Kent; instead he regarded him as a great painter
with whom none of his countrymen could compare. His blind
enthusiasm for his friend's meretricious talent in this branch of the
arts caused much dissatisfaction and jealousy among more gifted
painters. Henry Trench,[1] whom Burlington had patronized in
Rome and to whom he had promised great things on his return to
England, was much put out by being superseded by Kent. He was
silly enough to expostulate in writing to the Earl, who only read
his letter aloud to Kent amid much laughter. Trench was certainly
small fry; but when it came to preferring Kent to Thornhill and
procuring the job of painting the staircase at Hampton Court for
the former at the expense of the latter, Burlington showed positive
ill-judgment and unwisdom. Thornhill's son-in-law Hogarth knew
well enough how to hit back with a rough and ready weapon. So he
published a satirical engraving entitled 'Masquerades and Operas
Burlington Gate', in which he depicted the Earl as a common
mason carrying a hod up a ladder to Pope, who in the act of whitewashing a bust of Kent incidentally bespattered the Duke of
Chandos on the pavement below. Strangely enough Burlington's
inflated opinion of his protégé was endorsed by the select circle of
his friends in spite of the fact that the world at large had the bad
taste to prefer the works of Thornhill, who happened to be incom-

[1] Irish historical painter who settled in England, 1725. He died young in the following year.

parably the greatest baroque wall painter this island has produced. John Gay apostrophizing Kent in the *Epistle to Paul Methuen* of 1720 advised him, since his countrymen did not sufficiently appreciate his merits, to return to Rome and there rejoin the company of the immortal painters of whom he was their peer.

> *There on the walls let thy just labours shine,*
> *And Raphael live again in thy design.*
> *Yet stay awhile; call all thy genius forth,*
> *For Burlington unbyass'd knows thy worth;*
> *His judgment in thy master-strokes can trace*
> *Titian's strong fire and Guido's softer grace; . . .*

It is easy enough to guess that Gay could not tell a good from a bad painting. That Kent's talent should be compared with Raphael's and Titian's genius was as presumptuous as the suggestion was foolish that he, whose sole claim to fame up to date lay in a feeble adoption of pagan motifs, had any affinity with the sentimental religiosity of Guido Reni.

Vertue believed that Burlington over-reached himself in trying to advance Kent too far in royal circles, that royalty resisted and that in consequence Burlington out of revenge quitted his court posts. There may be an element of truth in the statement for Burlington did not readily brook opposition when he considered his views to be right ones. But the court had only to look down its nose at his lordship's protégé for society to take him to its bosom. Kent soon became the rage. Walpole observed that nothing was thought complete without his assistance or approbation: 'so impetuous was fashion, that two great ladies prevailed on him to make designs for their birthday-gowns. The one dressed in a petticoat decorated with columns of the five orders; the other like a bronze in a copper-coloured satin with ornaments of gold.' He turned into a highly gifted decorator, possibly the very greatest of that epicene race which can turn a hand to painting a ceiling, designing chairs, tables and every species of furniture, modelling ladies' dresses, laying out gardens, and even constructing a royal barge. Architecture was the last accomplishment to descend upon him. Whereas Burlington had erected a temple in 1717 Kent's first building, as distinct from decoration, was the addition of some wings to Esher Place as late as 1730 when he was already forty-five years old. By this date Burlington had already established English Palladianism on a sure footing. If then Burlington was the scholar who developed the theme, Kent was the artist who often provided the refinements. In other words Burlington lacked finesse but had

ng: Kent lacked depth but abounded in fertile imagination
was the complement of the other, and the two made a
marvellous combination.

They gloried in the united front they presented to the world
In a letter of 16th November, 1732, Kent reminded Burlington
that whereas the French considered the contemporary English a
hundred years behind them in civilization, Burlington and he were
a hundred years ahead of the average Englishman. And he proceeded to lash out against some ill-considered alterations then in
progress to Covent Garden church: 'By what I see doing in y'
Arcade in convent garding, Inigo thought proper to add a portico
of the Tuscan order, but these wise heads have put an Ionick
expencive portico in the rustick arches, for an entrance into the
absurd Building they have made, but so far they be in the right
being of a peice of what these Asses have done.' He was of
inestimable value in keeping an eye on Burlington's interests in
London and at Chiswick when the Earl was frequently away
attending to his Yorkshire estates. 'The new Buildings in Bond
Street,' he wrote in September 1745 when London was cowering
under the threat of a Jacobite invasion ('ye affaire in Scotland rather
augments to the Pretender') 'was going to make use of your wall
which I have stop'd.' Instead he had the wall raised another two
feet so as to hide the new buildings. 'The room you desir'd to have
painted is done before you come that you may be comfortable at
home in your own house, let me know you know I'll do my best,'
came from another letter written two months later, in relation to
Chiswick. Kent was well aware that in all matters of taste he saw
eye to eye with his patron, and so could safely assume authority
whenever he judged it expedient.

Most of Kent's letters to Burlington are in a very un-seriou
strain, full of nonsense and uninhibited fun. He did not write at
all in the deferential manner which the eighteenth-century patron
usually exacted from a protégé—Kent's parents had been working
class and the son in his youth was apprenticed to a coach-builder—
but on an equal footing as between boon companions. 'Am sorr
to hear you had so bad a cold,' is a typical sample of Kent'
inquiry after the Earl's health, 'Io spero che la purgazione ha
carryd all of before this time.' Burlington revelled in the other'
unaffected lack of restraint with him. He cherished his letters
endorsing them 'Mr. Kent's to be kept', and read them over an
over again. For Kent's character, like his talent, was the ver
opposite of his own. Where he was formal, dutiful, austere an
ascetic, Kent was easy-going, indolent, charming and addicted t

CHISWICK, THE EXEDRA
Sketch by William Kent in the Devonshire Collection, Chatsworth

Both reproduced by permission of the Trustees of the Chatsworth Settlement

CHISWICK HOUSE FROM THE SOUTH-WEST
Sketch by William Kent in the Devonshire Collection, Chatsworth

VILLA ROCCA PISANI, LONIGO
By Scamozzi, 1576

VILLA CAPRA, OR THE ROTONDA, VICENZA
By Palladio, 1550–53

the good things of life. He was moreover a character. He was accepted on terms first of tolerant amusement, then of affection by Burlington's closest friends. He loved to recount stories of the hilarious evenings he spent with them in Burlington's absence. He tells in one letter how he had dined with Lord Oxford, Pope and another off 'a pye got from Bath'. He was going to return their hospitality off a doe. As Burlington had gone away without leaving a drop of liquor in the house he 'bought . . . some excellent claritt and Scoth sack & cyprus esquisito, I have had but one feast in my room since you went, but I can assure you, was drank fourteen bottles of wine in one setting and neather I nor company was sick or sorry for the next day'. His letters are full of such unco-ordinated parentheses as: 'Sir Clement [Cottrell] desires his humble service to you. I have supp'd with his sister that's a good woman & talks very loud,' or 'Pope is ye greatest glutton I know . . . he told me of a soupe that must be seven hours a making . . . he was very drunk last Sunday.' The frequent references in Kent's correspondence to Pope's greediness and coming to see him 'in liquor' were mild jokes about the delicate poet's remarkable abstemiousness. Pope was well able to hold his own in this form of badinage as the following extract from a letter written to Burlington in 1740 from Bath testifies. 'If his Majesty's Principal Painter (for so I read again in my paper, the Gazeteer) would follow my example here for as many months (for so many at least it will take), to cleanse his pencil, and purify his pallat, from all that greasy mixture and fatt oyle they have contracted, he would paint like a Raphael, and look like an Angelo; whereas if he proceeds in his carnality and carnivoracity, he must expect not to imitate Raphael in any thing but his untimely end.' Kent well knew that Burlington delighted in the tittle-tattle which his behaviour and correspondence provoked. 'There are a hundred more wild things,' he ended one letter of gossip, 'that cannot be write.'

Burlington's marriage made not the slightest difference to their friendship. Lady Burlington adopted Kent as a necessary appendage to her large household. 'Pray let the Signor know,' she wrote from court in 1731, 'y^t His Majesty was yesterday full of Comendaions of ye two pictures & told me he once made him a visit with Sir Andrew Fountaine, & y^t he wou'd visit him very frequently if he knew when he shou'd meet the same sort of company'; and again from Bath where she was taking the waters in 1735, 'I hope the Signor has remembered about my tables and glasses.' The Signor or 'Signior', as Kent was known to all the Burlington House

9

circle, treated Lady Burlington exactly as he treated everyone else, that is to say with no ceremony and with plenty of boisterous humour. At court several ladies had fine necks, he assured her. 'I was told they call'd you Cupids Kettle drums.' After dinner when in his cups he wrote her some execrable impromptu 'Verses on the Countess of Burlington's Birth-Day':

> This is the Day deny it who can
> let us sing and be merry & call for a dram
> and drink to the health of this fine woman . . .
> Then whilst she is painting cha's beautiful eyes
> The Signor is drinking to be merry and wise,

and so it went rolling on.

Ultimately 'poor Kentino' overstepped the bounds of propriety in some respect which has not been specified. His last letter written from Paris in January 1749, not long before his death, to Lord Burlington is pathetically penitent. 'I should be asham'd evere to rem^r yf I left England with out paying y^r Lord my respects, & receaving y^r cõands, but for ye confidence I have in y^r goodnesse for my pardon. I know you are not ignorant of ye cause wch induc'd me to it, from a most unworthy proceeding; Therefore I shall say no more of it . . . But as I am sensible how little y^r Lord^p cares to wright, a line from you is a favour I can't hope for. But for this I doe, that you will be perswaded of ye respect & affection wch lyes me ever to be My Lord y^r Lord^{ps} most faithe obed^t hum^t servant & old friend.' This, like all Kent's letters, is in spite o most erratic spelling and phraseology written in a firmer hand than Burlington's, which it somewhat resembles, on quarto pape still glistening with the silver sand with which he sprinkled th bottom of each sheet before turning over. Kent left quite a lot o money, mostly to his relations and a natural child, but no toke of any kind to the Burlingtons who had befriended him all his life It is not for us to criticize him for ingratitude. He left them riche for his friendship and for the numerous creations of what he calle his 'gusto' in the shape of painted ceilings, decorations an furnishings of all sorts both at Chiswick and in London.

The Burlingtons were married on 21st March, 1721. On tha day his lordship's accountant handed him thirty pieces of gol valued at ten pounds each, to see him over his honeymoon Elkanah Settle, the poet and author of Cambyses King of Persia a Tragedy, composed as long ago as 1666, whose name crops u on several critical occasions in the Earl's life, was rewarded wit five guineas for an Epithalamium. Burlington was generous i presents to his bride for he bought her within the ensuing three months one large brilliant diamond worth £1,575, some lesser diamonds worth £1,000 and a diamond necklace worth £1,000. These were immensely large sums of money. Lady Dorothy Savile was the daughter of William, 2nd Marquess of Halifax. She was considered talented by her friends. She drew in pastel but the two portraits of her daughters now hanging at Chatsworth are not particularly accomplished. She also did caricatures for which she earned some renown. There is one of the squat, podgy, Italian soprano Cuzzoni looking up to the thin, cherub-faced castrato Farinelli while the ugly, sardonic impresario Heidigger sits beside them, which is very telling; and another of Pope sitting like a predatory hobgoblin in his grotto at Twickenham. She associated herself closely with her husband's interests, but without his cool detachment. She loved the stage and everything to do with it. She patronized actors, singers and dancers. When Violetti, the Viennese dancer, first came to England she took her to stay at Burlington House, and on her marriage to Garrick in 1749 provided her with a dowry. She was musical and such an enthusiastic opera-goer that during the celebrated fight in 1727 between the *prima donnas* Cuzzoni and Faustina, who pulled out each other's hair in fistfuls during a performance, she engaged in a shouting match with Lady Pembroke across the auditorium. Whereas the latter cat-called Faustina she as hotly hissed and reviled Cuzzoni. As lady-in-waiting to Queen Caroline she did all she could to encourage the court to adopt her husband's and Kent's schemes for the royal palaces and gardens. In 1735 she wrote to Burlington that the Queen talked of nothing but what she and he were to do at Greenwich. 'There is a new design going forward at Richmond in yͤ garden, & a building of Kent's design. I took yͤ liberty to differ with Mr. Bridgman & I daresay you wᵈ be of my opinion; I want to have you see it; he said that 3 slopes made it look bigger; I think one wou'd be not only handsomer, but look (in his style) more grande. I think it stands to reason yᵗ yͤ more breaks there are in any prospect yͤ shorter it looks.' She had very definite views on matters of taste and her letters to her lord contain frequent directions about the way she wanted her rooms decorated. 'I hope you will remember about my branch, to have it hung up, & the poize to be cover'd with green silk, of the same colour as the room, & likewise cord, & the weight to be in the form of a tassell.' Then there were the fabrics. Someone recommended that the gallery cushions at Chiswick should be of velvet. She thought a rich damask would be as handsome, more lasting and less expensive.

Besides, 'in any velvet that is much used, there will be always the print of people's sitting'. In the end she chose a beautiful velvet damask covering; 'The ground is gold colour, & ye flowers a bright crimson.'

There is little doubt that she loved her husband, even though she cherished a long infatuation for the Duke of Grafton, which was much talked about. On one occasion she so far lost control of herself as to weep over him in public. 'My God, I grow very old,' her lover complained wearily; whereat Lord Chesterfield, who happened to be present, remarked consolingly, 'Yes, but you are a glorious setting sun.' Her letters to Burlington are always affectionate. They either begin 'My dearest life', or 'My dear child'; and they express repeated concern for his well-being and safety. She orders a new suit of clothes for him, uncertain whether or not he wants the seams embroidered. She hopes to hear of his uneventful passage over the Humber on his way to the East Riding; and writes, 'I am glad my dear boy has such fine weather.' He too writes just as fondly to her. He hopes she is riding or taking exercise. He is sorry she has a recurrence of colic in spite of the Bath waters. Indeed her health seems to give her constant trouble. 'My cholick is quite over,' she says; instead of it she has a headache, and perhaps because of that leaves a huge blot on the paper through throwing the ink and not the sand over the page. She is ill from eating too many lampreys at a court ball; and her ankles swell towards evening still. Then to crown her misfortunes she injures her face with a branch while out riding and has to stop the bleeding with snuff.

Was she one of those people who have a perpetual grouse? It is true all persons can overstay their welcome and sometimes be bores, but the Rector of Tunbridge Wells 'has talk'd me almost to death'. Court life was hardly less tedious. 'I am just come from Court where I din'd,' she writes in September 1727: 'they talked of nothing but the Coronation.' The place 'in which one hears nothing' is how she describes it; then as though in contradiction proceeds to recount that a madman burst into St. James's Chapel during a funeral service to present a petition. 'Lady Gertrude told Mrs. Howard she was present and saw the coffin with the inscription,' and so forth; and Mrs. Howard told the Queen at her dressing. Such an incident is some little compensation for the dullness of the palace. She complains how she wants to be relieved from duty and how the other ladies just do not turn up nor inform the Queen beforehand, which she considers disrespectful, as well as inconvenient. Now she is kept awake all night by the gnats, and worst of all, is involved in a sad racket with the royal footmen, one of whom she has had to discharge for 'some vile practice, not fit for me to mention'.

Her rages on occasion were said to be appalling. Lord Hervey was unequivocal on the subject.

> *Let Dame Palladio, insolent and bold,*
> *Like her own chairman, whistle, stamp and scold.*

He thus apostrophized her. Lord Chesterfield who was present when she lost a favourite snuff-box was amazed, and rather disappointed, that she kept her temper. Horace Walpole recorded that even on her deathbed at Chiswick, 'in the corner room in the new house hung with Brussels tapestry', beneath the portraits of herself and Pope, she 'breaks out all over in—curses and blasphemies. Her maids are afraid of catching them and will hardly venture into her room'. She survived her husband by five years.

Her uncle Lord Winchilsea's opinion of his niece should be taken with caution since he was an extremely sour old man. 'The incumbrance of a wife,' he called her, 'the wickedest, mischievous jade upon earth. I can easily pardon the lady her coquetry and her intriguing . . . but lying and making mischief, abusing everybody, imposing upon her husband and exposing him only to show her own power.' These are such harsh words that it is quite a relief to learn that Dean Swift, who was by no means always charitable about his friends, came to hold her in high esteem. The first meeting just after her marriage was a formidable enough trial for a young wife. Burlington a little ungallantly neither introduced her nor mentioned her name to the Dean, seemingly for sport. After dinner Swift, having gathered who she was, said brusquely as if to try her, 'Lady Burlington, I hear you can sing: sing me a song.' She was nettled by his presumption and refused point blank. Swift then said she would sing, or he would make her. 'Why, madam, I suppose you take me for one of your poor hedge parsons; sing when I bid you!' Burlington only laughed at this freedom, but his wife burst into tears and left the room. Next time he saw her Swift remarked: 'Pray, madam, are you as proud and as ill-natured now as when I saw you last?' To which she answered with great good humour, 'No, Mr. Dean, I will sing to you, if you please.' From that moment on the crusty old man loved her. Pope too became genuinely fond of her ever since she showed extraordinary humanity towards his mother when she was dying. He admired her gift for caricature and composed some verses 'On the Countess of Burlington Cutting Paper'. He offered to edit the literary remains of her grandfather, George Savile, the 1st Marquess of Halifax, known as the 'Trimmer' from the pamphlet he circulated under that heading and his too easy adoption of political and constitutional opinions; and he exchanged with her nonsense letters—always a sign with Pope of affection for the recipient. He wrote to her in jest on 29th October, 1738, requesting the living of Eyam in Derbyshire for William Kent. 'He is totally ignorant of this address, nor do I know any motive he could have to accept of the living, save to get into a soft pulpit, where is a soft cushion, to lay his soft head, & rest his tender tail, from the fatigues of a horse, that now afflicts his soul, moves his very entrails (especially after dinner) & troubles all the bones within him; while not only the spirit is wearied, but the flesh that should cleave to these bones, cleaves to the saddle.'

Of the Burlington union there were three daughters, to whom both parents were devoted. From their earliest infancy the bills of Mr. Paul Girard 'the toyman' were a recurring item in the household expenditure.[1] Only two daughters grew up, and only one to womanhood. The elder, Lady Dorothy Boyle, was particularly beloved. She was of a sweet disposition and showed an aptitude for music. 'Pray bring Dolly's music book with you, which is in the room at London, where her spinette stands,' her mother writes to Lord Burlington in 1735. But Dolly's life was short and her end melancholy. She was married to Lord Euston, the Duke of Grafton's heir, who was licentious and brutal. Within seven months of her marriage and before her eighteenth birthday she was dead. She had contracted smallpox, but death was hastened by her husband's ill-treatment of her. Everyone, including Lady Mary Wortley Montagu who knew the story, was convinced of it. Lady Mary hinted that the mother was much to blame in having married Lady Dorothy to her lover's son in the first instance. Pope, in a letter to his friend Hugh Bethel, said Lord Euston 'has been absolutely her murderer. The sorrow of the father is inconsolable, but he bid me send you his good wishes'. Burlington challenged his son-in-law to a duel. Euston accepted but the duel was prevented. The heartbroken mother wrote upon a portrait of her daughter which she kept at Chiswick these words: 'She was the comfort and joy of her parents, the delight of all who knew her angelick temper, and the admiration of all who saw her beauty. She was married, October 18th, 1741, and delivered (by death) from misery, May the 2nd, 1742.'

---

[1] A toy shop in the early eighteenth century did not deal exclusively in commodities for children. It sold jewellery, ornaments and all sorts of trifles and bric-à-brac for adults.

Lady Charlotte, the younger sister—Cha or the Monkey her father called her—married Lord Hartington, son and heir to the Duke of Devonshire. She became Burlington's sole heir and ultimately brought to the Devonshire family all his lands, works of art, papers and eventually even his title. Lord Hartington was a very different son-in-law from the other. Burlington was from the first devoted to him. 'I shall make it the study of my life to do everything in my power, that may in any way contribute to your pleasure and happiness,' he wrote to him in 1745; and, again two years later, 'It is not possible for anyone to love another more sincerely than I do you.' When Hartington admired a specimen of Burlington's architecture the father-in-law could not conceal his contentment. To inspire in an undemonstrative man such spontaneous sentiments is evidence of an unusually endearing personality.

iii. Architectural Doctrines and Renown

The most fruitful period of Lord Burlington's life was between 1721 and 1735. The years when his influence was at its height were from 1730 to 1750. Thereafter a reaction set in. With the vogue of Robert Adam's delicate Pompeian decorations and the taste for linear Grecian architecture which followed, Burlington's robust and academic style was considered ponderous and pompous. Throughout the whole nineteenth century and even down to the 1920s it was reviled, when not totally ignored. So universal was the contempt for it that Burlington was either denied its authorship, or accused of misappropriating designs that were not his own. He was dismissed as a mere dilettante and dabbler in architecture and his buildings, unpopular though they were, were attributed to others. The amateur was held to be a trespasser upon the exclusive preserves of the professional, in spite of the fact that Inigo Jones and Wren, who were both amateurs, entirely escaped reproach on these grounds.

It is remarkable how quickly Burlington impressed contemporaries with his architecture and his powers. A man who is absolutely single-minded may earn more kudos than others whose works are more various, yet just as noteworthy. So we read in a letter from the Rev. Thomas Herring, an obscure young curate staying at Bishopsthorpe with his uncle the Archbishop of York in 1743, that Lord Burlington is the 'genius of the age'. Today we may deem this tribute extravagant. We may not acknowledge

Burlington to have been a genius, which is an extremely rare bird in any age. We may protest that he did not actually formulate a new architectural style, although admittedly he more than any other person fostered and developed its growth. Yet John Gay, who for several years lived under his roof and from close quarters watched his buildings rise, recognized that because of him something new and important in architecture was being introduced into the world.

> *While Burlington's proportioned columns rise,*
> *Does he not stand the gaze of envious eyes?*
> *Doors, windows, are condemned by passing fools,*
> *Who know not that they damn Palladio's rules.*[1]

Gay's lines imply that there was crass opposition to the Palladian innovations, and that there was danger ahead in the jealousy of professional men who were the Earl's inferiors in invention. Several years later Pope, who was a better judge of the architectural science than Gay, saw the situation reversed in that—he was addressing Burlington on the use of riches in Epistle IV of *Moral Essays*—

> *. . . (my lord) your just, your noble rules*
> *Fill half the land with imitating fools;*
> *Who random drawings from your sheets shall take,*
> *And of one beauty many blunders make;*
> *Load some vain church with old theatric state,*
> *Turn arcs of triumph to a garden-gate;*
> *Reverse your ornaments; and hang them all*
> *On some patch'd dog-hole eked with ends of wall;*
> *Then clap four slices of pilaster on't,*
> *That, laced with bits of rustic, makes a front:*
> *Shall call the winds through long arcades to roar,*
> *Proud to catch cold at a Venetian door;*
> *Conscious they act a true Palladian part,*
> *And if they starve, they starve by rules of art.*

The trouble then was that lesser architects were beginning to travesty his just and noble rules without grasping their proper implications. Ignorant copyists were bringing the master's splendid creations into disrepute because they were following the letter more literally than the spirit. Pope was jibing at the misuse of the truly imposing and magnificent in the erection of enormous white elephants, which were inconvenient and irrelevant. He doubtless

[1] In the *Epistle to Paul Methuen*, 1720.

had in mind newly built palaces, vast and sprawling, such as Wanstead and Wentworth Woodhouse. In addressing Burlington after the publication of his book on the Roman Baths he said,

> *You show us Rome was glorious, not profuse,*
> *And pompous buildings once were things of use.*

If the Earl's buildings were on the contrary of modest size they, like the Roman, were strictly utilitarian. All his houses were of the villa type and his few public buildings, whether the Westminster School Dormitory or the Assembly Rooms at York, were small, compact and carefully governed by the function for which they were destined.

In short, taste, Pope concludes, is the essential pre-requisite to great architecture; and this the Earl displayed to a degree that was indisputable. Taste was dependent upon sound common sense.

> *Something there is more needful than expense,*
> *And something previous even to taste 'tis sense.*

Pope's commendations of the Earl—they abound in his letters to him—are far too constant and heartfelt to be merely adulatory. Besides he praises him to others whom he exhorts to adopt his designs whether for houses, temples, or garden urns. In the case of the portico which he is adding to his own villa at Twickenham to Kent's design he must have the Earl's sanction of it before he proceeds. 'Your opinion of this,' he writes, after giving elaborate particulars of the proposals, 'will greatly oblige me.' Burlington's reply is rather tart. 'I have considered your front, and am of opinion that my friend Kent has done all that can be, considering the place, I hope you will forgive the shortness of this epistle, which I write in the middle of company and cards.' It was always the same story. The Earl hated writing letters, and when he did bring himself to do so, expressed himself stiffly.

Walpole who belonged to a later generation, and whose taste in building veered in a Gothic direction, nevertheless admired Burlington unfeignedly. He acknowledged him to be the reviver of true architecture in Britain—this was praise indeed—and considered his designs more chaste and classical than Kent's, which they were. But he was critical of his planning, which he thought ignored domestic convenience—how unlike Pope whose generation was blissfully indifferent to such considerations and interpreted convenience to mean use, not comfort—and of his fear of deviating from his models. Walpole regretted that Burlington knew 'the minute and mechanical parts of architecture too well' to allow his

o rove, a sentiment entirely contrary to that of the Earl's
nth-century detractors. Vertue classed him and another
ed nobleman, who is probably Lord Pembroke, 'in the first
rank' with those whose skill in geometry and architecture was
really beyond question. Not only were they 'great and true judges of
those sciences, but real practitioners of it in a fine degree and taste,
equal or above the professors who indeed may be said to be many.'

During his lifetime Burlington's reputation spread beyond these
shores. Antonio Cocchi dedicated to him a Life of Benvenuto
Cellini; and the Piedmontese architect, Filippo Juvara, a volume
of architectural fantasies. Scipione Maffei, the distinguished tragic
poet and antiquary of Verona, in presenting him with a copy of
Sanmichele's *Five Orders* inscribed it, 'A Mylord Conte di
Burlington il Palladio e il Jones de' nostri tempi'. In 1751 Count
Algarotti wrote from Berlin that he was recommending to Frederick the Great the adoption in Prussia of the architectural style
established by Burlington in England.

At home Burlington's advice was eagerly sought by others than
Pope; and usually it seems to have been given rather more readily.
His friend Thomas Coke received as much help in the design and
execution of his enormous palace of Holkham from the Earl as
from his architect, Kent. Of Wentworth Woodhouse Sir Thomas
Robinson wrote in 1734 that 'the whole finishing will be entirely
submitted to Lord Burlington'. And for the Mausoleum at Castle
Howard Burlington was kept informed of the progress of Hawksmoor's designs. When these were sent to him through the
intermediary Robinson, who was a professed disciple of Burlington, on Lord Carlisle's behalf, he criticized them severely. The
columns round the peristyle were too closely ranged to accord
with the augustan rules for a Doric temple, and the approaching
steps were faulty. Poor Hawksmoor was gravely offended. The
result was that after his death Daniel Garrett, who at the time was
Burlington's obedient clerk of the works, designed and built the
wide and spreading staircase which is a magnified, if modified,
reflection of that at Chiswick. It may, according to Dr. Wittkower,
even have been suggested by one of Juvara's drawings in the book
he dedicated to Burlington. Juvara's drawing in question was of a
circular temple with exterior staircase somewhat along these lines.

Burlington's advice was not however invariably adopted. When
the City of London besought him to recommend an architect for
their new Mansion House, he sent them instead a design by
Palladio. This they rejected on the grounds that Palladio was not a
freeman of the City, and was a notorious Papist to boot. Conse-

quently when a few years later they rashly returned to ask his approval of Roubiliac's carving for the pediment of the building which George Dance, senior, had raised for them in the meantime, they got short shrift. Anything was good enough for such a structure came the retort, which the minutes of the chastened Council transposed into 'The Earl of Burlington refused to inter-meddle therein'.

Burlington was absolutely uncompromising over style. Dedi-cated to his calling, which was the reinstatement in England of the ancient Roman canons of architecture as formulated by Vitruvius and practised by the apostles Palladio, Scamozzi and Inigo Jones, he yielded to no man in his conviction that other styles were inferior. Therein lay his limitations. Of rigid principles he was, as Pope described him to Swift, 'a positive man'. He condemned Michelangelo out of hand for not being correct. It is not altogether surprising that, such being his opinions and so great his influence, he played a sorry part in dismissing the aged Wren from the office of Surveyor-General. Wren might be eighty-six years old, a man of unimpeachable integrity, learning and proven duty towards the State, might in fact, to quote his own words, have 'made some figure in the world', nevertheless his style, an antiquated Carolean baroque of French derivation, was deemed to be pernicious and his authority consequently corrupting. Burlington was never actuated by rancour, only by a sense of right and wrong. His genuine contempt for Wren's architecture is expressed in a remark imputed to him as he watched the last stone laid to the old Surveyor-General's masterpiece, St. Paul's Cathedral: 'When the Jews saw the second Temple, they reflected upon the beauty of the first, and wept.'

The style Burlington revived and re-edited to suit his generation was followed throughout George II's reign with hardly any devia-tion. His influence can be traced in the most important buildings of his contemporaries and immediate followers. For example, his brand of Doric order was used by Kent and Vardy; his Palladian window of arched centre and flat flanking lights repeated in triplicate, and his Venetian lunette with mullions, both derived from Palladio, were employed by Kent, Flitcroft, Ware, Morris and Paine, his coffered vaults and semi-domes by Kent and others, his saucer domes by Ware and Morris. His Egyptian Hall, derived from Palladio, was adopted by Paine at Worksop, by Dance at the London Mansion House and even by Adam—who professed disapproval of him—at Kedleston: his vaulted spaces and niches in their variety by Kent at the Horseguards, by Paine, Carr and

Adam. Furthermore, a generous proportion of wall to window space, a preference for the single storey in villa architecture, a love of the temple form, and a dislike of the giant order soon became universal and were inspired by his architecture at Chiswick and elsewhere. His influence finally dispelled the baroque from England and prevented general acceptance of the rococo. The one never reached full maturity; the other was retarded at birth. Burlington succeeded in making the architecture of Wren, Vanbrugh and Archer look uncouth to his contemporaries, and Lord Chesterfield's *rocaille* decoration at Chesterfield House ridiculous. Isaac Ware, who was employed by Chesterfield, was so indoctrinated with Burlingtonian prejudices that he even protested in *The Complete Body of Architecture* at having been compelled by his patron to design ceilings in the French manner. Evidently a visit Burlington made to France in 1726 did not dispose him to favour the style current under Louis XV in any degree whatsoever.

iv. The Gardens at Chiswick

The gardens at Chiswick were begun ten years before Lord Burlington's new house, which was to earn him universal prestige as an architect. In the history of gardening they are of great importance, for they mark a departure from a long-accepted cosmopolitan style. They represent the slightly varying ideals of a number of persons who were to leave a deep impression upon the English landscape; and they illustrate within a strictly limited acreage the gradual process of a change in taste. Burlington took the gardens in hand in 1715 on his return from the grand tour. The consequence is that they are centred, not upon the Chiswick House of today, but upon a point slightly to the north-east where the previous Jacobean house was then standing. They were not completed until 1736.

The first we hear of the Earl's activities in this field is from John Gay, who at the time already had lodgings in Burlington House alongside Handel and Guelfi. He was one of several artists and men of letters to enjoy the sun of his youthful patron's favour. Unfortunately he had a habit of overstaying his welcome, without being the least aware of the fact. By the middle of the 1720s Lord and Lady Burlington had become rather bored by his presence and his everlasting escapades and scrapes. They were tending to neglect him, even when he was ill. Gay's friends were critical of the Burlingtons for not giving him enough to eat; and Dr. Arbuthnot declared that he found him one day in bed with a swollen face, eating his poultice for hunger. However, in his *Epistle to Lord Burlington*, composed somewhere in the west country while on a journey to Exeter in the autumn of 1715, the following lines occur:

> *While you, my Lord, bid stately piles ascend*
> *Or in your Chiswick bowers enjoy your friend;*
> *Where Pope unloads the boughs within his reach,*
> *Of purple vine, blue plumb, and blushing peach,*
> *I journey far.*

They suggest that Burlington, with Pope's help, was sole author of the improvements to the Chiswick gardens at this date. Kent was still abroad and was not to appear upon the scene for some years yet. On the other hand an important person called upon for advice at an early stage was undoubtedly Charles Bridgman. Throughout Queen Anne's reign and at the beginning of her successor's he was the acknowledged professional expert on garden layout. He had recently been working with Vanbrugh at Castle Howard. In 1720 he was to be made Royal Gardener and in 1724 was to collaborate with Pope and Bathurst over Mrs. Howard's garden at Marble Hill. He was the first to make use of the ha-ha and to bring cultivated fields into the purlieus of a country house demesne. He was in fact the first to abandon exact symmetry and what Horace Walpole termed 'verdant sculpture'. But it must be admitted that he did not go very far in this direction, for he still adhered to high clipped hedges, straight vistas and formal canals and pools for the bones of his landscape structures. Pope for one considered that he did not go far enough.

In his famous *Essay on Gardens*, anonymously published in the *Guardian* in 1713, Pope had made the novel appeal for a return to the simplicity of unadorned nature. The appeal was surprising because it was considered revolutionary and also frankly disingenuous. Although Pope's *Essay* first brought home to a wide public the cult of unadorned nature, it was not quite the first written work to broach the subject. The Earl of Shaftesbury in *The Moralist*, published in 1711, had advocated the cult from a philosophical rather than a horticultural approach. His theme was then taken up by Joseph Addison in several articles written for the *Spectator* in 1712. 'Why may not a whole estate be thrown into a kind of garden by frequent plantations, that may turn as much to the profit as the pleasure of the owner?' he asked. The question lay unanswered for a year. It was Pope who first showed how such a change could be brought about, and he did so, admittedly on a rather minute scale, with his own property at Twickenham.

Pope's ideal garden was only a degree less formal than what was generally considered suitable in Queen Anne's reign. But the degree was appreciable. It was high time that he made the stand he did. He was right to inveigh against the universally prevalent distortion of hedges and trees, which was a sort of recession from nature. 'We run into sculpture,' he said, 'and are yet better pleased to have our trees in the most awkward figures of men and animals, than in the most regular of their own.' Whereas men of taste appreciated nature in the raw and believed art to consist in the imitation of it, vulgar persons could not leave it alone. He gave an example to emphasize his point. 'I know an eminent cook, who beautified his country-seat with a Coronation dinner in greens.'

This was commendably pertinent. Pope was to repeat the argument years later in his *Epistle to Lord Burlington on Taste*:

> *To build, to plant, whatever you intend,*
> *To rear the column, or the arch to bend,*
> *To swell the terrace, or to sink the grot;*
> *In all let Nature never be forgot. . . .*
> *Consult the genius of the place in all;*
> *That tells the waters or to rise or fall.*

It was sound advice. The garden-maker must consider the acreage he intended to cover and adjust his layout to its dimensions. He must also observe the lie of the land and its precise contours before embarking upon improvements. Pope was quick to appreciate that an almost limitless park like Lord Bathurst's at Cirencester demanded a treatment entirely different from that of a circumscribed suburban area like Lord Burlington's at Chiswick. Taste, as he was never tired of pronouncing, was dependent upon sense; contrariwisely, lack of sense made Timon's villa garden so tasteless and utterly laughable.

It was when Pope and his associates urged people to plan gardens on the descriptions of those of the ancients as given by classical authors that they in their turn committed follies. In quoting Virgil's sketchy account of the garden of the old Corycian and Homer's of that of Alcinous as the perfect forms of layout, Pope really got his readers nowhere.[1] It is hard to imagine what Squire Allworthy in King George I's reign can have made out of these arbitrary interpretations. How was he, eager let us say to embellish the surroundings of Paradise Hall, expected to model them upon the following description?

[1] Virgil—*Georgics*, Book iv, 125–148: Homer—*Odyssey*, Book vii, 142–175

> *Close to the gates a spacious garden lies,*
> *From storms defended and inclement skies:*
> *Four acres was the allotted space of ground,*
> *Fenced with a green enclosure all around.*

It might mean anything. Suppose too the ground at his disposal covered less or more acreage than the allotted four.

> *Two plenteous fountains the whole prospect crowned;*
> *This through the gardens leads its streams around,*
> *Visits each plant, and waters all the ground.*

How simple, how correct, Pope exclaimed, how contrary to the modern way. Yes, Squire Allworthy might agree, if only his imagination were equal to the learned poet's. Perhaps after all it was easier to go on as his father had done before him clipping his yews and hornbeams into the monstrous figures of men and animals, especially if his hereditary seat happened to lie in flat country without the amenities of plenteous fountains.

What in fact Pope meant to advocate by the example of his own little garden at Twickenham and Lord Burlington's at Chiswick, hardly much larger, was a limitation of the scene in order that the visitor of taste and erudition might quickly capture from the landscape spread before him moods appropriate to his cast of mind at any given moment. He must be enabled to detect in it visions of grandeur, melancholy, sublimity, or gaiety. All these easily accessible visions had to be provided within a small compass. A garden should evoke literary associations; its aesthetic appeal, even its horticultural interest were only secondary. To achieve its purpose it had to abound in classical temples, columns, funerary urns, grottoes and cascades. There must be plenty of evocative inscriptions, chiefly in Latin, to bring tears of nostalgia, sorrow or patriotism to the eye, sometimes a gasp of wonder or admiration, and more rarely a smile to the lips. An elysium, an earthly paradise was the objective. This could not be presented by the old-fashioned grand manner of garden layout, which allowed no diversified scenes, where everything was exposed at a glance from the house, whence straight vistas radiated like the spokes of a wheel, and indeed where

> *No pleasing intricacies intervene,*
> *No artful wildness to perplex the scene;*
> *Grove nods at grove, each alley has a brother,*
> *And half the platform just reflects the other.*

Pope's landscape may not at first have departed noticeably from the landscape which he so severely criticized; the plan remained axial and formal in effect; but in between the straight vistas irregularities and wild, serpentine paths leading to groves and dells were deliberately introduced.

Burlington left no written account of his views on what a garden should be. We have to judge them from the remains of his Chiswick garden—which is by far the best guide—and by Robert Castell's *Villas of the Ancients*, which was published in 1728 at his entire expense. Castell was an impecunious young man whom Burlington encouraged and befriended, but not, it seems, to the extent of saving him from the debtors' prison, where he died the following year of smallpox. The book was dedicated to Burlington and there is little question that the views expounded in it coincided with those of the patron.

Like Pope's, Castell's ideal garden is derived from the classics. It is literary; it is evocative of the ancients' delight in rural life and the Sabine farm. Only Castell plunges far more deeply than Pope into the detailed purlieus of the ancients' garden. He opens the book by quoting Pliny's long letter to Gallus on health, in which an exact description is given of the historian's seaside villa garden at Laurentinum, near Rome. Castell supplies copious footnotes to the letter and draws a conjectural full-scale plan of what he imagines the garden looked like. He also quotes Pliny's letter to Apollinaris about his other seat in Tuscany under the Apennines. This he considers more appropriate to England than the first because the wintry climate of the Tuscan hills more closely resembles our own. In its interpretation of the Tuscan villa Castell's plan shows an avenue leading to the entrance side of the house, and an open space on the garden side. The space is terminated by a great semicircle of fir trees with a straight vista through to a temple at the far end of the grounds. Beyond the semicircle (or exedra) is a parterre or maze. On either flank of the straight vista are irregularly grouped spinneys and serpentining streams. Castell quotes Pliny's remark to Apollinaris, 'You would take delight in viewing the country' from the house, whence—and Castell himself now takes up the thread—'the whole must appear like one entire beautiful landskip, the distance allowing an opportunity of seeing all those parts at one view'. The house should be set, not on the top nor at the bottom of a hill, but on a middling height.

The significance of Pliny's Tuscan villa as seen through the eyes of Castell—and doubtless of Burlington—is that the garden of

CHISWICK VILLA

POPE IN HIS GROTTO AT TWICKENHAM
Sketch by Lady Burlington in the Devonshire Collection, Chatsworth
Reproduced by permission of the Trustees of the Chatsworth Settlement

Chiswick was made more or less to conform with it. Castell tried to prove that the most desirable type of ancient garden was that of which the 'beauty consists in a close imitation of nature where, though the parts are disposed with the greatest art, the irregularity is still preserved'. Here in the Tuscan garden was an 'agreeable disorder' aimed at and achieved. Here was the classical authority for irregularity in landscape. Castell's formula was an extension of that comparatively woolly one adumbrated by Pope fifteen years previously. At Chiswick it had for the first time been put to the proof, and Pliny's Apennine layout had been followed. A straight avenue of cedars, lined with terminal figures to give a true Roman air and known to Burlington's friends as the *Grande Allée*, led from the Chertsey road up to the house. On the opposite side of the house was an open space through which the Grande Allée continued to a domed temple in the far distance. Only the Exedra, formed of firs, is at Chiswick set a little to the left of the Grande Allée because it was intended to be a terminal feature to the view from Burlington's new villa added a little to the south-west of the old house in 1725. Within the Exedra were raised three antique statues, which had been excavated in Hadrian's garden at Tivoli, and stone seats placed between them. Within the triangular spaces formed by the Grand Allée and the several vistas which radiated from a point on a level with the Exedra, were the spinneys, intersected not with serpentining streams (for there was no water in this raised part of the garden) but paths. Pliny would surely have approved of the Chiswick layout which roughly approximated to his own, as described to his friend, Apollinaris.

The Chiswick garden did not end with the spaces immediately fronting the main south-east and north-west elevations of the house. A whole area to west and south was yet to be taken in hand. The author of this last part of the garden was William Kent. The area demonstrates a greater daring and freedom of design, and a more deliberate romanticism, which were Kent's contribution to the English garden landscape. Horace Walpole appreciated more than anyone has ever done what Kent's contribution amounted to, and has left some very perspicacious writing on the subject. Kent 'leapt the fence', he said, 'and saw that all nature was a garden'. By the time he appeared on the Chiswick scene however there was not a great deal of scope for fence-leaping. The gardens at Rousham are Kent's most complete memorial in his especial exercise. There his need for space, his love of perspective, his sense of light and shade, his sure grouping of trees

where clumps were required, and his delicate touch in placing
garden architecture which, as Walpole observed, appears 'more
the works of his pencil than of his compasses', are to this day to
be enjoyed. Moreover the Oxfordshire terrain, being undulating,
offered Kent advantages denied by the flat and circumscribed area
in Middlesex. At Chiswick he had a preliminary skirmish in the
art he was to perfect elsewhere. The river, or canal, is probably
his. It was made to wriggle in an irregular course until it swelled
into an informal pond with an island in the middle. It was an
absolute departure from the strictly rectangular sheets of water
which were thought indispensable by a former generation, and a
forecast of those studiedly informal streams and lakes which
Henry Hoare at Stourhead and Lancelot Brown all over England
were to fashion within the next fifty years. The cascade in the
shape of a grotto of larva-like stones from which the river flows
was not finished until 1738. Kent may have had in mind while
constructing it the Villa Pratalino, of which in 1714 he recorded in
his diary 'the very fine situation [a significant and unusual
observation for this date] very fine grotos adorned with shells &
petrified stones with pretty water works'.

In other words the element Kent brought to landscape layout
and so first of all to Chiswick, was the picturesque or, to be more
correct, the pictorial. During his Italian travels he had become
deeply impressed by the Italian and notably the Roman landscape
to which his eyes had first been opened by the paintings of
Salvator Rosa, Poussin and above all Claude. On his return home
he tried to transmit the scenes he had witnessed in nature (and on
canvas) to English soil. He fully realized that left to itself nature
could not, unassisted by man's art, achieve the purest forms, which
it was popularly supposed had existed before the fall of Adam.
Only the painter, who was akin to God the Creator, could do so
much. Consequently it was his bounden duty to treat the terrain
like one great canvas. Hence Horace Walpole's observation that
Kent's garden ornaments in the guise of Roman antiquities seemed
'more the works of his pencil than of his compasses'. They gave
the impression of having been painted rather than built into the
scenery. They resembled, as they were intended to do, those
temples and ruins from Tivoli or the Campagna reproduced by
Claude in his vast landscape compositions. We may be sure that
Kent advocated among his friends and contemporaries the
pictorial form of nature's embellishment. In this respect he
probably influenced Pope and, through Pope, the poets Thomson
and Dyer. Until the 1720s English poetry still echoed seventeenth

century Miltonic sentiments about nature, which was regarded as something like the jungle, tangled, hostile and to be kept at bay. During the 1720s, when Burlington's and Kent's garden at Chiswick was in the making, poetry changed from the subjective and occasional to the contemplative and didactic. The epic was replaced by descriptive verse, such as Thomson's *Seasons* and Dyer's *Grongar Hill*, wherein the muse of painting was first invoked. A landscape school of poets had arrived and nature was interpreted romantically in terms of pictures, so that we get descriptive stanzas about scenery like, for instance, this from Thomson's *Castle of Indolence*:

> *Sometimes the pencil, in cool airy halls,*
> *Bade the gay bloom of vernal landskips rise,*
> *Or Autumn's varied shades imbrown the walls:*
> *Now the black tempest strikes the astonish'd eyes:*
> *Now down the steep the flashing torrent flies:*
> *The trembling sun now plays o'er ocean blue,*
> *And now rude mountains frown amid the skies;*
> *Whate'er Lorraine light-touched with softening hue,*
> *Or savage Rosa dash'd, or learned Poussin drew.*

The distinction between that part of the Chiswick garden begun by the young Burlington (before his second journey to Italy) with the advice of Pope and Bridgman, and that completed by the mature Burlington in partnership with Kent is, alas, no longer very apparent on the site. A garden is the most ephemeral product of the arts. It is amazing that so much of the early eighteenth-century layout at Chiswick has survived at all, and it is greatly to the credit of the guardians of the place that the grounds are being sympathetically reinstated. Jean Rigaud's views of Bridgman's six vistas of trim paths between pleached hedges, at which smock-clad gardeners are perpetually stretching or kneeling to shear a few recalcitrant whiskers that have dared to sprout overnight, and fluffy trees trained to nod their branches or join together in bosky arches leading to a statue of Samson smiting the Philistine, the 'new casina', the domed temple, the Rustic House, the Doric column bearing the Venus de Medici, and the Deer house, still recall the classical seventeenth century. Kent's domain on the far side of his sinuous river was, it is true, focused upon the tall obelisk of which the base incorporates a Roman tombstone, carved with a husband and wife who gaze dully into eternity, unmindful of the child nestling at the father's feet. Walks radiated from this obelisk; but only two of them were straight and then ran, not between pleached hedges but through a spinney. The others were undulating and wound their way, one towards the cascade, another into nowhere particular, as if into infinity, regardless of the fact that the public road was a mere hundred yards distant behind a concealed boundary wall.

Even Kent's hazy sepia washes invest these secret groves with a sense of romantic isolation, which lies at the furthermost pole from the stiff, ceremonious world of Bridgman's regimented walks. He sketches a lady and a gentleman dancing. Three little dogs run up to them. A footman brings two glasses on a salver. A stone lion on a plinth between a pair of inscrutable herms smiles benignantly upon the solitary lovers. Again, a full moon shines through trees on to water. Two men talk in the distance, while in the foreground a party of rabbits gambol in happy disregard of human disturbance. The lovers, the stone lion and the rabbits are participants in a ghostly world of the imagination, arrested as it were for all time like the figures on Keats's Grecian Urn. The two sepia sketches conjure up a world absolutely remote from Bridgman's, a world which we associate rather with the romantic midnight canvases of Sebastian Pether and the novels of Walter Scott, sixty or even seventy years ahead.

At the end of Kent's longest straight ride is the miniature Ionic Pantheon, its columns copied from those of the Temple of Manly Fortune in Rome. One of Burlington's most sensitive and ethereal creations, it overlooks the circular pool, in the middle of which a small obelisk arises, and the open turf amphitheatre. Here in summertime round tubs of orange trees were aligned upon the grass terraces where exotic pheasants strayed and wild duck preened their wings after desporting themselves in the pool. Originally the Ionic Pantheon was flanked by two oblong sheets of water with apsidal ends, designed by Bridgman, but done away by Burlington and Kent, who disapproved of their formality. Indeed Burlington came, like all experienced gardeners, to look with shame upon the layout of his early youth. In his middle age he regretted that, were he to scrap his juvenile building and planting and begin all over again, there would be no time left to enjoy the full fruits of his labours.

v. The House at Chiswick

Burlington set about altering the Jacobean house at Chiswick as soon as he came of age in 1715. In Messrs. Graham & Collier's joint accounts which begin four years later there are many items of expenditure on work proceeding at Burlington House and Chiswick House simultaneously. Mr. Richard Wright, bricklayer, Mr. Hughes, plasterer, Edward Wethersby, painter, Thomas Morris, carpenter, Jonas Stevenson, paviour, are paid for work in 1719 at the latter house. The accounts are careful to add 'Mr.' where that equivocal honour was due and to omit it where it was not. And it is significant of the social position enjoyed by certain craftsmen that close to the south side of Chiswick church Mr. Richard Wright, the bricklayer, was buried in 1731 under an elaborate and costly tombstone, shaped like a sarcophagus with a central pediment, which could only have been designed by William Kent. In January 1720 'the Italians' (probably stuccoists) were paid fourteen shillings only for their lodging at Chiswick, whereas Mary Barton a week later received ten guineas for discovering in the Haymarket his lordship's gold chain and seals, after an advertisement of their loss had appeared in the *Daily Cour^t & Post*. In February the glazier's bill for work at Chiswick was settled, in March and April the cabinet-makers', Gumley for looking-glasses and Moore for branches and sconces.[1] At the end of this financial year the Earl's expenditure amounted to the enormous figure of £18,749 8s. 8d. A drawing by Jean Rigaud shows the face-lifting which the old house had received. It amounted on the south-west elevation to the addition of a classical portico, a Palladian window above it and a raised gable containing a mullioned lunette to crown the whole.

In 1725 a fire destroyed part of the old house at Chiswick. This disaster decided Lord Burlington to begin upon the new villa, plans of which he had been turning over in his mind ever since his return from Italy in 1719. The new villa was never intended to be a substitute for the old house to which it was connected by a link building, but to serve as a repository for the Earl's ever-increasing works of art and books, and as a place in which to entertain his friends and the many virtuosi from all over Britain and the Continent, whom he delighted to receive. It is still too generally assumed that Burlington modelled his Chiswick villa exclusively on Palladio's masterpiece, the Villa Capra (or Rotonda) outside Vicenza. Burlington undoubtedly derived much, but by no means everything from the Rotonda, which he knew well and admired greatly. On the other hand Colen Campbell, Burlington's first

---

[1] John Gumley *fl. c.* 1694–1729 and James Moore, *fl. c.* 1708–26, were very well-known cabinet-makers in their day. See Edwards and Jourdain, *Georgian Cabinet Makers*, 1944.

instructor in architecture, had anticipated his pupil's Chiswick Villa with Mereworth Castle in Kent, which was completed the very year in which Chiswick was begun, and which happened to be modelled far more closely on Palladio's prototype, both as to plan and elevations. Burlington not only re-examined Palladio's original schemes for the Rotonda, but introduced entirely new elements derived from other buildings by the master, as well as from some by Scamozzi and some by the ancient Romans. The variations in Chiswick Villa from the Rotonda are manifest. To begin with, instead of four porticos Burlington provided only one, and instead of four external staircases only two. Instead of a round saucer dome he raised an octagonal dome on a drum. His façades were entirely different; and he omitted an attic storey. His planning too was original. The circular central hall of the Rotonda gave place to an octagonal hall; and the disposition and shapes of the remaining rooms derived mostly from other sources.

Burlington's chief reason for having one, instead of four entrances, was practical. He was in no need of encouraging cool through draughts in Middlesex as architects were in warm Venetia, nor did he wish to darken his rooms by porticos on all four fronts. Where Palladio's four porticos are of the Ionic order with arched openings at the sides, Burlington's single portico is Corinthian with columns in the returns. The columns are fluted with magnificently carved capitals modelled on those of the Temple of Castor and Pollux in the Roman Forum, of which Palladio had written: 'I never saw any better work nor more delicately wrought.' His spaces between the columns are narrower than those of the Rotonda, coinciding with twice the diameter of each column at its widest, which was the measurement recommended by Palladio for the Corinthian order. Burlington also followed the Roman tradition of making all the intercolumniations equal, unlike Palladio and Campbell, who left the central one wider than the others. Nor do the portico stairs at Chiswick in any sense follow the Rotonda model. They are an elaborated form of Palladio's scheme for the Villa Malcontenta, in that the last flight of each pair divides into two. Much richness has been given them by the high quality of the turned balusters (which are of the Palladian waisted form) and the beautifully carved urns upon the newels. The stairs on the garden front are modelled upon those intended by Inigo Jones to lead from the double cube down to the riverside lawn at Wilton.

Another possible source of Burlington's portico stairs is those of Scamozzi's Villa Molin Moschini Dondi Dell' Orologio, which is situated upon the Battaglia Canal outside Padua.[1] When Burlington was in Venetia the portico of this villa had not been deprived of the winged flights which then descended to the waters. The central square tower of the Villa Molin may also have suggested to Burlington the treatment of his dome's drum at Chiswick, for each of the tower's four faces is lit by a lunette sub-divided by vertical mullions. This form of tripartite lunette—which is to be seen in some of Palladio's churches and was taken by him and Scamozzi from the Roman baths—was hitherto unknown in northern Europe and was regarded at Chiswick with astonishment. Lord Burlington's dome neither resembled Palladio's at the Rotonda, which was a shallow saucer, nor Campbell's at Mereworth, which was a tall Renaissance dome lit by four small windows. It was a Roman saucer dome with steps somewhat on the lines of the Pantheon dome and of Palladio's intended dome for the Villa Trissino at Meledo, which was never completed. Its nearest parallel however is that of Scamozzi's Villa Rocca Pisani at Lonigo. In fact both dome and octagonal drum (with the exception of the four lunettes lacking at the Villa Rocca where the only light falls through an open central eye) may have been deliberately taken from this source. Burlington may or may not have visited the Villa Rocca. He must certainly have known it from the illustration in D'Aviler's translation, published in 1713, of Scamozzi's *Five Orders of Architecture*.[2]

There are other resemblances at Chiswick to the Villa Rocca Pisani, namely in dimensions and elevations. Scamozzi's villa is square, as is Chiswick; of one storey, as is Chiswick; and has but one portico (not however projecting) between the same fenestration, as at Chiswick. The three remaining sides of the Villa Rocca, which are identical, correspond with the south-west front of Chiswick, in that they are composed of a central Venetian opening between two windows over a basement. The corresponding north-east front of Chiswick was, it must be remembered, attached to the Jacobean house. The north-west or garden front is however different from the Villa Rocca elevations and is Lord Burlington's sole invention.

The Chiswick garden front consists of three Venetian windows within relieving arches, separated by two little niches for urns. As Professor Wittkower has pointed out, their clean linear character

---

[1] Yet another suggestion is Rudolph Wittkower's that Juvara, the Piedmontese baroque architect, supplied the design when he was on a month's visit to London in 1720. Kent, who knew Juvara in Italy, must have introduced him to his patron either at Burlington House or Chiswick, or both (*Un Libro di schizzi Juvara a Chatsworth*, Bolletino Soc. Piedmontese d'Archaeologia e di Belle Arte, 1949).

[2] Moreover he possessed an elevation drawing and plan of the Villa Rocca Pisani in Scamozzi's own hand.

suggests that they have been cut from the bare flat wall with a sharp knife. This triple motif of Venetian windows within relieving arches was not Palladian, although Burlington may have assumed it to be so. He took it from a drawing in his possession purporting to be by Palladio of three such windows on a plain wall. As it happens the drawing was by Scamozzi. The motif had first been tried by Burlington in 1721 upon an elevation for Tottenham Park in Savernake Forest, a house belonging to Lord Bruce, who the previous year had married his sister. It was followed by Kent in his designs for the Houses of Parliament and carried out by him on the north front of Holkham Hall.

In the planning of Chiswick Villa Burlington departed signally from that of the Rotonda. In fact the only common theme was a central room under a dome, in Burlington's case octagonal, in Palladio's circular, with stairways in the angles. Whereas Palladio approached his central room through four passages from four porticos Burlington dispensed with all but one narrow passage from a single portico. Nevertheless the planning of Chiswick is strictly axial. The striking innovation is the gallery, lit by the triple Venetian windows on the garden front, and consisting of a rectangular apartment with apsed ends leading to two tribunes, the one circular and the other octagonal. All three apartments are studded with niches. Palladio rarely employed circular or polygonal forms for rooms in his villas (apart from the circular hall of the Rotonda they were square or rectangular), and only in one single case in a town palace. The exception is the Palazzo Thiene at Vicenza. It was the palace which Burlington admired above all others. There Palladio had intended to have on the *piano nobile* one long oval room with apses and alcoves and four octagonal corner closets with alcoves. Only two corner closets, one circular and the other octagonal, were actually constructed in the Palazzo Thiene. The long oval room never got further than the published plan in the *Quattro Libri*. Neither Inigo Jones nor John Webb had used polygonal forms; and Campbell at Mereworth in following the Rotonda ignored them likewise. His gallery, occupying the whole length of one front, was an unbroken rectangular chamber.

Even the rooms of the English baroque architects, Wren and Vanbrugh, were severely rectangular. So too were those of the house Burlington designed for General Wade in 1723. At Chiswick the three chambers forming the gallery on the garden front set a precedent in England which was to be followed by William Kent and Robert Adam. Burlington's interest in spatial forms extended to vaults. Until his day ceilings were flat, only occasionally diversified by coves. At Chiswick he introduced domes and half-domes which he coffered in the manner of Roman public buildings. Isaac Ware in the *Complete Body of Architecture* recognized them as the Earl's innovation. The possibility of their use in English architecture had perhaps first been suggested to Burlington by Kent's painted dome in recessed Roman coffering on the ceiling of the Cupola Room at Kensington Palace. At Kirby Hall and in the York Assembly Rooms the Earl continued the practice. At Chiswick these Roman ceiling features are unparalleled in grandeur and variety of forms in spite of the minuteness of the building's scale. Here Burlington was displaying a contradictory side to his character. In defiance as it were of his professed dislike of all baroque forms he struck a blow for looseness of plan and freedom of decoration which were in themselves baroque manifestations. His decorative elements, doubtless strongly encouraged when not positively introduced by Kent, comprised emphatic console scrolls, broken and split pediments, architraves with ears and other engaging unorthodoxies, which were baroque rather than strictly classical. For example the extraordinary ceiling with twin supporting consoles on the cornice of the Blue Velvet Room has a traceable baroque or at least mannerist origin. Among the drawings which Burlington bought from John Talman is one richly coloured of a ceiling of very similar design. It is signed by Cherubino Alberti (1553–1615) who executed works in oil and fresco for Roman churches and palaces.

Burlington's play upon spatial forms was his most individual contribution to British architecture. It was brought about through a direct return to ancient Rome by way of Palladio's drawings of the Roman baths. Consequently the shapes of the rooms at Chiswick were the outcome of his own researches and discoveries. They amount to the villa's greatest novelty. How far Burlington shares with Kent responsibility for the actual decoration we may never be absolutely certain. Nor does it greatly matter. The partnership of correct scholar and imaginative artist, neither of whom was afraid of venturing along unorthodox paths, was wonderfully successful. And it is surprising how Chiswick Villa, which is composed almost entirely of elements of plan derived from the Roman baths, and of decorative motifs from Palladio, Scamozzi, Inigo Jones (from whose buildings or drawings most of the ceilings and chimneypieces are deliberate adaptations) and other established masters, yet becomes an entity of remarkable originality as well as a work of inexpressible beauty.

The building had its detractors just as it has today. 'House! Do you call it a house?' exclaimed Lord Hervey on first viewing it. 'Why! it is too little to live in, and too large to hang to one's watch.' Sir John Clerk of Penicuik, fresh from outlandish Scotland, was with his cousin William Aikman the portrait painter entertained very graciously to dinner at Chiswick in May 1727. The new villa was barely finished. Yet Sir John decided at once that it was going to be 'rather curious than convenient'. Members of the Burlington circle thought otherwise. Pope wrote to its owner-architect in 1732: 'I assure you Chiswick has been to me the finest thing this glorious sun has shin'd upon. I have thrice made use of the obliging privilege your lordship allows me of bringing it admirers: & once I brought it a censurer, whose name I will not tell you (for his sake) till we meet.' It was perhaps just as well, for the Earl's retort was, 'I despise the whole race of censurers with or without names.' The house and its pictures were readily made available by ticket on those afternoons when, surprisingly enough, the family were in residence. The garden was no less visited in the summer, and the oranges in the Orangery, built to a design taken from Palladio's San Francesco della Vigna in Venice (Kent made a sketch of it in his travel diary) were so popular in blossom time that a fosse had to be dug to keep the public from damaging them.

Chiswick was Lord Burlington's favourite retreat, where he most loved to be and where he never tired of making some improvement or other, whether it were ordering Indian gauze embroidered with gold and silver flowers for Lady Burlington's dressing-table, having new fringe put on the state-bed, varnishing the pictures, redecorating the pantry, having pedestals made for the stone lions in the Grande Allée, or seeing that the fawns in the park were caught soon after birth and fed with cows' milk. No detail was too insignificant or too boring for him to supervise in person. When away he was always scheming how soon he could return. He was even known to dash down from Yorkshire to spend ten days at Chiswick, and back again. He slightly resented his family and friends being there without him. Kent was aware of this foible and when writing in November 1732 to assure his absent patron that all was well at Chiswick, added tactfully, 'I lay there the other night but though I love it, was too melancholy for want of you I wish to see.'

Ultimately Burlington removed all his most cherished belongings to Chiswick. From the various inventories that survive and from Dodsley's Environs of London (1761) we know practically every picture that hung in the new villa and furthermore the actual room in which it hung. A few still remain in the positions chosen for them by the Earl, such as the large portraits of Louis XIII and Anne of Austria and the allegorical pictures in the saloon. Many of the identical pieces of sculpture and busts, some antique, some by Guelfi and Scheemakers, are still there; several that were removed have lately been replaced in the very niches and on the brackets where they were set after their purchase nearly two hundred and fifty years ago. In the basement under the gallery was Lord Burlington's library, of which he had a catalogue made in 1742. Shelves were fitted round the walls for seven categories of books; four tables with shelves underneath took the folios, and in the circular tribune underneath the two windows stood four cases specially made for extra large volumes and portfolios. Many of the books were necessarily large and Lord Burlington lamented that owing to their size those which treated of different subjects had to be kept together. The subjects covered were state papers, history, travel, religion and poetry of which Shakespeare, Wycherley, Prior and all Pope were represented. Burlington was an avid reader of poetry and had been instrumental in collecting subscriptions to erect Kent's monument to Shakespeare in Westminster Abbey. He was a generous supporter of living authors and made arrangements with Lintot and Tonson, the well-known booksellers, that they were to supply him with his friends' volumes as soon as these were published. But the subjects most fully represented were of course the antiquities and architecture. There was an enormous number of illustrated volumes on buildings both ancient and modern. Several had been presented, with dedications, from the authors—such as 'A New and Accurate Method of the Different Orders in Architecture Englished from the Italian of O. R. Bruti by Thomas Malie, Gent, 1737': others, like Francesco Fanelli's *Varie Architetture* and Fréart's *Parallèle* were bought outright: some, like Leoni's second edition of *Palladio*, were subscription copies: and a few, like Kent's, Ware's and Castell's, had been published at his own expense. Many continental publications by eminent authorities were likewise to be found in the Chiswick shelves. Among all these volumes perhaps the most prized were Inigo Jones's two copies of *Vitruvius*, the one signed by him with the maxim 'Altro Diletto che imparar non trovo' on the verso of the fly-leaf, and the other copiously annotated in the margins by his almost indecipherable hand. At the end of the last volume Burlington wrote: 'This book belonged to Inigo Jones and the notes are of his hand writing.'

All Lord Burlington's books which survive are in mint

condition. None is torn, dog-eared, worn or appreciably thumbed, with the single exception of the copy of *Palladio* which he bought in Vicenza in 1719 and carried around with him on his pilgrimage to villas and churches in Venetia.

vi. Later Buildings and Declining Years

Chiswick Villa was by no means Lord Burlington's first mature specimen of architecture after the youthful essay of the 1717 casina in the gardens. Tottenham Park, long ago rebuilt, the Westminster School Dormitory, gutted by fire during the last war, and the house for General Wade in Great Burlington Street, demolished in 1935, were all built before Chiswick Villa was begun. A number of carefully finished drawings of Tottenham from 1721 to 1738 survive. They are in the accomplished hand of Henry Flitcroft who from about 1720 was Burlington's right-hand man (in the strictly subordinate capacity in which Roger Morris served Lord Pembroke). Flitcroft had begun life as a journeyman carpenter and is said to have come to Burlington's notice through a fall from a scaffold at Burlington House. Indeed there is the following item in Burlington's account book under the date 22nd October, 1719: 'To Surgeon re man who broke a leg from a fall from the scaffold, 10/6*d*.' During his recovery and convalescence, for which the Earl paid, Flitcroft greatly impressed him with his talent for drawing and general intelligence. He remained Burlington's draughtsman and assistant until 1726 when through his patron's influence he was appointed Clerk of Works to the Crown. Flitcroft never rebelled against his training and for the rest of his long life remained faithful to the Palladian style.

The shape of Tottenham, which Flitcroft supervised on Burlington's behalf, was little related to Chiswick. It was a four-sided block with angle towers after Inigo Jones's uncompleted wing at Wilton, with the addition of a central tower taken from Webb's Amesbury Abbey in the same county. As a prototype of English Palladianism Tottenham Park was extremely important. Here for the first time in the eighteenth century the Wilton towers with Venetian windows were revived. They were frequently to be repeated.

The Westminster Dormitory was likewise influenced by one of Inigo Jones's works, namely the unbroken arcades of Covent Garden square. But where Inigo used tall pilasters Burlington allowed no breaks of any kind. Instead he played a prolonged

sonata of identical parts. The vast uniform façade, with a tabernacle for a statue over each arcade, was considered a startling
innovation in northern Europe. Mr. Settle, now reduced to
extreme poverty in the Charterhouse and practically on his deathbed, composed a paean in praise of the design when it was made
known in 1721, for which he received a gratuity of ten guineas.
His lordship laid the first stone in 1722 and was the recipient of
very general acclamation. Owing however to his quickly over-
spending the sum allotted for the building and to the workmen
not receiving the regular payment due to them, the Dormitory was
not ready for use until 1729.

The elevation of General Wade's house was taken straight from
an unpublished drawing by Palladio in Burlington's possession.
It was the earliest instance of his deliberate reproduction of one of
the Italian master's designs. Beautiful and extraordinary it looked
in its London surroundings, being purely architectural, severe and
wholly rusticated. It was the first classical house in England to use
the Doric order for the *piano nobile*. James Ralph in his *Critical
Review of the Public Buildings in and about London* (1733) was
sparing in his praise of it. He called it 'one of the best things
among the new buildings: the general design, or plan, is intirely
chast and simple', and then continued, 'and yet the execution is
pompous and expensive'. The fact was that Burlington sacrificed
the planning entirely to the elevation which was not even his own.
Walpole wrote: 'It is worse contrived on the inside than is con-
ceivable, all to humour the beauty of the front. My Lord Chesterfield said, that to be sure [General Wade] could not live in it, but
intended to take the house over against it to look at it.' It was
literally true that the only direction Wade gave was to have a house
large enough to take Rubens's cartoon of Meleager and Atalanta;
but Burlington found it necessary to have so many correspondent
doors that no free space was left for the picture which the General
was obliged to sell to Houghton. Had Walpole and others realized
that the design was a flagrant plagiarism their criticism might have
been still less favourable.

Between 1725 and 1728 Burlington composed and Flitcroft
drew up a design for a villa for Lord Lincoln at Weybridge. The
building was probably never undertaken. It was a miniature,
single storey affair, supposedly Roman and certainly Palladian.
Several sources can be traced for the ingredients of this charming
but unpractical dwelling. The idea of a toy structure may have
been suggested by Campbell's Ebberston Lodge illustrated in
Vitruvius Britannicus, volume III. The pedimented portico of

three openings was based on that of the Villa Pisani at Bagnola d[
Lonigo; the heavily blocked window surrounds came from th[
Palazzo Thiene; and the ringed columns were copied from Inig[
Jones's rustic gateway at Oatlands Palace.

More important and more successful than these buildings—al[
of which apart from the shell of the Westminster Dormitory have
disappeared—are the Assembly Rooms at York. They belong to a
later decade, after Chiswick Villa was completed. In 1730 Lor[
Burlington, who for fifteen years had been Lord Lieutenant of th[
East Riding where his property of Londesborough lay, wa[
invited by a body of local landowners to submit designs. These
public spirited gentlemen had decided that it was high time a
provincial centre of the importance of York, where many of them
had town houses to which in the season they resorted far mor[
constantly than to distant London, should have a fitting meeting
place for balls and assemblies. The whole expense of the enterpris[
was borne by subscription. The same year the first stone was lai[
with much ceremony before the Mayor and Corporation to the pea[
of the Minster bells.

Francis Drake in his *Eboracum*, or history of York (1736) whic[
he dedicated to the Earl, declared that the accepted design for th[
Assembly Rooms 'was taken by that truly English Vitruvius
Richard, Earl of Burlington from Palladio; who gives the plan
but tells you that it never was executed out of Egypt'; and h[
called it an antique Egyptian Hall. In truth once again th[
Assembly Rooms find their inspiration directly in Palladio an[
indirectly in ancient Rome, without however owing anything a[
all to the land of the Nile. They are the outcome of Burlington'[
study of various prototypes in the *Quattro Libri*; and the finishe[
thing amounts in the words of Woolfe and Gandon[1] to 'a lastin[
monument of his lordship's taste in architecture'. Burlington wa[
immensely proud of the Rooms and presented Drake with th[
engravings of them for the historian's splendid book.

The large central ballroom has a continuous peristyle like tha[
of any Roman basilica. Over the columns a clerestory of pilaster[
has been introduced; both storeys are of the Corinthian order
The unusual arrangement of peristyle with clerestory was certainl[
suggested to the Earl by Palladio's plate in his second book, no[
of the 'Egyptian' hall which shows one storey only, but of what wa[
termed the courtyard to a Greek house. The disposition is th[
same down to the alternate rectangular niches and apsed alcove[
between the outstanding columns of the peristyle, the frieze o[

---

[1] Authors of *Vitruvius Britannicus*, vols. iv and v, 1767 and 1771.

cross-banded acanthus sheaves, and the windows between the pilasters of the clerestory. Nothing like this ballroom had been seen in England before. At night time the closely-packed columns which, as Clérisseau observed, distinguished classical from academic proportions, the richly carved capitals, and the regiment of magnificent Venetian glass chandeliers (the gift to the city from the architect) impart an illusion of magic and infinity. Round the ballroom Burlington carefully grouped a series of lesser rooms variously planned so as to produce contrasting effects. They and the entrance vestibule with its curved ends call upon an amazing variety of spatial themes—rectangles, circles, semicircles, ellipses, apses and niches both large and small—such as no architect in England before Burlington had ever dared to conjure up. The street elevation of the Rooms was likewise extremely interesting. Unfortunately it was much altered early in the last century when a portico was introduced. The width of the ballroom clerestory rose above the elliptical entrance front in three round-headed openings in a manner that was meant to recall the mausoleum of Santa Costanza outside Rome, which incidentally was illustrated in Palladio's fourth book. The openings of the elliptical entrance and of the side wings (which were given split pediments) were treated as columned screens with tripartite lunettes in the heads after those used in the Roman Baths.

No wonder that this sumptuous and unusual building provoked the jeers of the uninitiated and the admiration of those qualified to judge superior architecture. The old Duchess of Marlborough was quickly on the scene and loud in her dispraise. Only two years after it was begun she wrote (on 9th July, 1732) that 'the subscribers, I hear, are extremely weary of it, which I don't wonder at. For it exceeds all the nonsense and madness that I ever saw of that kind, and that is saying a great deal. It [the ballroom] is 98 feet long and 36 wide between the pillars, of which there are 44, which stands as close as a row of ninepins. Nobody with a hope [sic] petticoat can pass through them'. That dear old duffer Mr. Matthew Bramble in *Humphry Clinker* complained somewhat irrelevantly that there was nothing of the Arabic in its architecture and that the ballroom might just as well be a Roman church of idolatry. But Pope told Burlington that their mutual friend Hugh Bethel deemed it the finest building he had ever beheld, not excluding any in Italy; and Drake was not being merely fulsome when he opined that Roman Eboracum never boasted any building of greater nobility. The Mayor and Corporation of York to their credit publicly presented the noble architect with the freedom of the

City, while expending fifty guineas on the ceremony of investiture.

The Assembly Rooms were finished in 1736. It cannot therefore be to them that Burlington was referring in a letter to his wife of 6th June, 1735: 'tomorrow I dine at York about a new building which they have desired me to make a design for;' nor of course to the pavement in the Cathedral, which was laid the following year in 'a kind of mosaic work, thought properest for a Gothick building', and 'laid hollow to prevent the damp affecting of it'. For the purpose a local blue stone was taken, not from a quarry, but from uprooted gravestones cut to the dimensions required and laid face downwards. Within the aisles the outer border is a double Greek key pattern interlaced. The pavement was a small contribution to the Cathedral perhaps, but one which necessitated the tricky collaboration of several persons, clerics and artisans, as well as the formulation of a complicated design. Burlington was unaccountably satisfied with it in the way of artists who cherish an exaggerated love for those of their offspring the world accepts with indifference. It immediately became the stage as much of profane as of spiritual exercises, because it was customary for the ladies and gentlemen of the city to parade up and down the nave after service in summertime for want of a public recreation ground or park.

In 1732 Burlington designed a room, which Daniel Garrett, his then clerk of the works, carried out for Lord Harrington at Petersham. Queen Caroline went to see it in 1735. Lady Burlington told her husband in a letter that the Queen did not like it at all. 'She says 'tis horribly finished and the place very ill kept; the house she did not see, but dont believe you made that Room, wch I apprehend you did.' Other work of about this time included a wooden bridge at Euston for the Duke of Grafton; a house for the Duke of Richmond at Whitehall; a summer-house for Philip Southcott (a 'disagreeable, cherry-cheeked', jumped-up person according to Lord Hervey: he married the widow of the 1st Duke of Cleveland and contrived the first *ferme-ornée* style of garden in England) at Woburn Farm, Chertsey; the great hall at Raby Castle for the Duke of Cleveland; a hall for Lord Wilmington at Chiswick; and a house for Colonel Gee (composed of elements from designs by Webb) at Bishop's Burton, Yorkshire.

Two other buildings of Lord Burlington call for more than a mere passing mention. The first has disappeared: the second survives in a mutilated form. Kirby Hall at Ouseburn in the Vale of York was built about 1750 for Mr. William Aislabie. It was illustrated by Woolfe and Gandon in volume V of *Vitruvius Britannicus* (1771), and attributed to Lord Burlington and Roger

YORK
ASSEMBLY
ROOMS
Designed and
built by Lord
Burlington, 1730

JOHN GAY
Portrait by
Michael Dahl
*Reproduced by permission
of Lord Sackville*

Photo: Courtauld Institute of Art

WILLIAM KENT
Portrait by
Benedetto Luti, done
in Rome before 1719,
in the Devonshire
Collection, Chatsworth
*Reproduced by permission
of the Trustees of the
Chatsworth Settlement*

Morris. Certainly the plain exterior has a slightly Morris, or rather Pembroke, look, being of two storeys over a deep basement, its frontispiece of three bays crowned by a pediment. But at either side a single-storey and basement wing has been added, each with a lateral projection. These projections terminate four rooms of which two are planned as circles, one as an oval with niches, and one a rectangle with a semicircular bay. Whatever hand Roger Morris had in this house, it is fairly clear that only Burlington could have been responsible for the wings and the planning of their curved and polygonal apartments.

The design of the School and seventy Almshouses at Sevenoaks does not slavishly follow Palladio. Burlington's summary wash sketch and Flitcroft's finished drawing of the elevation agree in showing that only the arcaded wings resembled the connecting corridors of Palladio's Villa Emo at Fansolo. The high, rather ungainly central block had no counterpart in Italy, although it contained two prominent L-shaped staircases invented and illustrated by Scamozzi in Part I of his third book on the *Five Orders*.

The last of Lord Burlington's drawings are dated 1735. They are of some minor alterations to his own house, Londesborough Hall in the East Riding. The fairly extensive Yorkshire estate on the very edge of Easthorpe Wold was inherited by an early seventeenth-century forbear of the Earl through a Clifford heiress. Nothing of the house originally built by Robert Hooke in 1676 is visible today save the flat razed site, the red brick terrace with its moulded stone coping and curved steps—clearly identifiable in Knyff's view of Londesborough—leading to the vanished entrance, a few urns on plinths[1] and the sad relic of a garden arbour in a carved shell hood with two cornucopias spilling their fruitful produce upon this desert waste. The stables too remain in a fashion, and one can picture Burlington's horses, sweating and weary after the long journeys from London, being led through Hooke's classical doorway with the 1st Earl's cipher on the frieze. Londesborough claimed a good deal of Burlington's time and attention. Nearly all his surviving letters to his wife are addressed from there. On perusing the folded quarto sheets with their thick gilt edges, one gets the impression that it was duty rather than affection which took him so often to those distant parts often for weeks, and sometimes for months on end. His wife and daughters seem seldom to have accompanied him and their absence always made him look forward to leaving Yorkshire. Before setting ont

---

[1] On 29th June, 1753, Mr. Parsons, mason at Bath, was paid for twelve vases and six plinths sent to Londesborough.

from London he would send the servants ahead. £16 10s. 0d. was the regular fare paid for the York stage coach to take them up at Burlington House and put them with all their luggage down in the yard at Londesborough. The Earl evidently thought little of the journey which took him three days direct if he did not go out of his way to spend a night with his sister at the Bedingfelds' moated and towered hall in Norfolk. He often spent another night at Grantham or at Lincoln. Once only he referred to the chief terror of eighteenth-century roads in England. 'There are highwaymen about who have robbed the coaches between Brigden and Stilton,' still a lonely stretch of road after dark. Another hazard, which worried Lady Burlington in London, was his passage over the Ouse by the ferry east of Goole in order to avoid the far longer way round by the first bridge at Selby. In bad weather it took him as long as three and a half hours to be rowed across. Finally, a drive over flat and dull country abruptly ended in the thickly wooded grounds of Londesborough standing on the very edge of the wold.

'To pretend business in the life I lead here,' he writes to Pope in 1732, 'wou'd not bear water, and yet a constant hurry of doing nothing, is to be accounted for by those who experience it, but I am not to expect it shou'd be, by any that have not so great a stock of good nature as you are master of.' None the less he spent a good deal of time with his agent on the estate, draining the park, contriving elaborate water works, planting woods and laying out walks. Other occupations were hunting and shooting. There are in his letters to Lady Burlington references to having been out all day with the pointers until dark. The results were that she might expect by the York coach some red game and several brace of lapwing; and by Tuesday's coach 'a doe, which I suppose will be more for the Signors gola than anyones else'. The lengthening autumn evenings were often passed in playing whist with the Vicar whose impetuosity at cards caused a good deal of merriment and teasing. 'I keep the Vicar still in the dark about the Signors letter, and it operated so upon him, that he torments every body near him, with suspicions as to the author of such a calumny,' is an extract relating to some prank of Kent's, who had put it about that the worthy man was a Methodist in disguise. On another occasion he took the Vicar away with him on an expedition, but rather mischievously brought him back to Londesborough just in time for Sunday matins, from which the villagers were hoping for once to be excused. No bell-ringers being available Sir Edmund Langdale and his son were made to perform the office. It being late in the morning the Vicar tried to shorten his sermon, but in vain. He did not know how to abbreviate even when suffering the pangs of extreme hunger. Afterwards he felt quite ill and regretted that he had not been able to take at least a glass of wine and a jelly before preaching.

Paying visits and receiving visitors took up a deal of time. 'I had yesterday,' Burlington tells his wife on 3rd June, 1735, 'all the joys of the East Riding. The he Langdales, Sr Esmond and his delightful son, *Coozen* Breara, with his son, and the dismal Mr. Manby.' Friends and acquaintances had the habit of turning up unannounced and expecting hospitality, especially in the winter when they were apt to be at a loose end. Sir Edmund Langdale was a particular offender; and he was a bore into the bargain. No sooner had Burlington speeded one party of guests on a Sunday morning than, on his return from church, he found General Wade, Sir R. Clifton, Dan Draper, Colonel Moyser and two Stricklands[1] with others come to dine unannounced. Again, on returning late and tired from shooting one evening he was confronted with unbidden visitors. Sir Edmund, sure enough, was among them but this time 'by his ridiculous acc[ts] of his amour, has been much better company than I thought w[d] ever have fallen to his lot'. No wonder that the larder must be copiously stocked to meet such eventualities. After supper the host planted the guests at whist in order to write to 'My dear Child', as his letters to his wife invariably began: 'I have had a letter from the Signor, if possible, more in the clouds than ever,' but he had not yet had the opportunity of showing it to the Vicar.

The Vicar's rôle as well as being that of stooge was expected to be one of family mentor. 'The other day, my Warter [*sic*] neighbour came in, with his son, and two cubs from London. I thought him infinitely too low, to shew any resentment to him. . . . I hope I behaved well, for the Vicar told me at night, that he had observed me to use great civility, with the greatest coldness towards him.' Burlington's studied coldness, even towards a

[1] Sir William Strickland, 4th Baronet, and his wife, of Boynton Hall near Bridlington. It was either to the 4th baronet, or to his father, also Sir William, 3rd baronet, that Burlington gave 'a beautiful design, with a Palladian roof & an attic storey, instead of garrets & the old wretched & ugly roof of our Gothick ancestors—when the house was compleated, Sir Wm went down, pleasing himself that he had improv'd the bad taste of his County, & should be the object of the Envy of his neighbours, when alas he found the old fashion'd roof, and many other material alterations from the plan—he was not of a very passive disposition, & said everything that rage & disappointment could utter—att last the undertaker of the Building was allow'd to make his defense—wch was in few words, that he took it for *granted* the Architect had made a *mistake*, therefore he put on the sort of roof etc—of all Seats in that neighbourhood; no reply of Sir Wm's could however alterr the mistakes, & it was constant mortification to him while he lived——' Letter from Sir Thomas Robinson, Bart., to 2nd Earl Verney of Claydon, 10th September, 1768. The front of Boynton Hall remains to this day as the 'undertaker of the Building' bungled it.

Yorkshire bumpkin neighbour, must have impressed the two cubs from London as formidable indeed. Since an irreproachably correct manner to all men was habitual with him, he expected the same return with a leaven of deference whenever it was due. But there were limits to the conduct of inferiors and subordinates beyond which he would not tolerate any transgression. For example, when he found that Jean Rigaud was trying to cheat him by demanding more money for his Chiswick drawings than had been agreed upon, he dismissed him instantly without discussion or reference to the incident. His air of disapproval could be frigid, and his frown petrifying. He seldom found it necessary to raise his voice, or to expostulate in writing. When he fancied that the delivery of Lady Burlington's letters to Londesborough was being unnecessarily delayed, he took up his pen. 'I have sent the post master such a message,' he informed his wife, 'that I fancy the same accident will not happen again.' It is unlikely that it did.

On the whole, what with improvements to the estate and park, business expeditions to York, excursions to friends' houses, shooting, whist after supper by firelight, teasing the Vicar or baiting Sir Edmund Langdale, life at Londesborough was not too disagreeable. 'We have here a cielo di Napoli every day,' he wrote in the autumn of 1735, when his thoughts went back to Italy, now such a long way down the vistas of his memory. But was he still designing new buildings? There was that unspecified one he was asked to do in York for the Corporation. Whether it was actually undertaken we do not know. Certainly his interest in architecture never abated. 'I left a Scamozzi packt up, upon the table in my dressing room in towne,' he writes to his wife in 1739. 'I beg you to send it in a box by the coach.'

One thing is clear. He had seriously overspent himself, and was deep in debt. There are no references to his financial embarrassments in the letters to his wife, any more than there are to Dolly's death which had torn at his heart strings, for he was the most reticent and undemonstrative of men. But a friend of Jonathan Swift, that glutton for news of his friends' misfortunes, wrote to the Dean in 1738 that Burlington was selling all his estates in Ireland to pay off his creditors.

We hear comparatively little of Burlington throughout the 1740s. His active building period seems to have come to an end. He lived a retired sort of life between Londesborough and Chiswick. London did not call him quite so often as in former years. Nevertheless he spent just as much money on repairs and minor improvements to Burlington House as on his other houses. For instance, Stephen Wright,[1] who in the late 1740s occupied the post of chief clerk of the works formerly held by Daniel Garrett and before him by Henry Flitcroft, was paid annually for sundry work in London, such as 'for cleaning, mending and picking in of the grotesque ceiling in the Dineing and Glass Rooms'. Chiswick, which was Burlington's finest creation, delighted him most. There he was content to play his harpsichord, which Mr. Burkert Shudi tuned regularly, enjoy his pictures, read, add to his library, and receive his friends and distinguished visitors from the capital and overseas. The garden too held him in perpetual subjection. He continued to plant trees, commissioned a goat in Portland stone from Michael Rysbrack for the Grande Allée, and imported a herd of real cows from Alderney. In the last year of his life he was laying lead pipes from the engine house, through which water was to be pumped to the cascade. While the Signor was alive there was a limitless incentive to carry out improvements to the property. The Signor too was the chief link with the enthusiasms and the tenuous amusements of his early manhood. So long as he was about the Earl could not relapse into an irredeemable stateliness and impenetrable reserve. For the Signor's presence diffused the most endearing mixture of culture and sheer fun, to both of which attributes Burlington, though so brimful of the one and lacking in the other, immediately responded. He fairly expanded in the rays of Kent's badinage like the morning glory which opens to the first touch of sun, and he drooped like that ephemeral flower in the evening of Kent's absence. There exists the scrap of a petition, which must date from about 1741 and shows how the learned patron and venerated arbiter of taste, which is what he had now become in the public eye, could still be an enjoyer with his family and friends of the lighter sides of life. It is headed: 'The Petition of Dorothy Countess of Burlington, Dorothy & Charlot Boyle spinsters, Charles Duke of Grafton, Geo. Lord Euston, Sir Clem[t] Cottrel Knt., Alex[r] Pope gent. & Ch[s] Brunevall gent. and others— To the Right Honble. the Earl of Burlington.' It is easy enough to guess which of the signatories was draughtsman of the petition, which proceeds as follows: 'That whereas a Certain Tree lying, being and standing in or on the grounds of your Lordship, at or before or on one side or the other of a certain edifice of your Honour's called the Casino, hath possessed occupied and held, for the space of twenty or twenty one years, etc. . . . . And whereas a certain upstart Terras . . . hath, by the instigation of Sathan, & of

---

[1] Stephen Wright (d. 1780) built the University Library, Cambridge, 1754–8, and added wings to White Lodge, Richmond, 1758.

William Kent, his agent & attorney. . . . We, your Honour's humble petitioners who have for many years known, accustomed & frequented the said Tree, sitten, reposed or disported under the shade thereof and seen the said William Kent, the agent and attorney of the said Sathan, solace himself with syllabubs, damsels and other benefits of nature ... do ... petition & pray, that the said Tree may remain, subsist, continue & flourish in his place, during his or her natural life (not being absolutely certain of the sex of the said tree) to enjoy the small spot of ground on which God & your Lordships ancestors of ever blessed memory have placed it. . . .'

   Next to Kent in his affections came Pope, whom he had known since he was little more than a boy and for whom he had purchased during his grand tour the presents confiscated by the custom officials at Dover. He had certainly corresponded with him (admittedly most of the letters came from the poet) ever since 1716. In that year Pope sent him a well-known letter about the bookseller Lintot, which began: 'My Lord, if your mare could speak, she would give you an account of the extraordinary company she had on the road; which since she cannot do, I will,' and continued to narrate a ludicrous series of misadventures. Thereafter Pope was on neighbourly terms first with the Earl and then jointly with him and the Countess. He would send to Chiswick little missives begging the loan of a servant to notify some country relations of his father's death; or he would recommend a waterman for his friend's service, or an assistant secretary to the Westminster Bridge Committee in the person of a highly deserving writing-master from Westminster School, who—and this is characteristic of Pope—'is known to most of the young nobility & gentry who can write & read'. Then came further notes about the house he proposed to build on land he had rented behind Burlington House, complaining that Colen Campbell charged £200 beyond what he need spend if he built on his own. He eventually abandoned the scheme altogether as exceeding his means. He dispatched proofs of the *Dunciad* to Burlington who volunteered to submit them to a lawyer lest the author should expose himself to charges of libel, and then to become a joint publisher of the poem. He sent his friend the manuscript of the 'Epistle to Lord Burlington on Taste', and asked him not to show it to others in case he might still alter certain passages. After publication he confided in Burlington his concern lest people were interpreting Timon in the *Epistle* to be the Duke of Chandos, whereas 'that character of Timon is collected from twenty different absurditys and improprieties: and was never the picture of any one human creature'. What did his friend think? Then his zeal for the portico he was adding to his villa at Twickenham was the occasion of a mass of correspondence and desire for advice about cornices, moulds and stucco. 'Mr. Kent could tell you,' he wrote in December 1738, 'how often I talked of you, and wished for you; even at a time when I wish for few or none, when I am almost constantly with the greatest man I know, ever knew, or shall know,' meaning Lord Bolingbroke.

Burlington's terse replies are usually friendly, though less expansive. Whereas his earlier letters end stiffly enough 'My dear Pope, your affectionate humble servant', after twenty-five years' friendship a note of genuine feeling is allowed to creep in. The conclusion of one of his longer letters to the poet, written in 1732, is expressed, for Burlington, with unwonted fervour. 'I never can leave off without assuring you, that no mortal can be with more affection than I am my dear friend your most faithful servant.' Yet he was a poor correspondent. The essence of a good letter-writer is that, however busy he may be, he conveys the belief that all the time in the world is at his disposal. Burlington's letters constantly begin or end with an excuse: that he has been on the road for three weeks, that he is in the middle of company or cards, or is being badgered by people with requests for this or that—interruptions which in fact afflict bad and good correspondents alike, but which the latter feign to ignore. To bring himself to write at all was, we suspect, always an effort. He infuriated Dean Swift by not replying to the old man's demands that he should restore his ancestor's monument in St. Patrick's Cathedral. He even caused the flighty Signor to remonstrate with him for not acknowledging his epistolary effusions. 'Remember this is the third letter I have write,' is a postscript in 1738: and the very last letter Kent was to send, when in disgrace in Paris, contained the veiled reproach, 'I am sensible how little y^r Lord^p cares to wright.'

When he reached his late fifties Burlington was ailing. He was, according to the standards of the time, an old man. Pope was dead; the Signor was dead; so was Dolly; and Cha was now married. Yet his old mother went on living. So too did his wife. Lady Burlington with her grievances and her increasing tantrums was hardly the person to help revive the spent embers of his creative fire. By 1751 his signature had become noticeably shaky. In August of that year a special 'machine chair' was ordered from William Hallett, London's most fashionable cabinet-maker. Quantities of asses' milk, the rich invalid's tonic, were in frequent supply. On 23rd June, 1752, Horace Walpole reported that the

Earl had suffered another attack of palsy. He lingered on for over a year. On 1st September, 1753, he reached London from Londesborough, and on 3rd December he died at Chiswick. For some reason he was not to lie in the vault of Chiswick church where the Signor's bones were already mouldering. On 8th December £10 was paid to Mr. Allet, the minister at Londesborough for opening the family vault in that church and £5 was distributed to the poor of the parish. The body was taken to Londesborough on a slow and difficult winter progress. The coffin was escorted by the late peer's secretary, two footmen, two coachmen, two postillions, the chief undertaker and six lesser undertakers, all on horseback. On the 15th of the month Lord Burlington was buried among his Clifford ancestors at the east end of the church under the altar, within a stone's throw of Londesborough Hall.

That no monument was erected to him in Londesborough church can hardly be attributed to financial embarrassments, since his daughter inherited the residue of vast possessions and works of art beyond compare. His and his wife's only memorials are their coffin plates, beautifully engraved it is true with the inscriptions of their titles and dates of birth and death under blazoned arms. At some time or other they were removed from the vault and screwed to the north wall of the chancel. Beside them a framed plan indicates that the Earl's coffin measures six feet six inches in length.

A portrait by Knapton of Lord Burlington in the full panoply of his dignified middle age hangs in the Blue Velvet Room of Chiswick Villa. He is seated, wearing a red velvet coat and the blue sash and star of the Order of the Garter. His right hand holds an upright calf-bound folio—probably meant to represent his own edition of Palladio's drawings of the Roman Baths—on a marble-topped table. From the background Rysbrack's bust of Inigo Jones, which the Earl had commissioned, peers at him as though approvingly. Burlington's head is framed within the voluminous periwig which in the 1730s, when this portrait was painted, was beginning to grow out of fashion. It accentuates the Roman length of his nose, the tightness of his mouth, the narrowness of his chin and the judicial severity of his eyes which scrutinize the spectator. The carriage of the head is very patrician; and the expression of the face fastidious but by no means repellent. He was naturally a cold man, but capable of being warmed into a heartfelt humanity. 'Generous Burlington' Gay called him in *Trivia*. Nearly all his actions on a large or small scale prove this quality to a marked degree, whether he is ordering his gardeners to send pineapples to a sick friend, offering to pay Sir Hans Sloane whatever figure he proposes for his Inigo Jones gateway in Chelsea, or advancing the career of the useful Flitcroft to his own loss and detriment. Horace Walpole summed up his character in a sentence: 'Never was protection and great wealth more generously and more judiciously diffused than by this great person, who had every quality of a genius and artist, except envy.'

The greatness of this person lies, not on the social and political stage to which he was born and where he merits no special praise beyond having acted honourably, nor in the side wings of patronage where his enthusiastic promotion of every talent, literary, dramatic, musical or artistic was indeed scrupulous and just, but in the magical backgrounds of creation where it is allowed to few men to stray with profit to themselves or others. Burlington was an artist in spite of his exalted station, which in early Georgian times was no advantageous springboard to the flights of talent and genius. Pope acknowledged his claims to be such when he wrote to him without flattery: 'I need not be put in mind of you by the traces of your art, your buildings or your gardens: but so it is that a good writer is not more remembered by his works, than you by yours.' Burlington to his lasting credit overcame or overrode the prejudice of his equals in rank and the resentment of professional men against a rich nobleman becoming a serious performer in any one branch of the arts. On the contrary he was ready to compete openly with those socially inferior beings who had the advantage over him of hard practical training. It was with pride and a touching faith in his own scholarship and powers that he signed all his drawings, in that stiff and rather crabbed hand—'Burlington architectus.'

OXFORD IV

EDWARD HARLEY
2nd EARL OF OXFORD
(1689–1741)

---

i. Wanley and the Harleian Library

EDWARD HARLEY was a Tory through and through. Indeed it would have been surprising were he anything different in an age during which men's most consistent quality was traditional loyalty to a religious or a political creed. His father, Robert Harley, Chancellor of the Exchequer and Lord Treasurer, had been leader of the Tory party throughout the most critical years of Queen Anne's reign. For these services he was created an earl in 1711. He chose a little rashly the earldom of Oxford which only eight years previously had become extinct with the death of Aubrey de Vere, the 20th holder, after an unbroken descent since 1142, remarking that someone else would have the title within a month if he did not. At the same time as though to make amends for a lapse in good taste he took the additional title of Earl Mortimer.

Whereas today it is customary for a son to question, if not to spurn the professed principles of his father, in the reigns of Queen Anne and the early Georges such conduct was unusual. The Hanoverians alone seem to have been exceptional in that each elder son loathed his father and all he stood for, to the extent of behaving as Prince of Wales in a manner which amounted to resolute opposition to every paternal injunction whether wise or foolish, amicable or hostile. Only in the bitterness of this loathing can successive Hanoverians be termed consistently loyal to a tradition. Edward Harley's inherited Toryism however was unquestioned. It gave strength in a paradoxical sense to his otherwise weak character because, since only the first four years of his adult life coincided with Tory power—and not all of those with his father's supremacy—the remainder, when the Whigs were triumphant, enabled him largely to ignore politics, for which he had little bent, and to cultivate the arts and learning, to which he had a strong addiction.

He was born in 1689, the year in which his father first entered the House of Commons, and was educated at Westminster School. In 1707 he matriculated at Christ Church, Oxford, where he made the first of several lifelong friendships, namely with his tutor, Dr. William Stratford, who quickly fell a victim to his pupil's charm of manner and social position. In his last year at the University he was, on his father's becoming an earl, styled Lord Harley. In no other respects was he a distinguished undergraduate. There were complaints of his not attending lectures and of his running up debts, to nothing worse, it is true, than booksellers and bookbinders. On leaving Oxford in 1711 he was immediately elected Member of Parliament for Radnorshire, the seat which had been vacated by the Lord Treasurer on his elevation to the House of Lords. All the time he was in the Commons Harley made little contribution to debates. He kept his seat until the fall of the Tories after Queen Anne's death. For at least seven years, while his father was first in the Tower and then in the wilderness there was no opportunity of his procuring another had he wanted it. After Lord Oxford's release and nominal recovery of his position at court in 1722 Harley sat in Parliament again for Cambridgeshire. In 1724 he succeeded to his father's earldoms.

While the 1st Earl of Oxford was virtual ruler of England a brilliant marriage was arranged for Lord Harley and contracted in 1713. The bride was Lady Henrietta Cavendish-Holles, only daughter of the recently deceased John Holles, 1st Duke of Newcastle of the second creation, by Margaret third daughter and eventual heiress of Henry Cavendish 2nd Duke of Newcastle of the first creation. Whereas the Harleys were not a rich, although an ancient family, for long settled at Brampton Bryan in a remote northern pocket of Herefordshire, Lady Henrietta was the possessor of immense estates, of which the chief were Welbeck Abbey in Nottinghamshire and Wimpole Hall in Cambridgeshire. At first the bride's mother strongly favoured her daughter's match with the Lord Treasurer's son, but when she saw herself faced with the imminent surrender of a large part of the family revenues, which she had looked forward to enjoying for her life, she became bitterly opposed to it. Alas, she was too late, for matters were already out of her control. Determined to be united the young couple hurried on what she called 'the wicket marriage', which took place in the drawing-room at Wimpole. The Duchess refused to be present at the ceremony and parted with her daughter in a rage which she maintained until within a few months of her death in 1716. The consequence was that the Harleys' early years of married bliss were clouded by a trail of law suits with Henrietta's mother which involved them in constant worry and even some financial stringency. Added to this was the grief caused to Edward by the impeachment and imprisonment of his father by the Whigs after the accession of George I.

In spite of the Duchess of Newcastle's malice and Lord Oxford's misfortune the Harleys managed to live fairly comfortably. By 1714 they were established for a small part of each year at Welbeck, where Lord Harley freed from parliamentary duties reared Arab thoroughbreds and hunted his hounds in Sherwood Forest, and for longer periods at Wimpole or Dover Street in London. Estate management and sport however, which were what Welbeck afforded, appealed to him little more than politics had done. The preoccupation which engrossed him at Wimpole and in London from his earliest married years was his library. It was to become the be-all and end-all of his existence. Every other interest was subsidiary; and his pictures, engravings, coins and heterogeneous collections of antiquities were always secondary to his manuscripts and books.

Edward Harley's passion for these things was hereditary. It had first declared itself when he got into trouble for overspending at the University. The Earl of Oxford was hardly in a position to reprimand his son, considering that the weakness was one which he shared and indulged with the same results—namely debts. Books had in fact long been a family mania. The statesman's grandfather, Sir Robert Harley, when Brampton Bryan Castle was besieged and sacked by the Royalists in 1643, lost 'an extraordinary library of manuscript and printed books, which had been collected from one descent to another'. The Earl in the intervals of leading the Tory party, opposing Marlborough's wasteful campaigns, courting the confidence of his pig-headed mistress Queen Anne and parrying the machinations of his rival Bolingbroke, certainly did his best to repair the losses incurred by Sir Robert in the Civil War. His delight in books extended to those who wrote them. He loved to relax in the society of men of letters. Defoe was his secretary and confidant, his adviser of courses of political action. Pope was perhaps even more intimate with him. As well as appreciating his sound views on literature the poet sympathized with his liberal brand of Jacobite Toryism, and regarded him as a martyr sacrificed on the altar of Whiggish materialism and self-interest.

And sure if aught below the Seats divine
Can touch immortals, 'tis a soul like thine;
A soul supreme, in each hard instance tried,
Above all pain, all passion and all pride,
The rage of pow'r, the blast of public breath,
The lust of lucre, and the dread of death.

is how Pope addressed him on his release from prison. It was a noble tribute, only matched by the desire of that other Tory malcontent of letters, Jonathan Swift, to vindicate the Earl's honour by writing his biography. The intention came to naught, not through his fault but through the indecision of the son, who failed to supply him, in spite of his repeated requests, with the necessary papers.

Lord Oxford's love of literature was as sincere as his love of men of letters. It was due to a literary acquaintance that he had set about in earnest to buy rare books and manuscripts. In 1706 Humphrey Wanley suggested to him that he might purchase the library of Sir Simonds D'Ewes, which had been assembled over fifty years before and was then in the market. Sir Robert Harley, as he then was, consented, and authorized Wanley to negotiate the purchase on his behalf, which was accordingly done for the remarkably small sum of £500. Thus was the nucleus of the famous Harleian Library formed. By 1708 Wanley completed a catalogue of the collection and the grateful owner formally made him his 'library-keeper'.

Humphrey Wanley had been introduced to his patron in 1701. Until he was permanently employed by Lord Oxford his singular abilities had not been properly fulfilled. He had started life as a draper's apprentice in Coventry, but gave little satisfaction because every spare moment he could snatch from serving ribbon and lace was spent poring over whatever old tomes and documents he could beg, borrow or purloin. It is true that in 1696 he became an assistant in the Bodleian Library, but receiving no promotion retired of his own accord. In 1699 he was engaged by George Hickes, the non-juror, to prepare a catalogue of Anglo-Saxon manuscripts in Great Britain, a task which occupied him several years. In 1700 he was made Assistant-Secretary and in 1703 Secretary of the Society for the Propagation of Christian Knowledge, a post for which his sympathies were merely lukewarm. His engagement by Robert Harley gave him all he needed, a modest competence, uninterrupted opportunity for study and an outlet for his intense dog-like loyalty and devotion to a master. His

HUMPHREY
WANLEY
Portrait by
Thomas Hill, 1717

WANLEY
IENSIS

Photo: Bustin

WARD HARLEY,
2ND EARL
OF OXFORD
*eproduced by permission
Mr. Christopher Harley*

Edward Ha
the 2ª Earl of Oxf
and Earl Morti

MATTHEW
PRIOR
Portrait by
Thomas Hudson
after Jonathan
Richardson

JAMES GIBBS

invaluable services were thenceforth dedicated selflessly and un-
tiringly first to the statesman and then to his son. Wanley more
than anyone else was responsible for laying the practical foundation and raising the main structure of the Harleian Library, thanks
to the informed guidance, enthusiasm and confidence of its
successive owners. Nowhere, curiously enough, in all the voluminous papers, catalogues and journals kept by Wanley, is it
made absolutely clear to which of the two Harleys the library
belonged or where it was kept after the Lord Treasurer's disgrace.
We are left to deduce that the library begun by the father was
during his imprisonment taken over by the son, whose advantageous marriage had given him the means to maintain and the
space in which to keep it; that first of all it was kept in Lord
Harley's London houses in Marylebone and Dover Street, and
then moved by slow stages to Wimpole.

Wanley possessed some splendid qualities for a librarian. He
was honest, industrious and scholarly. In a corrupt age he stead-
fastly refused bribes, presents or vails. He drove hard bargains for
books and manuscripts in his masters' interest, at times slightly
overstepping the bounds of propriety expected of a purchaser. On
one occasion in his eagerness to acquire a volume for the library
he advised an agent to borrow it from the vendor and, armed with
this advantage, to haggle from a distance over the price. His
treatment of poor old Dr. Covel, the octogenarian Master of
Christ's College, Cambridge, who was reduced to parting out of
necessity with his life's collection of medals, curiosities and manuscripts, was peculiarly harsh. 'You have seen the world, and understand it as well as any man,' he told him on 13th September, 1715.
'Suffer me to advise you to sell your things yourself, and take the
ready money, now that you have it in your power.' And four
months later to a mutual friend he wrote brutally: 'Pray let the
Master of Christs know that really 'tis time for a man of his years
and supposed gravity to leave off trifling with a personage of
my noble lord's birth, quality and fortunes; and, in short, if he
doth not soon conclude'—whereupon Wanley subsided into a grim
humour habitual with him—'I will cause his statue to be erected
(made of Bath mettal) upon a leaden pedestal, and both sett on a
sandysoil. There he shall be represented, with the largest Spanish
spectacles, squinnying upon the most worm-eaten of all his manuscripts.' His catalogue of the Library in a neat and clear handwriting involved immense researches and labour. He could not
disguise his pride in it: 'the finest and most useful description
mine eies ever beheld,' he called it. The Library was his life's joy

and love. He entered into a special note-book those objects he considered desirable acquisitions, and their whereabouts in England and abroad. He grew to know exactly what was in Lord Harley's mind, and could choose additions to the collection without reference, if his master was away. From 1715 until within a fortnight of his death in 1726 he kept a journal which, far from being an exclusively dry-as-dust recital of book purchases, is full of enthusiastic exclamations. When for instance his agent Mr. Vaillant had bought at a sale a Virgil for £45 Wanley noted that 'he huzza'd out loud, and threw up his hat for joy, that he had bought it so cheap'. The journal is very enlightening on the methods by which he set about acquiring new material. Those passages which were clearly intended for Edward Harley's perusal were written in a rather formal and respectful style, as the following extracts show. 'His Grace the Duke of Devonshire thinks himself bound not to part with St. Athelwold's book, because given him by General Compton. . . . Mr. Smith of Venice writes that the Giustinianis will not part with their Greek manuscripts, and that he will not venture to send any of his own books to England yet.' And, 'Mr. Stevens the bookbinder came about four books he left here at 2 guineas. He (foolish man) offer'd me a gratuity to help him off with them. I told him he did not know me.'

Wanley held very definite views on the condition of the books in his charge. Binding was one of the most formidable expenses of the Library, for Edward Harley insisted upon all the books being uniformly bound in red morocco with a broad gold border, preferring whenever possible to make use of the doe or calf skins provided by his various parks until their supply was exhausted. Wanley would supervise the binders' work in the Library. When he found that imported leather from Cordova proved unsatisfactory he got his son-in-law to send some sample skins from Barbary as an experiment. He did not on any account favour sheeps' skins which, he maintained, bred worms. He also disapproved of the custom of 'scrawling' a book's title on the spine, for the strange reason in a well-ordered library, that the birds only pecked it off—the powdered cuttle-fish bone or silver pounce-box sand which glittered in the 'scrawl' proving irresistibly attractive to them.

From eight o'clock till eleven in the morning and from one o'clock till three and sometimes four in the afternoon, respectable persons were allowed to consult the Library and even to take out books and manuscripts on a signed receipt, provided Wanley approved their credentials. It was always at the back of Harley's mind, as the contents grew in size and rarity to make the Library over to the public, and only his desperate financial plight and early death prevented him from carrying out this laudable intention.

Wanley suffered from the confirmed bookworm's chronic ill health. He was forever catching colds and fevers. But then he never in any circumstances took exercise. Besides, he liked to drink more than was good for him. When in 1716 the old Duchess of Newcastle grudgingly consented on her deathbed to be reconciled with her daughter, Wanley admitted to celebrating the occasion by consuming a gallon of brandy and punch mixed with twelve lemons and snake-root. The lemons may have saved him from a serious hang-over whatever antidotal effect the snake-root was expected to have. The Harleys were exceedingly good to him and treated him as a friend. Lord Harley presented him with a silver tobacco pouch and some plate; Lady Henrietta gave Mrs. Wanley a silver teapot, kettle and lamp which were highly treasured. Their kindness was returned by unstinted services and unshakeable loyalty. Wanley, writing in 1716 to his wife, whom he often did not see for months on end while he was at Wimpole, begged her to send Lady Henrietta a recipe for her pease-pudding, which her ladyship had lately commended. The Harleys' literary friends were vastly entertained by Wanley's strange ways. If John Gay greeted the sallow, unhealthy librarian, 'O Wanley, whence com'st thou with shortened hair, And visage from thy shelves with dust besprent,' Pope would imitate his 'stilted turns of phraseology and elaboration of manner'. Matthew Prior, however, who genuinely loved the man, looked to him as his monitor in questions of literary style. In 1718 he submitted to Wanley for correction the proofs of his collected poems, 'as I ought with great reason to do everything concerning literature', exclaiming: 'My good and kind Wanley, I send you these sheets as looked over first by Mr. Bedford, and then by myself. . . . If you please to alter any thing, you know, and may use your dictatorial power.' Prior revered the sour, frowsty little man with lank uncombed hair, and in drab clothes, for his immense learning and unrivalled knowledge of the English language; and he relished the hours spent with him in the Library in argument about the usage of words, hours interspersed too with a good deal of merriment over the librarian's caustic stories of how he got the better of some dealer in Amsterdam or Geneva. He ended his long poem *Alma, or the Growth of the Mind* with these couplets,

If to be sad is to be wise,
I do most heartily despise
Whatever Socrates has said
Or Tully writ, or Wanley read.

wherein the recognition of jolly companionship could hardly convey a higher compliment from one learned man to another.

Worldly wisdom was not Wanley's outstanding virtue. The death of his wife in 1722—'my late grievous calamity'—left him so desolate that he took up with a woman who was as far beneath his deserts as she was beneath him in age. After four years of intermittent cohabitation and bickering he married, against his friends' strongly worded advice, this 'very young creature who had been his whore', as one of them bluntly described her. Within a fortnight he was dead at the age of fifty-five. To the second Mrs. Wanley, who was then barely twenty-nine, he left £234 17s. 4d., the plate, silver teapot, kettle and stand, given to him and his first wife by the Harleys, and a cornelian and gold chain which had belonged to his father.

Humphrey Wanley was a great antiquarian (he was a co-founder with John Talman of the London Society of Antiquaries), a great decipherer of manuscripts, a great palaeographer and a great Anglo-Saxon authority. It is not granted to many scholars, however renowned in their day, to be remembered by later generations. Wanley is hardly an exception. But if his dusty image is from time to time taken down from the overcrowded niches of England's pantheon of learning, and regarded with a little sympathy and a good deal of respect, it is solely on account of the large part he played in the creation of the Harleian Library.

Edward Harley's enthusiasm in adding to the Library begun by his father cannot be over-stressed. His incessant and often reckless purchases, not only of books and manuscripts but of all sorts of curiosities besides, largely contributed to his financial ruin. The earliest preserved letters addressed to him are concerned with his taste for the antiquities. For instance, Mr. John Urrey informs him in 1712 of the discovery at Stansfield, a village between Woodstock and Cornbury, of a fragment of a Roman pavement, being a Bacchus bestriding a tiger, and describes it as resembling a Persian carpet. He sends him a rough drawing he has made of it. Later in the year Mr. Urrey advises about a Chaucer manuscript which Harley has picked up. Mr. Stawell writes from Barcelona that when in Italy recently he searched the shops in vain for two books which Harley wanted, and has now asked a friend in Venice to try and find them there. Lord Harley was frequently making discoveries on his own, such as a Herodotus annotated by Erasmus. In Holland he purchased for a large price some leaves of the most precious biblical manuscript in the world, which long before had been stolen from the Royal Library in Paris. As soon as this was pointed out to him he promptly and in the most obliging manner possible sent the leaves back as a gift to where they properly belonged. Correspondents were constantly notifying him of collections about to come into the market. 'Mr. Thoresby, the great Leeds antiquary, being lately dead, his museum, books, and manuscripts will shortly be disposed of,' is a typical piece of information. Nearly always Lord Harley was known to ask his informant to buy the things for him *carte blanche*, which was promptly done, often on commission. In such a way he came upon the manuscript proclamation by Charles I to his People from Carisbrooke Castle of the 18th January, 1648, the Reverend Francis Peck having written out of the blue: 'I send your lorship enclosed a paper, and indeed a dirty one, but I daresay you will not despise it for being dirty, seeing it is every letter . . . King Charles I's own handwriting.' Certain years yielded a bumper crop. 1720 saw the addition to the Library by purchase of valuable manuscripts from John Warburton, the Somerset Herald, Archdeacon Batteley, and Pierre Séguier, Chancellor of France; also a bequest from Hugh Thomas. The dealers of course battened upon the easy-going and improvident peer who seemed never to care a fig about expenses. One of their order, Nathaniel Noel, derived £10,814 from him alone.

How much of a scholar Lord Harley was is questionable. Like many gifted amateurs he developed with experience an uncanny propensity for nosing out and running to ground desirable treasure. He was not merely satisfied with the successful conclusion of a hunt, but pored over the quarry he tracked down. He is said to have known precisely on which shelf of the Library each single book was kept, and in which box each paper. Considering that at the time of his death the Library comprised 50,000 printed books, 8,000 volumes of manuscripts, 41,000 prints and 350,000 pamphlets, his memory must have been prodigious. Prior who knew him intimately was certain that his bibliophile friend was also a voracious reader. There is a little volume (still at Wimpole) given to Prior by Lord Harley, on the fly-leaf of which the poet a few days before his death scribbled this distich:

Fame counting thy books, my dear Harley, shall tell
No man had so many, who knew them so well.

It must be confessed that Harley's rare letters are not very well composed; the lack of punctuation and the omission of the upper case at the beginning of a sentence are not compensated for by a polished style. Apart from the most casual jottings, his literary remains amount to some memoirs of a gossipy nature on certain members of the peerage written on the backs of letters addressed to himself, and a few *Bibliographical Notes* in a thick quarto volume. These scraps contain several crisp and pertinent observations on books and their authors, few of which are flattering. Of Elias Ashmole's *Memoirs*, he writes: 'Thin, and a very silly impertinent book,' and of the *Life of Thomas Firmin*: 'This fellow was a very proper man to give an account of religion, who had none himself.' Bishop Burnet[1] who in the *History of his own Times* wrote very partially and even falsely about the 1st Earl of Oxford, he calls 'That vile Scots lying rascal', and of John Pennyman the pseudo-Quaker, he remarks, 'The poor man seems to be very mad.' Against the titles of some books he is still more terse, scribbling 'Mere trifling', and 'Full of cant and spiritual pride'. For all their succinct depreciation the observations reveal at least a direct acquaintance with the books concerned.

When in 1743 the greater part of Lord Oxford's Library was disposed of by his widow an immense sale catalogue was prepared by the scholar, William Oldys, who in 1738 had been appointed his lordship's literary secretary at a salary of £200. To it was prefaced an anonymous *Account of the Harleian Library*, written by no less a person than Samuel Johnson. The eminent doctor, after explaining that his purpose was to record a great collection, which was about to be dispersed, paid high tribute to the 1st and 2nd Earls of Oxford. 'It will be no unpleasing effect of this account, if those that shall happen to peruse it, should be inclined by it, to reflect on the character of the late proprietors. . . . That our catalogue will excite any other man to emulate the collectors of this library, to prefer books and manuscripts to equipage and luxury, and to forsake noise and diversion for the conversation of the learned, and the satisfaction of extensive knowledge, we are very far from presuming to hope.' These rather puritanical misgivings might have been moderated by the question whether in the future any nobleman with the same taste for learning and distaste for

---

[1] There hangs a portrait of Bishop Gilbert Burnet in Wimpole Hall today. *The History of his own Times* was published posthumously in 1723-34.

equipage and luxury would have an equivalent amount of free money at his disposal.

Johnson went on to give brief descriptions of the subjects which the Library books comprised. Their great variety was surely a disclaimer of John Gay's remark in *Trivia* that 'Of ancients only hath Lord Harley care'. The subjects covered were sacred writings: history, ecclesiastical and civil, European and Asiatic: geography: travel: law: physic: philosophy: astronomy: mineralogy: mathematics: fortification: architecture: painting: prints: horsemanship: fencing: Greek and Roman literature and antiquities: sculpture: magic, sorcery and witchcraft. Upon the last three subjects there were a surprisingly large quantity of books, of which the titles were often long and tantalizing, such as: 'Strange News from Arpington near Bexly in Kent: being a true narrative of a young maid who was possest with several devils or evil spirits, one of which, by the prayers of a pious and religious doctor, who came to visit her, was fetcht out of her Body, and appeared in the Room in the likeness of a large snake, and twisted itself about the doctor's neck, whilst he was at his devotions'; and 'Strange, true and dreadful relation of the Devil's appearing to Th^os Cox, a hackney-coach man'.

Lord Oxford's curiosity was only matched by his credulity. Magic, sorcery and witchcraft fascinated him and no amount of rubbish on the subjects left him unmoved. Rubbish and junk of all sorts had for him indeed a fascination which could never be wholly assuaged, and accounted for much worthless stuff in books and other objects that found their way into his collections. His purchases, when not guided by Wanley's restraining hand, were at times injudicious, and also extremely costly. Early in 1742, a year before the books were sold, Lady Oxford got rid of the bric-à-brac. Horace Walpole wrote to Sir Horace Mann in the New Year: 'Lord Oxford's famous sale begins next Monday, where there is as much rubbish of another kind as in Her Grace's history [a reference to Sarah Duchess of Marlborough's Memoirs]. Feather bonnets presented by the Americans to Queen Elizabeth; elks' horns converted to caudle-cups; true copies of original pictures that never existed; presents to himself from the Royal Society, etc., particularly forty volumes of prints of illustratious personages; which collection is collected from frontispieccs to godly books, bibles and poems. . . . There are few good pictures, for the miniatures are not to be sold, nor the manuscripts; the books not till next year. There are a few fine bronzes, and a very fine collection of English coins.' It was of course exactly the sort of sale that most excited Horace, who attended it jubilantly. In March he wrote again to Mann that he had bought a number of things with which he was delighted. 'The things sold dear ... which no doubt cost him [Lord Oxford] more, for he gave the most extravagant prices.'

When the Library of printed books and pamphlets was on view to the public before their sale in 1743 it filled twelve rooms of Lord Oxford's house in Marylebone and two galleries which had to be built specially to accommodate them. It was bought in a single lot by Thomas Osborne, the bookseller, of Grays Inn Gate for a mere £13,000. Whether the sale was badly conducted, or Lady Oxford, who was most unmercenary, wished the business to be concluded with as much dispatch and little haggling as possible is not clear. At all events Vertue who had known the Library intermittently and loved its owner was deeply distressed. The total sum fetched was, he considered, but one-tenth the Library's true value, and did not even cover the cost of the bindings alone. The whole thing was a tragic sequel to Lord Oxford's improvidence and carelessness over money matters, made worse by the fact that Osborne, whom Wanley had in 1726 called 'as knavish as he is ignorant', resold the items separately at enormous profit to himself.

In 1753 the House of Commons reacted in a manner only too typical of the British legislature over matters relating to the arts and aesthetics. It thought fit piously to deplore the loss to the country of Lord Oxford's printed books and pamphlets which it could so easily have acquired ten years previously for a song. It expressed the wish to preserve for the nation what remained of the Library, that is to say the collection of manuscripts. On 19th March one of Lady Oxford's trustees conveyed to her the Government's miserable offer of £10,000 together with the ungracious observation, 'It is surmised that many manuscripts have come to hurt by damps and for want of fire to air them.' The Bishop of St. Asaph, who was the late Earl's nephew, also wrote pressing his aunt to comply. She, a little nettled by the ungenerous offer and the aspersion which accompanied it, was inclined to ask for £20,000, a sum still far below the manuscripts' worth. But she referred the matter to her daughter, the Duchess of Portland, giving her and her husband the 2nd Duke full authority to act as they thought fit. The Duchess to her lasting credit wrote directly to the Speaker, Arthur Onslow. 'Though I am told the expense of them was immense and that if they were to be dispersed they would probably sell for a great deal of money, yet as a sum has been named and as I know it was my father's and is my mother's intention that they should be kept together, I will not bargain with the public.' She accordingly agreed to accept the £10,000 on the understanding that 'this great and valuable collection shall be kept together in a proper repository . . . and be called by the name of the Harleian collection of manuscripts'. The terms having been settled the Government raised £10,000 by lottery and a further sum to purchase Montagu House, Bloomsbury, in which to preserve the papers.

In this way the country lost the Harleian Library of printed books and the British Museum acquired the Harleian collection of manuscripts in 7,639 volumes at no cost whatsoever to Parliament.

ii. Literary Friends and Down Hall

Of his contemporary peers Lord Oxford—for such in 1724 Edward Lord Harley became and such he should be entitled after this date—was without doubt the most devoted to learning for learning's sake. To its advancement he gave his energies and money to an extent that was selfless and unprecedented. He was the leading manager of the Society for the Encouragement of Learning. Bishop Warburton of Gloucester called him 'the most distinguished patron and friend of letters that this age can boast of'. And Vertue, who was for years the recipient of his patronage and friendship, wrote that 'Artists or men of superior skill allways meet with this good Lords Countenance and encouragement amongst men of Learning Prior Pope & Swift was his delight & his home & table its ornament. every branch of Learning and professors he kindly receivd & made himself acquainted with their merrit, & to his utmost promoted & protected them.' The arts and architecture were, as Vertue implied, by no means ignored by him, but they did not command the first place in his affections.

The scholars, antiquaries and divines whom he befriended and entertained were almost legion. The names of several crop up in the list of his regular correspondents, like Dr. Zachary Grey, Dr. James Tunstall, Dr. John Thorpe and Dr. Stratford, of whom the last a Canon of Christ Church and his old tutor, addresses him more letters than can be compressed within one volume of the Historical Manuscripts Commission.[1] In addition, Thomas Hearne writes to him about manuscripts and acknowledges a gift of £50. Allan Ramsay sends him 'the enclosed Pastoral Comedie' after the Earl's visit to Scotland in 1725. The Reverend Matthias Earbery

[1] Volume VII, Portland Manuscripts, gives a selection.

presumes to dedicate a book to him without permission (he receives a terrible drubbing for his pains). The Reverend Thomas Baker thanks him for a present of wine and chocolate. The great Dr. Richard Bentley addresses him from the Royal Library at St. James's Palace asking to borrow Oxford's manuscript of Lucan; and Dr. Robert Freind, who admired his lordship's portrait in Dahl's studio and thought it 'very like', ventures to suggest that Bentley's 'conversation is not the most polite, he made the women stare strangely, but to me he was often entertaining and instructive'. Dr. George Harbin, the non-juror, complains that his annuity is in arrears and hopes he is not therefore in disfavour (Lord Oxford instantly pays it); and writes again that 'Some of the East India ships have brought some curiosities from China greatly valued—most charming gold and silver fishes all alive and swimming in fine China cisterns, and the most beautiful cock pheasants.' William Elstob and his sister Elizabeth, scholars both of Anglo-Saxon, are grateful recipients of his bounty, the latter addressing him from Evesham where she supports herself by teaching the children of that small market town to read and write.

On the whole the letters of these learned pedagogues do not make lively reading. It is not surprising that Lord Oxford, whose mind though not so scholarly as theirs was a good deal sprightlier, liked to confer with most of them from a distance while receiving at Wimpole and in Dover Street the poets, artists and musicians (the composer Handel was a guest at his daughter's wedding) who entertained as well as edified him. George Vertue, the antiquarian, was an exception. Lord Oxford delighted in his company and took him on several tours round England, one from London to the south in September 1738 in the company of Lady Oxford and two young Harley nephews, Edward and Robert. Vertue kept brief records of each itinerary and made copious notes of the churches and country houses they visited. He even counted how many ancient buildings at Calais they could spy through a telescope from Deal. But then Vertue shared with the Earl an insatiable curiosity in everything that was old and unusual, whether it were buildings, portraits, tapestries, stained glass, coffin plates, coins, sarsen stones, cartularies or exhumed skulls in graveyards. His head teemed with heterogeneous information which was continually spilling out at all times of the day and night, and his talk was as amusingly disordered as his written English. There was nothing the least pedantic about him and he was moreover an artist, if a most delicate engraver on copperplate can be so designated. The Earl was devoted to him, gave him presents of plate and a seal ring of an onyx on which was graven the head of Socrates, because Vertue had taken a fancy to it, protesting that it could be 'of no great value to his L^dship'. In return, Vertue who though poor was no less generous, gave his patron a silver coffee pot and stand, and a pair of candlesticks.

Vertue never tired of interspersing among his disjointed magpie's nest of information on historic incidents and antiquarian finds little asides which rendered honour to his patron. He claimed that Lord Oxford had largely promoted the painters Michael Dahl and John Wootton, the architect James Gibbs, the sculptor Michael Rysbrack, the enameller C. F. Zincke and the engraver Christian Seal, not to mention George Vertue himself, who was proud to acknowledge the Earl's protection—and so had paved the way of their successes. Vertue strongly resented any slight offered to his patron. He denounced Scheemakers, who had the impertinence to criticize to Lord Oxford's face Francis Bird's effigy of the Duke of Newcastle's monument in Westminster Abbey, which the Earl had commissioned, as 'a little animal' and 'this creature'.

Lord Oxford was utterly indifferent to society, in which he played little or no part, and by which he was in consequence looked upon as an eccentric, if harmless outsider. He found no time whatever to spare for balls and routs, and grew more and more of a recluse as the years advanced. After his father's death he kept away from politics and the Court. He was the most unworldly of men. For a rich nobleman to be so averse to the ceremonial fatuities that regulated the lives of his equals in rank was deemed by them to be very stupid and by the intellectuals very wonderful. His single-minded dedication to the cause of learning earned him considerable renown even among scholars and writers of the Continent. It induced Voltaire during his visit to London in 1728 to beg for an interview. The famous philosopher and sage sent from the White Wig in Covent Garden, where he was staying, to Dover Street a short letter, which was adulatory if a trifle inaccurate. 'Though I am a traveller unknown to your lordship, the name of "Harlay" [sic] has been for many centuries so glorious among us French [a slight hyperbole] . . . that you must forgive the liberty of this letter.'

Lord Oxford's three most intimate friends were the three most distinguished poets of their day, namely Swift, Pope and Prior. Swift had known him since his boyhood and on the 1st Lord Oxford's death transferred to the son the full weight of that mountainous devotion, so large a share of which he had previously lavished upon the father. 'I am the only man since the first Villiers

Duke of Buckingham,' he wrote to him on one occasion, 'that ever succeeded in favour from a father to son.' Because they were members of the same literary club they addressed each other as 'Brother Harley' and 'Brother Swift', and ended their letters 'your affectionate brother'. Harley's proud wife being included in the charmed circle was even referred to by the Dean as 'Sister Harriette'. In 1718 the younger man gave his old friend a snuff-box of tortoiseshell inlaid with gold, and Swift the same year repaid the compliment by a reference to him as 'that person of the world for whom I have the greatest love and esteem'. Swift's affection never faltered and in 1736 he wrote in a letter to Pope, 'I hope you sometimes see my Lord and Lady Oxford. I love them dearly, but we seldom correspond of late, because we have nothing to say to each other.' The fault was Lord Oxford's, whose occasional letters were scrappy and uninformative, vouchsafing the barest morsels of family news for which the Dean in his Dublin isolation was craving. On the other hand he treasured those he received from Swift. When in 1724 the Dean first broached a wish to write the life of the 1st Earl, Oxford pressed him to do so, begging him to come over and stay at Wimpole for the purpose. He promised to send a portrait of his father and a ring in his memory. In reply to Swift's request for an autobiographical memoir he asserted that he could find no such document among his father's voluminous papers. These nevertheless he would dispatch to Dublin without fail. But Swift did not come over, and Lord Oxford did not send the papers. Perhaps the latter feared lest Swift's partisan championship of his father might be based upon incomplete evidence and —such was the son's fairness—might lead him to write some over-severe strictures about the statesman's enemies. Or perhaps, which is still more likely, sheer idleness deterred him from looking for, still less sorting, the documents. After several years of badgering Swift abandoned the proposition altogether. He was under no illusions about his friend's character. 'I have often panted for a letter from you, and I excuse you of any want of good will, but impute your silence wholly to your laziness' was a reprimand made in 1733. In spite of disappointment he posted to Lord Oxford some old Irish coins dug up in a Dublin churchyard. 'I must desire your lordship's pardon,' he said, 'if out of ignorance I send you medals that are perfect trash, but you have an easy remedy, to throw them out of the windows.' The Dean's later letters became more querulous. He was loud in his recrimination of England for her shameful treatment and exploitation of Ireland, 'this wretched and enslaved' nation, which 'is a mass of beggars, thieves, oppres-

sors, fools and knaves. All employments are in the hands of the
Kingdom's enemies'. And whose fault was that he would like to
know? Then he added in his bitterness, 'But what is all this to
your Lordship or to England?' By 1738 the clouds were beginning
to descend upon that turbulent and exacerbated brain. The old
man's letters ceased. Instead, a friend wrote to Lord Oxford from
Dublin: 'The Dean of St. Patrick's involves himself sometimes in
such strange, improper, insignificant oppositions to matters of a
public nature, that, by hanging out black flags and putting his bells
in mourning, he makes it impossible for one in my station to
converse much with him.' Even so the Earl predeceased him and
was never to receive the seals of Julius Caesar and Hercules which
were bequeathed to him 'because they belonged to her late most
excellent Majesty, Queen Anne, of ever glorious, immortal and
truly pious memory, the real nursing mother of her Kingdom'.

Swift had been a mere six years younger than Lord Oxford's
father. Pope was an exact contemporary of the son. In the postscript of a letter written from Twickenham by Swift to Lord
Oxford on 3rd July, 1726, Pope had scribbled: 'Indeed you are
very unreasonable. I never knew you so before. You say you will
quarrel with me if I keep the Dean here and let nobody see him.
Pray what hinders you? "Here we are to be seen" is the motto
over my house, but it is so written that none but such as are
worthy and enlightened can understand it. Pray show that you
do any day after Tuesday.' Petulance, fractiousness, banter and
familiarity form the tenor of this sentence which is typical of
many others addressed by the poet to the peer, and of his conduct
throughout their long relationship. Their love for one another was
firm enough to withstand any amount of irritation and display of
temper. Pope's letters to Oxford are not as long nor as interesting
as those to Bathurst and Bolingbroke, but they reveal that the poet
relied implicitly upon his friend's moral support which was always
to be called upon in any crisis of his life. When his mother was
desperately ill in 1724 he wrote to Oxford: 'At this season any one
to whom I can sit down to write a part of what fills my heart, must
have no small share of it.' Oxford's expressions of affection are no
less fervent. 'I will allow nobody to esteem, to value, or love you
more than I do, and I do so from the conviction that you are the
Best Poet, the truest friend, and the best natured man.' These
words must have flattered the recipient who was surely astute
enough to perceive that the last were just a little exaggerated. His
company was always welcome, the Earl continued, for 'I had
rather converse with you than any man living yet I would not

purchase it [at] so dear a rate as that it should put you to any pain. . . .'

So certain was Pope of the other's tolerance and good nature that he ceaselessly trespassed upon them. He was forever taking liberties. He would shamelessly ask Oxford for favours, bid him send this or that to a friend, and run errands in London on his behalf. Would Lord Oxford take and keep his manuscripts in the Wimpole Library? Would he help him in a dispute with his publisher? Could he, Pope, stay in Dover Street while his host and Lady Oxford were absent? There was a mutual understanding that the poet was to turn up at any time of the year, unannounced if needs be, at Wimpole where he might remain for as long as he chose to stay. Lord Oxford was constantly urging him to come and, like Lord Bathurst, relied upon his taste and advice in the improvements he was carrying out to house and garden. 'I am extremely busy at this place,' he wrote to the poet from Wimpole in April 1726, 'but I will not tell you what I am doing nor of my designs till you come to the place and see with your own eyes and you shall have power to alter and I am sure that will be amending, anything I shall think of.' Pope in a letter of the previous year called Wimpole 'the place to which I'm to leap, at an hours warning, from any other part of the land, the Neplus-ultra of this year, & in a word the next sign of my Zodiack.' He was the most exacting guest, and Lord Oxford the most patient and forgiving host. He made the freest possible use of the Library and then would take umbrage over something said, and sulk. Dr. Johnson in recounting Pope's later visits to Wimpole said: 'He was fretful and easily displeased, and allowed himself to be capriciously resentful. He would sometimes leave Lord Oxford silently no one could tell why, and was to be courted back by more letters and messages than the footmen were willing to carry.' He would quarrel with the other guests. Ugly scenes ensued. Lady Mary Wortley Montagu, that exasperating know-all, would provoke him by a fusillade of contradictions until one or other left the house, only to be sent for by the host and cajoled back again. Pope dispatched the footmen on such frequent and frivolous errands that they would refuse to undertake them. Instead of remonstrating with him Lord Oxford would discharge the servants. The housemaids when accused of neglecting their work would retort, with justice, that they had been employed by Mr. Pope. One of his foibles was to ring for coffee repeatedly throughout the night. An old maid of the Oxfords recalled that 'in the dreadful winter of 1740 she was summoned from her bed by him four times in one night, to supply him with paper, lest he should lose a thought' for a poem he was composing.

It is only fair to add that for these exacting services Pope liberally rewarded the old woman who ministered to him. Towards the end of his life he was in constant need of female attention. His sufferings were very pitiable. He was so sensitive to the cold that he wore a kind of fur doublet under a shirt of very warm coarse linen with cambric sleeves. When he rose in the mornings he would be clothed in a bodice made of stiff canvas, being hardly able to hold himself upright until it was tightly laced. He then put over it a flannel waistcoat. His legs were so thin that he padded them out with three pairs of stockings which were drawn on and off by the maid, for he could not dress nor undress himself. His extreme 'weakness made it very difficult for him to be clean'. Thus bolstered and stayed, wearing a velvet cap over a tie-wig, for his own hair was falling out, and sporting a ridiculous little sword, he would slowly descend the wide staircase, a stiff, jerky marionette, with a hunched back and the face of a tortured angel, to dine with the Oxfords.

Lady Oxford detested Pope. She could not, she averred, abide the wits that swarmed about her husband's table, and Pope, because of the trouble he caused her household and of his darting, acidulated tongue, was the most viperous of them all. In this intense dislike she was encouraged by her greatest confidante and for unspecified reasons, of which one may be that he had once dared to court and then to jilt her, Pope's bitterest enemy, Lady Mary Wortley Montagu. Why Lady Mary, no fool herself, was so fond of Lady Oxford, whose friendship she esteemed 'the greatest blessing and honour of her life' it is difficult to say. When it was suggested that her bosom friend was a stupid woman, Lady Mary would reply that, although not shining she had much more in her than many people could discern. High breeding and vast wealth were after all there for the whole world to apprehend in Lady Oxford. What profounder qualities lay buried beneath a natural taciturnity were perhaps fathomed by her husband, her daughter and the restricted few admitted to her intimacy. At any rate Lady Oxford's stupidity can hardly be held an excuse for the heartless terms in which she referred to Pope's death. 'It is true,' she wrote to Lady Mary, 'Pope is dead. I did not mention it, knowing the contempt you have for worthless people.' Had she then learned nothing from her husband's generosity of heart and the distinguished men in whose company he and she moved for nearly thirty years of married life? Admittedly she had a good deal to put up with from Harley's reckless and reprehensible extravagance. Of the £500,000, exclusive of the Wimpole estate, which she brought him, he is said to have gone through four-fifths, simply out of carelessness and simplicity. No wonder that the bride of eighteen whom Swift accounted a handsome girl 'with good sense but red hair' became before she was middle-aged care-ridden, deaf and subject to 'melancholy vapours'. At least she learnt one thing after the financial crash and her husband's death, and that was how to recuperate her seemingly infinite resources. By the most severe retrenchment and strict attention to the management of her property she put Welbeck and her other surviving estates on their feet again. Her old age was spent comfortably enough in retire-ment, employing a hundred men to embellish Welbeck by day-and candle-light, sorting ancestral portraits, poring over genea-logical trees and collecting snuff boxes, each of which Horace Walpole proclaimed so much uglier than the last that he once begged her to desist from showing them to him.

There had however been one of her husband's friends, and a wit to boot, of whom Lady Oxford was genuinely fond. It is true he died fairly early in her married life and so did not linger on to be a nuisance. Matthew Prior had returned her affection. He deeply loved both the Harleys. 'His lordship is really *amabilis*,' he once wrote, 'and Lady Harriette, *adoranda*.' In his will he left her a portrait of Queen Elizabeth, 'whole length with two or three figures behind'. Prior had been, like Swift to whose generation he belonged, the friend of Lord Oxford's father. In his youth a Whig he became a supporter of William III. With the advent of Queen Anne he veered over to the Tories in support of Robert Harley and Henry St. John against Marlborough and his protracted wars He remained, like Harley, only a moderate Tory by temperament Indeed he was moderate in all his opinions, and it is questionable whether he ever cherished many deep convictions. His humanity his tolerance and his cynicism prevented him taking other men' passions too seriously. For instance, they prevented him from healing the disastrous breach between Harley and St. John; a least this was the estimation of Swift, who contended that Prio was the only person who could have done so, had he only taken enough trouble, since he was deep in the confidence of both. Th fact was that life having treated Prior harshly, experience obliged him to trim his sails at times in order to subsist at all. The im pecunious son of a Dorset joiner, he owed his start in the world t the libertine poet, Charles Sackville Earl of Dorset. The career h adopted was diplomacy wherein, considering the tremendou handicap of his humble birth, he rose to distinction. In William's reign he acted the part of Minister to The Hague without being granted the title. Lacking official status, and with his pay continuously in arrears, he had to maintain a modicum of state and dignity in Dutch diplomatic circles. In spite of being instrumental in concluding peace terms with France in 1711 which led to the Treaty of Utrecht, known in London as 'Mat's Peace', he was prevented by that insufferably snobbish peer the Earl of Strafford from being accredited Ambassador to Versailles. Instead he was sent to France as a special plenipotentiary. So in order to keep his head above water he was driven to pay court to men in power, with the inevitable consequence that occasionally he betrayed those to whom he had once been beholden. On Queen Anne's death he found himself in disgrace with the Whigs for the extremely honourable part he had played in the Treaty of Utrecht and was, along with Harley, impeached and for a short term imprisoned. His speedy release was due to the caution and cunning he displayed when called before the committee set up to examine him.

In his career Prior's strongest suit was his humour and wit. At Versailles, the seat of the most intelligent and arbitrary government in Europe, the tall, thin Englishman of no breeding but remarkable shrewdness was respected and feared. Over high, florid cheekbones and on either side of a prominent, commanding nose —'ce visage de bois'—the brightest blue eyes twinkled and flashed. Between spasms of coughing—for he suffered from a slow consumption which eventually carried him off—he held his own by most devastating repartee in fluent French with the minister, de Torcy, and Louis XIV himself. The highly experienced statesman and the monarch were amazed and occasionally outwitted by the abilities of the low born emissary. Louis forgave him, relished his jokes and actually grew fond of him. Prior for his part had little reverence for the despot Sun King, of whom he was not the least in awe. 'The monarch as to his health is lusty enough,' he wrote to London in 1698, 'his upper teeth are out, so he speaks a little like old [Sir John] Maynard [a famous lawyer], and picks and shows his under teeth with a good deal of affectation, being the vainest creature alive even as to the least things. His house at Versailles is something the foolishest in the world; he is strutting in every panel and galloping over one's head in every ceiling, and if he turns to spit he must see himself in person or his Viceregent the Sun with *sufficit orbi*, or *nec pluribus impar*. I verily believe that there are of him statues, busts, bas-reliefs and pictures, above two

13

hundred in the house and gardens.' The high ranking official who on initiating Prior into the marvels of Versailles inquired if William III's palaces boasted similar evidences of glorious deeds, received the quick retort, 'The memorials of my master's actions are to be found everywhere but in his own houses.'

Prior's friends however did not esteem him on account of his distinctions in diplomacy which fell far short of his deserts in that field, but of his poetry. He on the contrary treated his muse lightheartedly. He declared that he was 'only a poet by accident', a verdict which was not wholly untrue. Dr. Johnson's appraisal of his verse is very nearly just. 'Whatever Prior obtains above mediocrity seems the effort of struggle and toil. He has many vigorous but few happy lines; he has everything by purchase, and nothing by gift; he has no "nightly visitations" of the muse, no infusions of sentiment or felicities of fancy.' And Johnson concluded: 'His verses always roll, but they seldom flow.' In other words he is not a major poet and not an artist of the first quality. He seldom enchants us with spontaneous magic, or bothers to refine his images with gold. Poor Mat, had circumstances only treated him a little more leniently! If he had not been obliged to earn his living as the subordinate of figureheads with a tithe of his intelligence and ability, but had enjoyed a leisure to devote to letters he might have become a greater poet than he was. Nevertheless I think his frosted genius is very conspicuous in the generous passage of *Alma* on Samuel Butler's style, a passage which shows an acute perception wherein the artistry of verse lies, and, notwithstanding Johnson's disclaimer, some astonishing felicities of phrase:

> *Yet he, consummate master, knew*
> *When to recede and where pursue;*
> *His noble negligences teach*
> *What others' toils despair to reach.*
> *He, perfect dancer, climbs the rope,*
> *And balances by fear and hope:*
> *If after some distinguish'd leap,*
> *He drops his pole, and seems to slip,*
> *Straight gathering all his active strength,*
> *He rises higher half his length.*
> *With wonder you approve his slight;*
> *And owe your pleasure to his fright.*

His wit—usually it must be confessed at the expense of women— is scarifying and Byronic, as the following couplets testify.

> *Women 'twixt sheets are best, 'tis said,*
> *Be they of holland, or of lead.*

and

> *As dames who native beauty want*
> *Still uglier look, the more they paint.*

where the rhyme is in truth more lively than happy.

At times a laconic cynicism anticipates Don Juan by more than a hundred years.

> *In Europe if a harmless maid,*
> *By nature and by love betrayed,*
> *Should e'er a wife become a nurse,*
> *Her friends would look on her the worse.*
> *In China, Dampier's travels tell ye*
> *(Look in his index for Pagelli)*
> *Soon as the British ships unmoor,*
> *And jolly long-boats row to shore;*
> *Down come the nobles of the land:*
> *Each brings his daughter in his hand*
> *Beseeching the imperious tar*
> *To make her but one hour his care.*
> *The tender mother stands affrighted,*
> *Lest her dear daughter should be slighted;*
> *And poor Miss Yaya dreads the shame*
> *Of going back the maid she came.*

Prior never married and his relations with women were of a sort to which the Oxfords, because they loved him, closed their eyes. Dr. Johnson who was more forthright than genteel pronounced that 'the woman with whom he co-habited' at the time of his death 'was a despicable drab of the lowest species'. Yet, lecherous old cynic that he was, Prior was capable of the most touching devotion to the other sex, especially if they happened to be children. All his letters to the Oxfords contain messages to their only child, to whom he refers as his 'little Margaretta', 'little Mistress Peggy' or 'little pearl'. Was she in good health, he inquired? Was she learning her lessons, and did she remember and spare a thought for her parents' old friend who laid his services unhesitatingly at her feet? Margaret Harley never forgot him. As an old woman and the Dowager Duchess of Portland she recalled with tears in her eyes how 'he made himself beloved by every living thing in the house—master, child, and servant, human creature or animal'. She inspired what is perhaps the best known of all Prior's lyrics and in any anthology of child poetry hardly has an equal:

> My noble, lovely, little Peggy,
> Let this my first epistle beg ye
> At dawn of morn and close of even
> To lift your heart and hands to Heaven.
> In double duty say your prayer: .
> 'Our Father' first, and then 'Notre Père'.
> And, dearest child, along the day,
> In every thing you do or say,
> Obey and please my lord and lady,
> So God shall love and angels aid ye.
>
> If to these precepts you attend,
> No second letter need I send:
> And so I rest your constant friend.

On his release from prison Prior's friends rallied to his assistance. The first to welcome him were Edward and Henrietta Harley, for Mat's political misfortunes were closely linked with those of the ex-Lord Treasurer and in a sense due to his standing by the disgraced statesman. The first thing to be done was to raise money for him; and this the Harleys managed with the help of other fond admirers, amongst whom were Lord Bathurst and Dr. Arbuthnot. Jointly they caused to be published a large folio volume of his collected verse. The sales realized the huge sum of three thousand guineas profit for the poet, which was soundly invested for him by Lord Bathurst. To this amount Lord Harley as a gift added an equal sum of his own to enable him to buy a house in return for its reversion. Prior was overjoyed with his friends' successful efforts on his behalf and agreed with eagerness to fall in with the suggestion of his 'dear Lord Harley', whom he found 'always the same good man, and [who] grows daily more beloved'. A house in the country was something to be desired almost beyond his wildest dreams. He had always taken the keenest interest in the improvements of his rich friends to their houses and gardens, and was even reckoned something of an authority on planting. Lord Halifax in 1713 wrote to him in Paris begging him to assist in the choice of trees for his orchard garden at Apps Court, and the following year thanked him for sending over some fruit trees and melon seed. Now at long last he would have the supreme satisfaction of choosing such things for his own plantations. In his recent publication he had actually given voice to this desire in song.

> Great Mother, let me once be able
> To have a garden, house and stable;
> That I may read, and ride, and plant,
> Superior to desire, or want;
> And as health fails, and years increase,
> Sit down, and think, and die in peace.

The years certainly were increasing for Prior—he was now fifty-five and his health was failing. There was little time to lose.

In actual fact the place of his dreams had for some time been waiting for him, and all that was needed was the money to pay for it. Down Hall stood between Harlow and Hatfield Broad Oak near the Hertfordshire border of Essex. It was very isolated and well situated on a wooded escarpment of the Downs facing westwards across flat, elm-studded country. Prior liked to imagine it conveniently half-way between London and Wimpole, so that the Harleys would have to stay with him on their frequent journeys to and from the capital. In a ballad which he composed and called *Down-hall* he recounted how he was first taken to see it by John Morley. Morley, originally a butcher of Halstead, was a land agent and jobber, who became business agent to the Harleys and was deep in their trust. His introduction to the great world had been through the merchant, Sir Josiah Child, who one day came upon him delivering meat to his house at Wanstead. Morley in later life recalled the occasion of his 'going to the parlour door . . . making a very low bow, with my hat in both my hands between my leggs, with a collar band and long shoe strings, in a Butcher's frock, and I think a gurdle, steel, and apron'. Within a short time the young butcher so ingratiated himself with the rich merchant that he helped him invest money in real estate and sell stock at East India House in the city. Whereupon the next time he called at Wanstead Sir Josiah 'ordered me buckles to my shoes, a Stenkirk neckcloth, and a wigg, and talked very kindly to me, and commanded me to sit downe in his parlor, and shew'd me to hold my hatt in an other manner, and not to stand at ye door, and showd me how to attend him at his table, when he came to Halstead'. One job as middle-man quickly led to another, and Morley waxed extremely rich. Swift strongly disapproved of him and the influence he wielded over Lord Oxford, holding him largely responsible for the Earl's wild speculations and ultimate undoing. Even Prior who employed him to negotiate the purchase of Down Hall finally grew suspicious

of his methods of conducting business. But on the bright spring
morning when the two men set out house-hunting from London
no such suspicions were in the poet's mind. Morley suggested
hiring a calash,

> But Matthew thought better; for Matthew thought right,
> And hired a chariot so trim and so tight.

And they proceeded, arguing whether to keep the window open
or shut.

> Draw up, quoth friend Matthew; pull down, quoth friend John,
> We shall be both hotter and colder anon.
> Thus talking and scolding, they forward did speed;
> And Ralpho [Prior's favourite horse] pac'd by under Newman
>   the Swede,

who was his servant.

> Into an old inn did this equipage roll,
> At a town they call Hodson, the sign of the Bull.

At Hoddesdon

> Then supper was served, and the sheets they were laid,
> And Morley most lovingly whispered the maid.

The next morning they leave after 'a breakfast so warm' and
come to Harlow, where they have 'tea, sugar and toast', and
engage a guide and a horse to take them the three remaining miles
of twisting lanes to their destination on the brow of the hill.
Presently Morley cries out:

> Oh here I spy Down, cast your eye to the west,
> Where a windmill so stately stands plainly confest.

But Prior is bitterly disappointed by his first glimpse through the
trees, and answers,

> O, now a low ruin'd white shed I discern,
> Until'd and unglazed; I believe 'tis a barn.

Whereupon the incensed Morley shouts,

> A barn! why you rave; 'tis a house for a squire,
> A justice of peace, or a knight of our shire.

Nevertheless Prior maintains that

A house should be built, or with brick, or with stone.
Why, 'tis plaster and lath; and I think that's all one;

only to receive the curt reply,

And such as it is, it has stood with great fame,
Been call'd a hall, and has given it name
> *To Down, down, hey derry Down.*

O Morley! O Morley! if that be a hall
The fame with the building will suddenly fall,

the unconvinced poet exclaims. And Morley quite out of patience
with his client's high falutin notions about correct architecture is
made to say:

With your friend Jemmy Gibbs about buildings agree;
My business is land; and it matters not me.
I wish you could tell what a deuce your head ails:
I show'd you Down-hall; did you look for Versailles?
And now, Sir, a word to the wise is enough.
You'll make very little of all your old stuff:
And to build at your age, by my troth, you grow simple!
Are you young and rich, like the master of Wimpole?
If you have these whims of apartments and gardens,
From twice fifty acres you'll ne'er see five farthings:
And in yours I shall find the true gentleman's fate;
Ere you finish your house, you'll have spent your estate.

which is the true philistine business man's counsel to the woolly-
headed aesthete.

Notwithstanding his disappointment that the house should be
old, timbered and plastered Prior buys it and instantly proceeds
to disregard the land-agent's advice, by calling in his friend Gibbs
to design him a new house on the site. By midsummer of 1719 he
is writing to Harley, 'To amuse the cares of life, I, like Solomon
have set my mind upon the magnificence of building, and my stairs
will be sawed out next week.' Prior's death prevented total
rebuilding, which in any case would have strained his resources to
the uttermost, and Gibbs's noble design never got further than
paper. There it may be seen reproduced in a splendid plate in his
Book of Architecture, published in 1728. It was to have been a
grand house in miniature, a centre block of three storeys with a
recessed portico and wings over a rusticated base. The flat parapet
would support graceful urns. A forecourt would be brought about
by two imposing pavilions for kitchens and stables connected to

the centre block by curving colonnades. It was the sort of house which today a city tycoon's family after demolishing both pavilions would find too large, but which in George I's reign a bachelor poet with an income of £300 a year seriously contemplated raising for his sole use.

Prior spent four months of this year at Wimpole immersed in plans and designs for his new seat and schemes for plantations and lawns. By 1720 work at Down did not seem to have got very far. The place was not yet fit for habitation, although in June Prior had the satisfaction of entertaining Harley to a meal cooked by his manservant. The proud owner was unable to do more than patch up and improve the existing house pending a time when Gibbs's scheme could be put in hand. On 2nd July he wrote to Harley: 'I have been at Down, surveyed the estate, and done everything— as to taking a rent-roll, discoursing my tenant, etc.—that Morley calls wisdom. It is impossible to tell you how beautiful a situation Down is, and how fine the wood may be made; but for the house, as all the cross unmathematicall devils upon earth first put it together, all the thought and contrivance of man cannot make a window to be looked out of; or a door to be shut, in case it were made otherwise habitable: so sooner or later I foresee *destruit domum*; but of this, as the divines say, at another opportunity . . .' A week later he told his friend, 'As to Down it is really fine; to make it habitable will be the question. *Deus provedebit*, to which I shall add all human means by commensuration, hortification, and edification, but nothing more than projection upon paper till I have seen you, which I very much desire to do.'

Confusion was reigning and Prior did not know where he stood. Was he to go on spending scarce money on patching an old house he wanted to do away with as soon as he had the means, or take the plunge now, demolish, and rebuild, in anticipation of funds forthcoming? Lord Bingley rebuked him for thinking of building at all on the site, and then gaily suggested his having a saloon thirty feet by thirty, an antechamber and a state bedchamber. 'All the world is paradox,' was Prior's comment. However, early in September one Mr. Cossens, presumably a builder, met him at Down 'to take my measures' and returned with him to Wimpole. On the 10th, 'I am with Gibbs and the virtuosi' at Wimpole still, with a view to a further consultation at Down with one of the virtuosi, probably Gibbs, and Mr. Cossens *ad opus inceptum et continuandum*. For on 13th he told Harley, 'Gibbs has built me a house, I will bring it over with me.' Was this yet another design —the architect is known to have produced two—perhaps the final one which Gibbs was to publish in his book? And was it an indication that Prior had decided once again to demolish the old house and rebuild *ab initio*? 'As soon as I shall have finished this letter I am going to sup with Dhayl [Michael Dahl the painter of aristocrats], Wooten [John Wootton the painter of thoroughbreds] and Gibbs to talk of buildings, pictures.' And on 17th he wrote, 'I have so far settled matters with my "virtuosi" that I shall see Down, and bring Gibbs over with me to Wimpole within eight days from this in which I write.'

The 'virtuosi' were that exclusive little group of Tory intellectuals and artists who revolved around Lord Harley in Dover Street and at Wimpole. Gibbs was busy over important additions and alterations to Wimpole Hall; Thornhill was preparing to decorate the new chapel; Bridgman was engaged upon the grounds; Dahl was painting his lordship's and her ladyship's portraits and Wootton their horses; Prior was celebrating their merits in verse. One or other of them, when not all together, was travelling from London to Cambridgeshire, stopping at Down either on the way there or back.

Towards the end of September Prior sets off from Westminster, after a very brief London sojourn, in a calash with Gibbs for Wimpole. He asks Harley to send his calash to meet theirs at Buntingford. After a day or two at Wimpole he and Gibbs, with Bridgman, whom they there pick up, proceed to Down, talking 'of nothing but canals, parades and vistas' on the road. Once again, alas, Prior's and Gibbs's daydreams of a new house vanish into thin air. Only the poet's garden is drastically altered, so that on 29th December he is able to write: 'We have laid out squares, rounds and diagonals, and planted quincunxes at Down.' These delightful fantasies have like the old house all disappeared. The only trace of Prior's and Bridgman's layout is the remains of what was until a few years ago a well maintained, long avenue of clipped hornbeams directed towards the steeple of Hatfield Broad Oak church.

Not until 1721 was Prior actually living at Down. Events had not turned out quite as he expected. The ideal new seat had not yet been raised. At least however he was installed under his own roof; and was at long last actually leading the bucolic existence of his dreams as squire of Down Hall. 'I am so employed that the day seems short,' he wrote to Harley in the summer, 'and so much in love with Down that I think I shall pardon my countryman Morley for being the innocent cause of turning my brain.' On 8th June he was at pains to persuade his noble friend to make regular use of his house. 'I may tell you that the best way to save your future dragons is to make your journey to Wimpole two days, and take Down for your half-way house, which I hope may be effected in eighteen months, for I have already lopped the tree that is to make the plank that is to saw the timber, that is to floor the room where I hope you will be within the time aforesaid . . .' If anticipation of pleasure is greater than its realization then Prior may have been the happiest of mortals when he penned these words. He went on: 'You may laugh at my solitude as much as you please, but I like it infinitely and shall do more so when the noise of the axes and hammers to the tune of five pound a week grows less tumultuous; but Down in itself considered I love more than Tully did his Tusculum, or Horace his Sabine field, nor would quit it for anything, but to be with you, or to serve you.' And his last letter of 14th was all about the stile he was erecting at the end of Great Hilly Field where the cattle forced a way into the garden and did 'a power of wrong, to be sure', and the brushwood he was putting under the old gate—Harley would know which he meant —'where they plaguy pigs crept into the pease-close.' These miniature worries were the surest measure of his ineffable content. 'The kitchen-garden this year,' he continued complacently, 'the apartment of three rooms the next, and what then?'

What then indeed? He was still at Down on 25th June. In August, perhaps sooner, he was at Wimpole, loitering in the library. His cough grew worse. On 18th September he quite suddenly died. Harley was stricken with grief, and Swift wrote from Dublin, 'I pray God deliver me from many such trials.' On Harley who was made one of his executors, and who inherited most of his small possessions, fell the burden of erecting the monument in Poets' Corner for which Prior had in his lifetime strangely made the extravagant provision of £500. He wrote a poem when he was fifty explaining what he had done.

> As doctors give physic by way of prevention,
>   Mat alive and in health, of his tombstone took care;
> For delays are unsafe, and his pious intention
>   May haply be never fulfill'd by his heir.

He directed the monument to be designed by his friend Gibbs, and his bust which Louis XIV had commissioned for him of Coysevox to be set upon it. Gibbs employed the young and practically unknown sculptor Rysbrack to carve the attendant figures on the tomb. Vertue was stung to remonstrate against Gibbs's meanness in only paying Rysbrack £35 for carving both figures, whereas he took from Lord Harley £100 for each figure which he had merely sketched out. ' 'Tis an unreasonable gripeing usage to a most ingenious artist (in his way) far more merit than Gibbs will ever be mr. of' was Vertue's growling comment. The fairly lengthy epitaph, recording in Latin the deceased's various diplomatic activities, was to be composed by Dr. Robert Freind, the head-master of Westminster School. All these injunctions the faithful Harley saw carried out at the cost of additional calls upon his own purse. The 'pious intention' was, then, conscientiously fulfilled by Mat's principal heir. The resulting monument is, to say the least, grandiose and possibly a little too solemn for the harum-scarum poet, whose sense of fun was overriding and sense of sin, according to Mr. Bonamy Dobrée, noticeably lacking. The ups and downs of Prior's life, so very variable and perverse, merely taught him to take things as they came with a philosophy best expressed in the final quatrain of the lines *For My Own Monument*, from which I have already quoted:

> *Now in equipage stately, now humbly on foot,*
> *Both fortunes he tried, but to neither would trust;*
> *And whirl'd in the round, as the wheel turn'd about,*
> *He found riches had wings, and knew man was but dust.*

According to the arrangement made with Prior, Harley came into the Down Hall property. He frequently resorted there for short spells of retirement; and he lent it occasionally to his literary friends who needed to get away from London for fresh air and tranquillity. Pope was at Down Hall by himself in the New Year of 1726. Evidently the old scheme to rebuild was still being mooted, to judge from a sentence in a letter of 22nd January from the poet to his absent host. 'I liked my lodging so well (both the apartments above, & the closet below) that I am utterly against Gibbs, & all his adherents for demolition. The rooms where I look up to the cieling, appear very lofty; & surely they are large enough, when both Lady Margaret has room to run about all the morning, in her chamber, & Mr. Thomas [Lord Oxford's chaplain] to sport with Bridgman, in his. I fear he will grow fat, now, for want of exercise, unless he betakes himself to hard study and painful preaching.' Pope, in spite of his Catholicism and Toryism, was no admirer of Gibbs's architecture, being himself Palladian-minded, nor did he greatly approve of Bridgman's old-fashioned taste in landscape gardening, as has appeared in an earlier chapter. But he need not have had immediate fears for the romantic old house of lath and plaster. Lord Oxford could no more afford to replace it with

Gibbs's imposing substitute than Prior, and apart from laying a new bowling green, cutting down some old trees to reveal vistas, and planting a young coppice round the spring, he made few alterations. When faced with financial ruin he was obliged to sell Down to a city merchant, Mr. Selwyn.

By their writings then, Swift, Pope and Prior frequently testified to the easy manner with which they treated Edward Harley as well as to the extent they were beholden to him. How dearly they loved his companionship and his never failing hospitality! Of their genuine fondness of him there can be no question. He was endowed with charm of manner, unbounded generosity and sheer goodness. John Gay referred to the last quality in *Trivia*, which he addressed to Pope,

> *Harley, whose goodness opens in his face,*
> *And shows his heart the seat where virtue stays,*

which rings like an unpremeditated exclamation of friendship. His old aunt Abigail Harley wrote in 1721, 'Could you look into my heart you would find the deepest impression of your kindness of which I have had numberless instances, and 'tis no small pleasure that you indulge a poor old scrub in writing often to you.' We may readily assume that this particular pleasure was not very regularly reciprocated. Dr. Zachary Grey for his part accorded all the cardinal virtues to Oxford, stressing in particular his courtesy, compassion and humility. Vertue quoted him as once saying, 'A man of humanity finds a secret pleasure in seeing all the world happy about him; and that pleasure is doubled, if he himself has contributed to that felicity.' His easy temper was, it must be confessed, enhanced by a congenital idleness, which ultimately led to most disastrous consequences. In earliest infancy this idleness was too readily apparent. In a letter from his grandfather Sir Edward Harley an admonitory sentence points to the incipient failing which was to grow with time into a prevailing vice. 'I have expected, Ned Harley Junior,' the old man complained in 1696 when the boy was only seven, 'this many weeks a letter from you, of your inditing, tho' not of your writing; 'tis time for you to learn to write, for wch you are already big enough.'

His dislike of refusing a favour frequently involved him in lending a total stranger precious manuscripts and volumes from the Library, when Wanley or his successor was off duty, and his indolence to his omitting to make a note of the loan. When conscientious friends brought books back he was often amazed, and when unscrupulous borrowers did not do so he seldom knew.

This casualness was unwise. It also led him to accept manuscripts from friends and strangers on approval and to forget either to pay for, or to return them. Sir John Dolben in 1733 inquired bitterly for information about some papers which he had offered to sell to Lord Oxford as long as ten years before. The case of poor Dr. Covel, the aged Master of Christ's, Cambridge, has already been mentioned. It was all very fine for Wanley brusquely to bid him accept his patron's offer. The Doctor complained that Oxford had kept the catalogue of his collection for a year and a half and would not make up his mind to buy the things. 'Matters lying in this uncertain condition,' he wrote most piteously, 'give me an unsupportable trouble, and it will certainly shorten my life . . .' He was well over eighty. 'Therefore for God's sake, give me your positive answer, or send me my catalogue with all possible and convenient speed.' This behaviour was unkind. Lord Oxford was guardian to his cousins Lord Barnard and his brothers and sisters. They were detestable children. Lord Oxford let them run wild and was too idle ever to check them. Their wretched tutor, Patrick Guthrie, wrote that their house was 'Bedlam, Drury Lane, Billingsgate, Mother Needhams all at once'. His charges abused him to his face as 'rogue, dog, scoundrel, pickpocket'. Guthrie begged at least for protection from their violence, if he could not have authority to direct their studies. The wretched tutor described a quarter of an hour spent with Lord Barnard as being 'as great an act of charity as feeding the hungry, cloathing the naked, or visiting the sick'. No, Lord Oxford could not be bothered to intervene, or even to reprimand his wards. This was surely most reprehensible. When it came to allowing rascally stewards and agents so to mishandle his affairs that a great part of his wife's estates, including Wimpole, yielding £20,000 per annum, had to be sold, while he sat back and took heavily to the bottle, his engrained indolence can only be condemned as criminal. And so Swift deemed it to be. 'His way of managing his fortune is not to be endured,' the Dean wrote in 1738 to a mutual friend, John Barber, in answer to his query, 'Is it not shocking? I say, is it not shocking?'

The ultimate catastrophe, which had long been foreseen by his friends, did not occur until the spring of 1740, by which time it was too late to expect any permanent reform of Lord Oxford's character. He sank into a decline of drink and apathy from which he could not even be roused to take one of his equestrian tours into the country.

iii. Architectural Tours

These tours had been fairly regular recreations over the years. Occasionally Lady Oxford accompanied her husband. More often he was attended solely by his chaplain, the Reverend Timothy Thomas (who succeeded Wanley as librarian), George Vertue, John Morley or some other male dependant, and a host of servants. The ostensible objective was the inspection of his wife's scattered and distant estates, the actual outcome visits to great country houses, churches and shrines of antiquarian interest. Lord Oxford loved these carefree itineraries. Sometimes it amused him not to disclose what part of England he was going to cover until the cortège had already set forth. Thus in August 1723 Mr. Thomas recorded that, having attended his master on horseback from Dover Street, until they passed Hyde Park Corner and were under the wall of Buckingham House, he 'was kept in the dark which way the excursion was intended'. It happened they journeyed to Kent. The chaplain who kept the journal jotted down in a somewhat obsequious and yet facetious style whatever he found of interest on the route. Many of his carefully considered observations strike us as rather trite, whereas some of his casual remarks are less commonplace to us than they were to him. For instance, he noted almost as a matter of course that the poor women of one village which they rode through strewed mint from their aprons upon the road in compliment to Lord Oxford; the inhabitants of Dartford were generally recognized to be the most skilled cricketers of Kent, that county being more renowned for the game than any other; and the main road from London to Canterbury was so narrow at intervals that two single horsemen could not pass conveniently, much less two carriages.

One of Lord Oxford's longest itineraries was through the northern counties to Scotland. It lasted from April to June 1725. The journal was again kept by Thomas, who was at great pains to explain that he recorded no observations which were not inspired by his master. The chaplain waited upon Lord Oxford in Dover Street on Saturday morning 10th April at six o'clock. Ever since Good Friday, 26th March he had kept away from the house at his lordship's express command on account of Lady Margaret developing smallpox. At seven o'clock the two of them set out for Wimpole. There they stayed ten days. On 20th April having been joined by John Morley they proceeded by coach with the servants, including a cook, and with twelve horses, including Bumper, Monkey, Buckskins and the one-eyed pad. Morley took care to stow in his luggage some bohea tea and loaf sugar in case of emergencies. They reached Stilton by one o'clock, and were much disappointed in the cheese, 'though an extravagant apologist might very properly cry it up for food for the Gods, for I verily think few human stomachs would care to devour it'. They visited Belvoir Castle, which was in process of having all its windows sashed, and passed Belton House, where a handsome new gravel walk was being laid through the garden at the end of which 'they were making a new "ah Ha!" ' In Lincolnshire the machine for measuring the mileage was put out of order by the deep ruts in the road. Near Ancaster they noticed oxen ploughing and even drawing carriages. Lincoln Cathedral was in very poor condition and approaching irredeemable ruin. Thomas recorded that James Gibbs had lately presented the Chapter with a scheme to avoid total collapse of the structure, and all the silly Dean had done was to pave the floor. The whole city of Lincoln was practically ruinous. How different from York where the Minster inside and out was well cared for by the Dean and where the enlightened Corporation was erecting a new Mansion House.

Castle Howard called for comment on account of the exorbitant amount of money being spent and the admirable use of Derbyshire marble in the fabric. The stucco work on the other hand looked ill and mean. On 2nd May they went to church in Thirsk and the chaplain was gratified by the congregation which was large and attentive. At Durham on 5th Bishop Cosin's library of books and manuscripts was visited. It was here that Thomas ventured upon an opinion of his own. 'The whole situation of the place is somewhat romantic, but to me seems not unpleasant, being altogether upon hills which have a descent to the river,' he observed intrepidly. But the poor man instantly corrected himself in that timorous and deferential manner that prejudices us against him. 'Others of better judgment [meaning his master] condemn this site, to whose opinion I always submit my own, to my great advantage and instruction.' The extent to which clergymen allowed themselves to be put upon by their social superiors in the eighteenth century was pitiful. Fielding was not exaggerating their subservience when he made Squire Western send Parson Supple all the way from London to Basingstoke to look for the tobacco box which the Squire fancied he might have left behind in the inn.

In Northumberland the roads were so bumpy that the coach was abandoned to the postillions. Thenceforth it was no uncommon thing to spend eleven hours of one day in the saddle. At Titlington Moor several gentlemen met the Earl by appointment to settle the boundaries of the manor lands which they were about to enclose. At Alnwick the strange method of creating a freeman of the town was commented upon. The candidate was obliged to wade through a deep, dirty, stinking pond, a barbarous custom established by King John out of malice because he happened to tumble off his horse into it. At Cambus in Berwickshire a somewhat similar accident befell Lord Oxford who was riding along the sea shore. His horse reared and threw him into the salt water, but happily only up to his middle. An honest servant rushed to his assistance. The Earl merely suffered a good soaking, which led the chaplain to thank Almighty God whenever he reflected upon the terrible incident. In Scotland conditions were so primitive and the tracks—there were no proper roads—so deplorable that Thomas could hardly bear to record them. Only the planting done at Dupplin by Lord Kinnoull, who was Lord Oxford's brother-in-law, earned the country a measure of praise. From Dupplin to Alloway the party spent eleven ghastly hours on horseback with no refreshment save one glass of wine each provided by the Governor of Stirling Castle.

On the return journey the road from Belford to Alnwick, a distance of fourteen miles, took the horsemen three and a half hours and the coach four hours and forty minutes. To cross the moors between Tosson and Rothbury experienced guides had to be hired to keep them to the track. As for the route from Hexham to Byermoor, near Gateshead, taken on 31st May, this was 'by far the worst days journey'. The track was so bad that no coaches traversed it except the Judge's once a year, and then at midsummer.

Appleby Castle was visited and Hornby Castle observed in passing. Back in Yorkshire they felt they had returned to civilization. At Fountains the canals in Mr. Aislabie's new landscape garden, which had just been finished, were grudgingly admired. When he visited Raynham in Norfolk in 1732 Lord Oxford thought Lord Townshend's place far superior to Mr. Aislabie's, 'which is very much cried up'. Lord Bingley's wonderful formal garden at Bramham, which survives today unaltered, received only scant recognition. This is rather surprising considering that it adhered to the old-fashioned baroque style of layout which Lord Oxford, as might be expected, preferred to the new picturesque style introduced by Burlington and Pope. The Reverend Timothy Thomas was not at all impressed by the cascade which to his eye seemed 'no other than a kind of stone ladder lying almost horizontally upon the ground with great penury of water distilling over the steps of it'. On 10th June the party reached

Welbeck and the tour was considered to be safely over. At 8 p.m., so the journal concludes, 'in your Lordship's chapel, we offered up a particular collect of humble acknowledgments for this great blessing by your Lordship's particular commands and direction to your poor chaplain.'

The few journals of tours kept by Lord Oxford himself make rather more lively reading, because they were not carefully composed like Mr. Thomas's to please a critical superior, but jotted down un-selfconsciously, sometimes in letter form to amuse Lady Oxford at home, or else in note form purely for private record purposes. Lord Oxford was unsparing in his condemnation of the country inns where he was obliged to spend many a weary night. At Harleston in Suffolk, he wrote in September 1732, 'Well for us it was that Lord Dupplin [his nephew] and the cook went before and got into the inn some time before us' to prepare a makeshift meal which they could at least swallow, the food of the house being absolutely uneatable. Of Diss in Norfolk he said in December 1737, 'the worst town and the worst inn I ever was at in Britain, for there was neither meat, drink nor beds fit for Christian people to make use of. Our supper and dinner was a crop of pork, this was the only tolerable thing, which proved to be a neck, beef steaks as black as a shoe and as tough'. And at the inn at Alresford in Hampshire in 1738 the fire smoked so badly that the windows of his bedroom had to be flung wide open. The wind and rain admitted then put the fire out. 'At last I got to bed; but such a bed, there were great bumps much bigger than my fist and as hard, the bed cloathes as heavy as lead, the bolster and pillows filled with new feathers that they stank like the devil.' He was an indefatigable sightseer and his observations are sometimes whimsical. At Bury St. Edmunds he remarked of a tomb, 'The lead coffin that covered the body was made like a skeleton to humour what was within.' He took nothing for granted and reached his own opinions, resolving as he put it, 'upon hearing the description of any places, not to form too high an idea of them'. Certainly he would not admire places just because previous travellers had done so, or because it might be expected of him. He found Stonehenge, which he came upon in a fog, 'unpleasant'. In other words antiquity for its own sake was not enough. Neither did he reverence indiscriminately the classical in architecture nor despise the Gothic. He thought the introduction of the Arch of Severus as a screen to the sideboard in the dining-room of Raynham Hall a preposterous affectation. On the contrary he considered the monastic gatehouse at Bury St. Edmunds and the steeple of

Salisbury Cathedral beautiful. Among modern buildings St. George's chapel at Yarmouth struck him as 'very handsome'. This is significant because St. George's, designed and erected by John Price in 1714–16, is in its astonishing plan of duplicated curves one of the most baroque churches in Great Britain. In all these respects he was indubitably no diehard Vitruvian. Indeed the most revealing parts of his journals are his views on architecture and his opinions of his Whig contemporaries, Lord Burlington and William Kent.

Lord Oxford's Tory predilection for the now outdated school of Wren whose work he admired (he found the unfinished Palace of Winchester one of the best buildings in England) and his contempt for the new Whig Palladianism are expressed unequivocally both in his 'Account of a Journey made through part of the Counties of Suffolk, Norfolk, and Cambridgeshire in the month of September 1732', and in the few alterations he made to Wimpole Hall. He intensely disliked Kent's form of painting and decoration. While staying at the Angel Inn in Bury St. Edmunds he remarked, 'The room we dined in is much decorated (as Mr. Kent's phrase is, and those that follow him) with the paintings or rather daubings of one Bryan Hill, nephew to our landlord. The works of this gentleman's hand are the only proper pieces to decorate the buildings of Mr. Kent or his great patron the Earl of Burlington, and I wish he was their sworn servant, only to attend them and their operations, that he might not fall in the way of any honest gentleman to cheat him of his money. But these wishes though well meant are like most others vain and of no effect.' They are certainly harsh wishes, but not by any means surprising in coming from one who had employed Kent's most implacable rival, Thornhill, to paint the chapel Gibbs had built for him at Wimpole. When he visited Raynham Hall, where Turnip Townshend greeted him at the front door very courteously with a drink of chocolate, he was confronted with samples of Kent's decoration. 'The rooms are fitted up by Mr. Kent,' he noted, 'and consequently there is a great deal of gilding; very clumsy over-charged chimney pieces to the great waste of fine marble.'

His reactions to Sir Robert Walpole's newly-built Houghton Hall were similar. 'This Houghton has made a great deal of noise, but I think it is not deserving of it . . . I think it is neither magnificent nor beautiful, there is very great expense without either judgement or taste.' He goes on to call it 'a composition of the greatest blockheads and most ignorant fellows in architecture that are', of whom he labels Colen Campbell, its principal creator, 'that ignoran rascal'. He even blames Gibbs, his own favourite architect, for having altered the roofs of the corner towers into domes, and so for having tried to mend the blunders of the blockheads. Rather uncharitably he attributes Gibbs's interference to a Scottish love of money. There are only two apartments in Houghton that can be described as such, namely the hall and saloon, the rest being small and poky closets. Even the hall is too crowded with statuary, and the niches contain unsuitable terms bearing busts. Furthermore it is made dark by the surrounding gallery which obstructs light from the upper and lower windows. The 'much talked of lanthorn' is too small and 'very ugly', but cost £170 at auction. The stair well is completely filled by the cast of the Gladiator on a clumsy pedestal, which Henry, Lord Pembroke's father, the 8th Earl, gave to Sir Robert. You cannot get far enough away to have a good view of it. The profusion of mahogany all over the house is 'most monstrous'. Kent is to be blamed for many of these shortcomings, in other words for pandering to the tastes of a vulgar parvenu. Although Lord Oxford modified his unfavourable opinion the next time he visited Houghton, which was in 1738, when indeed he was received by Sir Robert personally with great 'civility, good nature, freedom, ease and cheerfulness as I ever saw', and invited to spend the night, he never approved of what he considered the sacrifice of convenience to a cramping, over-exuberant splendour.

After Houghton on the 1732 tour came Narford Hall. This was the seat of that well-known connoisseur and patron, who was the friend of Lords Pembroke and Leicester, namely Sir Andrew Fountaine. Lord Oxford was fairly caustic about Narford. 'It is a pretty box,' he wrote. 'A great deal of gilding and painting done by very bad hands' is presumably a reference to the delightful panels of mythological scenes by Pellegrini who was patronized by the sort of people he disliked. 'Many pictures, most copies. The library is very smart and beauish, there are round the room the heads of several learned men, but very ill done. The joiners' work as well as the painters' is very bad; in short, all parts are most vilely finished by all workmen. . . . He carried us to see his china room, but took us through his kitchen, perhaps to show us that meat was cooking there, and more than ordinary because my Lord Lovel [Lord Leicester to be] was to dine with him.

'His china room is a most wretched place, set out upon shelves like a shop, no old china, a mere baby room. . . . There is here a small paddock with some Indian deer in it, mere affectation; he values himself much for a pretty design of a deer house, a ridiculous trifle, a thing of boards.'

And so he goes on, with hardly a good word said for anything he sees. It cannot be that Lord Oxford found it all so at variance with his notions of what was good art. He owned an enormous quantity of books on architecture which were very catholic as to styles and types. Yet his views on correct architectural style were extremely circumscribed, if we are to believe his own words. Why was this so? Why did he react so strongly against the taste of Burlington, Kent and Campbell and the men for whom they built and decorated houses? He was not by any means a naturally jealous or cantankerous person. On the contrary he was generous and good. He even regarded Lord Burlington as a friend, exchanged presents with him and frequented Burlington House. He owned a copy of Burlington's *Fabbriche Antiche* in which he inscribed that it was given him by the author. We have to remember that Lord Oxford was by birth and conviction a Tory peer, of wide political influence notwithstanding. Because of his wife's several estates he held control over numerous pocket boroughs. As a patron of letters and the arts he therefore felt constrained to favour writers and artists who belonged to his political party. Pope, the Tory writer, who was head and shoulders above his brethren, was almost alone in mixing freely with patrons of either persuasion; others like Defoe, Swift and Prior tended to consort with Tory lords almost exclusively. Tory artists such as Thornhill, Wootton and Gibbs did the same. It was both the weakness and the strength of letters and the arts in the reigns of the first two Georges that they were swayed by political partisanship and made the vehicles of political propaganda. It meant that a man of Lord Oxford's erudition scorned talented writers and artists who worked for the Whigs. But it equally followed that a patron gave special encouragement to those writers and artists who adhered to his own party, and thus spurred them to produce their best results in rivalry with their opponents.

iv. Gibbs and Wimpole Hall

James Gibbs was the typical example of an artist who worked almost exclusively for that political party to which he owed his advancement and success. Born a Scottish Catholic, he became a suspect Jacobite and a Tory. His early patron was the titular Duke of Mar who was the Old Pretender's avowed supporter and agent. Towards the end of Queen Anne's reign he fell in with the young and recently wedded Edward Lord Harley, newly possessed of the valuable Cavendish property in what was then north London, the far side of the present Oxford Street. The Queen's death, the accession of the House of Hanover, the downfall of Jacobite hopes and the triumph of the Whig party drew patron and architect together. In this atmosphere of mutual lamentation and sympathy their tastes in architecture coincided and developed. Gibbs, having received his early training in Rome from Carlo Fontana, always harked back to the triumphant baroque style of his Italianate youth. He tended to reproduce it in his architecture, where it is perhaps most perceptible in the church of St. Mary-le-Strand and the Radcliffe Camera in Oxford. As a prominent member of the group of 'virtuosi' who looked to Harley as their protector he helped impart a distant baroque flavour into the landscapes of Bridgman and the mural paintings of Thornhill. It was truly a diluted version of the continental; was much anglicized, rather old-fashioned and nostalgic, acknowledging in a half-hearted sort of way the lonely King over the Water, who aimlessly drifted from Versailles to Rome in ever-increasingly hopeless exile.

Gibbs's profession however was anything but hopeless. The Tories might be in the wilderness, but they were possessed of wealth and political influence, if not of power. Harley in developing his wife's London properties was able to employ Gibbs to great advantage. The architect began to lay out the streets and squares that bear the names and titles of the Harley and Cavendish families. He built the Oxford chapel, now styled St. Peter's church, in Vere Street. By the autumn of 1714 he was firmly established in the confidence of Lord Harley. On 23rd November he wrote to his patron, 'I was with Mr. Witton [Wootton] last night with whom I did drink your Lordships health and ladys & all ye familys, I am heartily glade to heare by him that all is weel in ye family. I hope he has pleased yʳ Lordship, he speaks very much of Your Lordship & lady's handshom treatment, not forgetting the excellent french claret affter supper, for which my Lord I am also infinitly obliged for doing me so great ane honor as remembring me so frequently. . . .' He then proceeded, 'Your house goes on very forward, and I wish I had ane answear about these locks, what sorts and sises you would pleas to have,' which is the first reference to work he was doing at Wimpole Hall. On 2nd February next he supervised the packing and dispatch of a cartload of books from Dover Street to Wimpole. Clearly he was by now enlisted among Harley's most trusted dependants.

Although work on the house at Wimpole may have been proceeding in the autumn of 1714, it soon came to a halt for reasons mentioned early in this chapter, namely the financial troubles involved with Lady Henrietta's mother, the truculent old Duchess of Newcastle. In 1718 plans for Wimpole's aggrandizement were still in the air. The aged Dr. Covel, not yet in desperation over Harley's casual treatment of his collections, referred in a letter to his lordship's intention to make of the house 'a Vatican' and a repository for books which would outvie 'the great Ptolemy himself' at Alexandria. Not until March 1721 does work seem to have been resumed in earnest. Prior wrote to Harley on 16th that at Wootton's house he had just met Gibbs, Bridgman and Thornhill who were on the point of setting out for Wimpole; and that Bridgman told him, 'he will make it the finest and noblest thing in England. The garden side I find he has a mind to be at; he does not open yet, but I think it is rather enlarging than much altering.' Two days later Prior wrote again: 'I believe you have your virtuosi by you while you receive this letter; as they were packed up in one coach, they must necessarily have come together, or else—if it were possible—Gibbs would have come about three hours after the rest,' a playful reference to that prosperous architect's enhanced stoutness and slowness of movement. 'Sir James [Thornhill], I presume has rather been speculating in the chapel he is to paint, than praying in the neighbouring church, and friend Bridgeman's devotion has consisted chiefly in contriving how the diagonal may take Waddon [Whaddon] steeple exactly in the middle.' In other words Edward Harley's major changes and improvements to Wimpole were at last well in hand.

The house which John Holles Duke of Newcastle had bought in 1710 and his daughter Henrietta conveyed to Edward Harley in 1713 was a large rectangular block built of red brick for Thomas Chicheley in 1632. Chicheley's son sold it in 1686 to Sir John Cutler of the Grocers' Company. He was an extremely rich City merchant of a most miserly disposition. Pope was to make a striking comparison between Cutler's mode of living at Wimpole and his friend Lord Oxford's in the following mention of the house:

> Where one lean herring furnished Cotta's board,
> And nettles grew, fit porridge for their lord,
> Where mad good nature, bounty misapplied,
> In lavish Curio blazed awhile and died.

On Cotta's, or rather Cutler's death in 1693 his daughter Lady Radnor succeeded to Wimpole and began making additions to the house and planting avenues in the park. Nothing further was done until the Harleys took up residence. Lavish Curio only slightly altered the main block, but considerably extended the house to east and west. In his eastern extension of the south front he formed a chapel and in the western a library, which he prolonged northwards, as well as an orangery. Vertue has left a very rough sketch of the south front as it looked when his patron had finished with it. The sketch coincides fairly closely with Gibbs's elevation drawing of what was intended. The Tory Lord Chancellor and 1st Earl of Hardwicke, to whom Lord Oxford sold Wimpole in 1738, refaced both the north and south fronts and redecorated most of the interior. He made still further extensions, which were even increased in the nineteenth century, when the house reached a truly formidable size. Some of these extensions have lately been demolished so that the house has resumed more reasonable proportions, and thereby greatly gained in beauty. Although the present exterior would be recognized by Lord Oxford, could he see it today, little within, beyond the chapel and the library, remains unchanged since his time. Bridgman's formal Versailles-like gardens were much modified by Capability Brown and finally swept away by Repton; but some of the splendid stone urns designed by Gibbs have been preserved and re-erected.

The Chapel and the Library are among the chief of Wimpole's glories. It is fortunate that they have survived, for they are our only material evidence of Lord Oxford's taste in architecture. Gibbs's sectional drawings for the Chapel prove that he outlined the design which Thornhill followed with his brush on walls and ceiling. The repetitive Palladian openings of the nave and the Pantheon-like coffers of the ceiling faintly recall the interior of St. Mary-le-Strand, generally considered the most Italian of Gibbs's baroque churches. Every inch of wall and ceiling space is covered; scene and architecture merge in one embracing pictorial *trompe-l'oeil*; the vividly coloured figures move against a putty background, of which the highlights are streaked in gold. For the east end altar-piece Thornhill chose as his subject the Adoration of the Magi and for the nave wall opposite the windows figures of the prophets within niches. Proudly the artist signed and dated his work 1724 over the entrance door to the gallery pew, where Lady Oxford's gigantic books of Common Prayer, bound in faded morocco and stamped with her arms and the Cavendish knot under her husband's coronet, still repose upon the velvet cushions of the ledge. The Chapel—a joint masterpiece of Gibbs and Thornhill—is baroque in its entirety. Here painting and furnishing (the altar rails of wrought iron and the table of gilt gesso adorned with carved angel heads are coeval) have been made the handmaids to architecture.

The Library at the opposite end of the house is solely Gibbs's contribution. This historic apartment was designed for the Harleian collection of books and manuscripts which were moved here from London as work proceeded. The Library was begun in 1719 and took eleven years to complete. Apart from the window which Sanderson Miller threw out at the north end in 1760 for Lord Chancellor Hardwicke there have been few alterations. The woodwork of the tall round-headed bookcases, painted a deep Prussian blue and picked out in gold, stand forth boldly from the grey walls. The ceiling was redecorated in 1840 possibly in the original shades of yellow, pink and blue. The magnificent carpet adorned with wreaths and floral patterns on a chocolate ground may be the very one Lord Oxford brought to the room, for which however it was not actually made, because it has been cut to fit. In this Library Wanley wearing his skull cap and dusty old coat once bustled from shelf to shelf; Prior passed the last days of his life scribbling verses to his dear Lord Harley upon the fly-leaf of a book, and romping with little Lady Peggy; Pope escaped in the sulks from the provocative rodomontades of Lady Mary Wortley Montagu; and Lord Oxford himself, driven at last to desperation by the importunities of creditors and duns, supervised the dismantling of his precious shelves before turning his back upon the scenes of his greatest happiness where, in the society of a handful of learned friends he had felt really free, so he told Pope, 'from the impertinence of this world'.

Lord Oxford's enjoyment of his Library between its completion and the final catastrophe of his affairs was brief. In November 1730 he wrote contentedly to Pope: 'I am very busie about my new room, there I hope to spend some days with you.' In less than eight years' time all the treasures which he had so carefully collected and so lovingly arranged were packed up and sent for storage to Welbeck. He never had them out again after he was obliged to part with Wimpole; nor did the manuscripts see the light of day until the guardians of the new British Museum exhibited them for the benefit of the public in Bloomsbury. Meanwhile Lord Oxford was blissfully set upon 'growing wise in retirement', as Pope put it, so as 'to like it better and better the longer you stay in it'. It was a fool's paradise. While away he always hankered to be back at the great house on the Cambridgeshire downs, where the horizons seem limitless and the sky is so omnipresent as to induce those who live beneath it to think themselves a part of infinity. And each time that on returning from London he rode up the two-mile elm avenue, with its ever-nearing vista of the great welcoming house at the far end, his heart rejoiced. Pope knew what home-coming meant to his friend and in a letter of 1730 drew a delicious picture of such an occasion. 'As soon as I imagine you at your journey's end, Wimpole, I send to welcome you. I put myself in the place of your wood-men or stewards (or rather the whole country and University), to hail your arrival. I will fancy I am standing on the stone-steps at the great door to receive you, & that I have just been setting the bells a-ringing in your parish church. I am impatient to follow you to the new-roofed Library, & to see what fine new lodgings the ancients are to have? I salute the little gods & antiquities in my way in the anti-room, wishing them joy of the new temples they are to be inshrined in, and I admonish that Prior's Lamp be set in a private corner. I advise; that two poets heads, which I see in another room, be always kept together, as being both odd-headed fellows (Cleveland and Another) & kept at a convenient distance from the Library, not to be of ill example to those who shall come to study there.' The one head was of John Clieveland, the eccentric cavalier poet who suffered in the Stuart cause, the other Rysbrack's of Pope which Lord Oxford had commissioned. The touchy subject referred to the last in a quatrain which hinted that some slight or sneer at his deformed little person had been intended:

> 'Tis granted Sir; the Busto's a damned head.
> Pope is a little elf.
> All he can say for't, is, he neither made
> The busto, nor himself.

Who knows that these lines did not move the generous and compassionate peer to some fresh act of conciliation and friendship?

Lord Oxford's friends agreed sorrowfully that after the financial crash of 1738 he was never the same man again. Vertue wrote that 'his affairs had for some time mortified his mind' as well as affected his health. Mrs. Delany who was the intimate confidante of his daughter declared that he found no enjoyment in life after the mismanagement of his finances, for which he rightly held himself chiefly responsible. That dependants had battened upon his generosity, that spongers had thriven on his bounty, and that dishonest stewards had profited from his casualness were no excuse for his abysmal lack of business acumen and his engrained indolence. That what he had lost was a large part of his wife's fortune and his daughter's inheritance made the consequences of his folly so much harder to bear. Not being a strong character he allowed his tribulations to overwhelm him. Both Vertue and Mrs. Delany gave terrible pictures of his decline in the last days. Vertue described his appearance so grievously altered from that of the plump, jolly figure he remembered, 'his colour and eyes turned to yellow, to a great degree, his stomach wasted and gone'. Mrs. Delany wrote that 'his whole mass of blood is corrupted, and one of his legs mortified'. Both attributed his condition to excessive drinking throughout the long days in hopeless endeavour to drown his wretchedness and remorse. Yet both were careful to add that in spite of his pitiable condition he remained invariably courteous to his servants, kind to his friends and affectionate with his wife and daughter. All who ministered to his sufferings were heartbroken. At last the engraver recorded how 'Jaundice and death speedily put an end to that life, that had been the support cherisher and comfort of many many others, who are left to lament. But none more heartily than Mr. Vertue'. He died on 16th June, 1741, in Dover Street at the age of fifty-two.

By his will he directed that his body should be buried without pomp and with the least expense. It was put into a leaden coffin, enclosed in another of wood which was covered with a velvet pall and removed to the Jerusalem Chamber at Westminster. It was buried in the vault under Gibbs's far too splendiferous monument which Lord Oxford had raised in the north transept of the Abbey to his father-in-law's fairly insignificant memory. That he made no provision for his own name to be inscribed either on the monument or even on the paving at its foot was typical of his diffident and self-depreciatory nature. His widow when the first transports of mourning were over viewed the course of her husband's past life dispassionately, and allowed her justifiable grievances to overcome any desire to perpetuate his memory in stone or marble.

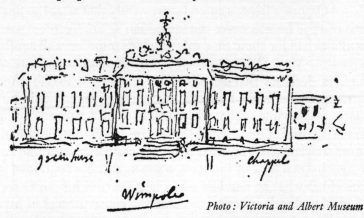

Photo: *Victoria and Albert Museum*

Wimpole Hall, Cambridgeshire. A sketch made by George Vertue in his notebook, November 1733

LEICESTER V

THOMAS COKE
1st EARL OF LEICESTER
1697–1759

i. Youth and the Grand Tour

THE COKE FAMILY are found settled in Norfolk at the very beginning of the thirteenth century as tenants of the Townshends of Raynham. In 1554 Robert Coke bought from Sir Roger Townshend a property at Mileham where four years previously his son Edward had been born. This Edward, who was to become Speaker of the House of Commons under Elizabeth and Lord Chief Justice under James I, was the undoubted founder of Coke greatness. One of the most learned of English lawyers, he was the implacable opponent of any encroachments by the royal prerogative upon the rights of the House of Commons. No man has been a more vociferous denunciator of abuses or a more righteous upholder of justice. But with these highly commendable virtues he combined the most unattractive qualities with which it is possible for an upright human being to be endowed. He was brutal, ruthless and pitiless. His temper was ungovernable, and he so browbeat prisoners in the dock that they were reduced through sheer terror to admit whatever charges were brought against them. His devotion to the Church of England was endorsed by a detestation of Papists which was wholly pathological. 'Not only do you kill your King, but you eat your God,' he screamed at the Gunpowder plotters as he sentenced them to savage penalties. When he died in 1634, piously ejaculating, 'Thy kingdom come, thy will be done!' he left his descendants the possessors of a vast Norfolk acreage, with all the privileges which were the recognized concomitants of land.

Lord Chief Justice Coke was not the owner of the Holkham property. It was acquired by his fourth son, John Coke, through marriage with an heiress, Merial Wheatley. John Coke by a process of buying up adjacent lands and reclaiming salt marshes from the sea became by 1659 sole lord of Holkham parish. Although he and his wife produced seven sons and seven daughters, none of their children begat heirs, and the Holkham property was eventually inherited by Robert Coke, the grandson of the Lord Chief Justice's fifth son. Eventually it came to pass that in 1707 Robert's grandson, Thomas Coke, succeeded at the age of ten to the Holkham estate with numerous other lands accumulated in Norfolk, Suffolk and Oxfordshire, as well as £22,000 of his father's debts.

Both Thomas Coke's parents died in 1707 while still in their twenties, his father Edward in April and his mother Cary in August. When after four months of mourning a consumption brought Cary Coke to her husband's grave, Tommy, his two brothers and two sisters were packed off to their maternal grandparents, Sir John Newton, Baronet, and Lady Newton of Barr's Court in Gloucestershire. For the rest of his childhood the boy enjoyed no settled home. Almost immediately Sir John arranged for him to be sent to a boarding school in Isleworth at a fee of £50 a year. The holidays, which did not amount to anything like the long spells of present-day holidays, appear to have been spent at the school with only occasional visits to the Newtons' town house in Soho Square. There were however frequent excursions with Mr. Brook, his tutor, to London. Before he had even reached his teens Tommy was showing prowess in those studies which were to distinguish him in later life. When he was only nine his proud mother had written to Sir John that the tutor 'gives him a great Character as to his Book and says hee is foreder than any of his age'. His future education and well-being were not neglected by his grandfather who was the chief of four guardians, all relations. At school he was provided with five servants as well as Mr. Brook. The family accounts for the next few years record additional payments to a French master, a writing master and a dancing master. There are also repeated payments for the lettering of his books which suggest that in these tender years the future bibliophile was laying the foundations of that library which was to bring him renown among scholars of the European nations. His passion for book-collecting was inherited from poor Cary who in her short married life between giving birth to and rearing five children had made quite a few well-chosen additions to the Lord Chief Justice's library housed at Holkham.

The young heir was not in fact deprived of anything thought conducive to his health, which was delicate, or to his recreation. A flannel 'to wheare at his stummack and strings to them' and quantities of asses' milk, Hungary water, wine, sack and physic were considered as necessary as articles of clothing, like garters, silk and cambric handkerchiefs, thread stockings and a pair of doe-skin gloves, or personal adornments, such as a periwig and ruffles when he was just thirteen, a string to his watch, rings and even lockets. Soon after their mother's death all the children were taken to see 'the strange birds and beest' and in 1708 'the drum-medare' at a travelling zoo in the metropolis. There were payments too 'for seeing the Moving Picture', 'for a shuttle and cock' and 'to the man that lett my master up into the gallery att Gild Hall'. Visits to the opera in 1711 are the first indication of a love of music which lasted throughout the years; also excursions to the cockpit initiated him into a lifelong addiction to his favourite sport. In April of this year owing to his failing health he was taken from the Isleworth school for good and sent to live with another guardian, his cousin Sir Edward Coke at Longford Hall in the bracing dales of Derbyshire. At the same time a governor in the person of a Mr. David Wilkins was engaged in the place of Mr. Brook to attend him for the next twelve months at a yearly salary of £200. The governor, or new tutor, expressed a high opinion of his pupil's acquaintance with the best Latin authors as well as the English poets, commended his good humour and obedience and only deplored 'that his delight is so much in cock fighting', which he felt constrained to limit to one day a week. Sightseeing now became part of his educational curriculum and in Mr. Wilkins's charge he paid a visit to Hampton Court before leaving London. Later on he was taken for a tour of the Midlands. 'Eden's Hole and the Devil's arse' were followed by country houses including Mel-bourne, Chatsworth, Lyme, Hardwick, and Bolsover, Warkworth and Nottingham Castles in July; and Hinchingbrooke, Kimbolton, Boughton, Burleigh and Kedleston in September. In February of 1712 he left Longford Hall and the cousin who had been so kind to him for London. A jaunt to the Tower, to the dome of St. Paul's and the top of the Monument was followed by a severe illness in April, entailing heavy expenses to a nurse and doctor for six long weeks.

Even before Tom Coke left Longford his anxious cousin Edward had written to Sir John Newton suggesting that the best course would be to send the boy abroad. 'This air agrees with my cosen's health' was the preamble to his letter of 27th October, 1711, 'for he grows tall, is plump, and looks fresh and vigorous . . . yet I can't prevent his conversing with my servants and ordinary people in the neighbourhood, which may have no good influence upon his morals, neither his going too often abroad an hunting with the Gentlemen about us, which I find makes him grow more cool to his studyes, and less tractable to his Governor; his passions are strong and violent, and should be early regulated, civilized and softened, and this requires a Governor of sound judgment and admirable addresse.' In other words the young man's character was beginning to shape itself along the very positive lines of his manhood, when his passions were indeed not always to be softened by his good qualities. Yet Sir Edward, had he only known it, need not have feared lest his cousin might abandon his studies. They were, as a matter of fact, never to be neglected in favour of all those forms of outdoor exercise which he so dearly loved, or of that habitual Georgian indulgence in copious drinking. Permission having been granted by Sir John, preparations were at once put in train for his grandson's prolonged journey overseas.

No precaution was considered too great and no expenditure too much to ensure the success of the grand tour for the young heir of Holkham. It is true that Tom Coke's father had left his affairs in a seemingly hopeless tangle of mortgages and debts. Nevertheless, because of the son's long minority and because of the extraordinary diligence and expert management of the family estates by the faithful agent, Mr. Humphrey Smith, matters had by 1712 enormously improved. Coke's spendable income was now in the region of £10,000 a year. The first thing his guardians felt obliged to do was to replace Mr. David Wilkins by a tutor and bear-leader of higher standing in the world of learning and polite society. Wilkins having been dismissed, Doctor Thomas Hobart was engaged in his stead. Hobart, who was probably of Norfolk origin and perhaps allied to the owners of nearby Blickling Hall, combined with his advantages of 'sound judgment and admirable addresse', as specified by Sir Edward Coke, the qualifications of a doctor of medicine. A learned and cultivated Fellow of Christ's, Cambridge, he was given by his college special leave of three years' absence to accompany his important young gentleman overseas. Accordingly in July Tom paid a fortnight's visit to his ancestral home at Holkham in order to bid a formal farewell to his own people. His arrival was greeted by the beating of drums and the pealing of church bells in the villages he passed through, in return for which handsome donations were distributed to the drummers and ringers, and by the firing of ships' guns as he approached the seaside town of Wells.

To judge from his age, which was only fifteen when he set forth on his travels in 1712, Tom Coke must have been an unusually forward boy. Lord Burlington, who was three years his senior in age, was not to embark upon his first continental tour until 1714 when he was nearly twenty. Coke's travels were far more extensive

WIMPOLE HALL, THE LIBRARY
By James Gibbs, 1719–1730

WIMPOLE HALL, THE CHAPEL
By James Gibbs and Sir James Thornhill, 1724

THOMAS COKE, 1st EARL OF LEICESTER
Bust by L. F. Roubiliac, 1759, on the tomb in Tittleshall Church

and lasted a much longer period. He remained abroad for nearly six years which were the most formative of his life and covered the transition from puberty to manhood. Practically every step of the journey can be traced by means of the meticulous records kept by a superior servant, Edward Jarrett, who paid all the bills. Jarrett's book is headed, 'An Acc^t of the Moneys that I Rec^d of Mr. Hobart upon acc^t of My Master Thomas Coke Esq Viz^t for Cloaths, Necessaries, Extraordinary Traveling Expenses and Other Payments from August the 21: 1712', which was the day the party set out, until 18th May, 1718, when it landed at Dover once again. Letters written home by Dr. Hobart and Coke to the grand-father, Sir John Newton, fill in many gaps which Jarrett's dry statements of facts otherwise leave bare. The story of the tour has by these means been told very fully by Mr. C. W. James[1] in his book on the Coke family and consequently does not call for detailed repetition. In a sense the tour resembles to a remarkable degree Lord Burlington's progress, with some differences. It was far less hurried, better conducted (because better prepared by Dr. Hobart than by Burlington's unknown bear-leader) and more purposeful. Whereas Burlington's objectives were the arts gener-ally, Coke's, even in his adolescence, were more specialized. Of course he set out to see and to purchase, wherever available, paintings, statues, and all other objects of virtu which took his fancy. But his primary quarry was rare books and manuscripts: his primary study that of architecture with a view to its practice at some future date. In this last respect he anticipated his noble contemporary whose specific interest in this branch of the arts was not to emerge until he had actually reached manhood.

It may be relevant notwithstanding to capitulate rather briefly the outline of Coke's continental journey with particular emphasis upon those incidents which largely shaped his future creation, Holkham, and its collections. The party left London with a coach and four horses, two grooms, of whom one was shortly to be replaced by a Frenchman, and a valet, Abraham. The faithful agent, Humphrey Smith, and his son Edward accompanied the young master, Dr. Hobart and Edward Jarrett as far as Dunkirk, whence having sped them on their way they returned to England and to Holkham. The travellers reached Paris on 24th September where they stayed six weeks. The Invalides, the Luxembourg Palace and Notre-Dame were visited. There were excursions to the gardens at Marly and Versailles. Dr. Hobart, grimly determined

[1] *Chief Justice Coke, His Family and Descendants at Holkham*, by C. W. James, Sometime Librarian at Holkham, 1929.

to avoid all social distractions and dissipations, moved his charge early in November to Angers. There they remained for five months, which in spite of lessons in riding at the Academy, in fencing, dancing and music, did not appeal to Tom. He complained ruefully to his grandfather of the fogs of Angers, the execrable French spoken by the inhabitants and the indifferent teachers. Dr. Hobart had occasion to mention the number of other young English bloods in the town and his fear of bad influences.

In April 1713 the party leave Angers. Throughout the summer they are almost perpetually on the move. Nantes, La Rochelle, Toulouse (where some rare little books are bought), Narbonne, Montpellier, Nîmes, Arles, Avignon and then Lyons do not delay them for more than a day or two each. Along the route Tom Coke pays his respects to governors, marshals and presidents of parliaments who presumably return their compliments to this bright adolescent. The cursory items in the account books remind us closely of Lord Burlington's expenditures. 'For a flute', 'for a flagiolet', 'for a trumpet' speak of Tom's indefatigable music exercises, interspersed with visits to the opera in the towns they pass through. Tips or 'vails' and gifts of charity to the poor, or the galley-slaves in Marseilles are regular and unavoidable exactions. 'For painting the shaze', for broken windows and new springs, and 'for a dog fowling a silk carpet' are no less familiar entries. Only the entry, 'given to too prety women, by my master's order', has no counterpart in the record of Burlington's unimpeachable conduct. On 4th November, 1713, they cross the Mont Cenis pass by mule and on 7th arrive in Turin. The next fourteen months are spent in Italy.

From the very start of the journey Turin Academy had been looked upon as a fitting seat of learning to claim the young traveller's studies. But it was not yet to mean a halt of more than a few weeks. Even so an excursion was undertaken by chaise to the Palazzo Stupinigi where the King of Piedmont sometimes resided. The party soon continued to Genoa, thence by sea to Lerici, and so to Pisa and Florence, where courtesies and presents were exchanged with the Grand Duke of Tuscany. In January 1714 they were in Venice where operas and masquerades were the rule. There was little loitering in the lagoons, however, and the beginning of February saw them at Ravenna and Rimini. By the 7th they were in Rome, and put up for their first two nights at the Golden Mountain Inn.

There is every indication that in Rome Tom Coke did much serious sightseeing between attending brilliant receptions, like that of the Queen of Poland. He visited the Villa Borghese, the Villa Ludovisi, the Palazzo Farnese, the Vatican and Quirinal palaces and gardens, the Palazzo Odeschalchi, the Palazzo Rospigliosi, the Palazzo Aldobrandini, the Palazzo Chigi and the Palazzo Spada, as well as countless churches by renaissance and contemporary architects. But, curiously enough, there is no mention of his studying the antiquities of the Forum or the remains of ancient temples. He had Italian lessons and bought pictures. He also engaged one Signor Giacomo, an 'architecture master for a month', and acquired 'instruments to learn architecture'. Then after a rushed visit of a fortnight to Naples he seems for the first time to have met, probably at the studio of the painter Benedetto Luti, and struck up a friendship with the thirty-year-old William Kent. Under 1st June in Jarrett's account book there appears the first of many entries relating to the man who was to wield such tremendous influence upon Coke's taste in the arts.—'Paid to Mr. Kent 60 pauls.' Almost immediately the cavalcade again left Rome for the north, this time taking Kent in its train. The very first entry in a scrappy journal which Kent began at this date records: 'Rome: I had ye honour to waite of Mr. Coke & Dr. Hubert. from thence June ye 6—on ye 8 whe came to Siena.' Since Kent's journal is concerned almost exclusively with pictures (he had learnt painting under Luti's tuition), it is just possible that Tom Coke's enthusiasm first turned the older man's interests in the direction of architecture. We learn that together they looked at Siena Cathedral and visited Giuliano da Sangallo the elder's villa at Poggio a Caiano, which had been taken by Inigo Jones as a model for the river front of his Queen's House at Greenwich. After Bologna they entered the Republic of San Marino. 'Whe returned,' Kent recorded in his halting but picturesque style, 'from ye Bright Republick with ye sounding of Trumpets & came to our calash & set out for Ravenna.' There they were much impressed by 'ye famous church of St. Vitale ye plan being an ottangle & they say ye form of St. Sabbena at Constantinople'. The neighbouring sepulchre of Galla Placidia was likewise inspected.

On 22nd July they reached Venice. The next day they visited St. Mark's (the Cathedral 'very much Gotic but ye great arches are round & all of mosaic upon ye frount without are four noble horses of a green gusto'); and in the afternoon crossed the water to San Giorgio Maggiore ('the architecture of Palladio, ye library in ye cieling divided into several divisions', Kent noted down). Santa Maria della Salute was seen, the canvases of Tintoretto and Titian receiving special praise. Kent made a rough plan of the octagon, and on the opposite page a half-elevation sketch of Palladio's San Francesco della Vigna. Before leaving Venice Coke, like Burlington seven months later, had his portrait done in pastel by Rosalba.

On 18th August they took what Kent calls a 'bootcello[1] very convenient to come by water' to Padua, stopping on the way 'to see the villa of yᵉ famous beauty, Motzenigo Procuratess', and admire the frescoes, 'some of Veronese's first manner things relating to yᵉ family'. At Padua the paintings of Giotto were—surprisingly—commended. Next came Vicenza, with its Palladian palaces and the Teatro Olimpico, 'ornamented with statues and basso relievos with fifty marble pillars' which Kent sketched. Then Verona with its Roman amphitheatre, and on 4th September Mantua, with the Palazzo del Té 'without yᵉ gate very fine, but most ruined by yᵉ Germans'. Kent approved the very fine grotto at the end of the garden—'ma per disgratia e per la vertu va tutte in ruina', the Signor breaks into Italian, ending the brief entry with, 'write this at yᵉ Peacock in Parma upon my bed not haveing more Room.'

At Padua Coke had parted from Kent who returned on 3rd October by slow stages to Rome, his expenses as far as Parma at least having been paid for by his young friend. Coke and Dr. Hobart proceeded to Turin where at last the youth—he was now seventeen—settled down for the winter at the Academy. From the account he gave to his grandfather he hated every moment of it. 'I did intend,' he wrote, 'to have desired you to defend me from being whip'd in this Academy, for I heard a very ill character of it, but I, having a Governour, am obliged to no rules. . . . I am sure you would not desire that I should be treated like a child, as the Piedmontese are in this Academy. . . . I think of all the Academies that I have seen, except at Rome and Naples, this is the worst'—which last sentence suggests that very few, if any, from his limited acquaintance with them, would have met with Tom's unqualified approval.

In the spring of 1715 they move, much to Tom's relief, from Turin into Savoy. At Aix-les-Bains the doctor takes the waters and his pupil lessons in geography, mathematics and again architecture. In July they are in Geneva and in August at Basle, where a chestful of books including *The Habits of Basel* and *The Death Dance of Holbrin* is purchased. Also the young master's head is shaved preparatory to his wearing a new wig. The party then proceeds by water to Frankfurt in the company of two new friends, a Mr. Warner and a Mr. Richard Mongoe, upon whom the

---

[1] By *bootcello* Kent meant *burchiello*, a large covered water omnibus with oars which plied between Venice and Padua at regular times.

YOUTH AND THE GRAND TOUR

cautious governor looks askance. Here a whole consignment of
volumes is bought through a Greek agent. By now the youthful
pupil is so well indoctrinated by his learned governor that a passion
for book collecting has taken firm hold of him. At Mainz three
boxes of books are packed. At Langres a missal is found; and at
Lyons for 3,000 livres some forty manuscripts are acquired from
the discalced Augustinians' convent of the Croix-Rousse. This
haul, which was Coke's first and most spectacular purchase of a
whole collection, comprised the famous library of Raphael de
Marcatellis, the natural son of Philip the Good. In December the
party are at Marseilles. On Christmas Day they leave the 'Bons
Enfans' hotel and pack themselves, the chaises and plenty of
provisions, including candles and two chests of Côte-rôtie, on
board a ship bound for Sicily.

January 1716 saw Mr. Coke in Palermo, which he thought a
beautiful city; but the inns of Sicily were so atrocious that it was
out of the question to settle comfortably in any of the island towns
for long. He saw Messina, Syracuse and Catania, and even crossed
to Malta for 'while things continue so troubled in England, one
can't keep too far from it', a sentiment inspired by the recent
change of dynasty and the menace of a Jacobite restoration. In May
he went to Naples where he met Kent again, who introduced him
to Solimena from whom he commissioned two pictures. More important still was his acquisition of the cream of the Giuseppe
Valletta collection of manuscripts. There are payments to Kent
for his journey to Naples, his lodgings and other necessaries as
well as 'for pictures and drawings that he bought for my master at
several times'. Together they went in June to Rome where they
put up at the Black Eagle. Numerous paintings by Procaccini,
Garzi, Conca, Luti as well as anonymous views of the city and its
palaces were bought. These adorn the walls of Holkham to this
day. The month of August and the first half of September were
particularly devoted to the study of architecture. Signor Giacomo,
'the Architect master', is again paid for his tuition and supply of
drawing paper; and is given a present 'for goeing about the town
with my master and larning of him architecture'. It is apparent
that Mr. Coke's intensive study, not only of the history but also of
the technicalities of the science, was done for an ulterior motive.
At the back of his mind in these early years of his life he cherished
a determination to rebuild, on the palatial lines which suited his
ever accumulating fortune, the home of his ancestors. There in a
suitably neo-classical setting he would display the magnificent
books, pictures and sculpture amassed during his travels.

He now began in all seriousness to buy marbles. A colossal bust of the Emperor Lucius Verus, found when the port of Nettuno was cleared, and a bas-relief were his first acquisitions in this department of the arts. On 12th September he left Rome for Florence and the northern cities, chiefly in pursuit of books, of which a rare edition of Livy was the prize. Kent accompanied the party and was taken ill at Modena where he was attended by doctors at Coke's expense. In January 1717 they were back in Rome for a stay of three busy months of sightseeing and collecting both pictures and statues. Signor Giacomo was paid for preparing plans of the Palazzo Farnese just as he had been paid the previous autumn for drawing Andrea Pozzo's rich altar of St. Ignatius Loyola in the Gesù. A 'Great Statue' of Jupiter was transported to Civitavecchia to be shipped to England, but the wagon carrying the colossal burden stuck fast in the snow. A headless statue of Diana, still in the gallery at Holkham—at the time highly prized but actually very stiff and dull—was dispatched to Leghorn. For its extradition out of the Papal States without a licence Coke was, according to Matthew Brettingham and Kent, very properly arrested and nearly imprisoned.

Before leaving Rome for the last time the *Cavaliere* Coke, as by now he was known all over Italy, had his portrait painted by Angelo Trevisani. He was then twenty years old, and by no means good-looking. He is represented sitting in a richly carved chair, his left hand resting on the head of a mastiff. Busts to indicate the young virtuoso's tastes are set in the background. The angular face is enveloped in a close-fitting wig. The nose is long and very prominent; the eyes are deep and earnest, the lips sensual; the chin is slightly receding. It is the portrait of a wilful but intelligent youth of a serious and brooding cast of mind.

Having said good-bye to Kent who was to remain in Italy for another two years Coke and Dr. Hobart departed for the north. Once more they passed through Florence where Coke commissioned Signor Biscioni, Prefect of the Laurentian Library, to collate the current printed text of the three decades of Livy with twenty-six manuscripts in the Library. The formidable task was not completed until 1728. Biscioni gave the young man an introduction to the scholar Apostolo Zeno in Venice, who reluctantly parted with several valuable manuscripts in return for a mere £60. Zeno and other Italian scholars of the early eighteenth century gravely resented their need to part with rare manuscripts to young milords from the north, most of whom, unlike Thomas Coke, had more riches than education. A brief excursion to Padua resulted in the purchase of a large section of the library of the Canons Regular of San Giovanni in Verdara which had been given them in the fifteenth century.

After being shown over a number of Venetian palaces by a specially hired guide Coke and his attendants left for Vienna, by way of Innsbrück and Salzburg, completing the journey down the Danube. In Vienna the *Cavaliere* made elaborate preparations to take part in a campaign then being waged against the city of Belgrade. Horses, tents, baggage and equipment of all sorts were mustered at heavy expense in a special room hired for the purpose, in spite of the remonstrances of Dr. Hobart. Alas, the glorious prospect of winning golden spurs was rudely scotched through the cunning instance of his governor, who had already warned the young man's guardians. Appalled, they ordered the governor to prevent this folly at whatever cost. Accordingly the wise Dr. Hobart, in order to diminish his pupil's recriminations against himself, urged the Austrian police forcibly to intervene. Abashed and disappointed the would-be warrior sought consolation in flute practice and gambling, after inditing a rather touching apology for his intemperate behaviour to his grandfather. The letter addressed from Prague began: 'I beg ten thousand pardons for what you may by this time be informed of, of my intention to see the Army in Hungary, notwithstanding Sir Edward Coke, in the name of my guardians had refused.' His excuse for having wanted to see active service at least showed spirit and his lack of resentment against the tutor a good-humoured and philosophic temper. 'Mr. Hobart (who in deference to my Guardians I forgive, they having recommended him) got the Governor of Austria to put me in arrest,' the letter continues. And then, 'Vienna is a very dull place' is followed by an equivocal description of the Emperor Charles VI's ladies of the court, whom His Imperial Majesty commands to shoot every afternoon at a target in the palace grounds. 'I can't call these Ladys Amazons, one must find a new name, for they, instead of one breast being cut off, have two as big as four other women can have. The sexes are so changed at Vienna, that as the Ladys shoot, the men are obliged to make curtsies.'

Perhaps after this disappointment it was just as well that the doctor and his pupil separated for a few weeks. After Dresden and Berlin, where valuable manuscripts and two illuminated Byzantine Gospels were bought from the library of Andreas Erasmus Seidel, Coke went alone to Hanover, Amsterdam and The Hague. There he joined forces with Lord Leslie and his brother. The three young men visited Brussels together where they joined Lord

Bruce. Finally, February 1718 saw *Cavaliere* Coke and Dr. Hobart in Paris. Thomas was nearly twenty-one years old and practically his own master. Dr. Hobart's responsibilities were accordingly nearing an end. Now the life the pupil chose to lead in Paris was his own affair. The situation was radically different from that five and a half years ago when the doctor had been at pains to keep him away from the dissipations that beset a boy from every quarter. He lived in luxurious apartments and was waited upon by four servants in livery. Lord Stair and Lord Essex were his constant companions; his young brother Neddy had joined him from London. He patronized expensive tailors, had his shirts ruffled and bought periwigs of the latest fashion. He went to balls and was sent a present of flowers by the King of France's gardener. He purchased more pictures, including the large equestrian portrait by Vandyke of the Comte d'Aremberg which hangs in the saloon at Holkham. In May there were great preparations for a return to England. Crates of books, pictures and statuary, not already dispatched from Civitavecchia or Leghorn by sea, had first to pass through the customs, then be corded and sealed. Two smart new berlins were bought to take the great quantities of luggage. The crates, boxes, trunks and packages, the servants, Dr. Hobart and, lastly, Mr. Coke himself all embarked at Calais. On 18th May they landed at Dover, where the faithful Humphrey Smith, come specially from Holkham, greeted his young master on the pier.

ii. Paterfamilias and Collector

One can only marvel at the satisfactory organization of young Thomas Coke's life up to date. Credit for the smooth way in which events turned out are largely due to his own persistence ever since as a boy of fifteen he persuaded his guardians to send him abroad. At the time there was understandable opposition to be broken down before consent could be obtained for the infant heir to vast estates to venture among the perils of the Continent. But he overcame it. Certainly his guardians chose for his companion a learned and sensible governor, who without nagging and without altogether forbidding those ranker pleasures of gaming, cockfighting and masquerades to which he had no mind himself, fostered his ward's better instincts and kindled those intellectual and artistic enthusiasms which eventually bore fruit to Coke's and posterity's lasting profit and delight. Tom Coke was a typical product of his generation and class; in other words he was equally

at home in the stable and the drawing-room. He found companionship in grooms and courtiers, philistines and artists, and
preferred one extreme to the other according to his mood of the
moment. He loved sport and the outdoor life just as heartily as the
whip-cracking, foul-mouthed Squire Western whose mind was as
empty of refinements as a sewer. Indeed the grosser half of his
character developed very much along the lines of that insensitive
figment of Fielding's imagination, for he could often be coarse and
cruel. He also passionately loved music and books, particularly the
Latin classics; his taste for architecture, painting and sculpture is
manifested in the superb palace he built and furnished at Holkham. In this temple of learning, art and beauty the gentle, civilized
side of his nature took refuge from the crude and savage side as
surely as the sybarite finds luxurious shelter within those velvet
walls from the biting winter winds, which sweep from the North
Sea across the exposed Norfolk landscape.

Coke so arranged matters that on his return to England a mere
month was to elapse before he came of age on 17th June. At last
he was absolutely free to look after his own estates and possessions.
Another fourteen days and he got married. This event can only
have been settled by letters to and from the Continent which have
not come down to us. It is difficult to believe that the highly suitable match can have been made entirely by his guardians in his
absence and without his consent. Submissive though the boy Tom
was to his grandfather and Cousin Edward, he was no doormat;
and with adolescence he showed a mind to go his own way which
is proved by the extravagant purchases frequently made in direct
opposition to his guardians' wishes. It is still less likely that the
match was a romantic one when we consider the short space of
time between his arrival in England and the wedding. The bride
selected was Lady Margaret Tufton, third daughter and co-
heiress of the 6th Earl of Thanet, and incidentally through her
Cavendish mother a first cousin of Henrietta Lady Oxford. She
was eighteen years old. In the eyes of Mr. Edward Smith, who
shortly succeeded his father Humphrey as trusted family factotum,
she was 'a Lady of great beauty, singular virtue and goodness'.

To judge from the bridegroom's generosity as recorded in
Edward Smith's journal book, Coke endorsed his agent's highly
flattering opinion of her. He gave Lady Margaret wedding presents
to the tune of £3,077 15s. 4d. They consisted of a necklace of
forty-eight stones, earrings, a buckle to her girdle, stay buckles
and tags, and a spray for her hair, all in diamonds; also an old gold
endowing purse, a green velvet saddle and, what is curious, two

wedding rings. For himself to mark the occasion he bought a gold watch, chain and swivel, an agate snuff box, a silver barber's basin in a shagreen case, a diamond ring, a silver buckle and pearl tassels sewn with diamonds and rubies. His wedding suit was of fine cloth of scarlet drab, embroidered with gold and silver lace; he wore a hat with feathers over a new periwig, and carried gloves and a sword.

After the wedding service which took place at the Tufton seat, Hothfield Place in Kent, the newly married pair proceeded to Lees Court, the home of Lady Margaret's elder sister Lady Sondes, amid the pealing of church bells from the villages they drove through. There the honeymoon was spent.

If her portraits are anything to go by Lady Margaret was tall and of good figure, with a well-shaped face of soft features. Whether this apparent softness ever really reflected her character, even before it became soured by her husband's brusque treatment, is questionable. Those who knew her judged her to be a faithful, submissive wife, gentle with the poor and generous to her servants, yet haughty with her neighbours. Everyone, with a single exception, recognized her strength of character. The exception was Admiral Boscawen who with a bluff sailor's obtuseness described her ineptly as 'a good sort of a Pyning kind of woman', which implies a browbeaten, ineffectual person, the very opposite of what she certainly turned out to be. On the contrary she ruled her household with efficiency. We have a glimpse of her shortly before her husband's death, giving orders to the servants in the kitchen at Holkham at six o'clock in the morning.[1] When she was left a widow and to the surprise of her friends absolute possessor for life of the Holkham estates, she carried on the decoration of the house as she knew her husband wished it to be completed. Once she was free from his dominance she became increasingly imperious. She took an instantaneous dislike to her heir, Wenman Coke, born Roberts and son of her husband's sister who had married beneath her, and left him no more than what she was obliged to leave. After enumerating in her will a list of chattels at her own disposal, she concluded, 'Some of these things above named I would have left to Wenman Coke, esquire . . . if his conduct to me had been such as I had just cause to expect.'

No sooner was the honeymoon over than the husband took his wife on a tour. Evidently the past five and a half years wandering on the Continent had made Tom Coke restless and loth to settle down. The young couple's goal was Longford Hall in Derbyshire

[1] Mrs. Lybbe Powys, Diaries, 1756.

to pay their respects to Sir Edward Coke, the kind cousin and guardian who had made a home for Tom after he left school. They started from London by way of Oxford and Blenheim Palace, where they met with a reverse. In spite of a handsome bribe of nineteen shillings to the servants word was sent them from Sarah Duchess of Marlborough, who was in residence, that they should not be admitted to the Palace. To add to this affront, which was inspired by no personal ill-will but by an habitual inclination to be disobliging, the inn at Woodstock charged them twenty shillings too much for stabling. They succeeded however in gaining admission to nearby Cornbury Park and Heythrop Hall: and, it appears, to Burley-on-the-Hill in Rutland, Burghley near Stamford, and to Kedleston and Sudbury in Derbyshire.

The early years of their married life were mostly spent at Thanet House in Great Russell Street, which they rented from Lady Margaret's father. Lord Thanet retained the use of an apartment in the house for so long as he lived, which was in fact another eleven years. There they set themselves up in considerable splendour. They kept fourteen indoor male and seven female servants, and ten stable servants. It is gratifying to know that Edward Jarrett was still in their employ as house steward at £140 a year. They spent large sums on improving the house, including twelve shillings 'to Mr. Southall for killing of Bugs'—Mr. Southall being later promoted to the permanent office of 'buggman'. More important items were to Gumley for looking-glasses, Paul Lamerie for plate, 'Mr. Vanstreten for cleaning pictures', and 'Mr. Gibs Architect for his design in the alteration of the house, his trouble and attendance in giving direct^{ns} to ye workmen, etc., & likewise his examination of the Workmen's Bills for the making of ye proper Abatements'. The last item in the accounts is of interest in showing that Coke was at this stage no more wedded to the exclusive Palladian style of architecture than his friend Lord Burlington, who the very same year was also employing the baroque Gibbs for alterations to Burlington House.

Ostensibly Thomas Coke passed his early manhood in leisure and indolence. In London balls and routs claimed most of his spare moments from gaming and cock-fighting; in the country the days were almost wholly devoted to 'hounds and cocks'. To be sure, as an hereditary Whig he affiliated himself to his chief, who was also his near neighbour in Norfolk, Sir Robert Walpole. As one with a large stake in the county and plenty of political influence it was incumbent upon him to assume his responsibilities by becoming a Member of Parliament. So without too much haste or enthusiasm he got himself elected for Norfolk in 1722. It was merely a matter of time before offices were thrust upon him. In 1726 he was made Serjeant-at-Arms in Ordinary, which entailed attendance upon the King's person, having the previous year been dubbed a Knight of the newly revived Order of the Bath. For someone of his breeding, splendid living and wealth, these honours were a step to further advancements in rank. In 1728 he was created Baron Lovel of Minster Lovel, a property embracing the picturesque monastic ruins on the banks of the Windrush in Oxfordshire, which had originally accrued to the Lord Chief Justice in James I's reign. To increase his vast private income he was given a reversionary grant of the lighthouse at Dungeness for thirty-one years, which in return for a rent to the Crown of £6 13s. 4d. brought him a penny a ton from every vessel which passed it. In 1733 he was made joint Postmaster-General at £1,000 a year, a sinecure which afforded the enjoyable privilege of perusing his friends' private letters as they passed through the Post Office. For these and other services of no very exacting sort he was in 1744, in accordance with a pledge made by his grateful friend Sir Robert Walpole, created Viscount Coke and Earl of Leicester.

The Cokes had been married on 2nd July, 1718. In February of the following year the illustrious doctor, Sir Hans Sloane, was paid five guineas for attending Lady Margaret during illness at Thanet House. Six months passed and her first and only child to survive was born. It was a son, and great was the jubilation of the young couple. The child was christened Edward. Every attention and every luxury were lavished upon him. The household account books speak loud and clear of the affection which was borne him by parents and servants alike. 'Mr. Neddy' he was called, and 'little Master', and often even 'tiny Master', for whom the most expensive toys in London were ordered. And what did this pampered son and heir, on whom his father and mother pinned their fondest hopes, become? As a baby he was pretty and engaging. As a boy sensitive and bright. As a youth wilful and rakish. As a man brutal, drunken and hopelessly debauched. Nearly all the later correspondence of Lord Leicester—we shall call him by this title now—refers to this overwhelming disappointment of his life, this tragedy which was to break him down into an embittered, lonely and despairing old man, and cause his ambitions to drop one by one into sourness and putrescence.

In vain the disillusioned parents looked for a remedy in marriage. Not until he was well within his twenty-eighth year would

Lord Coke consent to forego his independence. Unwisely the Leicesters produced—for their son was too indifferent to make his own choice—Lady Mary Campbell, a daughter of the 2nd Duke of Argyll. Nicknamed the 'Wild Cat' because of her dead white skin, albino hair, dark, sullen, fiery eyes and lack of eyebrows, Lady Mary was from the start as indifferent to the marriage as her suitor. She was well-read yet silly, romantic yet wrong-headed, and inflexibly determined upon self-martyrdom. At first the Duchess her mother was averse to the match because of 'Lord Leicester's notoriously violent and dissolute character', according to an intimate friend of the Campbell family.[1] The young man, spurred on at length by his parents to show some sort of interest in his bride-to-be, exercised his charm. He frequented the Duchess's tea-table, petted her cats and pugs and listened to her interminable stories. Lady Mary all the while sat in stony silence, looking upon her lover with unconcealed disdain. Her attitude was—to her ultimate cost—not disregarded by Lord Coke who at the time feigned total unconcern. The strange wooing being brought to an end the ill-assorted pair were united in 1747, she with loathing in her heart and he with revenge in his.

Lord Coke left his wife on his wedding night, resolutely declining to consummate the marriage. Instead he returned to his boon companions of the tavern, where he thenceforth spent the better part of the twenty-four hours of each day drinking and gaming. Lady Mary, who had asked for what she certainly got, was nevertheless gravely offended. 'She objects,' Horace Walpole wrote at the time, 'his loving none of her sex but the four queens in a pack of cards.' To her bitter chagrin her husband added insult to injury by addressing her whenever they did meet in public as 'My love! my life! my angel!' At first Lady Mary pretended to appear unmoved by his extraordinary conduct. Her father-in-law on the contrary was incensed against his son. He referred to him as 'this thoughtless Beast', deplored his 'brutish behaviour' and warmly espoused Lady Mary's cause. Piteously he besought his son by threats and then cajolery to behave as a husband should. But when Lord Coke made a half-hearted show of relenting, Lady Mary, exasperated beyond all bounds, refused to have him back. Lord Leicester in his extremity then took against her. Her refusal to cohabit with her husband was, he declared righteously, 'contrary to the laws of God and man'. One day while she was entertaining friends he arrived at her house, roundly abused her before the assembled company and raved like a lunatic. Lord Coke who

[1] Lady Louisa Stuart, *Some Account of John Duke of Argyll and His Family*, 1827.

accompanied his father announced that she must travel down to Holkham instantly where he 'would make her as miserable as he could'. Father and son combined to break her spirit; but this was easier said than done. They encouraged the servants to be rude to her and only laughed when they spoke of 'Our Virgin Mary'. The more the Cokes bullied the more obstinate she became. When Lord Coke besought her to be reconciled, she replied: 'There may be some things perhaps which one ought to do, but this I will not do!' Lord Leicester informed her that 'she was a piece of useless Lumber, fit only to be locked up in the garrat out of the way', a threat which he put into instant execution. For twelve months she was confined to an upper floor room of the Family Wing and not allowed to communicate with the outside world. Bent upon suffering as a means of ultimately attracting attention to herself, she declined to eat and made herself ill. Lord Leicester would not send for a doctor and declared her illness to be 'all damned affectation'. The Duchess of Argyll, alarmed by her daughter's silence, drove down to Holkham and was repulsed from the door. On her return to London she obtained a writ of Habeas Corpus. Lady Mary was accordingly released under a threat of criminal proceedings being taken against the Cokes. She thereupon applied for a divorce.

Scandal now broke over society in full fury. The injured wife arrived at the court carefully dressed in rags in order to enlist as much public sympathy as possible. The crowd of people assembled to see her was so great that the windows of her sedan chair were broken by their pressure. To crown her vexation her husband stood at the door. With diabolical cunning he had considered how best to humiliate her. He darted forward as though to protect her from the mob, and with the sweetest smile, exclaimed so that all might overhear, 'My dearest love, take care and do not hurt yourself!' The consequence of these dulcet words was that Lady Mary failed to substantiate her case of ill-usage from Lord Coke's hands. Her petition for a divorce was dismissed. She was merely allowed a judicial separation and ordered by the Court to live with her mother near Richmond.

The tragi-comedy was all but over. Still Lord Leicester was no nearer getting a grandson, which was all that he had now set his heart upon. There was no divorce and no longer the vestige of a hope of a reconciliation. Meanwhile Lord Coke drifted still further into dissipation, which turned to disease. Pathetically the father watched his condition from a distance. In 1750 he believed he detected a sign of improvement in his son's health, and wrote to a friend: 'so that Kennell of Bitches [meaning the Duchess and her daughter] who expect his death, will be disappointed, if he will be prudent enough, and not relapse into his idle courses of drinking.' But relapse he did and the kennel of bitches was satisfied. Mercifully Lord Coke died in 1753. His disconsolate parents continued to lead their solitary existence in the splendour of the Holkham they were creating—for what? All hopes of an heir were gone. The purpose of their brave efforts was extinguished. Gallantly Lord Leicester protested that his wife's unhappiness was the chief cause of his distress. 'Our time which is spared from Vertu is spent on Whist,' he wrote sadly.

There are portraits of Lord Coke and Lady Mary at Holkham, but rightly they are given little prominence. The almost full-face pastel of him by Rosalba is handsome and debonair. It is of a youth with an intelligent brow. It does not entirely belie the pathetic tribute which his mother had carved upon his memorial tablet—she did not dare inscribe the words before her husband was dead—'distinguished in two Parliaments by a steady conception, strong Memory and a most pcircing judgment.' Lady Leicester's touching hyperbole is not however borne out by a later full-length oil of her son by Andrea Casali. Here a receding chin, now much in evidence, gives him a slightly idiotic look. The artist has made him point to a background of the Holkham Hall which he was never to inherit. Lady Mary's small pastel is the portrait of a pretentious, simpering, affected miss; the long gauzy black veil which she has draped over her hair is typical of those romantic poses[1] which were to madden her friends until the day of her death at the advanced age of eighty-five.

There is little doubt that Lord Leicester's character deteriorated with adversity and self-indulgence. Mrs. Stirling[2] considered it on the whole inestimable. 'He inherited,' she wrote, 'in no small measure the less pleasing qualities of the Lord Chief Justice, notably Sir Edward's imperious spirit, acerbity and harshness of temper.' It must be confessed that his relations with his son and daughter-in-law confirm this unfavourable indictment. Lack of an heir and the utter dissolution of Edward Coke were not the sole causes of these shortcomings. Heavy drinking was another contributory factor. It was indeed the besetting weakness of his generation; and he was in no way singular in giving way to it. Unlike William Kent, whose naturally cheerful disposition was merely enhanced by a liberal application of the bottle, Lord

---

[1] Another pose was as the player of a theorbo or base lute, higher than herself, in a portrait by Allan Ramsay, now at Mountstuart.

[2] A. M. W. Stirling, *Coke of Norfolk*, 1908. Chapter II, entitled 'Thomas Coke and the Building of Holkham'.

Leicester was made choleric and quarrelsome. He could not bear his friends not to join with him in a drinking bout, and grew fractious when they declined. George Dodington in a letter to Henry Fox of 10th June, 1757, mentioned what must have been a recurrent experience. 'When we parted, I went to carry Lord Leicester to Ken-wood, who kept us drinking there till nine.' He was lucky to get away so early. Two years later when the Earl was sixty-three he became involved in a violent quarrel which actually was not caused by his intoxication. A neighbour, Colonel George Townshend,[1] accused him of having spoken disparagingly of the Militia Bill which the Colonel had piloted through Parliament. For once Lord Leicester, it seems, was more sinned against than sinning. The Colonel while in liquor himself dispatched a challenge to fight, which the Earl who was thirty years his senior declined in a sober yet dignified reply. His letter, rambling and diffuse though it was, did not lack sense or humour. 'It would grieve you much,' he wrote after a deal of irrelevant self-justification over coverts and the killing of foxes, 'if, unexplained, things were to be carried to extremity, where you could get no honour by vanquishing a man older than your Father and grown quite unwieldy and unfit for such encounters by a long lazy and inactive life and entire disuse of sword or file, not having for this twenty years wore a sword that could be of any use, and for a pistol I never could hit a barn door with a gun, so it would be difficult for me to choose weapons; and I think to begin to turn duellist in my grand climacterick would be a greater proof of indiscreet rashness than true courage, especially with an officer who is in the prime of his years and military exercise. . . .' Lord Leicester's candour had always been disarming, and by gently laughing at himself he evidently turned aside the younger man's wrath without injuring his own self-pride.

Passionate he had always been, but underneath warm-hearted and generous. His gifts of money were constant and unsolicited. The account books abound in entries such as 'For a gentleman of decay'd Fortune £1', 'For a poor man to keep him out of gaol 5 guineas', to prisoners at Derby, the galley-slaves at Marseilles and to a poor 'Man y^t bro^t home ye Lyon Dogg'. With his tenants he was popular because of his justice and liberality. And if his acquaintances found him imperious—he once declined, although Member of Parliament for the county of Norfolk, to dance with the Sheriff's pretty wife at the Norwich assembly—his intimates like the Dukes of Devonshire, Newcastle and Grafton were fond

---

[1] Later 4th Viscount and 1st Marquess Townshend, 1724–1807.

MARGARET TUFTON, COUNTESS OF LEICESTER
Portrait by A. Casali
Reproduced by permission of the Earl of Leicester

LADY MARY COKE
Portrait by Rosalba
*Reproduced by permission of
the Earl of Leicester*

EDWARD,
VISCOUNT COKE
Portrait by Rosalba
*Reproduced by permission of
the Earl of Leicester*

of him. The latter he nicknamed 'Baldassar' and the 'Gran Cor-
teggiano'. The Duke once began a letter to him 'My Angel Trott'
and even addressed it, surely in his cups, to 'Trott, Holkham'.
'The fat, laughing, joking peer' Admiral Boscawen called him,
who would sit up half the night gambling with his equals in rank
and riches—in the year 1723 for instance he won £2,445 and only
lost £146 by this means. Lord Hervey once described him as 'the
darling idol of the professed wits of this good city, tout ridicule
qu'il est'. He set out to be something of a wit himself in the making
of epigrams and brilliant conversation. But if he earned Swift's
commendation as the inventor of the word 'flam' to describe the
little love verses then in vogue, Horace Walpole declared that the
younger generation deemed his bon-mots antiquated and the silly
old fellow superannuated.

It is not however by his ephemeral witticisms, nor by his tantrums any more than it is, alas, by his generous deeds that Lord
Leicester will be remembered. It is amazing how quickly the
character of the creative man is forgotten, whereas that of the man
of action is minutely remembered as though it alone affected the
lives of others and shaped the destiny of posterity. Art historians
seldom bother themselves unduly whether painters or sculptors,
and still less whether architects and the makers of gardens and
landscape were good or bad, poetic or matter-of-fact men. As it
happens their creations are largely governed by their natures. The
earthy side of Lord Leicester's nature has been sufficiently
stressed, and the effect it had upon the creation of Holkham may
in due course become apparent. It determined the robust, commonsense, enduring quality of the great house's structure, about which
there is nothing finical or weak. The scholarly and the artistic side
of the man thereupon imposed itself upon this solid foundation.
When we consider the extrovert, boisterous, rough material—for
the boy Tom Coke, charming and frank as he then was, seemed
indistinguishable from the foolish sport addicts of his class and
generation—out of which the ardent bibliophile and art collector
was fashioned, we must give credit to Dr. Hobart. This learned
pedagogue was remarkably adept as a teacher. He may have
frowned upon gaming and cock-fighting, but he was sensible
enough not positively to discourage them. That would have been a
disastrous pitfall, but one into which the majority of pedagogues
tumble headlong. By some miraculous tutorial gift he succeeded
in inspiring his pupil with a sense of the fun of scholarship. The
pursuit of rare books and manuscripts he made as thrilling as the
hunt of a fox. Tom Coke's innate love of the chase instantly

responded; and we have already seen what some of his game amounted to. He quickly took to the classics for their own sakes, absorbed them and quoted them at length upon appropriate occasions. A Norfolk neighbour recorded how, after a long day's hunting the fox at Holkham, 'We often passed the Evening in reading the Ancient Authors: when the beauty of the language, the strength, the Justice of Their thoughts for ever glowing with a noble spirit of Liberty, made us forget not only the Pains, but the pleasures of the Day.' The bucolic picture thus brought to our eyes is civilized and sympathetic.

Dr. Hobart's intelligence was further evinced by his enlisting the services of another scholar to instruct the boy Tom Coke at an early stage of their travels. Domenico Ferrari's services are a little ambiguous. He was a Neapolitan of ancient lineage whom Coke is said to have befriended before they became intimate. His name is first mentioned in company with Dr. Hobart's in a letter from Tom to his grandfather from Angers in 1713. Shortly afterwards he was sent to England, but reappeared in Paris in 1718 as tutor to Tom's young brother Neddy. Lord Leicester certainly had a high opinion of him, and from 1737 onwards allowed him a salary of £100 as librarian at Holkham. When Ferrari died in 1744, so the *Gentleman's Magazine* stated by way of obituary notice, 'We hear that his body being opened, a large Stone the size of a Turkey's egg was extracted and that he left a valuable library to the Earl.'

Lord Leicester's collection of rare books and manuscripts continued to grow apace after his return to England. In 1719 he managed to buy from Italy the celebrated note-book of Leonardo da Vinci. In 1721 two-thirds of his Greek manuscripts were acquired through the agency of Consul Smith in Venice. His bookish interests were not confined to collecting. In 1723 he edited and published at his own expense in Florence the manuscript—it amounted to two volumes—of a Scot, Thomas Dempster, who had died a hundred years before; he entitled it 'De Etruria Regali', and supplied it with splendid copper plates of Etruscan urns and other finds. The result of the book's publication was to launch an Etruscomania which swept across Italy for many years to come.

His collection of pictures and statuary was hardly less valuable, if rather less reflective of his informed taste. He was by no means the only rich milord to skim the cream of those continental old masters which happened to come on the market. His purchases were certainly more selective than those of the majority of the English gentry. Rubens's Holy Family, Vandyke's Comte d'Aremberg, a pair of Claudes bought in 1750 out of Cardinal Albani's

bedroom, Bastiano de Sangallo's contemporary copy of Michelangelo's cartoon for the Council Chamber in Florence, and
Richard Wilson's views of Tivoli (no longer at Holkham) which
he commissioned from the artist, would be outstanding treasures
in any public collection. The sculpture of Holkham contains a
number of original works of greater rarity than anything hitherto
brought to an English country house. There is the figure of Diana
(the head and some fingers added by Camillo Rusconi), for the
exportation of which from the Papal States Leicester narrowly
escaped imprisonment: the Venus and Meleager bought from the
merchant, Belisario Amedei, in the Piazza Navona: the Faun
crowned with vine leaves, bought from Cardinal Albani: the bust
of Thucydides, accounted the earliest true portrait in Greek art:
the bust of Lucius Verus: and the seraphic head of Aphrodite
from the pedimental group of the Parthenon. Indeed, Matthew
Brettingham junior, having been sent to Italy in 1747—he had
previously fulfilled the same service for Sir Robert Walpole—
specially to look for statuary for the Sculpture Gallery, brought
home in 1754 in a single haul eleven statues, eight busts, a relief
and some mosaic slabs of varying merit, it is true. Works by the
baroque sculptors Algardi and Monaldi were likewise purchased.
These pieces of modern sculpture have unfortunately disappeared.
Lord Leicester also commissioned sculpture from contemporary
artists—Guelfi (certainly for repairs to some of his antiques, if not
for original work), Scheemakers, Rysbrack and Roubiliac, who
made a bust of the Lord Chief Justice which he presented to
Trinity College, Cambridge, and at least a pair of himself and
Lady Leicester which repose upon their tomb in Tittleshall
Church.[1] He was ever ready to patronize worth-while projects,
whether it meant commissioning a bust for a university college by
an artist unknown to him; or helping to found the Society of
Dilettanti. He would lend, when requested, his rare manuscripts
and books to accredited scholars—perhaps the most trusting and
generous action of a bibliophile. He would subscribe to the publication of expensive folios on architecture, like Leoni's *Palladio*
and Campbell's *Vitruvius Britannicus*. Musicians found in him
instant response to appeals for help. He was a regular subscriber
to Handel's operas and to the Royal Academy of Music. He paid
for the lessons of young musicians who could not afford them as
the following entries in his Domestic Accounts show—'Paid Mr.
Cowper the half of what he is to have for teaching the Boy

---

[1] Roubiliac apparently did a bust of Lord Leicester in a Roman toga. The original in plaster
is lost, but a marble copy made by Chantrey survives.

Robinson to blow the streight horn,' and 'To Anthony for teaching Phil Border to play upon the ffrench horn.'

iii. The Conception of Holkham

Lord Leicester (as plain Mr. Thomas Coke) had returned from the grand tour, come of age and married in the early summer of 1718. He brought with him from the Continent crates of rare books, pictures, statuary and every variety of works of art. He also brought with him drawings, prints and memories of the best architecture Italy had to offer, as well as a knowledge and theory of practical building. The financial muddles that had followed upon his father's death were sorted out; the debts settled; the estates made to pay handsomely; and he was in consequence extremely rich.

There is no written evidence but plenty of room for conjecture that during his grand tour the youth had in mind the rebuilding of his ancestral seat at Holkham, in order to assemble in it the treasures he was acquiring in such vast quantities. On the other hand there exist plans and drawings for the proposed new Holkham which date from fairly soon after his marriage. They make it plain that both house and grounds were of his conception, albeit the issue of several master minds. Why, we may well ask, did he not begin upon his life's task in the first flush of youth, and before the memories of Italian architecture began to fade? In the first place, being an idealist and ambitious to raise but one monument that should be perfect, he saw no particular reason for hurry, and wanted, before embarking, to be satisfied with the exact form it was to take. In the second place, less than five years after his marriage he was seriously in debt again, owing to reckless gambling in South Sea stock, which resulted in debts of over £70,000. These reverses delayed building operations at Holkham for a further six years or more.

The landscaping of the park, however, did not have to wait so long. Unspecified work upon the grounds was in progress as early as 1720. In 1722 Leicester reclaimed four hundred acres of marsh from the North Sea. In August of the following year he paid a visit to Lord Bathurst at Cirencester, which may have supplied some ideas for the layout of the grounds at Holkham. From 1727 onwards he was buying seeds and trees from his neighbours' gardeners at Wolterton, Blickling, Felbrigg, Oxburgh and Houghton (Sir Robert Walpole even making him a present of some trees).

In 1729 and '30 the kitchen garden precinct was being built, the ground before the future south front of the house levelled and the lake dug. Rapidly Holkham heath was being enclosed and turned to parkland of nearly a thousand acres. The great obelisk, eighty feet high, was already raised on its mound in the ilex grove. The facing stone had been fetched all the way from Bristol by sea to Wells by four men and fastened with iron cramps to a brick core cemented with liquid mortar. Originally to Kent's design the obelisk was altered to the plan of an equilateral triangle by Matthew Brettingham, who claimed that his changes received Lord Burlington's approval. The finished thing has a rather more acute apex than that shown in Kent's sketch, against which he scribbled queries whether the rock work should 'project beyond the plain part of the dado or no' (it does), and if the dado were cut away, whether the structure would be weakened. The obelisk is in fact the punctuating feature round which the whole of Lord Leicester's park was subsequently fashioned and upon which the new house was to be centred. Eight vistas were made to open from it in different directions: one due north to the new house; a second due south to a triumphal arch; a third north-west towards the old parish church on a steep wooded hill; a fourth south-west to the Temple; a fifth east to the town of Wells; and the remainder to distant plantations. Arthur Young who in 1767 stood at the obelisk site was loud in praise of the superb effects afforded by the vistas, which at that date were no longer to the taste of his generation. 'But,' he conceded, 'such a genius as Lord Leicester might be allowed to deviate from the fashion in favour of beauty and propriety.'

The formal scheme brought about by Lord Leicester was very much in the conservative manner of Lord Bathurst's planting. It is not a little strange therefore that only six or seven years later (on 30th December, 1736, to be precise) Leicester was writing to Lord Burlington: 'to think of those damned dull walks at Jo. Windhams, those cold and insipid straight walks which would make the Signor sick, which even Mr. Pope himself could not by description enliven . . .' words which might be taken to suggest unqualified disapproval of his own recent layout in that style. Little of it remained for more than a few years apart from the main north to south axis, because Capability Brown was called upon by Leicester's widow, even before Arthur Young's visit, to give the park at Holkham a new look, namely some informal spinneys and a serpentine twist to the lake. Capability was paid at the rate of 50 guineas a year to bring these amendments into effect.

The Triumphal Arch, totally rusticated in bold blocks formed by smooth flints on brick in a kind of frost-work pattern, is in Kent's most Vanbrughian manner, and would have been more effective still if the pyramids over the side arches had been carried out according to the architect's intention. The Temple too is probably to Kent's design, being an adaptation of Burlington's Chiswick orangery, which had been based on Palladio's San Francesco della Vigna façade of half pediments broken by the complete pediment of a towering frontispiece. The theme evidently impressed Kent who, while in Venice, made a sketch of the church in his journal. The octagonal dome introduced was taken from that of Chiswick house, and the Doric portico from de Chambray's *Parallèle de l'Architecture*, in which it is given as a design by Pirro Ligorio from an ancient fragment found at Albano. The deeply projecting cornice much impressed Lord Burlington who pronounced the portico the best piece of work executed in his time. Great trouble was taken over the Temple, the stone being fetched from Bristol and the mason from London in 1731. If the younger Brettingham's words[1] relating to Kent are to be trusted the Obelisk, the Arch, the Temple and in addition the Seat on the Mount, the Stone Bridge and other ornamental park buildings now destroyed, were all taken from Kent's sketches but considerably altered in the execution.

The Earl's contemporaries were by no means all impressed by the new park layout. Sir Thomas Robinson thought the site chosen deplorable. The owner, he wrote in 1731 to Lord Carlisle, 'has no other temptation than that his ancestors lived there, and having [been] left a large estate round an exceeding bad old house, for his water is to [be] brought, his plantations but just begun, and a house to be built, and not fifty pounds worth of wood within two miles of the place . . . His successors might reap an advantage, but life is too short for the first generation to receive much benefit, where there are so many disadvantages from nature, and the whole to be compassed only by art, time, and expense.' And Lord Hervey the same year observed, 'It is at present a most unpleasant place; but he comforts himself with a park in embryo, and a Burlington-house with four pavilions on paper.' Lord Leicester was himself only too well aware of the disadvantages of the terrain, which he was resolved to overcome, and which his optimism and vision accomplished; so it was with justifiable pride that he eventually raised over his front door a tablet, recording: 'This seat, on an open barren estate, was planned, planted, built, decorated, and

---

[1] *The Plans, Elevations and Sections of Holkham*, 2nd Edition, 1773.

inhabited the middle of the XVIIIth century by Th^{os} Coke, Earl of Leicester.'

Not until 1734 were the foundations of the new Holkham Hall dug. If Lord Hervey, who was no particular friend of Lord Leicester, knew well in advance the shape the house was to assume, it is clear that the project had been widely discussed among the Earl's intimates. 'A Burlington-house with four pavilions' is perhaps a vague, but not wholly inaccurate prognosis of what Holkham turned out to be. Burlington House, lately rebuilt, boasted two wings, it is true; Chiswick Villa, now on the point of being finished, had none. Yet the Burlington affinities with Holkham are to be sought in the latter house, for the very reason that Chiswick was as much Lord Burlington's invention as Burlington House was Palladio's. In other words the design of Holkham conceived by Lord Leicester, sketched on paper by William Kent and carried out by Matthew Brettingham the elder, son of a Norwich bricklayer, was chiefly inspired throughout its growth by Lord Burlington, as we shall shortly see.

The younger Matthew Brettingham in a second edition, published with the addition of a text in 1773, of his father's 'The Plans, Elevations and Sections of Holkham' (1761) stated that the general idea of a centre block and wings was first suggested by Palladio's unfinished Villa Trissino at Meledo, and then by his plan for Leonardo Mocenigo's villa on the Brenta. The Villa Trissino design with two pavilions attached by long curved colonnades was, Brettingham explained, found 'not to answer the situation or admit of offices adequate to the Earl's family and fortunes', and so was dropped in favour of the Villa Mocenigo plan, which indeed had four instead of two pavilions connected to the centre block by curved colonnades. But this plan was also dropped when Leicester with his passion for what he called 'commodiousness' found the curved colonnades an awkward and wasteful arrangement. He finally settled for four pavilions emerging straight from the four corners of the main block. In other words only in regard to its four pavilions can Holkham be said to derive indirectly from Palladio, since there were already in existence English houses with two, notably Burlington House and neighbouring Houghton Hall, both by Colen Campbell.

'The general idea,' the younger Brettingham explains, 'was first struck out by the Earls of Leicester and Burlington, assisted by Mr. W. Kent.' Brettingham has been accused, a little unjustly, ever since Horace Walpole first expostulated in writing, of claiming too much credit for the design of Holkham to his father. It is objected that the plans and elevations which the elder Brettingham published and attributed to himself were really Kent's. But as his son asserted with some justification, 'in the space of time which passed from the commencement of this villa, so many alterations indeed took place, that very few of the original thoughts remained untouched'; and moreover the final working plans and drawings were undeniably the father's. 'The care of proportioning the parts at large,' the son continued with splendid loyalty to his father's memory, 'and the detail of each member of the building in particular, was committed by the Earl of Leicester to the superintendence of his own architect, the late Mr. Matthew Brettingham of Norwich . . . who was allowed to equal, if not excel, all the professors of his time.' For these services the elder Brettingham was given a room in the house and a salary of a mere £50 a year until the Earl's death when it was doubled by the Countess. The fact is that the Brettinghams, whose status throughout their long Holkham association was kept thoroughly subservient so as to incite in them understandable resentment against the socially acceptable Kent, were a little too much inclined to overlook the importance of those 'original thoughts'.

We do not know when Leicester and Burlington first became friends. The probability is that as boys they did not know each other personally, although they would have known about each other. It is now fairly certain that the course of their grand tours never once coincided. Burlington must notwithstanding have learned a good deal about Tom Coke's activities when he met Kent for the first time in Rome in November of 1714. Probably they became acquainted in London before Burlington left for his second visit to Italy in 1719. Soon afterwards they were certainly often together. On 4th May, 1721, the younger man hired a horse to take him to Lord Burlington's ball at Chiswick and back to London again the next morning. Thereafter visits to Chiswick were frequent, and ideas upon landscape layout and architecture discussed and pooled. In the 1730s the two peers and William Kent were very intimate, to judge from the letters which passed to and fro. 'No compliments from me to Signor Cazzo vestito,' Leicester wrote to Burlington coarsely, 'who would not come to see me tho' I had Cherry Brandy from France on purpose for him wch he shall pay for.' Small wonder perhaps that the prim Burlington endorsed this effusion with the laconic words: 'Lᵈ Lovel not much in it.' The Signor makes several mentions of Lord Lovel, as Leicester then was, in his letters to Burlington. 'Now I am a going to paint a cieling for Lord Lovell here on cloth' is one reference,

and another: 'My Lord Lovell desires his service to you and this
day goes to Chiswick with Marchese Sacchette, my Lord told him
Michelangelo era un ignorante in Arch^{re}'—a somewhat startling
pronouncement to be directed at an erudite Italian visitor.

It is not difficult to believe that Leicester was about as well
versed in the science of building as Burlington. We have seen how
while abroad he took lessons in architecture from Signor Giacomo.
His library of architectural books even exceeded Burlington's in
their number and variety. The elder Brettingham[1] acknowledged
that 'the study of architecture became his chief amusement and
delight, during the greatest part of his life', and that 'his delight
and passion for architecture was such' that he intended to publish
a book of designs of houses, large and small. 'This was,' he
boasted, 'our joint study and amusement in the country, and the
drawings for this work have been made by me near twenty years.'
The younger Brettingham, who knew him no less well than the
father, wrote that his patron 'continued with uncommon diligence
to improve and elucidate the first sketches of the plans and elevations concerted with the Earl of Burlington and Mr. Kent; and in
this he was guided by those great luminaries of architecture,
Palladio and Inigo Jones.' His learning in the science was widely
recognized among the cognoscenti. A tablet in the back regions of
Coleshill House put up by the owner about 1735 recorded that
alterations to this Jonesian masterpiece had been made by the two
most eminent architects of their age, namely the Earls of Burlington and Leicester. After the deaths of Kent and Burlington
Leicester's reputation was unassailable. In 1748 he was invited to
take over the architecture of Euston Hall in Suffolk begun by Kent
for his friend the Duke of Grafton. In 1756 young Robert Adam
studying architecture in Rome with a view to launching himself in
a London practice, was warned that 'Lord Leicester is the Burlington of the times; that his condemnation or approbation is
sufficient either to raise a man in my way or knock him in the
head. . . .'[2]

At Holkham Lord Leicester left not the smallest detail to be
designed by his clerk of the works without first giving it his own
approval. The younger Brettingham acknowledged that his lordship 'co-operated not only in the choice and appropriation of every
member and ornament, before any part was given to the workmen
for execution'. If he approved every detail before it was carried
out then the elder Brettingham sadly neglected his duty of

---

[1] In the Preface to the first edition (1761) of the *Plans . . . of Holkham*.
[2] *Robert Adam and his Circle*, John Fleming, 1962.

supervision. Recent restorations have revealed a shocking amount of slipshod workmanship at Holkham, notably in the south portico where only one out of a hundred brackets was found to be intact. A photograph illustrates that the core of a random bracket was a roughly hewn block of wood secured by a single eight-inch nail driven into a mass of plaster above it. The block was studded like a porcupine with lesser nails upon which the outline of a bracket was built up in plaster reinforced with pieces of stick and string. No wonder that Leicester had complaints to make about the workmen; no wonder he protested to the Duke of Newcastle that he dared not leave Holkham, because he must see things finished 'under my own eye which alone I can trust'. Perhaps after all he was not being over querulous when towards the end of his life he grumbled to the younger Brettingham, 'Your father has built a house more to look at than to live in, for all the chimnies smoke and cannot be cured.'

By 1733 heavy expenses were being incurred by the brick kiln set up in the grounds. Lord Leicester, regardless of the fact that Norfolk was not a stone county, only decided that brick should be the material for his house because Vitruvius recommended it for villas. A brick earth at Burnham Norton on the estate turned out to be durable and to acquire more or less the colour of seasoned Bath stone. It so happened that one original Roman brick, which had been accidentally packed in a crate containing an ancient statue sent from Italy, exactly corresponded in texture with those being manufactured at Burnham Norton. Lord Leicester was delighted with this confirmation of his choice of material. He took the greatest care that the bricks, of which thirty different scantlings were used for the various joints and angles of the 'bird's mouth' rustication of the window lintels, sills, voussoirs and keys in the basement alone, were first moulded before baking. The same infinite care was taken in the preparation of the mortar. Having been ground between a pair of large millstones to make it particularly fine it was poured in a liquid state upon every course of the bricks. When in 1734 the foundations of the house were being dug it was said that as many bricks were laid below ground as would appear above. No timber was allowed below the level of the soil. Certainly no parts of the main walls were laid upon woodwork which might perish. Thus the strength of the whole fabric was hardly dependent upon timber. Arches and counter-arches were constructed to take the weight and thrust of the walls, and floor girders were not laid until the roof of the main part of the house had been raised. This did not take place until 1749. Nevertheless, as soon as the new house was partially habitable the Leicesters came to live in it; by 1741 they were comfortably installed in the south-west, or Family Wing.

Dr. Wittkower has established fairly conclusively that the manner in which the four Holkham pavilions are attached to the main block of the house has a precedent in Burlington's cunning device for linking the old house at Chiswick with his new villa. This device was later amplified by Burlington in the four wings which he added to his brother-in-law Lord Bruce's house at Tottenham Park in Savernake Forest.[1] The Tottenham scheme, carried out in the early 1730s, will then have been the model for Holkham. Lord Leicester had the opportunity of studying it on the site when he stayed with Lord Bruce on a journey to Bath in October of 1734. Its peculiarity lay in a short corridor of one bay forming the junction from house to pavilion; and in the division of each pavilion into three blocks under pediments, of which the central and higher pediment was split. This triple block theme which at Holkham results in an achievement of quite unwonted beauty was evidently much favoured by Burlington, for he also carried it out on a house at the north end of Savile Row (demolished in 1935). The split pediment was, he knew, regarded by Palladio as an ancient domestic feature.

In other respects the influence of Lord Burlington's architecture, particularly Chiswick House, is the more apparent the more one looks at both the exterior and the interior of Holkham. To take the exterior first: the centre block consists, as at Chiswick, of a main floor, or *piano nobile*, over a basement, without an attic or mezzanine floor. It belongs in fact to the villa type of English country house, notwithstanding its size which is that of a palace, in contrast with Houghton, for example, which has prominent mezzanine and attic storeys. The south portico of six Corinthian columns over a rusticated base follows very closely that of Chiswick. And the pattern of repeated Venetian windows within relieving arches on the north front is a deliberate transcript of the garden front of Chiswick.

Neither the south nor the north front was carried out exactly as Kent designed it, although the finished elevations are basically the same as those of his sketches. Whether they were altered by Leicester alone, or in consultation with Kent and Burlington there is now no means of telling. For instance, Kent intended that 'Gibbs' surrounds, or blocks, should be given to the pedimented windows, and relieving arches to the Venetian windows of the

[1] The wings have gone and the house was rebuilt in the nineteenth century.

towers. He meant the whole south front, including the towers, to be of rusticated stone, and the frieze to be adorned with heavy swags. He designed a perron to descend from the portico to the grass; one version was curved, the alternative in single flight, which at the landing branched at right angles into two arms—in other words somewhat after the Chiswick model. It seems however that no perron was ever actually constructed. The omission seriously detracts from the beauty as well as purpose of the portico and was deplored in 1767 by Arthur Young who wrote: 'When you advance near, you find no entrance to the house; there are no stairs up to the portico.' Young nevertheless found the south front to be 'as beautiful, light, airy (excuse tautology) and elegant a building as can be viewed'. Lightness and airiness are not in our eyes conspicuous qualities of Holkham, but we must remember that when the original sash windows were intact—their bars of burnished gold[1] glittering in the sunlight against the yellow brick background—the impression conveyed was very different. Now the gaping plate-glass voids tend to over-accentuate Holkham's thick-set stolidity, that characteristic of early-Georgian houses, which is reflective of the sturdy fibre of the squires who built and lived in them.

The north front did not please Young as much as the other although he considered it to be 'by far more of a piece with the wings', a point of view difficult to appreciate. This front remains (apart from the Victorian addition of the porte-cochère) pretty well as Kent's final drawing showed it. Originally he wanted the centrepiece and two towers to be wholly rusticated and their central Venetian windows to be given heavy Gibbsian voussoirs. The result would have been much too concentrated and rich, and the delicate recessions produced by the shallow relieving arches to the Venetian windows would have been largely thrown away.

One is seldom able to judge a great work of architecture of the distant past as its creator intended or even as he left it. The exterior of Holkham has been altered in two hundred years and the surroundings changed, but not so drastically that we cannot assess the house's wonderful merits. The basic structure is still absolutely intact. Later accretions are remarkably few. With a sweep of the hand the porte-cochère of the north front and the nineteenth-century terraces before the south front can easily be eliminated, so that we picture the deer once again grazing the rough grass right up to the portico and the windows of the basement. Only the fenestration needs to be restored by our imagina-

---

[1] A permanent burnisher was employed to keep the gilding in trim.

tion. And what do we have? From every viewpoint a consummate architectural achievement. I can think of no English country house with an exterior more purely and exquisitely architectural now that Coleshill, the acme of English classicism, has to the lasting discredit of our age been allowed to disappear off the face of the land. And the term *architectural*, as a quality and not as a woolly reference to buildings in general, needs clarification. I do not mean *architectonical*, that adjective with its tiresome technical flavour. I mean by the term *architectural* in this context something different from—I will not say beyond—beauty (the ultimate measure by which every work of art must come to be judged), something on the other hand which may even invest at certain moments of its long history the exclusively romantic, or irregular structure, just as a casual finger of sun- or moonlight may fortuitously touch the most commonplace scene with a sudden and evanescent magic, something even additional to beauty and regularity and indispensable to a truly monumental building. It is that justification of purpose, that meticulous solution of imponderable problems, that exactitude of balance, and that indefinable and accidental perfection which makes us gasp and cry aloud that the artist's powers can go no further in satisfying our sense of what is fitting. Holkham is not, as I have indicated, the most lovely English country house. To many people the material of which it is constructed is unsympathetic, and the surfaces appear grim and forbidding. But to the observer with a trained eye the mathematical precision of its every line and, without exaggeration, every brick, the balance of its every detail and the marvellous relation of voids to solids and of the smallest parts to the whole proclaim the years of careful thought which went into its conception and generation. The completeness of Holkham could no more have been brought about by several minds than the delicate mechanism of a clock by Jump or Vulliamy, although the culmination of centuries of experiment, could have been put together by several hands. Several minds, as we have seen, combined to propound the plan and design, but one co-ordinating mind directed them to finality. The genius of that mind lay in a willingness to glean ideas and motifs from past generations as well as from contemporaries. The scholarship and hedonism, the elegance and flamboyance, the delicacy and grossness of Thomas Coke are apparent in every contour of Holkham. There is nothing spiritual about the house. It is secular and pagan, classical and bucolic.

iv. The Creation of Holkham

On 20th December, 1736, Lord Leicester wrote from Holkham to Lord Burlington, 'I shall still wait on you with my Portfeüill, & make the Signor scold, for now we must think of the inside of the Rooms.' There is in his letter a tone of slight importunacy which is confirmed in a later sentence: 'Nothing but your goodness could have made you bear my Company at Bath.' Had Leicester then during a course of spa waters that autumn against the gout and the spleen—to say nothing of a disappointment in love which he did not hesitate to confide in his friend—again been badgering him for ideas on the decoration of his Norfolk palace? It is clear that he was still greatly dependent upon Burlington's advice and guiding hand, of which the marks are traceable in practically every part of the house. We can so well imagine the confabulations that must repeatedly have taken place at Holkham—Lord Burlington, aloof and stern, slim and upright, the Garter ribbon and star resplendent upon his breast, vouchsafing occasional opinions of considered import: Kent, large, voluble and merry, amplifying and illustrating them in his sketchbook with many an interspersed quip in the shape of a donkey or ostrich in the foreground: Leicester, heavily jowelled, ponderous and bluff, commenting upon them with approval or blowing them sky high with a coarse imprecation: and the elder Brettingham in the background, servile and resentful, yet watchful and quick to assimilate the opinions of his betters which he will assuredly turn to his own account one day, determined meanwhile to minimize the credit of his petted rival, the gifted amateur Kent who, he never tires of reminding others, lacks his professional training and shares his humble origin of birth. The son graciously acknowledged the rooms of the Family Wing to have been completed to the designs of Kent[1] 'without undergoing any material change'; which was tantamount to asserting that the decoration of no others was wholly his. But if not, the alterations are more likely to have been to Lord Leicester's dictation than to Matthew Brettingham the elder's.

The suite of state rooms is unparalleled in this country for splendour without ostentation. An extraordinary chastity not only of design but of decoration distinguishes them from others of the same period, and notably those at neighbouring Houghton, which are attributed to Kent. There the designs of walls and ceilings are more complex and the colour schemes more intricate. Here the

---

[1] The carver employed here for doorcases and woodwork was Marsden; the ceiling stuccoist Thomas Clark of Westminster; the carvers of marble chimneypieces Joseph Pickford and Thomas Carter.

unpainted ceilings are merely sub-divided into bare panels by flat ribs of the simplest moulds; and the walls when not hung with subdued red velvet or tapestry are painted a uniform ivory and gold. Sir William Chambers, whose cult of the simple was to some extent a protest against the exuberantly fussy patterns of his contemporaries the Adam brothers and James Wyatt, was moved to high encomiums of the Holkham rooms. 'With regard to the whole interior decoration,' he wrote,[1] 'it may certainly vie, in point either of magnificence, or taste, with anything now subsistent in England.' He found it bold, uncomplicated and pure. As for the proportion of the rooms, 'The Earl of Leicester's house at Holkham is a masterpiece in this respect, as well as in many others: the distribution of the plan in particular, deserves much commendation, and does great credit to the memory of Mr. Kent; it being exceedingly well contrived, both for state and convenience'. Arthur Young too emphasized the last quality. 'So convenient a house does not exist—so admirably adapted to the English way of living, and so ready to be applied to the grand or the comfortable stile of life.' This convenience, which 'renders it so different to all other great country houses', he attributed largely to the unseen staircases which discreetly descend from several hidden closets to the office in the basement. Curiously enough, although 'the English way of living' has changed today to an extent never contemplated by Chambers and Young, Holkham has proved itself 'very ready to be applied to the grand', by which is now interpreted use of the staterooms by the visiting public, and to 'the comfortable stile of life' for the present Lord Leicester in the detached and compact Family Wing, where the only modern change has been the insertion of a small kitchen in place of the vast and awkward barrack occupying the north-east pavilion at the furthermost end of the house.

The great Marble Hall occupies two-thirds of the width, one-third of the length and the whole height of the centre block. This latter dimension is taken full advantage of by the floor being at ground level. In other words entrance to the Marble Hall is by the front door in the basement. All the other staterooms which cluster round this huge and dominant apartment are on the raised first floor, or *piano nobile*. In consequence the hall's sheer height alone provides an extremely imposing introduction to the visitor to Holkham. Its novelty is undeniable. For the first time in the eighteenth century the traditional type of Inigo Jones hall, a cube with galleries supported by stout brackets, first used at the

[1] Sir W illiam Chambers, *Civil Architecture*, 1st edition, 1759.

Queen's House, Greenwich, and followed by Leoni at Moor Park and Campbell at Houghton, was abandoned. Matthew Brettingham junior affirms that the novel conception was solely Lord Leicester's, inspired by 'Palladio's example of a Basilica, or tribunal of justice, exhibited in his designs for Monsignor Barbaro's translation of Vitruvius'. A glance at the plan in the third book of Palladio's *Quattro Libri* must confirm the tenor of this statement. But Leicester can only have derived the general idea, namely of a rectangular basilica of nave and aisles separated by columns, an apsed end (even concealed stairs in the angles flanking the apse) and wall niches for statues of the gods, from Palladio. The proportions of Leicester's basilica are quite different and on a far smaller scale; moreover, the entrance end is devoid of columns and the apsed end, approached by nineteen steps, is so arranged that the columned aisles continue into it. Since Palladio omitted to give a section of his conjectural Roman basilica, Lord Leicester had to look elsewhere for ideas how to space his colonnade. What was more natural than that he should turn to his friend Lord Burlington's Assembly Rooms in York? From them he took the relation of two to one between the width of his aisles and the diameter of his columns.[1] Now Burlington's influence upon the Marble Hall at Holkham is still further to be found in the treatment of the apse, and inner *exedra*. The continuation of the screen of columns into the apse is a fulfilment of that treatment by Palladio of the sanctuaries of his Venetian churches, which Burlington greatly admired. Of San Giorgio Maggiore Burlington had written, 'behind the great altar there is an open inter-column: which discovers the choir, it ends in a semi-circle and is one of the most beautiful buildings in the world.' Now at last he was able to persuade Lord Leicester to introduce this dazzling effect. The intercolumn is there within the semicircle and it 'discovers', not of course a choir, but an exedra with a semi-dome coffered in the Chiswick manner—and a through view of the great saloon beyond. According to Kent's preliminary sketch of the Marble Hall an immense statue of Zeus was to be raised on a socle in, as it were, the place of the altar at the foot of the steps; but the arrangement was not carried out.

In their faithful quest of classical authority the trio of friends, Leicester, Burlington and Kent raked through still further sources. The fluted Ionic columns of the screen, the entablature moulds and frieze of swags suspended between naked boys, the candelabra

---

[1] A measurement which, inciden tally, Burlington had derived from Palladio's design for an Egyptian Hall.

HOLKHAM HALL, THE SOUTH FRONT

HOLKHAM HALL, THE TRIUMPHAL ARCH
From a design by William Kent

HOLKHAM HALL

HOLKHAM HALL

and rams' skulls, were copied in meticulous detail from Antoine Desgodetz's plates of the Temple of Fortuna Virilis in *Les Edifices Antiques de Rome*,[1] plates which were far more exact than Palladio's rough woodcuts. Desgodetz's book likewise supplied the recessed coffered panels of Rome's Pantheon dome for the ceiling coves in the Marble Hall, which were followed more or less accurately by Thomas Clark of Westminster, a craftsman 'bred in the school of Lord Burlington'. The pattern for the actual flat of the ceiling in thick, deep, carved ribs was taken from a design by either Inigo Jones or John Webb, in Lord Burlington's possession.

The magnificent columns of a variegated Derbyshire alabaster ranging in colour from a blood red to a livid green were carved by Joseph Pickford, a superlative statuary mason whose name crops up continually in the correspondence and accounts of Burlington and Kent. The former held him in great regard and when negotiating with Sir Hans Sloane over the purchase of the Inigo Jones gateway for Chiswick, offered to send Pickford to make a valuation. The latter employed him to carve several chimneypieces for No. 44 Berkeley Square as well as for Holkham. Pickford was likewise responsible for the band under the columns and the skirting of the Marble Hall in damson purple marble with the Vitruvian scroll and the Greek key pattern raised in white relief. These horizontal courses make a powerful contrast with the dado between them, which is of the same alabaster as the columns. Neither Kent in his preliminary sketch nor the Brettinghams in their plates illustrate the existing metal balustrade to the screen, which was put up by Messrs. Tapenden & Hanley for Lady Leicester as late as 1761. Kent in a detailed drawing had suggested turned marble balusters of waisted outline, which would have been more in character than the pretty fern and feather balustrade executed in wrought iron. But that the metal balustrade was also of Kent's design is borne out by the staircase balusters of his 44 Berkeley Square which are of the identical pattern, and which were incidentally reproduced by Flitcroft at Milton Hall near Peterborough.

If the Marble Hall at Holkham was derivative in several particulars, it was also extremely original. To Lord Leicester—with or without his friends—is due the brilliant expedient of giving height to the apartment by putting the floor on basement level and raising the colonnade on a deep plinth. Arthur Young was not a connoisseur and his observations on art were naturally not assound as those on his speciality, agriculture, which was the paramount

1 Published 1682.

purpose of his tours of country estates. But he often hit the nail with his blunt and commonsense pen directly on the head. To look from the landings between the alabaster columns mounted on their great alabaster plinth down 'into the area, it appears', he remarked, 'exactly like a bath'. And this is how 'it' does appear. So much marble and cold, white ceiling and walls, where the only furnishing is the antique statues and plaster casts arrested seemingly for all time in the alcoves, and the only ornament the classic moulds of frieze and ribs, calls for water to fill the great empty well and give some rippling movement and life to an overwhelmingly static composition.

A step into the Saloon and the contrast is immediate and comforting. Here we have the most ornate decoration of Holkham, otherwise remarkable for chastity in the design of its rooms. Even so the colour scheme of doorways and ceilings is confined to dulled white and gold relief, a combination noted by Mrs. Lybbe Powys during her visit in 1756. Then the room had only just been finished, 'many capital pictures standing there to be put up'. Two years previously Thomas Clark was still plastering the ceiling; and two years hence Lord Leicester himself would be dead. Warmth is imparted to this room by the wall hangings of crimson Genoese velvet, or cassoy as it was described at the time, the cut background now dimmed to gold, and by the gilt suite of Kent's armchairs upholstered in original green Genoa velvet; and richness too by the Composite entablature and foliage frieze adapted from Palladio, and by the diminishing octagonal panels of rosettes in the ceiling coves taken from Desgodetz's Temple of Peace. On either side of the great central door, from the pediment of which glowers a bust of Juno bought in Rome by the younger Brettingham, is a fireplace in Sicilian marble with bas-reliefs worked by Thomas Carter. Under two of four double oval pier-glasses with branched arms for candles are tables with antique mosaic tops found in Hadrian's Villa. On the walls hang the 'Continence of Scipio', a large historical composition painted in Rome by Giuseppe Chiari for Lord Leicester who, then a youth, was made to figure in the scene as the princely Allutius: Rubens's Flight into Egypt, wherein the Virgin Mary was described by Arthur Young as 'a female mountain': and the noble Vandyke equestrian portrait of the Comte d'Arembourg bought in Paris. The dimensions of the Saloon, forty-two by twenty-seven feet, are strangely arbitrary, and the resulting proportions are not entirely satisfactory.

The neighbouring Drawing-room likewise faces south across the garden and park towards the Obelisk. It too is hung with crimson cassoy of a lighter tone than the walls of the Saloon. Here the flat ceiling of ribs covered with fruits, foliage and masks at the intersections is from Inigo Jones's or Webb's design; Pickford's chimneypiece is taken from Inigo Jones, and the griffins of the frieze come from Desgodetz's plates of the Temple of Antoninus and Faustina. Nearly all the pictures in the room—the large Claude was bought by Leicester in Rome—are those listed by the Brettinghams. The table of *alabastro Palombaro* was bought in Rome by the younger Brettingham.

In the Sculpture Gallery which runs along the entire west front of the house we have overwhelming evidence of Lord Burlington's influence. With its great central Venetian window, apsed ends and two corner tribunes a magnified version of the Chiswick gallery has been brought about. Only here the shape of both tribunes is octagonal, as were those which Palladio planned for the Palazzo Thiene in Vicenza, the original theme of this particular fugue. Mrs. Powys called the Gallery 'the most superbly elegant I ever saw . . . painted a dead white, with ornaments of gilding', and Arthur Young, 'without exception, the most beautiful room I ever beheld'. The walls today are toned by time from white to coolest green. 'The ceiling,' Young went on, 'the only plain one in the house (they are all gilt fret work and mosaic) not accidentally; it appears to me a stroke of propriety and true taste.' Soberness is indeed the keynote of this exquisitely chaste apartment, where the only conscious ornament is in the Corinthian cornices (taken from Palladio) and in the lozenge panels of the semi-domes (taken from the Temple of the Sun and Moon in Palladio's fourth book) picked out in gold. John Neal, gilder, was paid for this work in 1755. Pickford's veined statuary marble chimneypiece with Siena tablet is to Inigo Jones's design. Additional colour is provided by the gilt suite of sofas and chairs, upholstered in a rich tomato Genoa velvet, which were designed by Kent and made by the cabinet-maker Goodison.[1] Within the unadorned wall niches of the Gallery and the two tribunes stand full-length statues, some of them antiques, bought in Rome by the younger Brettingham specially to fill the spaces. All the statues in the niches are those illustrated in the plates of the younger Brettingham's book.

The Great Dining-room faces north; and when the park trees were but nurslings the windows 'commanded the sea which is often enriched by the number of ships that pass that way'.[2] This room which, exclusive of the apse for a sideboard, is a cube, also has

[1] Benjamin Goodison *fl. circa* 1727–67. See Edwards and Jourdain, *Georgian Cabinet Makers*, 1944.
[2] *Vitruvius Britannicus*, Vol. V, 1771.

unadorned walls. Above the fireplace an eagle holds in its talons stucco drapery which falls in loops over a roundel sheltering the famous head of Lucius Verus. The pair of chimneypieces with trusses of Sicilian jasper and central reliefs—in the western tablet Young noticed that 'the nose of the sow is broke off'; it has not been replaced—are by Carter, who also carved the scrolls of foliage on the open pilasters of the recess, not in marble but in lime wood. The ceiling design, adapted from Inigo Jones, is echoed in the Axminster carpet.

The South Dining-room, the Landscape Room, the Green State Bedchamber and Dressing-room, the Brown State Bedroom and Dressing-room and the State Sitting-room occupy the eastern half of the centre block. They are scarcely less magnificent than the rather more important rooms already described, but they were finished after Lord Leicester's death. Their ceilings and chimney-pieces are mostly taken from the designs of Jones and Webb; their walls are hung with velvet damasks or, in the case of the Green State Bedchamber, with Brussels and Soho tapestries. The massive canopied bed and suite of furniture in this room were designed by Kent and upholstered in green Genoa velvet.

We are now left with the Library and Chapel which are situated at the opposing ends of the south-west and south-east pavilions. Standing with one's back to the north-west Library window one can look, if all the intervening doors are open, across the long enfilade of twelve apartments to the east window of the Chapel at the far extremity of the house, three hundred and forty-four feet away. So exact is the alignment and so mathematically precise the joinery of the silky mahogany doors that, were they all to be shut and the locks of the keyholes opened, we could, it is authorita-tively stated, see daylight from end to end.

The Library being in the Family Wing was one of the first rooms to be finished. It was typical of Lord Leicester that he put it next to his private apartments so that he could resort there at any hour of the day or even night in his 'undress', if needs be, without the risk of encountering guests or servants had his beloved books been kept in one of the state rooms. The thick ribbed ceiling and the Siena marble chimneypiece are both to Kent's design. In fact this room is wholly Kent's, although not decorated quite so fully as he intended. For each lunette and spandrel over the bookcases was to have been filled with large-scale arabesques and a naked figure reclining on a shell. These omissions need not however be regretted, for Kent's decorative paintings were feeble as well as fussy. The shelves are as he designed them, except that the dados have been removed to accommodate additional folios. The whole room is painted white, the relief ornament of ceiling, cornice, overmantel, shelves and doors being picked out in burnished gold.

The Chapel on the other hand was somewhat altered from Kent's design, which provided tabernacles along the upper part of the walls, now however bare save for a few religious panels in inset frames. These alterations were carried out by Lady Leicester in 1762. The lower part of the walls is lined with veined alabaster of a subdued green, and girdled by a key mould. The Chapel lacks colour and gilding and, like the hall, conveys the impression of a deep, empty swimming pool. The screen to the family pew of cedarwood inlaid with carved lime tree is from a design by Inigo Jones.

v. Disenchantment and Death

The death in 1753 of Edward Lord Coke without an heir sounded the knell of Lord Leicester's disappointed and miserable old age. Besides, by this date the two co-begetters of Holkham and companions of his youth, Kent and Burlington, were also dead. The Earl never fully recovered his spirits, but continued perfunctorily and at a slackening pace with the decoration of the vast palace which now was never to be peopled with his own issue. The elder Brettingham hinted in the Dedication of his book (1761) to the Duke of Cumberland that only His Royal Highness's encouragement had made his patron persevere with the work which had once been the joy and chief purpose of his existence. Leicester must at times have regretted that he ever launched upon the undertaking which had entailed years of expense and continuous discomfort, all, as it turned out, to no purpose. Life at Holkham became very dull and there were few visitors. The change in its tempo is reflected in the Account Books, still punctiliously kept up to date. There were no longer those entries, once so delightfully indicative of Lord Leicester's curiosity in all natural phenomena, such as 'Extraordinary expenses—for killing a pole cat', or 'bringing a strange fish to show my Lord'; for new gadgets—'from Mr. Brettingham a microscope & perspective glass'; for good living— 'an hogshead of French claret of Lord Herbert', and its consequences, 'Jesuits bark & vomiting powder', to say nothing of sport, hunting and cockfighting; or music—'for songs, hautboy and bassoon'; or pets—'for keeping the macaw and two parrots', and for 'a vomit for the Chinese Boy Houli Kan'. The items in the late 1750s relate almost solely to wages and domestic provisions of the dreariest sort.

Nothing any longer interested the master of Holkham very much. One of the last letters he wrote to the younger Brettingham sounded a note of sadness: 'It is a melancholy thing to stand alone in one's own Country. I look around, not a house to be seen but my own. I am Giant, of Giant Castle, and have ate up all my neighbours—my nearest neighbour is the King of Denmark.' Could anything be more depressing? He would stand for hours at the Library window on still evenings, gaze vacuously across the lake, and listen to the Canadian geese croaking like a pack of unearthly hounds, and the deer in the park coughing like tired old men. Then he would turn and cast a dull eye over his precious manuscripts—the *Libro della Natura* written and illustrated by Leonardo da Vinci's own hand, no less: the Dante which had belonged to Aenias Sylvius, or the Boccaccio illustrated by Taddeo Crivelli for Alberto d'Este—and as he fingered these treasures would wonder how their discovery and acquisition had once meant as much to him as the most thrilling victory in the cockpit. In January of 1759 he was momentarily shaken out of his apathy. There was that explosion of rage and challenge to a duel brought post-haste from Raynham. Lord Leicester gathered himself together to pen a tactful and humorous rebuttal of young Colonel Townshend's truculent accusations. The affair caused a good deal of tongue-wagging in Norfolk. Try as he might to laugh it off he was more upset than he cared to admit. Whether or not it hastened his end who can tell. There were neighbours who opined that it did. At any rate the shadows fell; and on 29th April he died.

Lady Leicester now came into her own as widows do whose years of married life have not been unadulterated bliss. 'Notwithstanding the contempt with which he always treated her,' as Lady Mary Wortley Montagu remarked, she got the firm of C. Atkinson in London to erect in the south-east corner of the chancel of Tittleshall church an expensive monument to her departed lord. The design took the appropriate shape of a large Palladian tabernacle over a raised sarcophagus all in marble, above which was set a florid escutcheon with mantling. An impressive epitaph recorded the Coke family's ancient lineage and alliances, and Lord Leicester's virtues and honours. He 'received the most conspicuous marks of royal favour and affection', whereas she preserved 'inviolable the most perfect impressions of conjugal and parental affection'. Roubiliac's splendid bust of the deceased had been modelled during a visit to Holkham in the last year of the Earl's life. It portrays him wearing his own hair. The features are heavy, the chin is double. The mouth is still libidinous; the Roman nose rather pinched and thin. The expression is one of disdain and disenchantment.

To the last Lady Leicester remained implacably hostile to Wenman Coke and his son. 'Young man,' the formidable old woman addressed her great-nephew when he paid his respects to her, 'you are now for the first time at Holkham, and it is probable that you will one day be master of this house, but understand I will live as long as I can.' Until her death at the age of seventy-five she enjoyed her life interest in Holkham, together with £2,000 a year provided by her husband exclusively for the purpose of carrying on the building and decoration of the house. Faithfully she supervised the work which the two Brettinghams completed. It entailed plastering the ceiling and marbling the dado of the great hall and setting up the statues in the niches: decorating and furnishing from scratch several of the staterooms, such as the Brown State Bedroom and the Chapel, and practically all the rooms in the Strangers Wing. The furnishing of these rooms she was obliged to do out of her own pocket, the £2,000 a year not stretching beyond the requirements of building and decorating. The 'platform' before the north front of the house was raised, and the stables were built under Lady Leicester's directions, so that on her death in 1775 there was virtually nothing further to be done. No wonder that the great-nephew[1] who inherited Holkham from his father in less than a year's time, and was to reign there for sixty-six years, exclaimed: 'I shall never venture rashly to interfere with the result of years of thought and study in Italy.' Fortunately his descendants have felt the same way, with the result that Holkham has survived to be one of the least spoilt and most perfect specimens of a great Palladian country house dating from the reign of George II.

---

[1] His father having taken the name of Coke in lieu of Wenman, he became Thomas William Coke, known as 'Coke of Norfolk', who was made Earl of Leicester of the second creation in 1837.

BIBLIOGRAPHY

INTRODUCTION

Allen, B. Sprague—*Tides in English Taste*, 1619–1800: 1958.
Brett, R. L.—*The Third Earl of Shaftesbury*, 1951.
Carritt, E. F.—*A Calendar of British Taste*, 1600–1800: 1949.
Dobrée, Bonamy—*English Literature in the Early Eighteenth Century*, 1959.
Hogarth, William—*The Analysis of Beauty*, 1753.
Hussey, Christopher—*The Aesthetic Background to the Art of William Kent* (Preface to M. Jourdain's *William Kent*, 1948).
Pope, Alexander—*Essay on Gardens*; No. 173, The Guardian, II, 29th September, 1713.
Richardson, Jonathan—*Theory of Painting*, 1715.
Shaftesbury, 3rd Earl of—*Characteristicks of Men, etc.*, 1711.
Shaftesbury, 3rd Earl of—*The Beautiful*, 1712.
Summerson, Sir John—*The Classical Country House in eighteenth-century England*: Journal of Roy. Soc. of Arts, July 1959.
Walpole, Horace—*On Modern Gardening* (Chapter XXIII of *Anecdotes of Painting*, vol. III, ed. 1876).
Williams, Basil—*The Whig Supremacy*, 1939.

CHAPTER I

THE EARL BATHURST

Angus, W.—*Views of the Seats of the Nobility and Gentry*, 1787.
Annual Register, The, 1775 (for character of Lord Bathurst, pp. 22–5).
Ashton, John—*Social Life in the Reign of Queen Anne*, 1897.
Atkyns, R.—*History of Gloucestershire*, 1712.
Baddeley, W. St.Clair—*History of Cirencester*, 1924.
Baker, George—*History of Northamptonshire*, ii., pp. 202–3. 1822–41.
Bathurst, 7th Earl—*Catalogue of Collections at Cirencester Park*, 1908.
Bigland, R.—*Gloucestershire*, 1791.
Brayley, E. W. and Britton J.—*Gloucestershire*, 1803.
Burke, Edmund—Speech in the House of Commons of 22nd March, 1775.
Campbell, John, Lord—*Lives of the Lord Chancellors* (for 2nd Earl Bathurst), v., pp. 433–6, 1846.
Country Life—Articles on Cirencester Park, 8th August, 1908, and 16th and 23rd June, 1950.
Delany, Mary Granville, Mrs.—*Correspondence* of 24th October, 1733; ed. 1861.
Historical Manuscripts Commission—*Bathurst Papers* and others.
Jones, Barbara—*Follies and Grottoes*, 1953.

Layng, Henry, Rev.—Version of *G. B. Gelli's Circe*, 1744 (dedicated fulsomely to Lord Bathurst).

Montagu, Lady Mary Wortley—*Correspondence*, Everyman's Library, first published 1906.

National Biography, Dictionary of—Entry on Allen Bathurst 1st Earl Bathurst.

Neale, J. P.—*Views of Seats*, 2nd Series, vol. ii., 1825.

Pope, Alexander—*Correspondence*, 5 vols., edited by George Sherburn, 1956.

Pope, Alexander—*Epistle III of Moral Essays* addressed to Allen Lord Bathurst.

Rudder, Samuel—*Gloucestershire*, 1779.

Stanhope, 5th Earl—*History of England*, 1836–63.

Sterne, Laurence—*Letter to Eliza* of March 1767.

Swift, Jonathan—*Correspondence* of, ed. by F. E. Ball, 6 vols., 1910–14.

Torrington, 5th Viscount (Hon. John Byng)—*Diaries*, 1787.

Vertue, George—*Note Books*, published by Walpole Society 1929–50.

Walpole, Horace—*Correspondence*.

Warton, Thomas—*Life and Literary Remains of Ralph Bathurst, M.D.*, 1761.

Wentworth Papers—Selections from, edited by J. J. Cartwright, 1883 (including several letters from 1st Earl Bathurst to Thomas Wentworth, 1st Earl of Strafford).

CHAPTER II

THE EARL OF PEMBROKE

Anonymous—*The Downfall of Westminster Bridge, or My Lord in the Suds, a new Ballad, to the Tune of King John, and the Abbot of Canterbury*, 1747.

Chesterfield, 4th Earl of—*Correspondence*, ed. Lord Mahon, 1892.

Cobbett, R. S.—*Memorials of Twickenham*, 1872.

Collins' *Peerage*, edition iii, 142–5, 1812.

Colvin, H. M.—*Dictionary of Architects*, 1954 (for entries on The Earl of Pembroke and Roger Morris).

Country Life—Articles, 25th March, 1916, and 28th January, 1944 (for Wilton Palladian Bridge): 24th February, 1900 (for plan of Garden at Marble Hill).

Cresy, Edward—*Encyclopaedia of Civil Engineering*, pp. 422–5, 1856.

Downes, Kerry—*Hawksmoor*, 1959.

Doyle, J. W. E.—*Official Baronage of England*, 1886.

Foster, J.—*Peerage*, etc., 1880–2.

Goodison, Ingleson—*English Interior Decoration*; article in Architectural Review, vol. 34, 1913.

Green, David—*Blenheim Column of Victory*—Architectural Review, vol. 107, April 1950.

Historical Manuscripts Commission—*Marquess of Lothian Papers* (Cd 2319) 1905, and other volumes (with references to Lord Pembroke and Lady Suffolk).

Howard, Henrietta, Countess of Suffolk—*Correspondence*, 1712–67, in 2 vols., ed. 1824.

Lenygon, F.—*Decoration in England from* 1660–1770, published 1914.

London County Council—*Survey of London; Parish of St. Margaret, Westminster*, 1930 (for Lord Pembroke's house, Whitehall).

Mac Coll, D. S.—*Richmond Hill and Marble Hill*; article in Architectural Review, July 1901.

Marble Hill House—London County Council leaflet, 1954.

Morris, Robert—*Essay in Defence of Ancient Architecture*, 1728.

Morris, Robert—*Lectures on Architecture*, 1734, 1736.

Morris, Robert—*Rural Architecture*, 1750.

National Biography, Dictionary of—Entries on Henry Herbert 9th Earl of Pembroke and Henrietta Howard, Countess of Suffolk.

Nichols, John—*Literary Anecdotes*, 1782–1812, 9 vols., 1815.

Parliamentary Papers, Reports of Select Committees, vol. vi., 1844.

Pembroke versus Thorpe. Hil. 13. Geo. 2, 29th March, 1740. Chancery Case.

Pembroke, 9th Earl's *House Book*, 1733–49.

Piggott, Stuart—*William Stukeley*, 1950.

Smith, H. Clifford—*Marble Hill House*, 1939.

Swift, Jonathan—*Dialogue between Richmond Lodge and Marble Hill*, 1727.

Thomson, G. Scott—*Letters of a Grandmother* 1732–5: 1943.

Vertue, George—*Note Books*, published by Walpole Society, 1929–50.

Vitruvius Britannicus, vol. iii, 1725 (Plate 48, Lord Herbert's House, Whitehall, and Plate 93, Marble Hill).

Walpole, Horace—entry on 9th Earl of Pembroke in *Anecdotes of Painting*, vol. III, 1876.

Walpole, Horace—*Correspondence*.

Walpole, Horace—*Memoirs of the Reign of King George II*, ed. Lord Holland, 3 vols., 1846.

Warburton, E.—*The Earl of Peterborough and Monmouth*, 1853.

CHAPTER III

THE EARL OF BURLINGTON

Burlington, 3rd Earl—*Fabbriche Antiche disegnate da Andrea Palladio Vicentine*, 1730.

Burlington, 3rd Earl—*Correspondence of:* British Museum, Sloane MSS., 4055, folio 349; and B.M. Additional MSS., 32,696, folio 438.

Burlington, 3rd Earl—*Correspondence of:* Unpublished letters mostly from Lord Burlington to Lady Burlington (in the possession of The Earl Spencer at Althorp).

Burlington, 3rd Earl—*Correspondence of:* Unpublished letters and papers (in the possession of the Duke of Devonshire at Chatsworth).

Castell, Robert—*Villas of the Ancients*, 1728.

Charlton, John—*Chiswick House and Gardens*: H.M. Stationery Office, 1958.

Clark, H. F.—*Lord Burlington's Bijou at Chiswick*: Architectural Review, vol. 95, 1944.

Colvin, H. M.—*Dictionary of Architects*, 1954 (for entry on The Earl of Burlington).

Complete Peerage, the (for entry on 3rd Earl of Burlington).

Country Life—Articles on Chiswick House, 9th February, 1918, and on Burlington House, 3rd May, 1924.

Coxe, W.—*Life of John Gay*, 2nd ed. 1797.

Cunningham, Allan—Chapters on William Kent and The Earl of Burlington (from vol. iv of *Lives of the British Painters*, 1831).

Deutsch, O. E.—*Handel, A Documentary Biography*, 1955.

Dodsley, R. and J.—*London and Environs*, vol. ii, 1761 (for a catalogue of Lord Burlington's pictures).

Drake, Francis—*Eboracum, or the History and Antiquities of the City of York*, 1736.

Esdaile, K. A.—*Signor Guelfi, an Italian*; Burlington Magazine, vol. 90, November 1948.

Falk, Bernard—*The Royal FitzRoys*, 1950.

Flower, Newman—*George Frideric Handel*, 1947.

Gay, John—*Epistle on Journey to Exeter* (addressed to Lord Burlington), *c.* 1720.

Gay, John—*Epistle to Paul Methuen*, 1720.

Gay, John—*Trivia, or Mr. Pope's Welcome from Greece, c.* 1720.

Hervey, John, Lord—*Memoirs of Reign of George II*, ed. by J. W. Croker, 1848.

Historical Manuscripts Commission—various Papers.

Honour, Hugh—*John Talman and W. Kent in Italy*; Connoisseur, August 1954.

Jourdain, Margaret—*The Work of William Kent*, 1948.

Kimball, Fiske—*Burlington Architectus*; R.I.B.A. Journal, 15th October, and 12th November, 1927.

Kimball, Fiske—*William Kent's Designs for the Houses of Parliament*; R.I.B.A. Journal, 1932.

Leoni, Giacomo—*Architecture of A. Palladio in Four Books*, 1715.

Lodge, E.—*Irish Peerage*, i, pp. 177–8, 1789.

Macky, J.—*Journey through England*, I, 1724.

National Biography, Dictionary of—Entry on Richard Boyle 3rd Earl of Burlington.

Neale, J. P.—*Views of Seats*, 2nd Series, vol. v, 1829.

Nichols, J.—*Literary Anecdotes*, 1782–1812, 9 vols., 1815.

Pococke, Richard—*Travels Through England* (Camden Soc.), i. 1888.

Pope, Alexander—*Epistle IV* (on Taste) *of Moral Essays*, addressed to Richard Boyle, Earl of Burlington, 1731.

Smollett, T.—*Humphry Clinker*, 1771.

Spiers, R. P.—*Alterations to Burlington House*; Architectural Review, xxx, 1911.

Spiers, R. P.—*Burlington House*, I and II; Architectural Review, xvi, 1904.

Swift, Jonathan—*Correspondence of*, ed. by F. E. Ball, 6 vols., 1910–14.

Tipping, H. Avray—*Four Unpublished Letters of William Kent*; Architectural Review, vol. 63, 1928.

Tipping, H. Avray—*Letters of William Kent to the Earl of Burlington*; Country Life, 10th May, 1924.

Vallese, Tarquinio—*Paolo Rolli in Inghilterra*, 1938.

Vertue, George—*Note Books* (particularly vol. xxii, Walpole Society.)

Vitruvius Britannicus, vol. iii, 1725 (Plate 10, *General Wade's House*, and Plates 22-26 *Burlington House*), vol. iv, 1767 (*York Assembly Rooms*).

Walpole, Horace—Entry on The Earl of Burlington in *Anecdotes of Painting*, vol. iii, 1876.

Walpole, Horace—*Journals of Visits to Country Seats* (*Chiswick* 1760); Walpole Society, vol. xvi, 1927-8.

Webb, G.—*Letters and Drawings of N. Hawksmoor*; Walpole Society, vol. xix, 1930-1.

Webb, M. I.—*Giovanni Battista Guelfi*: Burlington Magazine, vol. xcvii, May 1955.

Wheatley, H. B.—*Round About Piccadilly*, 1870.

Wittkower, R.—*Pseudo Palladian Elements*; Warburg and Courtauld Institute Journal, 1945.

Wittkower, R.—*The Earl of Burlington and William Kent*; Archaeological Journal cii, 1945.

Wittkower, R.—*Un Libro di schizzi Juvara a Chatsworth*; Bolletino Soc. Piemontese d'Archaeologia e di Belle Arte, 1949.

York-Long, Alan—*George II and Handel*; History Today, October 1951.

CHAPTER IV

THE EARL OF OXFORD

Barwick, G. F.—*Humphrey Wanley and the Harleian Library*; The Library, 1902.

Barwick, G. F.—*The Formation of the Harleian Library*; The Library, 3rd Series, vol. i, 1910.

Bickley, Francis—*The Life of Matthew Prior*, 1914.

Complete Peerage, the (for entry on 2nd Earl of Oxford), 1945.

Country Life—Articles on Wimpole Hall, 15th February, 1908, and 21st May, 1927.

Delany, Mary Granville, Mrs.—*Correspondence*, vol. ii, ed. 1861.

Douglas, D. C.—*English Scholars* (for H. Wanley), 1939.

Edwards, Edward—*Lives of the Founders of the British Museum*, Part I, 1870.

Gay, John—*Prologue to the Lord Viscount Bolingbroke*, 1714.

Genealogist (new series i, 114, 178, 256) 1884—*Wanley's Harleian Journal*.

Gibbons, Rev. T. G.—*John Morley of Halstead*; Essex Review xi, 145, 193: 1902.

Gibbs, James—*Book of Architecture*, 1728.

Goulding, R. W.—*Henrietta, Countess of Oxford*; Trans. Thoroton Society, vol. xxvii, 1923.

Grey, Zachary—*Memoir of Harley Family*; Brit. Mus. Addit. MS., 5834, f. 286: 1765.

Harley, Edward, Lord—*Account of a Journey . . . through . . . Suffolk, Norfolk, and Cambridgeshire*, 1732; Historical Manuscripts Commission, Portland, vol. vi.

Historical Manuscripts Commission—*Letters to 2nd Earl of Oxford*; Portland MSS, vols. v and vi; also Bath MSS, vols. i and iii.

Hulsband, Robert—*Life of Lady Mary Wortley Montagu*, 1956.

Johnson, Samuel—*An Account of the Harleian Library*; Preface to *Catalogus Bibliothecae Harleianae*, 1743.

Johnson, Samuel—chapters on Prior and Swift (from *Lives of the Poets*), 1779–81.

Ketton-Cremer, R. W.—*Matthew Prior*, 1957.

Lathom, Charles—entry on Wimpole Hall from *English Homes*, iii, 1909.

Legg, L. G. Wickham—*Matthew Prior*, 1921.

Library Chronicle, i, 87, 110, for extracts from *H. Wanley's Journal*.

Little, Bryan—*James Gibbs*, 1955.

National Biography, Dictionary of—entry on Edward Harley 2nd Earl of Oxford.

Nichols, John—*Literary Anecdotes*, vol. i, pp. 86–94, 1782.

Notes and Queries—for entries on the Harleian Library and H. Wanley; 1st Ser. viii, 335, 1853: 2nd Ser. i, 325–7, 1856: 2nd Ser. ix, 417–21, 1860: 2nd Ser. xi, 441, 1861: 6th Ser. vii, 212, 1883: 7th Ser. xi, 341, 1891.

Pope, Alexander—*Correspondence*; vols. 2 and 3, edited by George Sherburn, 1956.

Pope, Alexander—*Epistle to Robert, Earl of Oxford and Earl Mortimer*, 1721.

Prior, Matthew—*Down Hall*, Ballad of, 1715.

Prior, Matthew—*Letters of, to Edward Lord Harley*; Historical Manuscripts Commission, Harley MSS.

Roscoe, E. S.—*Robert Harley, Earl of Oxford*, 1902.

Swift, Jonathan—*Correspondence of*, ed. by F. E. Ball, 6 vols., 1910–14.

Turberville, A. S.—*History of Welbeck Abbey*, vol. i, pp. 291–387, 1938.

Vertue, George—*Note Books* (pub. Walpole Society, 1929–50) for constant references to 2nd Earl of Oxford.

Walpole, Horace—*Correspondence*.

Wanley, Humphrey—*Account of the Harleian Library*; Nicolson's Historical Libraries, p. vi, 1736.

Wanley, Humphrey—*Journal from 2nd March, 1715, to 23rd June, 1726*; Brit. Mus., Lansdowne MSS., 771–2.

Wren Society—Volumes xii, 1935, and xvii, 1940, for *Wimpole Hall*.

CHAPTER V

THE EARL OF LEICESTER

Brettingham, Matthew—*Plans and Elevations of the late Earl of Leicester's House at Holkham*, 1761. (Second edition produced by his son, Matthew Brettingham, 1773.)

Chambers, Sir William—*Decorative Part of Civil Architecture*, 1791 (for descriptions of Holkham).

Dawson, J.—*The Stranger's Guide to Holkham*, 1817.

Desgodetz, Antoine—*Les Edifices Antiques de Rome*, 1682.

East Anglian, the, vol. ii, 1866.

Hassall, W. O.—*Portrait of a Bibliophile*; The Book Collector.

Historical Manuscripts Commission—various volumes for references to 1st Earl of Leicester of the first creation.

Hussey, Christopher—section on Holkham (*Early Georgian Country Houses*, 1955).

James, C. W.—*Chief Justice Coke, His Family and Descendants at Holkham*, 1929.

Jarrett, Edward—*Accounts* (in manuscript) kept of Thomas Coke's Grand Tour, 1712–18.

Jourdain, Margaret—*The Work of William Kent*, 1948.

Kent, William—*Journal of*, in Italy, 1714 (in manuscript); Bodleian Library, MS. Rawl, D 1162.

Ketton-Cremer, R. W.—*The Phantom Duel* (chapter in *Norfolk Assembly*, 1957).

Michaelis, A.—*Ancient Marbles in Great Britain*, 1882.

Neale, J. P.—*Views of Seats*, vol. i, 1818.

Powys, P. Lybbe, Mrs., *Passages from the Diaries of*, 1756.

Smith, Edward—A Journal kept by, of payments made for Thomas Coke, from 13th May, 1718.

Stirling, A. M. W.—*Thomas Coke and the Building of Holkham* (Chapter II of Coke of Norfolk), 1908.

Stuart, Lady Louisa—*Some Account of John Duke of Argyll and His Family*, 1827.

Tipping, H. Avray—article on Holkham in *English Homes*, Period V, vol. i, Early Georgian, 1921.

Vitruvius Britannicus, vol. v, 1771 (description and plate of Holkham).

Walpole, Horace—*Correspondence*.

Watts, W.—*Views of the Seats of the Nobility and Gentry*, 1780.

Young, Arthur—*A Six Weeks' Tour*, 1767.

INDEX

Abbot, Rebecca, Mrs., 65

Adam, Robert (architect), 68, 135, 139, 140, 152, 249

Addison, Joseph (poet and essayist), 13, 141

Aikman, William (portrait painter), 154

Ailesbury, Charles Lord Bruce, 3rd Earl of, 104, 105, 152, 232, 251

Aislabie, John (of Fountains, Yorks), 208

Aislabie, William (of Kirby Hall, Yorks), 160

Albani, Cardinal (Roman collector), 242–3

Alberti, Cherubino (fresco artist), 153

Alfred the Great, King, 45

Algarotti, Francesco, Count (author), 138

Allworthy, Squire (Fielding's *Tom Jones*), 142–3

Amedei, Belisario (Roman merchant), 243

Amesbury Abbey, Wiltshire, 97, 156

Anne, Queen, 22, 23, 34, 104, 175

Anstis, John (Garter King of Arms), 97

Antiquaries, London Society of, 180

Appleby Castle, Westmorland, 208

Apsley, Sir Allen (King's Falconer) and Lady, 22

Apsley, Peter, 22

Arbuthnot, John (physician and wit), 25, 75, 140–1, 196

Archer, Thomas (architect), 86, 140

Argyll, Jane Warburton, Duchess of (wife of 2nd Duke), 237, 238

Argyll, John Campbell, 2nd Duke of (General), 61, 237

Arundel, Honble. Richard (stepbrother of 9th Earl of Pembroke), 99

Ashmole, Elias (antiquary and astrologer), 182

Asser (10th cent. monk), 45

Atkinson, Charles (monumental mason), 262

Atkyns, Sir Robert (Gloucestershire historian), 38

Atterbury, Francis, Bishop of Rochester, 13, 24, 25, 45

Badminton, Gloucestershire, 38–9

Bagnola di Lonigo, Villa Pisani, 158

Baker, Rev. Thomas (Cambridge antiquary), 186

Barbaro, Daniele (Palladio's client), 125

Barber, John (friend of Swift), 205

Barber-Surgeons' Hall, London, 126

Barnard, Henry Vane, 3rd Lord, 205

Bathurst, Allen Bathurst, 1st Earl, 11, 14, 21–56 (chapter on), 73, 76, 80, 105, 141, 142, 189, 190, 196, 244, 245

Bathurst, Sir Benjamin, M.P. (Lord Bathurst's father), 22, 23, 33

Bathurst, Benjamin (Lord Bathurst's brother), 26

Bathurst, Catherine Apsley, Countess (wife of 1st Earl), 22–3 (described), 34–5

Bathurst, Frances Apsley, Lady (Lord Bathurst's mother), 22

Bathurst, George (Lord Bathurst's grandfather), 21–2

Bathurst, Henry, 2nd Earl (Lord Chancellor), 25, 26, 28, 36, 55

Bathurst, Ralph (President of Trinity Coll., Oxford), 22

Batteley, Oliver (divine), 181

Beaufort, Henry Somerset, 3rd Duke of, 38

Beaufort House, Chelsea, 126

Bedford, Diana Spencer, Duchess of (1st wife of 4th Duke), 67, 93, 95

Bedford, John Russell, 4th Duke of, 94, 95

Bedingfeld, Lady Elizabeth (sister of Lord Burlington), 104

Beggar's Opera, The, by John Gay, 76

Belton House, Lincolnshire, 207

Belvoir Castle, Rutland, 207

Benson, William (Surveyor of Works), 35, 116

Bentley, Dr. Richard (scholar and critic), 186

Berkeley, Honble. George, 73, 74 & n. 91

Berkeley Square, London, No. 44, 257

Bertram, Charles (literary forger), 62n.

Bethel, Hugh (friend of Pope), 134, 159

Bigland, R. (Gloucestershire historian), 56

Bingley, Robert Benson, Lord (diplomatist), 37, 200, 208

Bird, Francis (sculptor), 187

Biscioni, Signor (Laurentian Librarian), 230

Bishops Burton, Yorkshire, house for Col. Gee at, 160

Blenheim Palace, Oxon, 235

Blenheim Column of Victory, 92

Blickling Hall, Norfolk, 71, 74, 89, 224, 244

Blount, Martha ('Patty', friend of Pope), 42, 49, 74, 84

Blount, Teresa (Patty's sister), 42

Bolingbroke, Henry St. John, 1st Viscount, 23, 24, 29, 31, 32, 48-9, 53, 73, 166, 175, 189, 192

Boscawen, Honble. Edward, Admiral, 234, 241

Boyle, Lady Henrietta (wife of Henry Boyle), 104

Boyle, Lady Jane (Lord Burlington's sister), 104

Boynton Hall, Yorks, 163n.

Bramble, Matthew (Smollett's *Humphry Clinker*), 159

Bramham Park, Yorkshire, 37, 208

Brampton Bryan Castle, Herefordshire, 174, 175

Branchi, Pietro (? Roman dealer), 110

Brandon, Henry (? Lord Burlington's tutor), 107, 111

Brettingham, Matthew, snr. (architect), 85n., 230, 245, 247-59 (at Holkham)

Brettingham, Matthew, jnr. (architect), 243, 246 & n., 247-59 (at Holkham), 262

Bridgman, Charles (landscape gardener), 14, 39, 80, 90, 131, 141 (described), 147, 148, 201, 203, 213, 214, 215

Brook, Mr. (Lord Leicester's tutor), 222-3

Brown, Lancelot or 'Capability' (landscape gardener), 39, 146, 215, 245

Bruce, Charles, Lord (*see* Earl of Ailesbury)

Bruce, Lady Juliana Boyle (wife of Charles, Lord Bruce), 104

Buckinghamshire, John Hobart, 2nd Earl of (Ambassador), 85

Buononcini, G. B. (composer), 114-5 (described), 122

Burgess, E. (Minister in Venice), 123

Burlington, Dorothy Savile, Countess of (wife of 3rd Earl), 104n., 105, 129-35 (marriage), 140, 154, 160, 162-4 (letters to Londesborough), 165, 167

Burlington, Juliana Noel, Countess of (mother of 3rd Earl), 104, 167

Burlington, Richard Boyle, 3rd Earl of, 11, 12, 14, 15, 16, 40, 56, 68, 69, 76, 86, 88n., 96, 103-69 (chapter on), 208, 210, 212, 224, 225, 226, 245-59 (at Holkham), 261

Burlington House, Piccadilly, London, 69, 82, 103, 105, 106, 112, 113, 115, 116-21 (described), 131, 149, 151n., 156, 162, 164, 212, 235, 246-7

Burke, Edmund (statesman), 26, 55

Burnet, Gilbert, Bishop of Salisbury, 182 & n.

Bute, James Stuart, 2nd Earl of, 37

Butler, Samuel (satirist), 194

Byng, Honble. John (later 5th Viscount Torrington, diarist), 56

Byrom, John (shorthand teacher), 114

Camden House, Kensington, 104n.

Campbell, Colen (architect), 11, 69, 70, 81, 88, 116, 117–21 (Burlington House), 149, 150, 152, 157, 166, 210, 212, 243, 247, 256

Campbell, Jack (later 4th Duke of Argyll), 81

Campbell, Honble. Mary Bellenden, Mrs. Jack, 80–1, 82

Canons Park, Middlesex, 114

Capra, Giulio (Vicenzan nobleman), 87

Capra, Villa (*see* Vicenza, Rotonda)

Carlisle, Charles Howard, 3rd Earl of, 47, 92, 138, 246

Caroline, Queen (Princess of Wales 1714–27, wife of George II), 66, 70–1, 72, 73, 77, 78, 131, 160

Carr, John (architect), 139

Carracci, Annibale (painter), 109

Carter, Thomas (marble carver), 254n., 258, 260

Carteret, John Carteret, 2nd Lord (later 1st Earl Granville), 26

Carvilius Maximus (Roman Consul), 62n.

Casali, Andrea (portrait painter), 239

Castell, Robert (*Villas of the Ancients*), 144–5

Castle Howard, Yorks, 47, 138, 141, 207

Castor and Pollux, Temple of, Rome, 150

Castrucci, Pietro (violinist), 113

Chambers, Sir William (architect), 68, 69n., 255 & n.

Chambray, Roland Fréart de (*Parallèle*), 246

Chandos, James Brydges, 1st Duke of, 56, 114, 126, 166

Chantrey, Sir Francis (sculptor), 243n.

Charles VII, Emperor of Austria, 231

Cheere, John (statuary), 92

Chesterfield House, London, W.1, 140

Chesterfield, Philip Dormer, 4th Earl of (letter writer), 12, 13, 15, 26, 64, 66, 67, 68, 73, 78 (Lady Suffolk), 99, 105, 132, 133, 140, 157

Chiari, Giuseppe (Roman painter), 258

Chicheley, Thomas (builder of Wimpole Hall), 214

Child, Sir Josiah (banker), 197

Chiswick, hall for Lord Wilmington at, 160

Chiswick House, or Villa, 105, 109, 110, 119, 123, 124, 133, 145, 148–156 (section on), 158, 165, 168, 246, 247, 251, 259

    Gardens, 39, 40, 126, 140–8 (section on), 165

    The 'new casina', 121–2, 147, 156, 165

    Ionic Pantheon, 148

Cirencester Abbey, Glos., 33

Cirencester House, Glos., 22, 31, 32, 33–7 (section on)

    Alfred's Hall, 42, 44–5, 54

    Hexagon, 50–1, 52

    Horseguards, 53

    Ivy Lodge, 48, 54

    Park, 37–56 (section on), 142, 244

    Pope's Seat, 42, 48, 50, 51

    Queen Anne's Column, 42, 52, 53

    Round House, 48, 54

    Seven Rides, 42, 48, 52

    Silvan Bower, 42–3

    Square House, 48, 54

Cirencester, Richard of (14th cent. monkish chronicler), 62n.

Clark, Thomas of Westminster (stuccoist), 254n., 257, 258

Claude Lorraine (landscape painter), 16, 146, 147

Clérisseau, Charles-Louis (designer), 159

Clerk, Sir John, Bart., of Penicuik, 154

Clermont, Andien de (grotesque painter), 63, 85

Cleveland, Charles FitzRoy, Duke of, 160

Clieveland, John (cavalier poet), 217

Clifford of Lanesborough, 4th Baron (3rd Earl of Burlington), 103 & n.

Cobham, Sir Richard Temple, Viscount (statesman), 34, 105

Cocchi, Antonio (Italian biographer), 138

Coke, Cary (Lord Leicester's mother), 222

Coke, Sir Edward (Lord Chief Justice), 221 (described), 225n., 236, 239, 243

Coke, Edward (Lord Leicester's father), 222

Coke, Sir Edward (of Longford Hall), 223, 224, 231, 233, 234

Coke, Edward ('Neddy', brother of Lord Leicester), 232

Coke, Edward Coke, Viscount (son of Lord Leicester), 236–9 (described), 261

Coke, John (acquired Holkham), 221

Coke, Lady Mary (Campbell), 237–9 (described)

Coke, Thomas (see Leicester, 1st Earl of)

Coke, Thomas William ('Coke of Norfolk', later 1st Earl of Leicester of second creation), 263 & n.

Coke, Wenman (nephew of Lord Leicester), 234, 263

Coleshill House, Berkshire, 249, 253

Combe Bank, Kent, 81

Congreve, William (dramatist), 29

Cork, Richard Boyle, 4th Earl of (3rd Earl of Burlington), 103

Cossens, Mr. (builder), 200

Cotterell, Sir Clement (Master of Ceremonies), 129, 165

Covel, Dr. John (Master of Christ's, Cambridge), 177, 205, 214

Covent Garden, St. Paul's Church, London, 126, 128

Coysevox, Antoine (French sculptor), 202

Craggs, James (Secretary of State), 115

Croftes, Daniel (garden contractor), 90

Cromwell, Richard (Lord Protector), 55

Cutler, Sir John (London merchant), 214

Cuzzoni, Francesca (operatic soprano), 131

Dahl, Michael (portrait painter), 34, 122, 186, 187, 201

Dance, George, snr. (architect), 139

Danvers, Sir John (regicide), 33

de Caux, Isaac (water engineer), 97

D'Ewes, Sir Simonds (antiquarian), 176

Defoe, Daniel (novelist), 175, 212

Delany, Mary Granville, Mrs. (letter writer), 45, 217, 218

De La Warr, Charlotte McCarthy, Countess (wife of 1st Earl), 95

Dempster, Thomas (miscellaneous writer), 242

Denham, Sir John (poet-architect), 117, 118, 119

Desgodetz, Antoine (Edifices de Rome), 257, 258, 259

Designs of Inigo Jones, by William Kent, 126

Devall, John (mason), 97

Devoto, — (decorative painter), 120

Digby, Edward (publisher of Pope's Dunciad), 32

Dobrée, Bonamy (man of letters), 203

Dodington, George Bubb (later Lord Melcombe Regis), 240

Dolben, Sir John, Bart (divine), 205

Dormer, James, Lieut.-General, 77

Dorset, Charles Sackville, 6th Earl of (poet), 192

Dover Street, London, Lord Oxford's house in, 175, 177, 186, 187, 190, 201, 206, 213, 218

Down Hall, Essex, 197–205 (section on)

Down-hall, ballad by Prior, 197–205

Drake, Francis (York historian), 88n., 158, 159

Dryden, John (poet), 14

Dubois, Nicholas (French architect), 116

Dunstall Castle, Croome, Worcs., 44

Dupplin, Thomas Hay, Viscount (later 9th Earl of Kinnoull), 209

Dyer, John (poet), 146–7

Earbery, Rev. Matthias (author), 185–6

Ebberston Lodge, Yorks., 157

Edgehill Tower, War., 44
Ellis, John (painter), 63
Elstob, Elizabeth (Anglo-Saxon scholar), 186
Elstob, William (divine and Saxon scholar), 186
Esher Place, Surrey, 127
Essex, William Capell, 3rd Earl of, 48-9, 111, 232
Etheridge, William (carpenter), 98
Etty, William (designer and carver), 88n.
Euston, Dorothy Boyle, Countess of, 134 (described), 164, 165
Euston, George FitzRoy, Earl of, 134 (described), 165
Euston Hall, Suffolk, 160, 249

Fabbriche Antiche, etc., by Lord Burlington, 125 & n., 168, 212
Fane, Colonel John (later 7th Earl of Westmorland), 81
Fansolo, Villa Emo, 161
Farinelli (Carlo Broschi, castrato), 131
Faustina Bordoni (operatic soprano), 131
Fenton, Elijah (poet and translator), 29
Ferrari, Domenico (Holkham librarian), 242
Fielding, Henry (novelist), 207, 233
Firmin, Thomas (philanthropist), 182
Fitton, Mary, Countess of Pembroke (wife of 3rd Earl of Pembroke), 59
Fleming, John (architectural historian), 249n.
Fletcher, Joshua (mason), 118
Flitcroft, Henry (architect), 139, 156 (described), 157, 161, 165, 169, 257
Fontano, Carlo (Roman architect), 213
Foscari, Signor (of Malcontenta), 124
Foudrinier, Paul (engraver), 63
Fountaine, Sir Andrew (virtuoso), 62-3, 86, 91, 129, 211
Fountains Abbey, Yorks., 208
Fox, Henry (later 1st Lord Holland), 240

Franks, Kent, 21 & n.
Frederick, Prince of Wales, 53, 63, 66, 115
Frederick the Great, King of Prussia, 138
Freind, Dr. Robert (headmaster of Westminster), 186, 203

Gandon, James (architect), 158 & n., 160
Garrett, Daniel (architect), 138, 160, 165
Garrick, David (actor), 131
Gay, John (poet and playwright), 28, 29, 31, 41, 45, 76-7 (Lady Suffolk), 80, 84, 89, 119-20 (on Burlington House), 127, 136 (Lord Burlington), 140-1 (at Burlington House), 168, 179 (Wanley), 183, 204
Gee, Colonel (house for), 160
George I, King, 71, 83, 104, 113, 114
George II, King (Prince of Wales, 1714-27), 28, 63, 66, 71, 72, 73, 74, 80, 81, 83, 89, 105, 115
George III, King, 25, 44
Germain, Lady Betty (friend of authors), 85
'Giacomo, Signor' (architectural teacher), 227, 229, 230, 249
Gibbons, Grinling (carver), 82
Gibbs, James (architect), 70, 81, 117, 118, 120, 187, 199, 200-1 (Down Hall), 202-3, 204, 207, 210, 211, 212-18 (at Wimpole Hall), 235
Girard, Paul (toyman), 134
Goodison, Benjamin (cabinetmaker), 259 & n.
Goupy, Lewis (French fan-painter), 107, 111
Grafton, Charles FitzRoy, 2nd Duke of, 132, 160, 165, 240-1, 249
Greenwich, Queen's House at, 256
Grey, Dr. Zachary (antiquary), 185, 204
Griffier, John (painter), 63
Guardian, The, Pope's *Essay on Gardens*, 40, 141
Guelfi, G. B. (sculptor), 113, 115 (described), 140, 155, 243
Gulliver's Travels by Swift, 36, 77

Gumley, John (cabinet-maker), 149 & n., 235

Guthrie, Patrick (tutor), 205

Hagley Hall, Worcestershire, 97

Hagley Tower, 44

Halifax, George Savile, 1st Marquess of ('The Trimmer'), 134

Halifax, William Savile, 2nd Marquess of, 131

Hallett, William (cabinet-maker), 167

Handel, George Frederick (composer), 60, 104, 106, 113–15 (Lord Burlington), 119, 140, 186, 243

Harbin, Dr. George (non-juror), 186

Hardwicke, Philip Yorke, 1st Earl of (Lord Chancellor), 215, 216

Harleian Library, the, 173–85 (section on), 216 (at Wimpole)

Harley, Abigail (aunt of 2nd Earl of Oxford), 204

Harley, Sir Edward (Governor of Dunkirk), 204

Harley, Edward, Lord (see 2nd Earl of Oxford)

Harley, Robert (see 1st Earl of Oxford)

Harley, Sir Robert (Parliamentarian), 175

Harrington, William Stanhope, 1st Earl of, 160

Hartington, Charlotte Boyle, Marchioness of, 135, 165, 167

Hartington, William Cavendish, Marquess of (later 4th Duke of Devonshire), 135, 240

Hawksmoor, Nicholas (architect), 86, 92, 98n., 138

Haym, Nicola Francesco (cellist and librettist), 106

Hayman, Francis (painter), 122

Hearne, Thomas (historical antiquary), 185

Heidigger, John James (impresario), 131

Herbert, Henry, Lord (see 9th Earl of Pembroke)

Herbert, Honble. Robert (brother of 9th Earl of Pembroke), 66

Herring, Rev. Thomas, 135

Hertford, Lady, 31n.

Hertford, Lord, 53

Hervey of Ickworth, John Hervey, Lord (courtier and memoir writer), 63, 71, 72, 73, 115, 133, 154, 160, 241, 246, 247

Hervey, Mary Lepell, Lady, 82

Hickes, George (non-juror), 176

Hill, Bryan (painter), 210

Hillsborough, Trevor Hill, 1st Viscount, 64

Hoare, Henry, Mr. of Stourhead, 146

Hobart, Elizabeth Maynard, Lady (wife of Sir Henry, 4th Bart.), 74

Hobart, Dr. Thomas (Ld. Leicester's tutor), 224–32 (on Grand Tour), 241–2

Hobart Papers, at Norwich, 81, 86

Hogarth, William (painter), 120, 126

Holbein, Hans (painter), 59

Holdenby House, Northants, 95

Holkham Hall, Norfolk, 14, 85n., 138, 152, 221–2, 225, 229, 230, 232, 233, 234, 238, 239, 242 (pictures at), 243 (sculpture at), 244–53 (The Conception of), 254–61 (The Creation of), 262–3

Homer (Greek poet), 40, 142 & n.

Hooke, Robert (architect), 161

Hopper, Thomas (architect), 44

Horace (Roman poet), 44, 50n., 202

Hornby Castle, Yorks., 208

Horseguards, the, Whitehall, 139

Hothfield Place, Kent, 234

Houghton Hall, Norfolk, 89, 118, 157, 210–11 (Lord Oxford at), 244, 247, 254, 256
  Water-house, the, 69, 70 (described)

Howard, Henrietta Hobart, Honble. Mrs. Charles (see Suffolk, Countess of)

Hussey, Christopher (architectural historian), 14n., 15, 38

Islay, Archibald Campbell, Earl of (later 3rd Duke of Argyll), 12, 61, 81, 82, 90, 94, 117

James, C. W. (Holkham Librarian), 225 & n.

James, John of Greenwich (architect), 98

Jarrett, Edward (Lord Leicester's accountant), 225, 227, 235

Jersey, William Villiers, 2nd Earl of, 28

Jervas, Charles (portrait painter), 74, 107, 118

Johnson, Dr. Samuel (sage and lexicographer), 32, 182–3, 190, 194, 195

Johnston, James (Secretary for Scotland), 70

Jones, Inigo (architect), 14, 35, 59–60, 69, 70, 89, 116, 118, 121, 125, 126 (Burlington), 135, 139, 150, 152, 153, 155 (his copy of Vitruvius), 168, 227, 249, 257, 259, 260, 261

Jourdain, Margaret (furniture and decoration expert), 14n.

Juvara, Filippo (Baroque architect), 138, 151n.

Kedleston Hall, Derby., 139, 223, 235

Kensington Palace, Cupola Room, 153

Kent, William (architect), 16–17 (described), 39, 40, 41, 68, 69, 107, 109 (in Rome), 120, 122–35 (the Burlingtons), 137, 138, 139, 141, 145–8 (Chiswick gardens), 151n., 152–5 (Chiswick Villa), 165, 166, 167, 210, 211 (Lord Oxford on), 212, 227, 230 (in Italy with Coke), 239, 245–59 (at Holkham)

King, James (carpenter), 98

King, Thomas (lutemaker), 63

Kinnoull, G. H. Hay, 8th Earl of (Lord Oxford's brother-in-law), 208

Kirby Hall, Yorks., 123, 153, 160–1 (described)

Knapton, George (portrait painter), 168

Kneller, Sir Godfrey (portrait painter), 32, 34, 122

Knole Park, Kent, 85

Labelye, Charles (engineer), 98–99

Lambert, George (landscape painter), 94

Lamerie, Paul (silversmith), 235

Langdale, Sir Edmund (Yorkshire squire), 162, 163, 164

Langley, Batty (architect), 98

Lansdowne, George Granville, Lord (poet and dramatist), 29

Lees Court, Kent, 234

Leicester, Margaret Tufton, Countess of (wife of 1st Earl), 233–4 (described), 236, 243, 245, 248, 257, 261, 262–3 (reigns at Holkham)

Leicester, Thomas Coke, 1st Earl of, 11, 12, 14, 16, 109, 138, 211, 221–63 (chapter on)

Le Nôtre, André (landscape gardener), 39

Leoni, Giacomo (architect), 37, 87, 116, 117, 118, 243, 256

Leslie, John Leslie, Lord (afterwards 9th Earl of Rothes), 231

Lewis, Erasmus (diplomatist), 27

Ligorio, Pirro (Renaissance architect), 246

Lincoln, Henry Clinton, 7th Earl of, house for, 157–8

Lintot, B. B. (publisher), 166

Londesborough Park, Yorks., 104, 158, 161–4, 168

Longford Hall, Derbyshire, 223, 234

Lonigo, Villa Rocca Pisani, 151 & n.

Louis XIV, King of France, 193, 201

Lovel, Lord (secondary title of 1st Earl of Leicester), 211, 236

Luti, Benedetto (Roman portrait painter), 227

Macky, John (Government spy), 121

Maffei, Scipione (poet), 138

Malcontenta, Villa on Brenta, 111, 124, 150, 228

Mann, Sir Horace, Bart. (Envoy at Florence), 65, 99, 183–4

Mansion House, London, 138–9

Mantua, Palazzo del Té, 228

Mar, John, 6th Earl and titular Duke of (Old Pretender's Agent), 24, 212

Maratta, Carlo (Baroque painter), 110

Marble Hill, Middlesex, 27, 68, 70–79 (Lady Suffolk at), 79–92 (section on), 93, 120, 141

Marcatellis, Raphael de (library of), 229

Marlborough, John Churchill, 1st Duke of, 23, 92, 175

Marlborough, Sarah Jennings, Duchess of (wife of 1st Duke), 67, 92–96, 98, 159, 183, 235

Marsden, — (wood carver), 254n.

Mary II, Queen, 22

Maser, Villa, near Asolo, 125

Mason, Rev. William (poet and scholar), 24

Massingberd, Burrell (patron of Kent), 122

Maynard, Sir John (Judge), 193

Mead, Dr. Richard (physician), 125

Meledo, Villa Trissino, 151, 247

Mereworth Castle, Kent, 81, 150, 151, 152

Michelangelo Buonarroti (architect), 139, 249

Miller, Sanderson (amateur architect), 44, 216

Milton, John (poet), 13

Milton Hall, Northants, 257

Mocenigo, Leonardo (Villa of on Brenta), 247

Molin Moschini Dondi Dell'Orologio, Villa, near Padua, 150–1

Montagnana, Villa Pisani, 88
      Villa Thiene, 94

Montagu, Elizabeth, Mrs. (society bluestocking), 13

Montagu, John Montagu, 2nd Duke of (courtier), 64

Montagu, Lady Mary Wortley (letter writer), 28, 32, 43, 54, 134, 190, 191, 216, 262

Montagu House, Bloomsbury (British Museum), 185, 216

Montgomery, Earl of (secondary title of Earls of Pembroke after 1630), 59

Moor Park, Herts., 256

Moore, James (cabinet-maker), 149 & n.

Moral Essays by A. Pope, 60

Morley, John (agent to 2nd Lord Oxford), 197, 201, 206–7

Morpeth, Henry, Viscount (later 4th Earl of Carlisle), 111

Morris, Robert (architectural writer), 86–87, 88, 90

Morris, Roger (architect), 61, 81 (described), 82–87 (Marble Hill), 92, 93, 94, 97, 139, 156, 160–1

Mortimer, Earl of (secondary title of Earls of Oxford), 173

'Mosquita, Bendetto' (Roman dealer), 109

Nadder river, Wiltshire, 96, 97

Narford Hall, Norfolk, 63 & n., 211 (Lord Oxford on)

Nash, John (architect), 44

Neal, John (gilder), 259

Newburgh, Anne Poole, Countess of, 23

Newcastle (-on-Tyne), Henry Cavendish, 2nd Duke of, 174

Newcastle (-on-Tyne), John Holles, 1st Duke of, 174, 187, 214, 218

Newcastle (-on-Tyne), Margaret, Duchess of (widow of 1st Duke), 174–5, 179, 214

Newcastle (-under-Lyme), Thomas Pelham-Holles, 1st Duke of (Prime Minister), 240, 250

Newton, Sir John, Bart. (Lord Leicester's grandfather), 222, 223, 224, 225

Nichols, John (printer and author), 65

Noel, Honble. Henry (grandfather of Lord Burlington), 104

Noel, Nathaniel (dealer), 181

Nollekens, Joseph (sculptor), 34

Oakley Grove (now Cirencester Park House), 23, 33, 35

Oakley Wood, Cirencester, 30, 38, 40, 41, 42, 43, 45, 46, 48, 53, 54

Oatlands Palace, Surrey, 158

Oldys, William (herald and antiquary), 182

Onslow, Arthur (Speaker, House of Commons), 184

Orford, Earl of, (see Sir Robert Walpole)

Orkney, Elizabeth Villiers, Countess of (wife of 1st Earl), 106

Orleans House, Twickenham, 70 & n.

Osborne, Thomas (bookseller), 184

Oxburgh Hall, Norfolk, 104, 244

Oxford, Aubrey de Vere, 20th Earl of, 173

Oxford, Edward Harley, 2nd Earl of, 11, 12, 14, 27, 63n., 96, 97n., 129, 173–218 (chapter on)

Oxford, Henrietta Cavendish-Holles, Countess of (wife of 2nd Earl), 174, 179, 183, 184, 186, 188, 191–2 (described), 206, 209, 215, 233

Oxford, Robert Harley, 1st Earl of (statesman), 23, 24, 29, 32, 173, 175–7 (Harleian Library), 182, 187–8, 192, 193

Page, Sir Gregory, Bart., 94

Paine, James (architect), 139

Palladio, Andrea (architect), 11, 69, 70, 86, 87, 94, 97, 117, 118, 121, 122, 123, 124, 125, 138, 139, 150–6 (Chiswick Villa), 157 (General Wade's house), 158 (York Assembly Rooms), 247, 249, 251, 256, 259

Palmer, Samuel (printer), 65

Parsons, Mr., of Bath (urn purveyor), 161

Pastoral Dialogue, A, by J. Swift, 68, 83

Peck, Rev. Francis (antiquary), 181

Pellegrini, Gianantonio (mural artist), 211

Pembroke, Henry Herbert, 2nd Earl of (married Mary Sidney), 59

Pembroke, Henry Herbert, 9th Earl of, 11, 14, 59–100 (chapter on), 120, 138, 156, 211, 261

Pembroke, Mary Fitzwilliam, Countess of (wife of 9th Earl), 66–7, 91, 131

Pembroke, Mary Howe, Countess of (3rd wife of 8th Earl), 60

Pembroke, Mary Sidney, Countess of (wife of 2nd Earl), 59

Pembroke, Philip Herbert, 4th Earl of (Inigo Jones's patron), 59

Pembroke, Thomas Herbert, 8th Earl of (virtuoso), 59, 60, 211

Pembroke, William Herbert, 1st Earl of (Holbein's patron), 59

Pembroke, William Herbert, 3rd Earl of (Shakespeare's patron), 59

Pembroke House, Whitehall, 69 & n. (described), 70, 88n.

Pendarves, Mrs. (see Delany, Mrs.)

Pennyman, John (pseudo-quaker), 182

Peterborough, Charles Mordaunt, 3rd Earl of (admiral, general, diplomatist), 27, 79, 80, 111

Petersham, Surrey, room for Lord Harrington, 160

Pether, Sebastian (moonlight artist), 148

Picart, B. (architectural draughtsman), 117

Pickford, Joseph (marble carver), 254n., 257, 259

Pingo, Thomas (engraver of medals), 63

Pisani, Francesco (client of Palladio), 88

Pliny, the Elder (1st century historian), 16, 144, 145

Pope, Alexander (poet), 13, 14 (described), 15, 16, 25, 27, 28, 29–33 (friendship with Bathurst), 36–56 (creation of Cirencester), 60, 68, 71, 73, 74, 75–6 (Lady Suffolk), 77, 80–92 (Marble Hill), 112, 118, 126, 129 (William Kent), 131, 133–4 (Lady Burlington), 136 (Lord Burlington), 139, 141–8 (Chiswick gardens), 154, 159, 162, 165, 166–7 (Lord Burlington), 175–6 (1st Earl of Oxford), 179 (Wanley), 185, 187, 188, 189–92 (2nd Earl of Oxford), 203, 204, 208, 212, 214, 216, 217, 245

Porteous, John (Captain, Edinburgh city guard), 26

Portland, Jane Martha Temple, Countess of (widow of 1st Earl), 65

Portland, Margaret Harley, Duchess

of (wife of 2nd Duke), 184–5, 195–6, 203, 206, 216
Portland, William Bentinck, 2nd Duke of, 184
Poussin, Nicolas (painter), 16, 146, 147
Powys, Caroline Girle, Mrs. Lybbe (diarist), 234n., 258, 259
Pratolino, Villa, 146
Pretender (James Stuart), The Old, 24, 25, 111, 212
Price, John (architect), 210
Prior, Matthew (poet), 27, 29, 179–80 (Wanley), 181, 185, 187, 192–204 (2nd Lord Oxford), 212, 214, 216, 217
Prior Park, Somerset, 97
Purcell, Henry (composer), 114

Quattro Libri dell'Architettura, by Andrea Palladio, 87, 118, 123, 152, 158, 256
Queensberry, Catherine Hyde, Duchess of (wife of 3rd Duke), 75, 76

Raby Castle, Durham, 160
Radcliffe Camera, Oxford, 213
Radnor, — Cutler, Countess of (wife of Lord Robartes, 2nd Earl), 214
Ralph, James (Critical Review), 157
Ramsay, Allan (Scottish painter), 239
Ramsay, Allan (Scottish poet), 185
Raynham Hall, Norfolk, 208, 209, 210, 221, 262
Repton, Humphrey (landscape gardener), 215
Revett, Nicholas (architect), 13n.
Ricci, Sebastian and Marco (mural painters), 120
Richards, James (carver), 82, 89, 120
Richardson, Jonathan (portrait painter), 122
Richmond, Charles Lennox, 2nd Duke of, 160
Richmond Lodge, Surrey, 68, 83, 84
Rigaud, Jean (draughtsman), 147, 149, 164

Riskins, Buckinghamshire, 27, 31 & n., 33, 49, 51, 53, 80
Rivella di Monselici, Villa Maldara, 88
Robinson, Sir Thomas, Bart. (architect), 138, 163n., 246
Rolli, Paolo (Italian poetaster), 60, 67, 114
Rome,
  Santa Costanza, 159
  Villa Borghese, 109, 227
Rosa, Salvator (romantic painter), 146, 147
Rosalba Carriera (Venetian portrait painter), 111, 228, 239
Ross, Charles (joiner), 85n.
Rosset, François (French picture dealer), 110
Roubiliac, L. F. (sculptor), 61, 63, 100, 139, 243 & n., 262
Rousham, Oxfordshire, 39, 145
Royal, The Princess (Anne, later Princess of Orange), 73, 115
Royal Academy of Music, 114–5, 122, 243
Royal Lodge (now White Lodge), Richmond, Surrey, 70, 165n.
Rubens, Sir Peter Paul (painter), 89
Rudder, Samuel (Glos. historian), 46
Rudgell, E. (solicitor), 80
Rusconi, Camillo (Milanese sculptor), 115, 243
Rysbrack, John Michael (sculptor), 115, 165, 168, 187, 202, 217, 243

St. John, Henry (see Bolingbroke, 1st Viscount)
St. Mary-le-Strand, London, 213, 215
St. Paul's Cathedral, London, 139
St. Peter's, Vere Street, London, 213
Santa Sofia, Villa Serego, 121
Sapperton Manor, Glos., 38, 44, 46, 53
Savile Row, London, house by Burlington in, 251
Scamozzi, Vincenzio (architect), 69, 87, 88, 139, 150, 151 & n., 152, 153, 161, 164
Scheemakers, Peter (sculptor), 63, 155, 187, 243

Seal, Christian (engraver), 187
Seidel, Andreas Erasmus (library of), 231
Selwyn, William (City merchant), 204
Settle, Elkanah (poet), 130, 157
Sevenoaks, School and Almshouses, Kent, 161
Shaftesbury, Anthony Ashley Cooper, 3rd Earl of (philosopher), 14–16 (described), 141
Shakespeare, William (poet), 59, 63, 155 (monument)
Shannon, Henry Boyle, 1st Earl of, 104
Shudi, Burkert (harpsichord maker), 165
Sidney, Mary (see Countess of Pembroke)
Sloane, Sir Hans, Bart. (physician and connoisseur), 126, 169, 236, 257
Smith, Edward (Holkham agent), 225, 233
Smith, Joseph (Consul in Venice), 242
Smith, Humphrey (Holkham agent), 224, 225, 232, 233
Smollett, Tobias (novelist), 13
Soldani, Massimiliano (bronze sculptor), 113n.
Solimena, Francesco (Neapolitan painter), 229
Somerset House, Strand, London, 70
Southall, Mr. (bugman), 235
Southcott, Philip (landscape gardener), 160
Stainborough (Wentworth Castle), Yorks., 37n.
Stair, John Dalrymple, 2nd Earl of (Field Marshal), 232
Stanhope, Charles (Secretary to Treasury), 99
Stanhope, James, General (later 1st Earl Stanhope), 111
Stanton Harcourt, Oxon., 41
Sterne, Laurence (humorist and sentimentalist), 55
Stirling, A. M. W. (authoress), 239 & n.
Stoke Bruerne Park, Northants, 121

Stonehenge, Wilts., 62, 209
Stourhead, Wilts., 51, 146
Stowe Park, Bucks., 50, 97
Stra, Palazzo Pisani, 111
Strafford, Thomas Wentworth, 3rd Earl of, 12, 23, 24, 26, 28, 37, 47, 49–50, 51, 53, 54, 193
Strafford, Countess of (wife of 3rd Earl), 27
Stratford, Dr. William (Oxford tutor), 174, 185
Strawberry Hill, Twickenham, 71, 74, 78
Strickland family, of Boynton, Yorks, 163 & n.
Stuart, James (architect), 13n.
Stuart, Lady Louisa (biographer), 237n.
Stukeley, Dr. William (antiquarian), 62, 98
Suffolk, Charles Howard, 9th Earl of, 71 (described), 72, 84
Suffolk, Henrietta Hobart, Countess of (wife of 9th Earl), 14, 27–28, 32, 49, 54, 66, 67, 68, 70 & n., 71–79 (section on), 79–92 (builds Marble Hill), 132 (Lady Burlington), 141
Summerson, Sir John (architectural historian), 36, 86
Swift, Jonathan, Dean (poet and man of letters), 13, 25, 28, 29, 36, 37, 45, 47, 53, 55, 63, 65, 68, 73, 74, 75, 77–92 (Lady Suffolk), 133, 164, 167, 176, 185, 187–9 (2nd Earl of Oxford), 192, 197, 202, 204, 205, 212, 241
Switzer, Stephen (horticulturist), 63
Sylvius, Aenias (Pope Pius II), 262

Talman, John (collector), 125 & n., 153, 180
Talman, William (architect), 125n.
Tapenden & Hanley, Messrs. (ironworkers), 257
Thames and Severn Canal, 44
Thanet, 6th Earl of, 233, 235
Thanet House, London, 235, 236
Thomas, Rev. Timothy (Lord Oxford's chaplain), 203, 206, 207, 208, 209

Thomson, James (poet), 14, 146–7

Thoresby, Ralph (antiquary of Leeds), 181

Thornhill, Sir James (mural painter), 120, 126, 201, 210, 212, 213, 214, 215 (Wimpole chapel)

Thorpe, Farmer, 65

Thorpe, Dr. John (Kent antiquary), 185

Torcy, J. B. Colbert, Marquis de (French statesman), 193

Tottenham Park, Savernake, Wilts., 152, 156 (described), 251

Townesend family (Oxford builders), 35

Townshend, Charles, 2nd Viscount ('Turnip Townshend'), 208, 210

Townshend, Colonel George (later 1st Marquess Townshend), 240 & n., 262

Townshend, Sir Roger (of Raynham), 221

Trench, Henry (historical painter), 126 & n.

Trevisani, Angelo (portrait painter), 230

Tunstall, Dr. James (divine and classical scholar), 185

Twickenham, Pope's villa at, 31, 33, 137, 142, 143, 167

Upton, Anne, 75

Urrey, John (Chaucerian scholar), 180

Utrecht, Treaty of, 23, 193

Valletta, Giuseppe (MSS. collection), 229

Vanbrugh, Sir John (architect), 86, 92, 116, 140, 141, 152

Vanderbank, John (portrait painter), 63

Vandyke, Sir Anthony (painter), 59, 89

Vardy, John (architect), 139

Venice,
    San Giorgio Maggiore, 123, 227, 256
    San Francesco della Vigna, 154, 228, 246
    Santa Maria della Salute, 227

Veronese, Paolo (Venetian painter), 120

Versailles Palace, 39, 193–4, 199

Vertue, George (antiquarian), 60, 62, 63, 68, 106, 109, 113, 115, 127, 138, 184, 185, 186–7 (described), 202–3, 204, 206, 215, 217–18 (Lord Oxford)

Vicenza,
    Palazzo Chiericati, 123–4
    Palazzo Iseppo di Porti, 117–8, 123
    Palazzo Thiene, 123, 152, 158, 259
    Rotonda (or Villa Capra), 124, 149–52 (Chiswick Villa)
    Teatro Olimpico, 228

Vignola, Jacopo Barozzi (Renaissance architect), 69

Villiers, George (1st Duke of Buckingham), 187–8

Vinci, Leonardo da (artist), 242, 262

Vintlema, Joseph (Roman dealer), 109

Violetti (David Garrick's wife), 131

Virgil (Latin poet), 40, 142 & n.

Vitruvius Britannicus, vols. i–v, 69, 70, 88, 93, 116 (described), 117, 121, 157, 158, 160, 243, 259n.

Vitruvius Pollio (Augustan architect), 14, 16, 96, 125, 139, 250

Voltaire, F.-M. Arouet (French sage),187

Wade, General, house for in London, 152, 156, 157 (described)

Walpole, Horace (letter writer), 24, 25, 39 & n., 41, 44, 49, 65, 67–8, 71, 72, 74, 75, 78, 79, 85, 89, 90, 93, 99–100, 110, 121, 127, 133, 137, 145–6, 157, 167, 169, 183–4, 192, 237, 241

Walpole, Horatio, 1st Lord (diplomatist), 65

Walpole, Sir Robert, Prime Minister (later 1st Earl of Orford), 12, 24, 25, 66, 73, 76, 105, 210–11, 235, 236, 243, 244

Wanley, Humphrey (librarian), 173–185 (section on), 204, 205, 206, 216

Wanley, 1st Mrs., 179
Wanstead House, Essex, 69, 137, 197
Warburton, John (herald), 181
Warburton, William, Bishop of Gloucester, 185
Ware, Isaac (architect), 139, 140, 153
Webb, John (architect), 60, 121, 125, 126, 152, 156, 160, 257, 259, 260
Welbeck Abbey, Notts., 174, 175, 192, 209, 216
Wentworth, Lady (aunt of Lord Bathurst), 28
Wentworth Castle, Yorks., 37, 47
Wentworth Woodhouse, Yorks., 137, 138
Westcombe House, Blackheath, 94–96 (described)
Western, Squire (*Tom Jones*), 207, 233
Westminster Bridge, 86, 98–99 (described)
Westminster School Dormitory, 137, 156–7 (described), 158
Whitehall Palace, 118, 121
Whitton Park, Twickenham, 81, 82, 90, 94
Wilbury Park, Wilts., 35, 116
Wilkins, David (Lord Leicester's governor), 223, 224
Wilmington, Spencer Compton, 1st Earl of, 160
Wilton House, Wiltshire, 59, 63, 66, 68, 86, 89, 91, 93, 96, 150, 156
    Palladian Bridge, 68, 96–97 (described)
Wimbledon House, Surrey, 93–94 (described), 96, 98
Wimpole Hall, Cambridgeshire, 12, 44, 120, 174, 175, 177, 179, 181, 182n., 186, 190, 192, 199, 200,
201, 202, 205, 206, 210, 212–18 (section on)
Winchester Palace, Hants., 210
Winchilsea, Daniel, 8th Earl of, 133
Windham, Joseph (of Waghen Hall, Yorks.), 245
Wittkower, Dr. Rudolph (architectural historian), 138, 151 & n., 251
Woburn Farm, Chertsey, 160
Woodroffe, B. (? chaplain to Lord Pembroke), 64
Woolfe, John (architect), 158 & n., 160
Wootton, John (painter of horses), 187, 201, 212, 213, 214
Wordsworth, William (poet), 16
Wren, Sir Christopher (architect), 35, 60, 116, 135, 139, 140, 152, 210
Wright, Richard (bricklayer), 149
Wright, Stephen (architect), 165 & n.
Wyatt, James (architect), 44, 255

Yarmouth, Great, St. George's Chapel, 210
York,
    Assembly Rooms, 88n., 125, 137, 153, 158–60 (described), 256
    Cathedral pavement, 160 (described)
    Lord Mayor's House, 88n., 207
York House Watergate, Strand, London, 120
Young, Arthur (agriculturist), 245, 252, 255, 257, 258, 259, 260

Zeno, Apostolo (Venetian scholar), 230
Zincke, C. F. (enameller), 187